D0361871

ITALY

TOP SIGHTS, AUTHENTIC EXPERIENCES

Marc Di Duca, Cristian Bonetto, Peter Dragicevich,
Duncan Garwood, Paula Hardy, Virginia Maxwell, Regis
St Louis, Donna Wheeler, Nicola Williams

Contents

Baci (kisses)
FILIPPO GIULIANI/SHUTTERSTOCK ©

Plan Your Trip
Italy's Top 12

S BORISOV/SHUTTERSTOCK ©

Rome

Italy's hot-blooded capital is an inspiring city

Once capital of the world, Rome was legendarily spawned by a wolf-suckled boy, grew to be Europe's first superpower, became the spiritual centrepiece of the Christian world and is now the repository of over two millennia of art and architecture. From the Pantheon and the Colosseum (pictured above; p38) to Michelangelo's Sistine Chapel (pictured right; p52) and countless works by Caravaggio, there's simply too much to see in one visit. So toss a coin in the Trevi Fountain and promise to return.

1

Venice

A city of marble built on a lagoon

A maze of skinny streets and waterways, Venice straddles the middle ground between reality and sheer fantasy. This is a city of ethereal winter fogs, fairy-tale domes and Gothic arches fit for an opera set. Look beyond its sparkling mosaics and brooding Tintorettos and you'll discover the other Venice; a living, breathing organism studded with secret gardens, sleepy campi (squares) and well-worn bacari (small bars) filled with the fizz of *prosecco* and the sing-song local dialect.

Top: Grand Canal (p164); Bottom: Palazzo Ducale (p168)

2

Florence

An exquisite city packed with art

According to Unesco, Florence contains 'the greatest concentration of universally renowned works of art in the world'. The Tuscan capital is where the Renaissance kicked off and giants such as Brunelleschi, Michelangelo and Botticelli rewrote the rules of creative expression. The result is a city laden with artistic treasures, blockbuster museums and jewel-box churches. Its flawless medieval streets and lanes teem with wine bars, trattorias and elegant boutiques. Duomo (p102)

3

4

Tuscany

A wildly diverse, soulful, earth-driven region

With its lyrical landscapes, world-class art and a superb *cucina contadina* (farmer's kitchen), Tuscany is Italy's most romanticised region, and one tailor-made for fastidious aesthetes. Florence is the main draw, but beyond its flawless Renaissance streetscapes sprawls an undulating landscape of sinuous cypress trees, olive groves and coveted regional treasures, from the Gothic majesty of Siena and the Manhattan-esque skyline of medieval San Gimignano to the vineyards of Italy's most famous wine region, Chianti.

5

Pompeii

Roman city frozen in its death throes

The time-warped ruins of Pompeii hurtle you 2000 years into the past. Wander through chariot-grooved Roman streets, lavishly frescoed villas and bathhouses, food stores and markets, theatres, and even an ancient brothel. Then, in the eerie stillness, your eye on ominous Mt Vesuvius, ponder Pliny the Younger's terrifying account of the town's final hours: 'Darkness came on again, again ashes, thick and heavy. We got up repeatedly to shake these off; otherwise we would have been buried and crushed by the weight'.

Naples

Italy's boisterous southern metropolis

Nowhere else in Italy are people as conscious of their role in the theatre of everyday life as in Naples. And in no other city does daily life radiate such drama and intensity. Naples' ancient streets are a stage, cast with boisterous matriarchs, bellowing baristi and tongue-knotted lovers. To savour the flavour, dive into one of the city's markets – loud, lavish operas of fruit vendors, wriggling seafood and the aroma of just-baked *sfogliatelle* (ricotta pastries).

6

Amalfi Coast

Italy's most celebrated coastline

This stretch of southern coast is a gripping experience: coastal mountains plunge into creamy blue sea in a vertical scene of precipitous crags, sun-bleached villages and lush woodland. Between sea and sky, mountain-top hiking trails deliver Tyrrhenian panoramas fit for the gods. While some argue that the peninsula's most beautiful coast is Liguria's Cinque Terre or Calabria's Costa Viola, it is the Amalfi Coast that has seduced and inspired countless greats, from Richard Wagner to DH Lawrence.

7

8

Cinque Terre

Five dramatically picturesque fishing villages

For the sinful inhabitants of the Cinque Terre's five sherbert-coloured villages – Monterosso, Vernazza, Corniglia, Manarola and Riomaggiore – penance involved a hike up the vertiginous cliff side to the sanctuary to appeal for forgiveness. Scale the same trails today through terraced vineyards, and as the heavenly views unfurl, it's hard to think of a more benign punishment. Those seeking less exertion can hop from one village to the next on the train.
Manarola (p157)

9

Italian Lakes
The dramatic lakes of northern Italy

If it's good enough for George Clooney, it's good enough for mere mortals. Nestled in the shadow of the Rhaetian Alps, dazzling Lago di Como is the most spectacular of the northern lakes, its art-nouveau villas home to movie moguls, fashion royalty and Arab sheikhs. Over the regional border in Piedmont, Lago Maggiore has been seducing visitors since its heyday as a fashionable belle-époque retreat and Ernest Hemingway found inspiration for his WWI romance, *A Farewell to Arms.* Far left: Lago Maggiore (p220); Left: Bellagio (p216)

MARCO OSSINO/SHUTTERSTOCK ©

CHICCODODIFC/SHUTTERSTOCK ©

QUANTHEM/ISTOCK/GETTY IMAGES ©

Sicily

An island of diverse flavours

Sour, spicy and sweet, Sicily's flavours reflect millennia of cross-cultural influences. Indeed, no other regional Italian cuisine is quite as complex and intriguing. Tuck into golden *panelle* (chickpea fritters) in Palermo and chilli-spiked chocolate in Modica. From Palermo's Mercato di Ballarò to Catania's La Pescheria, market stalls burst with local delicacies: Bronte pistachios, olives, swordfish and nutty Canestrato cheese. But leave room for a *cannolo* or a slice of *cassata*.

10

KAVALENKAVA/SHUTTERSTOCK ©

Milan

Italy's financial and fashion capital

The de facto capital of northern Italy wows with its cosmopolitan, can do atmosphere, vibrant cultural scene and sophisticated shopping options. The city's legendary boutiques, contemporary galleries and dedication to cutting-edge design make for a stylish, forward-looking city. But Milan is not all about models and money; see historic sights including Leonardo da Vinci's *The Last Supper,* the immense Duomo (pictured above) and La Scala opera house.

MITCHOTO/SHUTTERSTOCK ©

Sardinia

Wild island of peaks and beaches

Words fail to accurately describe the varied blue-green hues of the sea surrounding Sardinia. While models, ministers and perma-tanned celebrities wine, dine and sail along the glossy Costa Smeralda, much of Sardinia remains a wild, raw playground. Slather on that sunscreen and explore the island's rugged coastal beauty, from the hilltop citadel in Cagliari to the haunting caves of Grotta di Nettuno and out-of-this-world beaches.

Plan Your Trip
Need to Know

When to Go

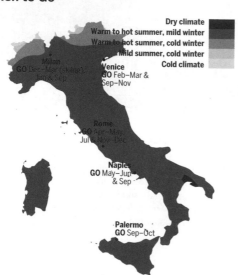

Dry climate
Warm to hot summer, mild winter
Warm to hot summer, cold winter
Mild summer, cold winter
Cold climate

Milan
GO Dec–Mar (skiing),
Jun & Sep

Venice
GO Feb–Mar &
Sep–Nov

Rome
GO Apr–May,
Jul & Nov–Dec

Naples
GO May–Jun
& Sep

Palermo
GO Sep–Oct

High Season (Jul–Aug)
○ Queues at big sights and on the road, especially August.

○ Prices also rocket for Christmas, New Year and Easter.

○ Late December to March is high season in the Alps and Dolomites.

Shoulder (Apr–Jun & Sep–Oct)
○ Good deals on accommodation, especially in the south.

○ Spring is best for festivals, flowers and local produce.

○ Autumn provides warm weather and the grape harvest.

Low Season (Nov–Mar)
○ Prices up to 30% less than in high season.

○ Many sights and hotels closed in coastal and mountainous areas.

○ A good period for cultural events in large cities.

Currency
Euro (€)

Language
Italian

Visas
Generally not required for stays of up to 90 days (or at all for EU nationals); some nationalities need a Schengen visa.

Money
ATMs are widespread in Italy. Major credit cards are widely accepted, but some smaller shops, trattorias and hotels might not take them.

Mobile Phones
Local SIM cards can be used in European, Australian and some unlocked US phones. Other phones must be set to roaming.

Time
All of Italy occupies the Central European Time Zone, which is one hour ahead of GMT. When it is noon in London, it is 1pm in Italy.

Daylight-saving time (when clocks move forward one hour) starts on the last Sunday in March and ends on the last Sunday in October.

Italy operates on a 24-hour clock, so 3pm is written as 15:00.

Daily Costs

Budget: Less than €100

- Dorm bed: €20–35

- Double room in a budget hotel: €60–130

- Pizza or pasta: €6–12

Midrange: €100–250

- Double room in a hotel: €110–200

- Local restaurant dinner: €25–45

- Admission to museum: €4–15

Top end: More than €250

- Double room in a four- or five-star hotel: €200 plus

- Top restaurant dinner: €45–150

- Opera ticket: €40–210

Useful Websites

Lonely Planet (www.lonelyplanet.com/italy) Destination information, hotel bookings, traveller forum and more.

Trenitalia (www.trenitalia.com) Italian railways website.

Agriturismi (www.agriturismi.it) Guide to farm accommodation.

ENIT (www.italia.it) Official Italian government tourism website.

The Local (www.thelocal.it) Has English-language news from Italy, including travel-related stories.

Opening Hours

Opening hours vary throughout the year. We've provided high-season opening hours; hours will generally decrease in the shoulder and low seasons. 'Summer' times generally refer to the period from April to September or October, while 'winter' times generally run from October or November to March.

Banks 8.30am–1.30pm and 2.45–4.30pm Monday to Friday

Bars and clubs 10pm–4am or 5am

Cafes 7.30am–8pm, sometimes until 1am or 2am

Restaurants noon–3pm and 7.30–11pm or midnight

Shops 9am–1pm and 4–8pm Monday to Saturday, some also open Sunday

Arriving in Italy

Rome Leonardo da Vinci The express train (€14) takes 30 minutes and runs between 6.23am and 11.23pm. Buses (€5 to €7) take an hour and run between 5am and 12.30am; night services run at 1.15am, 2.15am and 3.30am. Taxis (set fare €48) complete the journey in 45 minutes.

Malpensa Airport (Milan) The express train (€13) takes 50 minutes and runs between 5.40am and 10.40pm. Buses (€10) take 50 minutes and run between 5am and 1.20am. Taxis (set fare €90) take 50 minutes.

Marco Polo Airport (Venice) The ferry (€15) takes 40 to 60 minutes and runs between 6.15am and 1.15am. Buses (€8) take 20 minutes and run between 5.20am and 12.50am. Water taxis (from €110) take 30 minutes.

Naples International Airport (Capodichino) Shuttle buses (€4) take 20 to 35 minutes and run between 6am and 11.40pm. Taxis (set fare €19) take 20 to 35 minutes.

Getting Around

Transport in Italy is affordable, quick and efficient.

Bus Cheaper and slower than trains. Useful for more remote villages not serviced by trains.

Car Handy for travelling at your own pace, or for visiting regions with minimal public transport. Not a good idea for travelling within major urban areas.

Train Reasonably priced, with extensive coverage and frequent departures. High-speed trains connect major cities.

For more on getting around, see p343 ➡

Plan Your Trip
Hot Spots For...

SHAIITH/SHUTTERSTOCK ©

Architecture

Italy boasts some of the world's most instantly recognisable buildings, the unrivalled legacy of centuries of master builders, from Roman times to the Renaissance.

Rome (p34)
The Italian capital is all about the wonderfully preserved ancient ruins that dot the city centre.

The Colosseum (p38)
Take a tour of the world's best-known Roman site.

Venice (p160)
Venice's palaces and townhouses perched on tens of lagoon islands are a unique spectacle.

Palazzo Ducale (p168)
The Gothic home of medieval Venice's rulers, the doges.

Pisa (p132)
Pisa's Piazza dei Miracoli is one of the world's most attractive urban spaces.

Leaning Tower (p132)
Pisa's famous tower leans 3.9 degrees off the vertical.

D.BOND/SHUTTERSTOCK ©

Seaside Fun

With over 7600km of sun-kissed coastline, it's little wonder many head to Italy for beach holidays by the Mediterranean and Adriatic. Escaping the summer crowds is also easier than you might imagine.

Sardinia (p296)
Italy's second-biggest island is famous for its kilometres of glorious sandy beaches.

Alghero (p300)
Alghero's curving strand is a short walk from the Old Town.

Cinque Terre (p148)
Possibly Italy's most picturesque stretch of coastline, the Cinque Terre is made up of five villages.

Monterosso (p156)
This village has a gloriously long beach on which to laze.

Amalfi Coast (p260)
Turquoise seas and postcard-perfect piazzas await on this famous stretch of Italy's west coast.

Positano (p264)
The Amalfi Coast's most photogenic town.

Food

No one's taste buds can fail to be impressed by Italy's cuisine. From hearty Alpine dishes to the lemons of Sicily, Italy is a place to take your appetite on holiday.

KILTEDARAB/SHUTTERSTOCK ©

Rome (p34)
Roman fare is perhaps the most underappreciated of all Italy's cuisines but is a vital piece in the jigsaw.

Tripe (p85)
The capital's signature dish, mostly eaten on Saturdays.

Tuscany (p126)
Meat, herbs and olive oil come together in Tuscany to create some of the country's finest dishes.

Bistecca alla fiorentina (p324)
This Florence steak is served in slabs 'three fingers thick'.

Naples (p226)
The southern sun and volcanic soils combine to produce ingredients such as citrus fruits and tomatoes.

Pizza (p242)
Naples is best-known for its thick-crust *margherita* pizza.

Art

Art lovers should make at least one pilgrimage in their lives to Italy, the epicentre of ancient and Renaissance art and home to some of the planet's most celebrated works.

S-F/SHUTTERSTOCK ©

Florence (p94)
A feast of art awaits in the home of the Renaissance, where galleries are packed with the finest works.

Uffizi Gallery (p98)
Big-name masterpieces in a 16th-century *palazzo*.

Rome (p34)
The Vatican possesses a huge collection of artworks, displayed in several museums.

Sistine Chapel (p52)
Michelangelo famously painted this chapel's ceiling.

Milan (p192)
The northern metropolis isn't all about fashion – the city also boasts an impressive collection of art.

The Last Supper (p200)
One of da Vinci's most viewed works, painted in the 1490s.

Plan Your Trip
Local Life

CASIMIRO PT/SHUTTERSTOCK ©

Activities

Blessed with mountains, lakes and 7600km of coastline, Italy is like one giant, pulse-racing playground. Whether you're after adrenalin-charged skiing in the Alps, hard-core hiking in the Dolomites, coastal climbs in Sardinia, white-water rafting in Calabria or low-key cycling through Piedmont – *Madre Natura* (Mother Nature) has you covered. Every region of Italy has something and there are plenty of companies, guides and hire centres to help you get out there and at it.

Shopping

Italy is behind some of the world's most coveted fashion, design, crafts and culinary products, making shopping here richly rewarding. Different crafts or items are often associated with a particular city, town or area. For instance, Murano (Venice) is famed for its glassware, Como for its silk, Florence for its handmade leathergoods

and the Amalfi Coast for colourful majolica ceramics. All of this makes Italy one of the best places on earth to pick up superb souvenirs, though don't expect many bargains. Beware of cheaper foreign imitations; they are not only inauthentic, but also pose a threat to Italy's rich artisan traditions.

Eating

One of the world's most revered cuisines, Italian food is a handy umbrella term for the country's cache of regional cuisines, which differ wildly. Together they reflect Italy's extraordinary geographic and cultural diversity. The common thread between all is an indelible link between food, the land and the locals' sense of identity. From the quality of the produce to the reverence for tradition, eating here is all about passion, pride and *godere la vita* (enjoying life). In tourist hot spots look beyond the pasta-pizza-gelato trio to discover that region's authentic fare.

ELESI/SHUTTERSTOCK ©

Drinking & Nightlife

Historical cafes, cosy *enoteche* (wine bars) and trendy cocktail and craft-beer hot spots: Italy's drinking venues are diverse and commonly multipurpose. Here, quiet daytime cafes might transform into buzzing evening bars with bands or DJ-spun tunes, while wine bars are often just as popular for their food. Despite a rise in binge drinking, most Italians remain moderate imbibers, almost always consuming alcohol with food, whether with pre-dinner *aperitivo* snacks or a proper meal. A guide to Italy's wine would be far thicker than this book and is an unmissable part of the Italian experience. And when it comes to partying, Italy has everything from smooth nightspots to retro discos – late starts to the evening are the norm.

Entertainment

Whether you're hankering for opera in an ancient amphitheatre, arias at a gilded opera house, or nailbiting football matches at

a famous *stadio* (stadium), you'll find it in Italy. Summer is an especially lively time for alfresco arts events and festivals, among them **Verona's Opera Festival** (☏045 800 51 51; www.arena.it; Via Dietro Anfiteatro 6; ☺late Jun-late Aug) and multi-arts events like **Estate Romana** (www.estateromana.comune. roma.it; ☺Jun-Oct) in Rome and **Ravello Festival** (☏089 85 84 22; www.ravellofestival.com; ☺Jul-Sep) on the Amalfi Coast. Year-round you'll have to book tickets well in advance for especially popular events.

From left: Shoppers in Galleria Vittorio Emanuele II (p197), Milan; Al fresco dining in Palermo (p282)

Plan Your Trip
Month by Month

FRANCESCA SCIARRA/SHUTTERSTOCK ©

January
♣ Regata della Befana
Witches in Venice don't ride brooms: they row boats. Venice celebrates Epiphany on 6 January with the Regatta of the Witches, complete with a fleet of brawny men dressed in their finest *befana* (witch) drag.

🎿 Ski Italia
Italy's top ski resorts are in the northern Alps and the Dolomites, but you'll also find resorts in Friuli, the Apennines, Le Marche and even Sicily. The best months of the season are January and February.

February
♣ Carnevale
In the period leading up to Ash Wednesday, many Italian towns stage pre-Lenten carnivals, with whimsical costumes, confetti and festive treats. Venice's Carnevale (www. carnevale.venezia.it) is the most famous.

March
♣ Settimana Santa
The pope leads a candlelit procession to the Colosseum on Good Friday and blesses from St Peter's Square on Easter Sunday. Fireworks explode in Florence's Piazza del Duomo, with notable processions taking place in Procida and Sorrento, Taranto, Trapani and Iglesias.

✖ Taste
For three days in March, gourmands flock to Florence for Taste (www.pittimmagine. com), a bustling food fair held inside the industrial-sleek Stazione Leopolda. The program includes culinary-themed talks, cooking demonstrations and the chance to sample food, coffee and liquor from more than 300 Italian artisan producers.

April
☆ Maggio Musicale Fiorentino
Established in 1933, Italy's oldest arts festival (www.operadifirenze.it) brings world-class performances of theatre, classical

music, jazz, opera and dance to Florence's opera house and other venues across the city. Events run from April to June.

May

☉ La Biennale di Venezia

Held from mid-May to late November, Europe's premier arts showcase (www. labiennale.org) is actually held annually, though the spotlight alternates between art (odd-numbered years) and architecture (even-numbered years). Running alongside the two main events are annual showcases of dance, theatre, cinema and music.

✿ Maggio dei Monumenti

As the weather warms up, Naples rolls out a mammoth, month-long program of art exhibitions, concerts, performances and tours around the city. Many historical and architectural treasures usually off limits to the public are open and free to visit.

♟ Wine & The City

A three-week celebration (www.wineand thecity.it) of regional vino in Naples, with

> ### ★ Best Festivals
>
> Settimana Santa, March–April
>
> La Biennale di Venezia, May–November
>
> Estate Romana, June–October
>
> Il Palio di Siena, July & August
>
> Truffle Season, November

free wine degustations, *aperitivo* sessions and cultural events in venues as diverse as museums and castles, art galleries, boutiques and restaurants.

June

☆ Ciclo di Rappresentazioni Classiche

Ancient intrigue in an evocative Sicilian setting, the Festival of Greek Theatre (www. indafondazione.org) brings Syracuse's 5th-century-BC amphitheatre to life with performances by Italy's acting greats. The season runs from mid-June to early July.

From left: Procida's Settimana Santa procession; Carnevale

♣ Napoli Teatro Festival Italia

Naples celebrates all things performative with one month of theatre, dance and literary events. Using both conventional and unconventional venues, the program (www.napoliteatrofestival.it) ranges from classic works to specially commissioned pieces. Held from early June to early July.

July

♣ Il Palio di Siena

Daredevils in tights thrill the crowds with this chaotic bareback horse race around Siena's medieval piazza. Preceding the race is a dashing medieval-costume parade. Held on 2 July and 16 August.

☆ Estate Romana

From June to October, Rome puts on a summer calendar of events that turn the city into an outdoor stage. Dubbed Estate Romana (www.estateromana.comune.roma.it), the program encompasses music, dance, literature and film.

August

♣ Ferragosto

After Christmas and Easter, Ferragosto, on 15 August, is Italy's biggest holiday. It marks the Feast of the Assumption, but even before Christianity the Romans honoured their gods on Feriae Augusti. Naples celebrates with particular fervour.

☆ Venice International Film Festival

The Venice International Film Festival (www.labiennale.org/en/cinema) is one of the world's most prestigious silver-screen events. Held at the Lido from late August to early September, it draws the international film glitterati with its red-carpet premieres and paparazzi glamour.

September

☻ Expo del Chianti Classico

There is no finer opportunity to taste Tuscany's Chianti Classico than at Greve in Chianti's annual Chianti Classico Expo (www.expochianticlassico.com), on the second weekend in September. All of the major producers are represented, with supporting events including musical performances.

♣ Regata Storica

In early September, gondoliers in period dress work those biceps in Venice's Historic Regatta (www.regatastoricavenezia.it). Period boats are followed by gondola and other boat races along the Grand Canal.

♣ Venice Glass Week

This recently established festival (www.theveniceglassweek.com) in Venice showcases the work of Murano's finest glass-blowers. The week-long event also offers a peek into previously off-limits furnaces.

October

☆ RomaEuropa

From late September to late November or early December, top international artists take to the stage for Rome's premier festival (https://romaeuropa.net) of theatre, opera and dance. Performances are held at numerous venues across the city.

November

☆ Opera Season

Italy is home to four of the world's great opera houses: La Scala in Milan, La Fenice in Venice, Teatro San Carlo in Naples and Teatro Massimo in Palermo. The season traditionally runs from mid-October to March, although La Scala opens later on St Ambrose Day, 7 December.

✘ Truffle Season

From the Piedmontese towns of Alba (www.fieradeltartufo.org) and Asti, to Tuscany's San Miniato and Le Marche's Acqualagna, November is prime truffle time, with local truffle fairs, events and music.

December

♣ Natale

The weeks preceding Christmas are studded with religious events. Many churches set up nativity scenes known as *presepi*. Naples is especially famous for these. On Christmas Eve the pope serves midnight mass in St Peter's Square.

Plan Your Trip
Get Inspired

VASANTY/SHUTTERSTOCK ©

Read

The Italians: A Full Length Portrait Featuring Their Manners and Morals (Luigi Barzini; 1964) Revealing portrait of the Italian character.

The Leopard (Giuseppe Tomasi di Lampedusa; 1958) Masterpiece about tumultuous 19th-century changes.

The Italians (John Hooper; 2015) Italy correspondent assesses modern Italy.

Gomorrah (Roberto Saviano; 2006) Unputdownable epic about the Neapolitan Camorra (mafia).

History (Elsa Morante; 1974) War, sexual violence and a mother's struggles define this controversial novel.

Watch

La Dolce Vita (1960) Federico Fellini's tale of hedonism, celebrity and suicide in 1950s Rome.

Bicycle Thieves (1958) Vittorio di Sica's poignant tale of an honest man trying to provide for his son in postwar Rome.

Il Postino (1994) Massimo Troisi plays Italy's most adorable postman.

Gomorrah (2008) In-your-face mafia exposé based on Roberto Saviano's bestseller.

Videocracy (2009)Chilling documentary about Italy's celebrity- and television-infused culture.

La Grande Bellezza (2013) Set in Rome, Paolo Sorrentino's wonderful Fellini-esque peer into modern Italy's psyche.

Listen

La Traviata (1955) Diva Maria Callas embodies Verdi's fallen woman in La Scala's production by film-maker Luchino Visconti.

Crêuza de mä (Fabrizio de André) Bob Dylan–style poetry in Genovese dialect.

Mina (Mina) Best-selling album from Italy's foremost female rocker.

Stato di Necessità (Carmen Consoli) Guitar riffs and soulful lyrics from Sicily's favourite singer-songwriter.

Suburb ('A67) Neapolitan rock-crossover group 'A67 collaborate with anti-mafia activists.

Above. *Biscotti*

Plan Your Trip
Five-Day Itineraries

A Slice of the South

Sample the best of Italy's sun-kissed south on this five-day trip from Naples to Sicily. Naples' fiery streets and majestic sights will warm you up for the road ahead, which takes in amazing ancient ruins and brooding volcanoes, as well as sublime food at every turn.

Naples (p226) Begin your southern getaway with two days in hyperactive Naples with its baroque splendour and unparalleled pizza.
⚱ 12 hrs to Catania, 🚌 2 hrs to Mt Etna

Palermo (p282) Spend your last day getting to grips with Palermo's highly charged streets and magnificent hybrid architecture, sampling *arancini* (fried rice balls) as you go.

Valley of the Temples, Agrigento (p280) Sicily's single-most popular attraction is centred on a series of fantastically preserved Greek temples.
🚌 2½ hrs to Palermo

Mt Etna (p278) Dedicate your first day in Sicily to scaling Mt Etna, the island's legendary volcano.
🚌 3 hrs to Agrigento

Milan & the Italian Lakes

Formed at the end of the last ice age, and a popular holiday spot since Roman times, the Italian Lakes have an enduring, beguiling beauty. By contrast, Milan is all about the urban pleasures of fashion shopping and restaurant hopping.

Bellagio (p216) The most attractive and popular town on Lake Como with its waterfront of bobbing boats and quaint architecture.

Lago di Como (p222) Surrounded by wooded slopes, Lake Como is the most spectacular of the region's three major lakes. 🚗 1¼ hrs to Bellagio

Lago Maggiore (p220) The largest lake in the region, picturesque Maggiore is shared between Italy and Switzerland. 🚗 1 hr to Como

Milan (p192) Begin this northern tour with a dash around the north's de facto capital, fashion-concious Milan. 🚗 1 hr to Lago Maggiore

Plan Your Trip
10-Day Itinerary

Rome to the Italian Lakes

This 10-day road trip through central and northern Italy offers a vivid snapshot of the country's beauty. From Rome's ancient wonders to Tuscan treasures, a spectacular stretch of coastline and the far north's romantic lakes, it's a spellbinding journey.

Italian Lakes (p212) End with a couple of days lakeside. Take your pick between the belle-époque charms of Lago Maggiore or scenic Lago di Como.

Milan (p192) Home to the outlandishly Gothic Duomo, legendary La Scala and da Vinci's *The Last Supper*. 🚊 30 mins to 1 hr to Como

Lucca (p140) This charming walled city boasts the striking Cattedrale di San Martino and a lively *passeggiata*. 🚊 30 mins to Pisa

Florence (p94) Brunelleschi's Duomo cupola, Botticelli's *Birth of Venus* and Michelangelo's *David* – just some of Florence's treasures. 🚊 1½ hrs to Lucca

Cinque Terre (p148) Italy's coastal scenery is a sight to behold on the Cinque Terre, a glorious stretch of coastline. 🚊 4 hrs to Milan

Pisa (p132) A must on anyone's Tuscan itinerary where the Leaning Tower is attraction *numero uno*. 🚊 1½ hrs to Cinque Terre

Siena (p136) Like a huge open-air museum, Siena wows visitors with its architecture. 🚊 1¼ hrs to Florence

Rome (p34) Michelangelo's Sistine Chapel artworks, St Peter's Basilica, Piazza Navona, the Pantheon and the Colosseum – it all awaits in Rome. 🚊 4 hrs to Siena

Plan Your Trip
Two-Week Itinerary

Classic Cities

Taking in much of the boot, this two-week tour of Italy's greatest hits leads from Milan to the Amalfi Coast by way of the country's headline cities. On the way you'll encounter artistic masterpieces, inspiring city-scapes and stunning natural scenery.

Milan (p192) Kick off with a day in Italy's great northern metropolis, marvelling at its art, fashion and architecture. 🚆 2½ to 3½ hrs to Venice

Venice (p160) Check off must sees such as the Basilica di San Marco, Palazzo Ducale and the Grand Canal. 🚆 2¼ hrs to Florence

Florence (p94) Two or three days are hardly enough in Tuscany's Renaissance capital. 🚆 1¼ hrs to Siena

Siena (p136) The Piazza del Campo, Museo Civico and the city's astonishing landmark *duomo* are top sights in Siena. 🚆 4 hrs to Rome

Rome (p34) With just a couple of days to spare, you'll have to move fast to cover the basics in the eternal city. 🚆 2 to 2½ hrs to Naples

Naples (p226) The main city in southern Italy is a boisterous but fascinating mix. Circumvesuviana 🚆 1¼ hrs to Sorrento, then 🚆 40 mins to Positano

Amalfi Coast (p260) After two weeks on the road, Italy's most spectacular stretch of coastline makes the ideal finale.

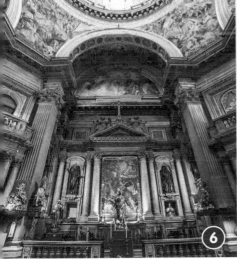

Plan Your Trip
Family Travel

Italy for Kids

Italian family travels divide into two camps: urban and rural. Cities in Italy are second to none in extraordinary sights and experiences, and with the aid of audioguides and some inventive tours, parents can find kid-appeal in almost every attraction.

Away from urban areas the pace slows and good, old-fashioned fresh air kicks in. Sandcastles, sea swimming and easy beachside ambles are natural elements of coastal travel while mountains and lakes inland demand immediate outdoor action from kids aged five and over.

Best Regions for Families

Rome & Lazio Ancient Roman ruins and world-class museums make Rome interesting for older children.

Naples & Campania Gold for every age: subterranean ruins in Naples, gladiator battlefields in Pompeii and Herculaneum, and natural high drama – think volcanoes, thermal pools and coastal caves.

Sicily Volcano climbing for sporty teens and beachside fun for sand-loving tots, alongside ancient ruins, hilltop castles and traditional 18th-century puppet theatre to inspire and entertain all ages.

Sardinia Alfresco paradise overflowing with dazzling beaches, water-sports action, horse riding and scenic hikes suitable for all ages and abilities.

Family Dining

Children are welcomed in most eateries, especially in casual trattorias and *osterie* – often family-owned with indulgent waiters. A *menù bambini* (children's menu) is fairly common. It's also acceptable to order a *mezzo piatto* (half-portion) or a simple plate of pasta.

Italian families eat late. Few restaurants open their doors before 7.30pm or 8pm, making pizzerias – many open early – more appealing for families with younger children. High chairs are occasionally available.

TORESS/SHUTTERSTOCK ©

Family-Friendly Accommodation

Italy's down-to-earth *agriturismi* (rural farm stays) are perfect for families: think self-catering facilities, green space to play around in and stacks of outdoor activities alongside traditional rural pastimes such as olive picking, feeding the black pig, making bread in ancient stone ovens and cultivating saffron. In southern Italy, kids enjoy accommodation in circular, whitewashed *trulli* and quiet, often luxurious *masserias* (farm stays).

In cities and towns countrywide, family and four-person rooms can be hard to find and should be booked in advance. Increasingly, boutique B&Bs offer family rooms and/or self-catering apartments suited to families with young children.

Need to Know

Baby formula and sterilising solution Available at all pharmacies.

★ Best Destinations for Kids

Sicily (p274)

Venice (p160)

Sardinia (p296)

Rome (p34)

Amalfi Coast (p260)

Disposable nappies (diapers) Available at supermarkets and pharmacies.

High chairs Available at many restaurants.

Change facilities Rare outside airports and more state-of-the-art museums.

Cots Request ahead at hotels.

Strollers Bring your own.

Infant car seats Reserve at car-rental firms.

From left: Hiking the Dolomites; Swimming in Sardinia (p296)

Roman Forum (p54)

Ceiling fresco in Museo e Galleria Borghese (p60)

Arriving in Rome

Leonardo da Vinci (Fiumicino) Airport Leonardo Express trains to Stazione Termini 6.23am to 11.23pm, €14; slower FL1 trains to Trastevere, Ostiense and Tiburtina stations 5.57am to 10.42pm, €8; buses to Stazione Termini 6.05am to 12.30am, €6.

Ciampino Airport Buses to Stazione Termini 4am to 11.15pm, €5; private transfers €25 per person.

Stazione Termini Airport buses and most trains arrive at Stazione Termini.

Where to Stay

Rome is expensive and busy; book ahead to secure the best deal. Accommodation ranges from palatial five-star hotels to hostels, B&Bs, *pensioni* and private rooms. Hostels are the cheapest, with dorm beds and private rooms: around Stazione Termini several budget hotels also offer 'dorm beds', meaning you can book a bed in a shared double, triple or quad hotel room. B&Bs and hotels cover every style and price range.

For more information about where to stay, see p93.

Interior of the Colosseum

Colosseum

A monument to raw, merciless power, the Colosseum is the most thrilling of Rome's ancient sights. It was here that gladiators met in mortal combat and condemned prisoners fought off wild beasts in front of baying, bloodthirsty crowds. Two thousand years on and it's Italy's top tourist attraction, drawing more than five million visitors a year.

Great For...

ℹ Need to Know

Colosseo; Map p68; ☎06 3996 7700; www. coopculture.it; Piazza del Colosseo; adult/reduced incl Roman Forum & Palatino €12/7.50; ⊙8.30am-1hr before sunset; Ⓜ Colosseo

★ **Top Tip**

Beat the queues by buying your ticket at the Palatino (Via di San Gregorio 30).

Built by Vespasian (r AD 69–79) in the grounds of Nero's vast Domus Aurea complex, the arena was inaugurated in AD 80, eight years after it had been commissioned. To mark the occasion, Vespasian's son and successor Titus (r AD 79–81) staged games that lasted 100 days and nights, during which 5000 animals were slaughtered. Trajan (r AD 98–117) later topped this, holding a marathon 117-day killing spree involving 9000 gladiators and 10,000 animals.

The 50,000-seat arena was originally known as the Flavian Amphitheatre, and although it was Rome's most fearsome arena it wasn't the biggest – the Circo Massimo could hold up to 250,000 people. The name Colosseum, when introduced in medieval times, was a reference not to its size but to the Colosso di Nerone, a giant statue of Nero that stood nearby.

With the fall of the Roman Empire in the 5th century, the Colosseum was abandoned and gradually became overgrown. In the Middle Ages it served as a fortress for two of the city's warrior families, the Frangipani and the Annibaldi. Later, during the Renaissance and baroque periods, it was plundered of its precious travertine, and the marble stripped from it was used to make huge palaces such as Palazzo Venezia, Palazzo Barberini and Palazzo Cancelleria.

More recently, pollution and vibrations caused by traffic and the metro have taken their toll, but the first stage of a €25-million clean-up, the first in its 2000-year history, has once again revealed the creamy hues of the Colosseum walls.

Exterior

The outer walls have three levels of arches, framed by Ionic, Doric and Corinthian columns. These were originally covered in travertine, and marble statues filled the niches on the 2nd and 3rd storeys. The upper level, punctuated with windows and slender Corinthian pilasters, had supports for 240 masts that held up a huge canvas awning over the arena, shielding spectators from sun and rain. The 80 entrance arches, known as vomitoria, allowed the spectators to enter and be seated in a matter of minutes.

☑ Don't Miss

The hypogeum's network of dank tunnels beneath the main arena. Visits require advance booking and cost an extra €9.

VLADISLAV GAJIC/SHUTTERSTOCK ©

Arena

The arena originally had a wooden floor covered in sand to prevent the combatants from slipping and to soak up the blood. It could also be flooded for mock sea battles. Trapdoors led down to the hypogeum, a subterranean complex of corridors, cages and lifts beneath the arena floor.

Stands

The *cavea*, for spectator seating, was divided into three tiers: magistrates and senior officials sat in the lowest tier, wealthy citizens in the middle, and the plebeians in the highest tier. Women (except for vestal virgins) were relegated to the cheapest sections at the top. As in modern stadiums, tickets were numbered and spectators assigned a seat in a specific sector – in 2015, restorers uncovered traces of red numerals on the arches, indicating how the sectors were numbered. The podium, a broad terrace in front of the tiers of seats, was reserved for the emperor, senators and VIPs.

Hypogeum

The hypogeum served as the stadium's backstage area. Sets for the various battle scenes were prepared here and hoisted up to the arena by a complicated system of pulleys. Caged animals were kept here and gladiators would gather here before showtime, having come in through an underground corridor from the nearby Ludus Magnus (gladiator school).

✕ Take a Break

Cafè Cafè (☏06 700 87 43; www.cafecafe bistrot.it; Via dei Santi Quattro 44; meals €15-20; ⊗9.30am-8.50pm; ☐Via di San Giovanni in Laterano) is the perfect venue for a post-arena break, for tea and cake or a light meal.

Pantheon

A striking 2000-year-old temple that's now a church, the Pantheon is Rome's best-preserved ancient monument and one of the most influential buildings in the Western world.

In its current form the Pantheon dates to around AD 125. The original temple, built by Marcus Agrippa in 27 BC, burnt down in AD 80, and although it was rebuilt by Domitian, it was struck by lightning and destroyed for a second time in AD 110. The emperor Hadrian had it reconstructed between AD 118 and 125, and it's this version that you see today.

Exterior

These days the facade is somewhat the worse for wear, but it's still an imposing sight. The monumental entrance **portico** consists of 16 Corinthian columns, each 13m high and made of Egyptian granite, supporting a triangular **pediment**. Behind the columns, two 20-tonne **bronze doors** – 16th-century restorations of the original portal – give onto the central rotunda. Rivets and holes in the building's brickwork

Great For...

☑ **Don't Miss**

The 7m-high bronze doors, which provide a suitably grand entrance to your visit.

PHANT/SHUTTERSTOCK ©

Piazza della Rotonda

◉ Pantheon

Via della Rotonda — Via della Minerva

Corso Vittorio Emanuele II

Largo di Torre Argentina Via del Plebiscito

Via del Corso

❶ Need to Know

Map p72; www.pantheonroma.com; Piazza della Rotonda; ⏰8.30am-7.15pm Mon-Sat, 9am-5.45pm Sun; 🚇Largo di Torre Argentina **FREE**

✕ Take a Break

Get caffeinated at **Caffè Sant'Eustachio** (Map p72; www.santeustachioilcaffe. it; Piazza Sant'Eustachio 82; ⏰8.30am-1am Sun-Thu, to 1.30am Fri, to 2am Sat; 🚇Corso del Rinascimento), known to serve some of the best coffee in town.

★ Top Tip

Mass is celebrated at the Pantheon at 5pm on Saturday and 10.30am on Sunday.

indicate where marble-veneer panels were originally placed.

Inscription

For centuries the inscription under the pediment – M:AGRIPPA.L.F.COS.TERTIUM.FECIT or 'Marcus Agrippa, son of Lucius, consul for the third time built this' – led scholars to think that the current building was Agrippa's original temple. However, 19th-century excavations revealed traces of an earlier temple and historians realised that Hadrian had simply kept Agrippa's original inscription.

Interior

Although impressive from outside, it's only when you get inside that you can really appreciate the Pantheon's full size. With light streaming in through the **oculus** (the 8.7m-diameter hole in the centre of the dome), the cylindrical marble-clad interior seems vast.

Opposite the entrance is the church's main **altar**, over which hangs a 7th-century icon of the *Madonna col Bambino* (Madonna and Child). To the left are the tombs of the artist Raphael, King Umberto I and Margherita of Savoy.

Dome

The Pantheon's dome, considered to be the Romans' most important architectural achievement, was the largest dome in the world until Brunelleschi beat it with his Florentine cupola. Its harmonious appearance is due to a precisely calibrated symmetry – its diameter is exactly equal to the building's interior height of 43.3m. At its centre, the oculus, which symbolically connected the temple with the gods, plays a vital structural role by absorbing and redistributing the dome's huge tensile forces.

The dome inside St Peter's Basilica

St Peter's Basilica

In this city of outstanding churches, none can hold a candle to St Peter's, Italy's largest, richest and most spectacular basilica.

Great For...

Cipro-Musei Vaticani

Via Cipro

Via Ottaviano

Ottaviano-San Pietro

Via Crescenzio

Valle Aurelia

St Peter's Basilica

Vatican Gardens

St Peter's Square

❶ Need to Know

Basilica di San Pietro; ☎06 6988 5518; www. vatican.va; St Peter's Square; ⏱7am-7pm summer, to 6.30pm winter; ☖Piazza del Risorgimento, ⓂOttaviano-San Pietro FREE

★ **Top Tip**
Strict dress codes are enforced, which means no shorts, miniskirts or bare shoulders.

Facade

Built between 1608 and 1612, Maderno's immense facade is 48m high and 118.6m wide. Eight 27m-high columns support the upper attic on which 13 statues stand representing Christ the Redeemer, St John the Baptist and the 11 apostles. The central balcony, the **Loggia della Benedizione**, is where the pope stands to deliver his *Urbi et Orbi* blessing at Christmas and Easter.

Interior

At the beginning of the right aisle is Michelangelo's hauntingly beautiful *Pietà*. Sculpted when the artist was 25 (in 1499), it's the only work he ever signed; his signature is etched into the sash across the Madonna's breast.

Dominating the centre of the basilica is Bernini's 29m-high **baldachin**. Supported by four spiral columns and made with bronze taken from the Pantheon, it stands over the **high altar**, which itself sits on the site of St Peter's grave.

Above the baldachin, Michelangelo's **dome** soars to a height of 119m. Based on Brunelleschi's cupola in Florence, it's supported by four massive stone **piers** named after the saints whose statues adorn the Bernini-designed niches – Longinus, Helena, Veronica and Andrew.

At the base of the **Pier of St Longinus** is Arnolfo di Cambio's much-loved 13th-century bronze **statue of St Peter**, whose right foot has been worn down by centuries of caresses.

St Peter's Basilica and St Peter's Square

Dome

From the **dome** (with/without lift €8/6; ⊙8am-6pm summer, to 5pm winter) entrance on the right of the basilica's main portico, you can walk the 551 steps to the top or take a small lift halfway and then follow on foot for the last 320 steps. Either way, it's a long, steep climb and not recommended for anyone who suffers from claustrophobia or vertigo. Make it to the top, though, and you're rewarded with stunning views.

Museo Storico Artistico

Accessed from the left nave, the **Museo Storico Artistico** (Tesoro, Treasury; adult/

> ☑ **Don't Miss**
>
> Climbing the (numerous, steep and tiring, but worth it) steps of the dome for views over Rome.

BRIAN KINNEY/SHUTTERSTOCK ©

reduced €7/5; ⊙8am-6.50pm summer, to 5.50pm winter) sparkles with sacred relics. Highlights include a tabernacle by Donatello; the *Colonna Santa*, a 4th-century Byzantine column from the earlier church; and the 6th-century *Crux Vaticana* (Vatican Cross), a jewel-encrusted crucifix presented by the emperor Justinian II to the original basilica.

Vatican Grottoes

Extending beneath the basilica, the **Vatican Grottoes** (⊙8am-6pm summer, to 5.30pm winter) **FREE** contain the tombs and sarcophagi of numerous popes, as well as several columns from the original 4th-century basilica The entrance is in the Pier of St Andrew.

St Peter's Tomb

Excavations beneath the basilica have uncovered part of the original church and what archaeologists believe is the **Tomb of St Peter** (✆06 6988 5318; www.scavi. va; €13, over 15yr only). In 1942 the bones of an elderly, strongly built man were found in a box hidden behind a wall covered by pilgrims' graffiti. And while the Vatican has never definitively claimed that the bones belong to St Peter, in 1968 Pope Paul VI said they had been identified in a way that the Vatican considered 'convincing'.

The excavations can only be visited by guided tour. For further details, and to book a tour, check out the website of the **Ufficio Scavi** (Excavations Office; Fabbrica di San Pietro; ✆06 6988 5318; www.scavi.va; ⊙9am-6pm Mon-Fri, 9am-5pm Sat; ⊠Piazza del Risorgimento, ⊠Ottaviano-San Pietro).

> ✕ **Take a Break**
>
> With more than 200 teas to choose from, you'll find the perfect cuppa at **Makasar Bistrot** (✆06 687 46 02; www.makasar.it; Via Plauto 33; ⊙noon-midnight Mon-Thu, to 2am Fri & Sat, 5pm-midnight Sun; ⊠Piazza del Risorgimento).

Vatican Museums

Founded in the 16th century, the Vatican Museums boast one of the world's greatest art collections. Highlights include spectacular classical statuary, rooms frescoed by Raphael, and the Michelangelo-decorated Sistine Chapel.

Housing the museums are the lavishly decorated halls and galleries of the Palazzo Apostolico Vaticano. This vast 5.5-hectare complex consists of two palaces – the Vatican palace (nearer to St Peter's) and the Belvedere Palace – joined by two long galleries. You'll never cover it all in one day, so it pays to be selective.

Pinacoteca

Often overlooked by visitors, the papal picture gallery displays paintings dating from the 11th to 19th centuries, with works by Giotto, Fra' Angelico, Filippo Lippi, Perugino, Titian, Guido Reni, Guercino, Pietro da Cortona, Caravaggio and Leonardo da Vinci.

Look out for a trio of paintings by Raphael in Room VIII – the *Madonna di Foligno* (Madonna of Folignano), the *Incoronazione della Vergine* (Crowning of the Virgin) and *La*

Great For...

☑ Don't Miss

The Sistine Chapel, Stanze di Raffaello, *Apollo Belvedere, Laocoön* and *La Trasfigurazione*.

ℹ️ Need to Know

Musei Vaticani; ☎06 6988 4676; www.musei
vaticani.va; Viale Vaticano; adult/reduced
€16/8, last Sun of month free; ⊗9am-6pm
Mon-Sat, 9am-2pm last Sun of month, last
entry 2hr before closing; 🚌Piazza del Risorgimento, Ⓜ️Ottaviano-San Pietro

✕ Take a Break

Snack on a scissor-cut square of pizza or
a rice croquette from Pizzarium (p87).

★ Top Tip

Avoid queues by booking tickets online (http://biglietteriamusei.vatican.
va/musei/tickets/do); the booking fee
costs €4.

Trasfigurazione (Transfiguration), which was
completed by his students after his death in
1520. Other highlights include Filippo Lippi's
*L'Incoronazione della Vergine con Angeli,
Santo e donatore* (Coronation of the Virgin
with Angels, Saints, and donors), Leonardo
da Vinci's haunting and unfinished *San
Gerolamo* (St Jerome) and Caravaggio's
Deposizione (Deposition from the Cross).

Museo Pio-Clementino

This stunning museum contains some of
the Vatican Museums' finest classical statuary, including the peerless *Apollo Belvedere*
and the 1st-century *Laocoön*, both in the
Cortile Ottagono (Octagonal Courtyard).
Before you go into the courtyard, take a
moment to admire the 1st-century *Apoxy-
omenos*, one of the earliest known sculptures to depict a figure with a raised arm.

To the left as you enter the courtyard, the
Apollo Belvedere is a 2nd-century Roman
copy of a 4th-century-BC Greek bronze.
A beautifully proportioned representation
of the sun god Apollo, it's considered one
of the great masterpieces of classical
sculpture. Nearby, the *Laocoön* depicts a
muscular Trojan priest and his two sons in
mortal struggle with two sea serpents.

Back inside, the **Sala degli Animali** is
filled with sculpted creatures and some
magnificent 4th-century mosaics. Continuing on, you come to the **Sala delle Muse**,
centred on the *Torso Belvedere,* another of
the museum's must-sees. A fragment of a
muscular 1st-century-BC Greek sculpture,
it was found in Campo de' Fiori and used
by Michelangelo as a model for his *ignudi*
(male nudes) in the Sistine Chapel.

The next room, the **Sala Rotonda**,
contains a number of colossal statues,
including a gilded-bronze *Ercole* (Hercules)
and an exquisite floor mosaic.

Museo Chiaramonti & Braccio Nuovo

This museum is effectively the long corridor that runs down the lower east side of the Palazzetto di Belvedere. Its walls are lined with thousands of statues and busts representing everything from immortal gods to playful cherubs and ugly Roman patricians.

Near the end of the hall, off to the right, is the **Braccio Nuovo** (New Wing), which contains a celebrated statue of the Nile as a reclining god covered by 16 babies.

Museo Gregoriano Egizio

Founded by Pope Gregory XVI in 1839, this Egyptian museum displays pieces taken from Egypt in ancient Roman times. The collection is small, but there are fascinating exhibits, including a fragmented statue of the pharaoh Ramses II on his throne, vividly painted sarcophagi dating from around 1000 BC, and a macabre mummy.

Museo Gregoriano Etrusco

At the top of the 18th-century Simonetti staircase, this fascinating museum contains artefacts unearthed in the Etruscan tombs of northern Lazio, as well as a superb collection of vases and Roman antiquities. Of particular interest is the *Marte di Todi* (Mars of Todi), a black bronze of a warrior dating to the late 5th century BC.

Galleria delle Carte Geografiche & Sala Sobieski

The last of three galleries – the other two are the **Galleria dei Candelabri** (Gallery

Sala Rotonda

of the Candelabra) and the **Galleria degli Arazzi** (Tapestry Gallery) – this 120m-long corridor is hung with 40 huge topographical maps. These were created between 1580 and 1583 for Pope Gregory XIII based on drafts by Ignazio Danti, one of the leading cartographers of his day.

Beyond the gallery, the **Sala Sobieski** is named after an enormous 19th-century painting depicting the victory of the Polish king John III Sobieski over the Turks in 1683.

> ★ **Local Knowledge**
>
> Tuesdays and Thursdays are the quietest days to visit, Wednesday mornings are also good, and afternoons are better than mornings. Avoid Mondays, when many other museums are shut.

VVOLF/SHUT ERSTOCK ©

Stanze di Raffaello

These four frescoed chambers were part of Pope Julius II's private apartments. Raphael himself painted the Stanza della Segnatura (1508–11) and the Stanza d'Eliodoro (1512–14), while the Stanza dell'Incendio (1514–17) and Sala di Costantino (1517–24) were decorated by students following his designs.

The first room you come to is the **Sala di Costantino**, which features a huge fresco depicting Constantine's defeat of Maxentius at the battle of Milvian Bridge.

The **Stanza d'Eliodoro**, which was used for private audiences, takes its name from the *Cacciata d'Eliodoro* (Expulsion of Heliodorus from the Temple), an allegorical work reflecting Pope Julius II's policy of forcing foreign powers off Church lands. To its right, the *Messa di Bolsena* (Mass of Bolsena) shows Julius paying homage to the relic of a 13th-century miracle at the lakeside town of Bolsena. Next is the *Incontro di Leone Magno con Attila* (Encounter of Leo the Great with Attila) by Raphael and his school, and, on the fourth wall, the *Liberazione di San Pietro* (Liberation of St Peter), another Raphael masterpiece.

The **Stanza della Segnatura**, Julius' study and library, was the first room that Raphael painted, and it's here that you'll find his great masterpiece, *La Scuola di Atene* (The School of Athens), featuring philosophers and scholars gathered around Plato and Aristotle. The seated figure in front of the steps is believed to be Michelangelo, while the figure of Plato is said to be a portrait of Leonardo da Vinci, and Euclide (the bald man bending over) is Bramante. Raphael also included a self-portrait in the lower right corner – he's the second figure from the right.

> ★ **Top Tip**
>
> Most exhibits are not well labelled. Consider hiring an audio guide (€7) or buying the *Guide to the Vatican Museums and City* (€14).

The most famous work in the **Stanza dell'Incendio di Borgo** is the *Incendio di Borgo* (Fire in the Borgo), which depicts Pope Leo IV extinguishing a fire by making the sign of the cross. The ceiling was painted by Raphael's master, Perugino.

Sistine Chapel

The jewel in the Vatican's crown, the **Sistine Chapel** (Cappella Sistina) is home to two of the world's most famous works of art: Michelangelo's ceiling frescoes and his *Giudizio Universale* (Last Judgment).

The chapel was originally built for Pope Sixtus IV, after whom it's named, and was consecrated on 15 August 1483. However, apart from the wall frescoes and floor, little remains of the original decor, which was sacrificed to make way for Michelangelo's two masterpieces. The first, the ceiling, was commissioned by Pope Julius II and painted between 1508 and 1512; the second, the spectacular *Giudizio Universale,* was painted between 1535 and 1541.

Michelangelo's ceiling design, which is best viewed from the chapel's main entrance in the far east wall, covers the entire 800-sq-metre surface. With painted architectural features and a cast of colourful biblical characters, it's centred on nine panels depicting scenes from the Creation, the story of Adam and Eve, the Fall, and the plight of Noah.

As you look up from the east wall, the first panel is the *Drunkenness of Noah,* followed by *The Flood* and the *Sacrifice of Noah.* Next, *Original Sin and Banishment from the Garden of Eden* famously depicts Adam and Eve being sent packing after accepting the forbidden fruit from Satan, represented by a snake with the body of a woman coiled around a tree. The *Creation of Eve* is then followed by the *Creation of Adam.* This, one of the most famous images in Western art, shows a bearded God pointing his finger at Adam, thus bringing him to life. Completing the sequence are the *Separation of Land from Sea;* the *Creation of the Sun, Moon and Plants;* and the *Sep-*

aration of Light from Darkness, featuring a fearsome God reaching out to touch the sun. Set around the central panels are 20 athletic male nudes, known as *ignudi.*

Opposite, on the west wall is Michelangelo's mesmeric *Giudizio Universale,* showing Christ – in the centre near the top – passing sentence over the souls of the dead as they are torn from their graves to face him. The saved get to stay in heaven (in the upper right); the damned are sent down to face the demons in hell (in the bottom right).

Near the bottom, on the right, you'll see a man with donkey ears and a snake wrapped around him. This is Biagio de Cesena, the papal master of ceremonies, who was a fierce critic of Michelangelo's composition. Another famous figure is St

Original Sin and Banishment from the Garden of Eden

Bartholomew, just beneath Christ, holding his own flayed skin. The face in the skin is said to be a self-portrait of Michelangelo, its anguished look reflecting the artist's tormented faith.

If you can tear your eyes from the Michelangelos, the chapel's walls also boast superb frescoes. Painted between 1481 and 1482 by a crack team of Renaissance artists, including Botticelli, Ghirlandaio, Pinturicchio, Perugino and Luca Signorelli, they represent events in the lives of Moses (to the left looking at the *Giudizio Universale*) and Christ (to the right). Highlights include Botticelli's *Temptations of Christ* and Perugino's *Handing over of the Keys*.

★ Michelangelo's Ceiling

When Pope Julius II first approached Michelangelo – some say at the suggestion of his chief architect, Bramante, who was keen for Michelangelo to fail – he was reluctant to accept. He regarded himself as a sculptor and had no experience of painting frescoes. However, Julius persisted and in 1508 he persuaded Michelangelo to accept the commission for a fee of 3000 ducats (more or less €1.5 to €2 million in today's money).

☑ Visitors with Disabilities

Free guided tours are available for blind and deaf visitors. For further details, see the Services for Visitors section of the museums' website.

SISTINE CHAPEL CEILING (1508-12), THE FALL OF MAN, 1510 (FRESCO) (POST RESTORATION), BUONARROTI, MICHELANGELO (1475-1564) / VATICAN MUSEUMS AND GALLERIES, VATICAN CITY / BRIDGEMAN IMAGES ©

Tempio di Antonino e Faustina (p56)

Roman Forum

The Roman Forum was ancient Rome's showpiece centre, a grandiose district of temples, basilicas and vibrant public spaces. Nowadays, it's a collection of impressive, if badly labelled, ruins that can leave you drained and confused. But if you can get your imagination going, there's something wonderfully compelling about walking in the footsteps of Julius Caesar and other legendary figures of Roman history.

Great For...

❶ Need to Know

Foro Romano; Map p68; ☎06 3996 7700; www.coopculture.it; Largo della Salara Vecchia, Piazza di Santa Maria Nova; adult/reduced incl Colosseum & Palatino €12/7.50; ⊙8.30am-1hr before sunset; ☐Via dei Fori Imperiali

★ **Top Tip**

Get grandstand views of the Roman Forum from the Palatino and Campidoglio.

Originally an Etruscan burial ground, the Forum was first developed in the 7th century BC, growing over time to become the social, political and commercial hub of the Roman Empire. In the Middle Ages it was reduced to pasture land and extensively plundered for its marble. The area was systematically excavated in the 18th and 19th centuries and work continues to this day.

Via Sacra Towards Campidoglio

Entering the Forum from Largo della Salara Vecchia, you'll see the **Tempio di Antonino e Faustina** (Map p68) ahead to your left. Erected in AD 141, this was transformed into a church in the 8th century, the **Chiesa di San Lorenzo in Miranda** (Map p68). To your right is the 179 BC **Basilica Fulvia Aemilia** (Map p68).

At the end of the path, you'll come to **Via Sacra** (Map p68), the Forum's main thoroughfare, and the Tempio di Giulio Cesare, which stands on the spot where Julius Caesar was cremated.

Heading right brings you to the **Curia** (Map p68), the original seat of the Roman Senate, though what you see today is a reconstruction of how it looked in the reign of Diocletian (r 284–305).

At the end of Via Sacra, the **Arco di Settimio Severo** (Arch of Septimius Severus; Map p68) is dedicated to the eponymous emperor and his sons, Caracalla and Geta. Close by the **Colonna di Foca** (Column of Phocus; Map p68) rises above what was once the Forum's main square, Piazza del Foro.

The eight granite columns that rise behind the Colonna are all that survive of the **Tempio di Saturno** (Temple of Saturn;

Arches of Basilica Giulia

Map p68), an important temple that doubled as the state treasury.

Tempio di Castore e Polluce & Casa delle Vestali

From the path that runs parallel to Via Sacra, you'll pass the stubby ruins of the **Basilica Giulia** (Map p68), which was begun by Caesar and finished by Augustus. At the end of the basilica, three columns remain from the 5th-century-BC **Tempio di Castore e Polluce** (Temple of Castor and Pollux; Map p68). Nearby, the 6th-century **Chiesa di Santa Maria Antiqua** (Map p68; currently closed) is the oldest Christian church in the Forum.

Back towards Via Sacra is the **Casa delle Vestali** (House of the Vestal Virgins; Map p68), currently off limits, it was the home of the virgins who tended the flame in the adjoining **Tempio di Vesta** (Map p68).

Via Sacra Towards the Colosseum

Heading up Via Sacra past the **Tempio di Romolo** (Temple of Romulus; Map p68), you'll come to the **Basilica di Massenzio** (Basilica di Costantino; Map p68), the largest building on the Forum.

Beyond the basilica, the **Arco di Tito** (Arch of Titus; Map p68) was built in AD 81 to celebrate Vespasian's and Titus' victories against rebels in Jerusalem.

☑ Don't Miss

The Basilica di Massenzio, to get some idea of the scale of ancient Rome's mammoth buildings.

VALERY ROKHIN/SHUTTERSTOCK ©

Roman Forum

A HISTORICAL TOUR

In ancient times, a forum was a market place, civic centre and religious complex all rolled into one, and the greatest of all was the Roman Forum (Foro Romano). Situated between the Palatino (Palatine Hill), ancient Rome's most exclusive neighbourhood, and the Campidoglio (Capitoline Hill), it was the city's busy, bustling centre. On any given day it teemed with activity. Senators debated affairs of state in the ❶ **Curia**, shoppers thronged the squares and traffic-free streets and crowds gathered under the ❷ **Colonna di Foca** to listen to politicians holding forth from the ❷ **Rostri**. Elsewhere, lawyers worked the courts in basilicas including the ❸ **Basilica di Massenzio**, while the Vestal Virgins quietly went about their business in the ❹ **Casa delle Vestali**.

Special occasions were also celebrated in the Forum: religious holidays were marked with ceremonies at temples such as ❺ **Tempio di Saturno** and ❻ **Tempio di Castore e Polluce**, and military victories were honoured with dramatic processions up Via Sacra and the building of monumental arches like ❼ **Arco di Settimio Severo** and ❽ **Arco di Tito**.

The ruins you see today are impressive but they can be confusing without a clear picture of what the Forum once looked like. This spread shows the Forum in its heyday, complete with temples, civic buildings and towering monuments to heroes of the Roman Empire.

TOP TIPS

➡ Get grandstand views of the Forum from the Palatino and Campidoglio.

➡ Visit first thing in the morning or late afternoon; crowds are worst between 11am and 2pm.

➡ In summer it gets hot in the Forum and there's little shade, so take a hat and plenty of water.

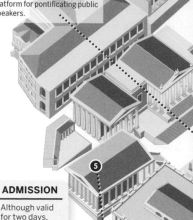

Colonna di Foca & Rostri

The free-standing, 13.5m-high Column of Phocus is the Forum's youngest monument, dating to AD 608. Behind it, the Rostri provided a suitably grandiose platform for pontificating public speakers.

Campidoglio (Capitoline Hill)

ADMISSION

Although valid for two days, admission tickets only allow for one entry into the Forum, Colosseum and Palatino.

Tempio di Saturno

Ancient Rome's Fort Knox, the Temple of Saturn was the city treasury. In Caesar's day it housed 13 tonnes of gold, 114 tonnes of silver and 30 million sestertii worth of silver coins.

IASCIC/SHUTTERSTOCK®

VIACHESLAV LOPATIN/SHUTTERSTOCK®

Tempio di Castore e Polluce

Only three columns of the Temple of Castor and Pollux remain. The temple was dedicated to the Heavenly Twins after they supposedly led the Romans to victory over the Latin League in 496 BC.

Arco di Settimio Severo

One of the Forum's signature monuments, this imposing triumphal arch commemorates the military victories of Septimius Severus. Relief panels depict his campaigns against the Parthians.

Curia

This big barn-like building was the official seat of the Roman Senate. Most of what you see is a reconstruction, but the interior marble floor dates to the 3rd-century reign of Diocletian.

Basilica di Massenzio

Marvel at the scale of this vast 4th-century basilica. In its original form the central hall was divided into enormous naves; now only part of the northern nave survives.

JULIUS CAESAR

Julius Caesar was cremated on the site where the Tempio di Giulio Cesare now stands.

Via Sacra

Tempio di Giulio Cesare

Casa delle Vestali

White statues line the grassy atrium of what was once the luxurious 50-room home of the Vestal Virgins. The virgins played an important role in Roman religion, serving the goddess Vesta.

Arco di Tito

Said to be the inspiration for the Arc de Triomphe in Paris, the well-preserved Arch of Titus was built by the emperor Domitian to honour his elder brother Titus.

Museo e Galleria Borghese

Housing what's often referred to as the 'queen of all private art collections', this spectacular gallery boasts some of the city's finest art treasures, including sensational sculptures by Bernini and important paintings by the likes of Caravaggio, Titian and Raphael.

Great For...

☑ Don't Miss

Tear yourself away from Bernini's mythical sculptures to admire Canova's *Venere Vincitrice,* his sensual portrayal of Paolina Bonaparte Borghese.

The museum's collection was formed by Cardinal Scipione Borghese (1579–1633), the most knowledgeable and ruthless art collector of his day. It was originally housed in his residence near St Peter's, but in the 1620s he had it transferred to his new villa just outside Porta Pinciana. And it's here, in the villa's central building, the Casino Borghese, that you'll see it today.

Entrance & Ground Floor

The **entrance hall** features 4th-century floor mosaics of fighting gladiators and a 2nd-century *Satiro Combattente* (Fighting Satyr). High on the wall is a gravity-defying bas-relief of a horse and rider falling into the void by Pietro Bernini (Gian Lorenzo's father).

Sala I is centred on Antonio Canova's daring depiction of Napoleon's sister, Paolina Bonaparte Borghese, reclining topless as *Venere Vincitrice* (Venus Victrix; 1805–08).

Bernini's *Ratto di Proserpina*

WJAREN/SHUTTERSTOCK ©

Viale dell'Uccelliera

Museo e Galleria Borghese

Piazzale del Museo Borghese

Viale del Museo Borghese

Via Pinciana

❶ Need to Know

📞 06 3 28 10; www.galleriaborghese.it;
Piazzale del Museo Borghese 5; adult/reduced
€15/8.50; ⏰9am-7pm Tue-Sun; 🚇Via Pinciana

✕ Take a Break

There's a bar in the basement entrance
area, but for a more memorable meal
head across the park to the **Caffè delle
Arti** (📞06 3265 1236; www.caffedellearti
roma.com; Via Gramsci 73; meals €40-45;
⏰8am-5pm Mon, 8am-midnight Tue-Sun;
🚇Piazza Thorvaldsen).

★ Top Tip

Remember to pre-book your ticket,
and take ID when you pick it up.

Goliath; 1609–10) – Goliath's head is said
to be a self-portrait.

But it's Gian Lorenzo Bernini's spectacular sculptures – flamboyant depictions of
pagan myths – that really steal the show.
Just look at Daphne's hands morphing into
leaves in the swirling *Apollo e Dafne* (1622–
25) in **Sala III**, or Pluto's hand pressing into
the seemingly soft flesh of Persephone's
thigh in the *Ratto di Proserpina* (Rape of
Proserpina; 1621–22) in **Sala IV**.

Caravaggio, one of Cardinal Scipione's
favourite artists, dominates **Sala VIII**. You'll
see a dissipated *Bacchino malato* (Young
Sick Bacchus; 1593–94), the strangely
beautiful *La Madonna dei Palafrenieri*
(Madonna of the Palafrenieri; 1605–06),
and *San Giovanni Battista* (St John the
Baptist; 1609–10), probably his last work.
There's also the much-loved *Ragazzo col
Canestro di Frutta* (Boy with a Basket of
Fruit; 1593–95) and dramatic *Davide con
la Testa di Golia* (David with the Head of

Picture Gallery

With works representing the best of the
Tuscan, Venetian, Umbrian and northern
European schools, the upstairs picture
gallery offers a wonderful snapshot of
Renaissance art.

In **Sala IX** don't miss Raphael's extraordinary *La Deposizione di Cristo* (The Deposition; 1507) and his charming *Dama con
Liocorno* (Lady with a Unicorn; 1506). In
the same room you'll find Fra' Bartolomeo's
superb *Adorazione del Bambino* (Adoration
of the Christ Child; 1499) and Perugino's
Madonna col Bambino (Madonna and
Child; early 16th century).

Other highlights include Correggio's
Danäe (1530–31), two self-portraits by
Bernini in **Sala XIV** and Titian's early masterpiece *Amor Sacro e Amor Profano* (Sacred and Profane Love; 1514) in **Sala XX**.

Emperors' Footsteps

Follow in the footsteps of an ancient Roman on this whistle-stop tour of the city's most famous ruins.

Start Colosseum
Distance 1.5km
Duration 4 hours

6 No emperor ever walked the massive mountain of white marble that is **Vittoriano** (p67), but it's worth stopping off to take the panoramic lift to the top, from where you can see the whole of Rome beneath you.

4 The Michelangelo-designed **Piazza del Campidoglio** (p67), one of Rome's most beautiful piazzas, sits atop the Campidoglio (Capitoline Hill), one of the seven hills on which Rome was founded.

5 Flanking Piazza del Campidoglio are two stately *palazzi* (mansions) that together house the **Capitoline Museums** (p67). These, the world's oldest public museums, boast an important picture gallery and a superb collection of classical sculpture.

Take a Break... Hidden away in the Capitoline Museums but accessible by its own entrance, the **Terrazza Caffarelli** (☎06 6919 0564; ⊙9.30am-7pm) is a refined spot for a coffee with magical views.

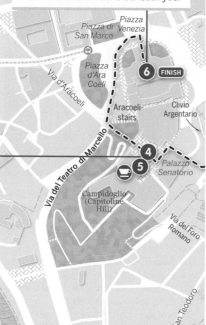

2 The **Palatino** (p66) was ancient Rome's most sought-after neighbourhood, site of the emperor's palace and home to the cream of imperial society.

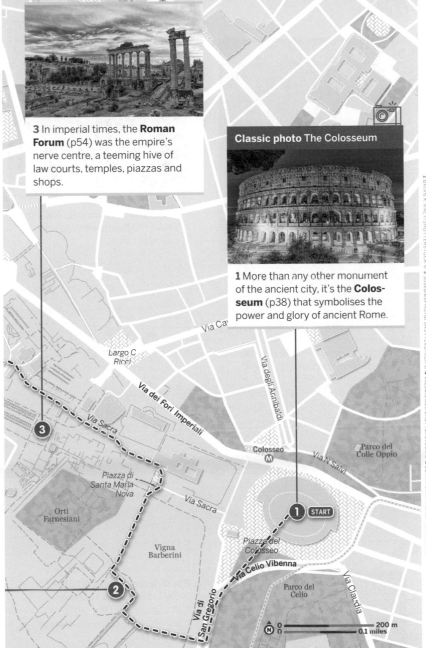

3 In imperial times, the **Roman Forum** (p54) was the empire's nerve centre, a teeming hive of law courts, temples, piazzas and shops.

Classic photo The Colosseum

1 More than any other monument of the ancient city, it's the **Colosseum** (p38) that symbolises the power and glory of ancient Rome.

Via Ca'

Largo C Ricci

Via dei Fori Imperiali

Via Sacra

3

Via degli Arnibaldi

Colosseo
Ⓜ

Parco del Colle Oppio

Via N Salvi

Piazza di Santa Maria Nova

Via Sacra

Orti Farnesiani

1 START

Vigna Barberini

Piazza del Colosseo

2

Via Celio Vibenna

Parco del Celio

Via di San Gregorio

Via Claudia

Ⓝ 0   200 m
0   0.1 miles

Centro Storico Piazzas

Rome's *centro storico* boasts some of the city's most celebrated piazzas, and several lovely but lesser-known squares. Each has its own character, but together they encapsulate much of the city's beauty, history and drama.

Start Piazza Colonna
Distance 1.5km
Duration 3½ hours

Classic Photo Piazza della Rotonda with the Pantheon in the background.

4 It's a short walk along Via del Seminario to Piazza della Rotonda, where the **Pantheon** (p43) needs no introduction.

5 Piazza Navona (p70) is Rome's geat showpiece square, where you can compare the two giants of Roman baroque – Gian Lorenzo Bernini and Francesco Borromini.

Piazza Navona

Corso del Rinascimento

Salita dei Crescenzi

4

Via della Rotonda

5

Via degli Staderari

Via dei Canestrari

Via Monterone

Piazza di San Pantaleo

Corso Vittorio Emanuele II

Via dei Cappellari

Via del Baullari

6

Via del Monserrato

7

FINISH

Via dei Farnesi

Via dei Giubbonari

Lgt dei Tebaldi

Take a Break... Those in the know head to Forno di Campo de' Fiori (p82) for some of Rome's best *pizza bianca* (white pizza with olive oil and salt).

7 Just beyond the Campo, the more sober **Piazza Farnese** is overshadowed by the austere fa-cade of the Renaissance **Palazzo Farnese** (p71).

1 Piazza Colonna is dominated by the 30m-high Colonna di Marco Aurelio and flanked by Palazzo Chigi, the official residence of the Italian prime minister.

Piazza di Montecitorio

1 START

2 Via di Pietra

Via dei Pastini

3 Via del Caravita

Via del Seminario

Via di Sant'Ignazio

Via della Minerva

2 Follow Via dei Bergamaschi to **Piazza di Pietra**, a refined space overlooked by the 2nd-century Tempio di Adriano.

3 Continue down Via de' Burro to **Piazza di Sant'Ignazlo Loyola**, a small piazza with a church boasting celebrated *trompe l'œil* frescoes.

6 On the other side of Corso Vittorio Emanuele II, **Campo de' Fiori** (p71) hosts a noisy market and boisterous drinking scene.

⊙ SIGHTS

They say that a lifetime's not enough for Rome (*Roma, non basta una vita!*). There's simply too much to see. So the best plan is to choose selectively, and leave the rest for next time. Note that many of Rome's major museums and monuments, including the Capitoline Museums and all four seats of the Museo Nazionale Romano, host regular exhibitions. When these are on, ticket prices are increased slightly, typically by about €3.

⊙ Ancient Rome

Arco di Costantino   Monument

(Map p68; Via di San Gregorio; ⓂColosseo) On the western side of the Colosseum, this monumental triple arch was built in AD 315 to celebrate the emperor Constantine's victory over his rival Maxentius at the Battle of the Milvian Bridge (AD 312). Rising to a height of 25m, it's the largest of Rome's surviving triumphal arches.

the world's oldest public museums

Capitoline Museums

Palatino   Archaeological Site

(Palatine Hill; Map p68; ☎06 3996 7700; www.coopculture.it; Via di San Gregorio 30, Piazza di Santa Maria Nova; adult/reduced incl Colosseum & Roman Forum €12/7.50; ⊗8.30am-1hr before sunset; ⓂColosseo) Sandwiched between the Roman Forum and the Circo Massimo, the Palatino (Palatine Hill) is an atmospheric area of towering pine trees, majestic ruins and memorable views. It was here that Romulus supposedly founded the city in 753 BC and Rome's emperors lived in unabashed luxury. Look out for the **stadio** (stadium), the ruins of the **Domus Flavia** (imperial palace), and grandstand views over the Roman Forum from the **Orti Farnesiani**.

Imperial Forums   Archaeological Site

(Fori Imperiali; Map p68; Via dei Fori Imperiali; ☐Via dei Fori Imperiali) Visible from Via dei Fori Imperiali and, when it's open, Via Alessandrina, the forums of Trajan, Augustus, Nerva and Caesar are known collectively as the Imperial Forums. These were largely buried when Mussolini bulldozed Via dei Fori Imperiali through the area in 1933, but

VVOE/SHUTTERSTOCK ©

excavations have since unearthed much of them. The standout sights are the **Mercati di Traiano** (Trajan's Markets), accessible through the Museo dei Fori Imperiali, and the landmark **Colonna Traiana** (Trajan's Column; Map p68).

Mercati di Traiano
Museo dei Fori Imperiali   Museum

(Map p68; ☎06 06 08; www.mercatiditraiano.it; Via IV Novembre 94; adult/reduced €11.50/9.50; ⊗9.30am-7.30pm, last admission 6.30pm; 🚇Via IV Novembre) This striking museum brings to life the **Mercati di Traiano**, emperor Trajan's great 2nd-century complex, while also providing a fascinating introduction to the Imperial Forums with multimedia displays, explanatory panels and a smattering of archaeological artefacts.

Sculptures, friezes and the occasional bust are set out in rooms opening onto what was once the Great Hall. But more than the exhibits, the real highlight here is the chance to explore the echoing ruins of the vast complex. The three-storey hemicycle was originally thought to have housed markets and shops – hence its name – but historians now believe it was largely used to house the Forum's administrative offices.

Rising above the markets is the **Torre delle Milizie** (Militia Tower; Map p68; 🚇Via IV Novembre), a 13th-century red-brick tower.

Capitoline Museums   Museum

(Musei Capitolini; Map p68; ☎06 06 08; www.museicapitolini.org; Piazza del Campidoglio 1; adult/reduced €11.50/9.50; ⊗9.30am-7.30pm, last admission 6.30pm; 🚇Piazza Venezia) Dating to 1471, the Capitoline Museums are the world's oldest public museums. Their collection of classical sculpture is one of Italy's finest, including crowd-pleasers such as the iconic *Lupa capitolina* (Capitoline Wolf), a sculpture of Romulus and Remus under a wolf, and the *Galata morente* (Dying Gaul), a moving depiction of a dying Gaul warrior. There's also a formidable picture gallery with masterpieces by the likes of Titian, Tintoretto, Rubens and Caravaggio.

 Passeggiata on Via del Corso

The *passeggiata* (traditional evening stroll) is a quintessential Roman experience. It's particularly colourful at weekends when families, friends and lovers take to the streets to strut up and down, slurp on gelato and window-shop.

To partake in the spectacle, head to Via del Corso around 6pm. Alternatively, park yourself on the Spanish Steps and watch the theatrics unfold beneath you on Piazza di Spagna (p71).

Via del Corso
J.JFARQ/SHUTTERSTOCK©

Ticket prices increase when there's a temporary exhibition on.

Piazza del Campidoglio   Piazza

(Map p68; 🚇Piazza Venezia) This hilltop piazza, designed by Michelangelo in 1538, is one of Rome's most beautiful squares. There are several approaches but the most dramatic is via the graceful **Cordonata** (Map p68; Piazza d'Aracoeli) staircase up from Piazza d'Aracoeli.

The piazza is flanked by **Palazzo Nuovo** and **Palazzo dei Conservatori**, together home to the Capitoline Museums, and **Palazzo Senatorio**, the seat of Rome city council. In the centre is a copy of an **equestrian statue** of Marcus Aurelius.

The original, which dates to the 2nd century AD, is in the Capitoline Museums.

Vittoriano   Monument

(Victor Emanuel Monument; Map p68; Piazza Venezia; ⊗9.30am-5.30pm summer, to 4.30pm winter; 🚇Piazza Venezia) **FREE** Love it or

Ancient Rome

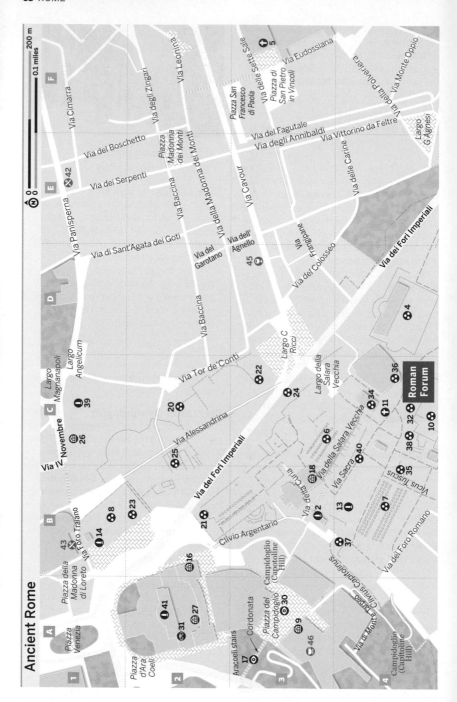

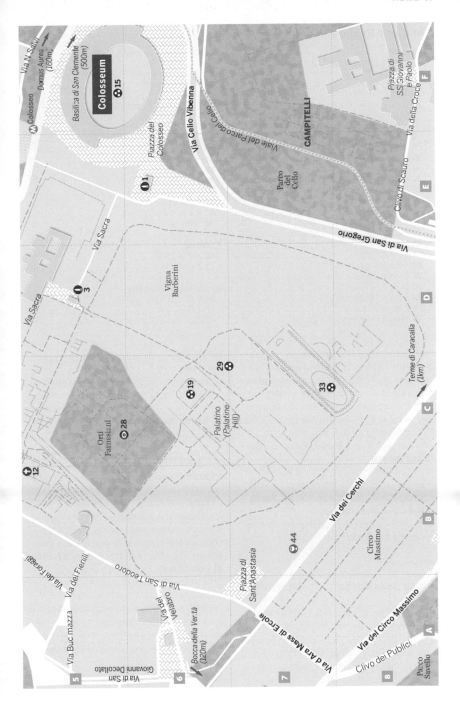

Via N. Salvi
Domus Aurea
(160m)
M Colosseo
Basilica di San Clemente
(500m)
Colosseum
⊗ 15
Piazza del
Colosseo
Via Celio Vibenna
Via del Parco del Celio
Piazza di
SS Giovanni
e Paolo
Via della Croce
CAMPITELLI
Parco
del Celio
Clivo di Scauro
Via di San Gregorio
❶ 1
Via Sacra
Vigna
Barberini
Via Sacra
❶ 3
Terme di Caracalla
(1km)
29 ⊗
❸ 19
Palatino
(Palatine
Hill)
33 ⊗
Orti
Farnesiani
◉ 28
✚ 12
Via dei Cerchi
Circo
Massimo
Via del Foraggi
Via Buc mazza
Via dei Fienili
Via dei Fienili
Bocca della Verità
(120m)
Via del Velabro
Via di San Teodoro
Piazza di
Sant'Anastasia
⊖ 44
Via del Circo Massimo
Via di San
Giovanni Decollato
Via d Ara Mass di Ercole
Clivo dei Publici
Parco
Savello

Ancient Rome

loathe it, as many Romans do, you can't ignore the Vittoriano (aka the Altare della Patria, Altar of the Fatherland), the massive mountain of white marble that towers over Piazza Venezia. Begun in 1885 to honour Italy's first king, Victor Emmanuel II – who's immortalised in its vast equestrian statue – it incorporates the **Museo Centrale del Risorgimento** (Map p68; ☏06 679 35 98; www.risorgimento.it; adult/reduced €5/2.50; ☺9.30am-6.30pm), a small museum documenting Italian unification, and the **Tomb of the Unknown Soldier**.

For Rome's best 360-degree views, take the **Roma dal Cielo** (Map p68; adult/reduced €7/3.50; ☺9.30am-7.30pm, last admission 7pm) lift to the top.

Bocca della Verità   Monument
(Mouth of Truth; Piazza Bocca della Verità 18; ☺9.30am-5.50pm; ▣Piazza Bocca della Verità)
A bearded face carved into a giant marble disc, the *Bocca della Verità* is one of Rome's most popular curiosities. Legend has it that if you put your hand in the mouth and tell a

lie, the Bocca will slam shut and bite your hand off.

The mouth, which was originally part of a fountain, or possibly an ancient manhole cover, now lives in the portico of the **Chiesa di Santa Maria in Cosmedin**, a handsome medieval church.

◎ Centro Storico

Piazza Navona   Piazza
(Map p72; ▣Corso del Rinascimento) With its showy fountains, baroque *palazzi* (mansions) and colourful cast of street artists, hawkers and tourists, Piazza Navona is central Rome's elegant showcase square. Built over the 1st-century **Stadio di Domiziano** (Domitian's Stadium; Map p72; ☏06 4568 6100; www.stadiodomiziano.com; Via di Tor Sanguigna 3; adult/reduced €8/6; ☺10am-7pm Sun-Fri, to 8pm Sat), it was paved over in the 15th century and for almost 300 years hosted the city's main market. Its grand centrepiece is Bernini's **Fontana dei Quattro Fiumi** (Fountain of the Four Rivers; Map p72), a flamboyant fountain featuring an

Egyptian obelisk and muscular personifications of the rivers Nile, Ganges, Danube and Plate.

Basilica di Santa Maria Sopra Minerva   Basilica

(Map p72; www.santamariasopraminerva.it; Piazza della Minerva 42; ⊙6.40am-7pm Mon-Fri, 6.40am-12.30pm & 3.30-7pm Sat, 8am-12.30pm & 3.30-7pm Sun; 🚇Largo di Torre Argentina) Built on the site of three pagan temples, including one dedicated to the goddess Minerva, the Dominican Basilica di Santa Maria Sopra Minerva is Rome's only Gothic church. However, little remains of the original 13th-century structure and these days the main drawcard is a minor Michelangelo sculpture and the magisterial, art-rich interior.

Campo de' Fiori   Piazza

(Map p72; 🚇Corso Vittorio Emanuele II) Noisy, colourful 'Il Campo' is a major focus of Roman life: by day it hosts one of Rome's best-known markets, while at night it morphs into a raucous open-air pub as drinkers spill out from its many bars and eateries. For centuries the square was the site of public executions, and it was here that philosopher Giordano Bruno was burned for heresy in 1600. The spot is marked by a sinister statue of the hooded monk, which was created by Ettore Ferrari in 1889.

Palazzo Farnese   Historic Building

(Map p72; www.inventerrome.com; Piazza Farnese; €9; ⊙guided tours 3pm, 4pm & 5pm Mon, Wed & Fri; 🚇Corso Vittorio Emanuele II) Home of the French Embassy, this formidable Renaissance *palazzo*, one of Rome's finest, was started in 1514 by Antonio da Sangallo the Younger, continued by Michelangelo and finished by Giacomo della Porta. Inside, it boasts a series of frescoes by Annibale and Agostino Carracci that are said by some to rival Michelangelo's in the Sistine Chapel. The highlight, painted between 1597 and 1608, is the monumental ceiling fresco *Amori degli Dei* (The Loves of the Gods) in the Galleria dei Carracci.

Jewish Ghetto   Area

(Map p72; 🚇Lungotevere de' Cenci) Centred on lively Via Portico d'Ottavia, the Jewish Ghetto is a wonderfully atmospheric area studded with artisans' studios, vintage clothes shops, kosher bakeries and popular trattorias.

Chiesa del Gesù   Church

(Map p72; ☑06 69 70 01; www.chiesadelgesu. org; Piazza del Gesù; ⊙7am-12.30pm & 4-7.45pm, St Ignatius rooms 4-6pm Mon-Sat, 10am-noon Sun; 🚇Largo di Torre Argentina) An imposing example of Counter-Reformation architecture, Rome's most important Jesuit church is a fabulous treasure trove of baroque art. Headline works include a swirling vault fresco by Giovanni Battista Gaulli (aka Il Baciccia), and Andrea del Pozzo's opulent tomb for Ignatius Loyola, the Spanish soldier and saint who founded the Jesuits in 1540. St Ignatius lived in the church from 1544 until his death in 1556 and you can visit his private rooms to the right of the main building in the Cappella di Sant'Ignazio.

◉ Tridente, Trevi & Quirinale

Trevi Fountain   Fountain

(Fontana di Trevi; Map p76; Piazza di Trevi; MBarberini) The Fontana di Trevi, scene of Anita Ekberg's dip in *La Dolce Vita,* is a flamboyant baroque ensemble of mythical figures and wild horses taking up the entire side of the 17th-century Palazzo Poli. After a Fendi-sponsored restoration finished in 2015, the fountain gleams brighter than it has for years. The tradition is to toss a coin into the water, thus ensuring that you'll return to Rome – on average about €3000 is thrown in every day.

Piazza di Spagna & the Spanish Steps   Piazza

(Map p76; MSpagna) A magnet for visitors since the 18th century, the Spanish Steps (Scalinata della Trinità dei Monti) provide a perfect people-watching perch. The 135 steps, gleaming after a recent clean-up, rise from Piazza di Spagna to the landmark **Chiesa della Trinità dei Monti** (Map p76;

Centro Storico

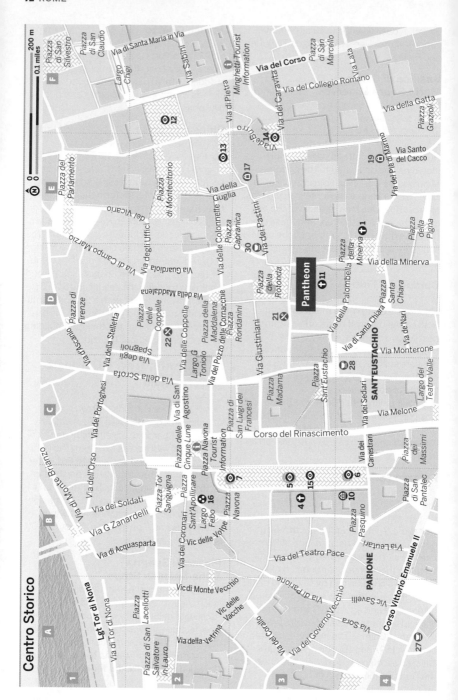

200 m
0.1 miles

Lgt Tor di Nona

Via di Tor di Nona

Piazza di San Salvatore in Lauro

Via di Monte Brianzo

Via dell'Orso

Via dei Soldati

Piazza Tor Sanguigna

Via G Zanardelli

Via di Acquasparta

Via dei Coronari

Piazza Sant'Apollinare

Largo Febo 16

Piazza Navona

Tourist Information

Piazza delle Cinque Lune

Via di San Agostino

Piazza di San Luigi dei Francesi

Via di Portoghesi

Via della Scrofa

Via della Stelletta

Piazza di Firenze

Piazza di San Lacellotti

Vic delle Volpe

Vic di Monte Vecchio

Vic delle Vacche

Via della Vetrina

Via del Corallo

Via del Governo Vecchio

Via di Parione

Via del Teatro Pace

Via Sora

PARIONE

Vic Savelli

Via Leutari

Corso Vittorio Emanuele II

Piazza di San Pantaleo

Piazza dei Massimi

Via dei Canestrari

Corso del Rinascimento

Piazza Madama

Piazza Sant'Eustachio

SANT'EUSTACHIO

Via dei Sediari

Via Melone

Via Monterone

Largo del Teatro Valle

Via de'Nari

Via di Santa Chiara

Piazza Santa Chiara

Via della Palombella

Pantheon

Piazza della Rotonda

Via Giustiniani

Piazza Rondanini

Via del Pozzo delle Cornacchie

Piazza della Maddalena

Largo G Toniolo

Via delle Coppelle

Piazza delle Coppelle

Via degli Spagnoli

Via della Maddalena

Via della Guardiola

Via degli Uffici del Vicario

Via di Campo Marzio

Via della Guglia

Via delle Colonnette

Piazza Capranica

Via dei Pastini

Piazza della Minerva

Via della Minerva

Piazza della Pigna

Via di Pietra

Piazza di Montecitorio

Piazza del Parlamento

Piazza di Pietra

Via di Santa Maria in Via

Via di San Claudio

Piazza di San Silvestro

Largo Chigi

Via Sabini

Minghetti Tourist Information

Via del Corso

Via del Caravita

Via del Tritone

Via del Collegio Romano

Piazza di San Marcello

Via Lata

Via della Gatta

Piazza Grazioli

Via Santo del Cacco

Via del Piè di Marmo

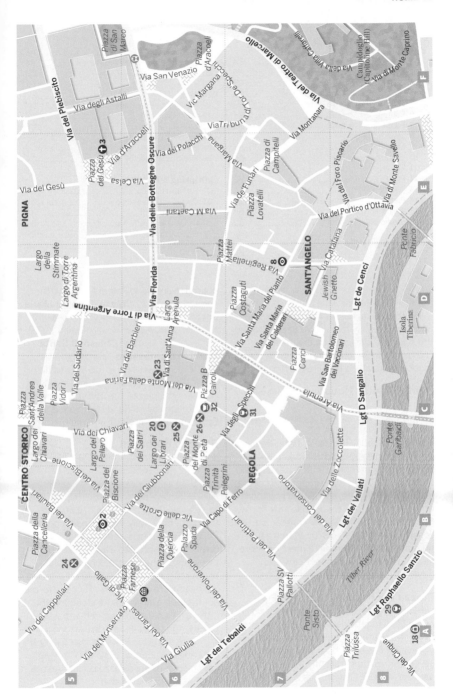

Centro Storico

⏻06 679 41 79; Piazza Trinità dei Monti 3;
☺7.30am-8pm Tue-Fri, 10am-5pm Sat & Sun).

Piazza di Spagna was named after the
Spanish Embassy to the Holy See, although
the staircase, designed by the Italian
Francesco de Sanctis, was built in 1725 with
money bequeathed by a French diplomat.

Keats-Shelley House   Museum

(Map p76; ⏻06 678 42 35; www.keats-shelley-
house.org; Piazza di Spagna 26; adult/reduced
€5/4; ☺10am-1pm & 2-6pm Mon-Sat; ⓜSpagna)
The Keats-Shelley House is where Romantic poet John Keats died of tuberculosis at
the age of 25, in February 1821. Keats came
to Rome in 1820 to try to improve his health
in the Italian climate, and rented two rooms
on the 3rd floor of a townhouse next to the
Spanish Steps, with painter companion
Joseph Severn (1793–1879). Watch a film
on the 1st floor about the Romantics, then
head upstairs to see where Keats and
Severn lived and worked.

Piazza del Popolo   Piazza

(ⓜFlaminio) This dazzling piazza was laid
out in 1538 to provide a grandiose entrance
to what was then Rome's main northern
gateway. It has since been remodelled
several times, most recently by Giuseppe
Valadier in 1823. Guarding its southern

approach are Carlo Rainaldi's twin 17th-
century churches, **Chiesa di Santa Maria
dei Miracoli** (Via del Corso 528; ☺6.45am-
12.30pm & 4.30-7.30pm Mon-Sat, 8am-1.15pm
& 4.30-7.45pm Sun) and **Chiesa di Santa
Maria in Montesanto** (Chiesa degli Artisti;
www.chiesadegliartisti.it; Via del Babuino 198;
☺5.30-8pm Mon-Fri, 11am-1.30pm Sun). In the
centre of the piazza, the 36m-high **obelisk**
was brought by Augustus from ancient
Egypt; it originally stood in Circo Massimo.

Palazzo Barberini   Gallery

(Galleria Nazionale d'Arte Antica; Map p76; ⏻06
481 45 91; www.barberinicorsini.org; Via delle
Quattro Fontane 13; adult/reduced €5/2.50, incl
Palazzo Corsini €10/5; ☺8.30am-7pm Tue-Sun;
ⓜBarberini) Commissioned to celebrate
the Barberini family's rise to papal power,
Palazzo Barberini is a sumptuous baroque
palace that impresses even before you
clap eyes on the breathtaking art. Many
high-profile architects worked on it, including rivals Bernini and Borromini; the former
contributed a large square staircase, the
latter a helicoidal one. Amid the masterpieces, don't miss Pietro da Cortona's *Il
Trionfo della Divina Provvidenza* (Triumph
of Divine Providence; 1632–39), the most
spectacular of the *palazzo* ceiling frescoes
in the 1st-floor main salon.

Palazzo del Quirinale   Palace

(Map p76; ☑06 3996 7557; www.quirinale.it;
Piazza del Quirinale; 1¼hr tour €1.50, 2½hr tour
adult/reduced €10/5; ⊗9.30am-4pm Tue, Wed
& Fri-Sun, closed Aug; MBarberini) Overlooking
Piazza del Quirinale, this immense palace
is the official residence of Italy's head of
state, the President of the Republic. For
almost three centuries it was the pope's
summer residence, but in 1870 Pope Pius
IX begrudgingly handed the keys over to Italy's new king. Later, in 1948, it was given to
the Italian state. Visits, by guided tour only,
should be booked at least five days ahead
by telephone (collect tour tickets at the
nearby Infopoint at Salita di Montecavallo
15) or buy online at www.coopculture.it.

Museo dell'Ara Pacis   Museum

(☑06 06 08; www.arapacis.it; Lungotevere in
Auga; adult/reduced €11/9; ⊗9.30am-7.30pm
Mon-Sat; MFlaminio) The first modern construction in Rome's historic centre since
WWII, Richard Meier's controversial and
widely detested glass-and-marble pavilion
houses the *Ara Pacis Augustae* (Altar of
Peace), Augustus' great monument to
peace. One of the most important works of
ancient Roman sculpture, the vast marble
altar – measuring 11.6m by 10.6m by 3.6m
– was completed in 13 BC.

⊚ Monti, Esquilino & San Lorenzo

Basilica di Santa Maria Maggiore   Basilica

(Map p76; ☑06 6988 6800; Piazza Santa Maria
Maggiore; basilica free, adult/reduced museum
€3/2, museum & loggia €5/4; ⊗7am-7pm,
loggia guided tours 9.30am-5.45pm; ☐Piazza
Santa Maria Maggiore) One of Rome's four
patriarchal basilicas, this monumental
5th-century church stands on the summit
of the Esquiline Hill, on the spot where
snow is said to have miraculously fallen
in the summer of AD 358. To commem-
orate the event, every year on 5 August
thousands of white petals are released
from the basilica's coffered ceiling. Much
altered over the centuries, it's an architectural hybrid with 14th-century Romanesque
belfry, 18th-century baroque facade, largely
baroque interior and a series of glorious
5th-century mosaics.

Museo Nazionale Romano: Palazzo Massimo alle Terme   Museum

(Map p76; ☑06 3996 7700; www.coopculture.
it; Largo di Villa Peretti 1; adult/reduced €7/3.50;
⊗9am-7.45pm Tue-Sun; MTermini) One of
Rome's great unheralded museums, this is a
fabulous treasure trove of classical art. The
ground and 1st floors are devoted to sculpture with some breathtaking pieces – check
out the *Pugile* (Boxer), a 2nd-century-BC
Greek bronze; the graceful 2nd-century-BC
Ermafrodite dormiente (Sleeping Hermaph-
rodite); and the idealised *Il discobolo* (Discus
Thrower). It's the magnificent and vibrantly
coloured frescoes on the 2nd floor, however,
that are the undisputed highlight.

Museo Nazionale Romano: Terme di Diocleziano   Museum

(Map p76; ☑06 3996 7700; www.coopculture.
it; Viale Enrico de Nicola 78; adult/reduced
€7/3.50; ⊗9am-7.30pm Tue-Sun; MTermini) The
Terme di Diocleziano was ancient Rome's
largest bath complex, covering about 13 hectares and able to accommodate some 3000
people. Today its ruins house a branch of the
impressive Museo Nazionale Romano. Exhibits, which include memorial inscriptions,
bas-reliefs and archaeological artefacts,
provide a fascinating insight into Roman
life. Outside, the vast cloister, constructed
from drawings by Michelangelo, is lined with
classical sarcophagi, headless statues and
huge sculptured animal heads, thought to
have come from the Foro di Traiano.

Domus Aurea   Archaeological Site

(Golden House; ☑06 3996 7700; www.coopcul
ture.it; Viale della Domus Aurea; adult/under 6yr
€14/free; ⊗9am-4.45pm Sat & Sun; MColosseo)
Nero had his Domus Aurea constructed after the fire of AD 64 (which he is rumoured
to have started to clear the area). Named
after the gold that lined its facade and interiors, it was a huge complex covering up to
a third of the city. Making full use of virtual

Trevi & Esquilino

reality, superb state-of-the-art guided tours shed light on just how grand the Golden House – a lavish villa with porticoes – was. Advance online reservations are obligatory.

Basilica di San Pietro in Vincoli
Basilica

(Map p68; Piazza di San Pietro in Vincoli 4a; ◷8am-12.30pm & 3-7pm summer, to 6pm winter; MCavour) Pilgrims and art lovers flock to this 5th-century basilica for two reasons: to marvel at Michelangelo's colossal *Moses* (1505) sculpture and to see the chains that

supposedly bound St Peter when he was imprisoned in the Carcere Mamertino (near the Roman Forum). Access to the church is via a flight of steps through a low arch that leads up from Via Cavour.

◎ San Giovanni & Testaccio

Basilica di San Giovanni in Laterano
Basilica

(Piazza di San Giovanni in Laterano 4; basilica/ cloister free/€5 with audio guide; ◷7am-6.30pm, cloister 9am-6pm; MSan Giovanni) For a thousand years this monumental cathedral was the most important church in Christendom. Commissioned by Constantine and consecrated in AD 324, it was the first Christian basilica built in the city and, until the late 14th century, was the pope's main place of worship. It's still Rome's official cathedral and the pope's seat as the bishop of Rome.

The basilica has been revamped several times, most notably by Borromini in the 17th century, and by Alessandro Galilei, who added the immense white facade in 1735.

Basilica di San Clemente   Basilica

(www.basilicasanclemente.com; Piazza San Clemente; excavations adult/reduced €10/5; ⊘9am-12.30pm & 3-6pm Mon-Sat, 12.15-6pm Sun; ▣Via Labicana) Nowhere better illustrates the various stages of Rome's turbulent past than this fascinating multilayered church. The ground-level 12th-century basilica sits atop a 4th-century church, which, in turn, stands over a 2nd-century pagan temple and a 1st-century Roman house. Beneath everything are foundations dating from the Roman Republic.

Terme di Caracalla   Archaeological Site

(☑06 3996 7700; www.coopculture.it; Viale delle Terme di Caracalla 52; adult/reduced €6/3; ⊘9am-1hr before sunset Tue-Sun, 9am-2pm Mon; ▣Viale delle Terme di Caracalla) The remains of the emperor Caracalla's vast bathhouse complex are among Rome's most awe-inspiring ruins. Inaugurated in AD 216, the original 10-hectare site, which comprised baths, gyms, libraries, shops and gardens, was used by up to 8000 people daily.

Most of the ruins are what's left of the central bathhouse. This was a huge rectangular edifice bookended by two **palestre** (gyms) and centred on a **frigidarium** (cold room), where bathers would stop after spells in the warmer **tepidarium** and dome-capped **caldaria** (hot room).

◎ Southern Rome

Via Appia Antica   Historic Site

(Appian Way; ☑06 513 53 16; www.parcoappiaantica.it; ⊘Info Point 9.30am-sunset summer,

9.30am-1pm & 2-5pm Mon-Fri, 9.30am-5pm Sat & Sun winter; ▣Via Appia Antica) Named after consul Appius Claudius Caecus, who laid the first 90km section in 312 BC, ancient Rome's *regina viarum* (queen of roads) was extended in 190 BC to reach Brindisi on Italy's southern Adriatic coast. Via Appia Antica has long been one of Rome's most exclusive addresses, a beautiful cobbled thoroughfare flanked by grassy fields, Roman structures and towering pine trees. Most splendid of the ancient houses was **Villa dei Quintili** (☑06 3996 7700; www.coopculture.it; Via Appia Nuova 1092; adult/reduced incl Terme di Caracalla & Mausoleo di Cecilia Metella €6/3; ⊘9am-1hr before sunset Tue-Sun), so desirable that emperor Commodus murdered its owner and took it for himself.

Basilica di San Paolo Fuori le Mura   Basilica

(☑06 6988 0803; www.basilicasanpaolo.org; Via Ostiense 190; adult/reduced €4/3; ⊘7am-6.30pm; ⓜBasilica San Paolo) The largest church in Rome after St Peter's (and the world's third-largest), this magnificent basilica stands on the site where St Paul was buried after being decapitated in AD 67. Built by Constantine in the 4th century, it was largely destroyed by fire in 1823 and much of what you see is a 19th-century reconstruction.

Chiesa del Domine Quo Vadis   Church

(☑06 512 04 41; Via Appia Antica 51; ⊘8am-7.30pm summer, to 6.30pm winter; ▣Via Appia Antica) This pint-sized church marks the spot where St Peter, fleeing Rome, met a vision of Jesus going the other way. When Peter asked, *'Domine, quo vadis?'* (Lord, where are you going?), Jesus replied, *'Venio Roman iterum crucifigi'* (I am coming to Rome to be crucified again). Reluctantly deciding to join him, Peter tramped back into town where he was arrested and executed. In the aisle are copies of Christ's footprints; the originals are in **Basilica di San Sebastiano** (Via Appia Antica 136; ⊘8am-1pm & 2-5.30pm; ▣Via Appia Antica).

From left: Tempio di Esculapio, Villa Borghese (p80); Terme di Caracalla (p77); Mosaics in Basilica di Santa Maria in Trastevere

Catacombe di San Callisto
Catacomb

(📞06 513 01 51; www.catacombe.roma.it; Via Appia Antica 110-126; adult/reduced €8/5; 🕙9am-noon & 2-5pm Thu-Tue Mar-Jan; 🚌Via Appia Antica) These are the largest and busiest of Rome's catacombs. Founded at the end of the 2nd century and named after Pope Calixtus I, they became the official cemetery of the newly established Roman Church. In the 20km of tunnels explored to date, archaeologists have found the tombs of 16 popes, dozens of martyrs and thousands upon thousands of Christians.

◎ Trastevere & Gianicolo

Piazza di Santa Maria in Trastevere
Piazza

(🚊Viale di Trastevere, 🚊Viale di Trastevere) Trastevere's focal square is a prime people-watching spot. By day it's full of parents with strollers, chatting locals and guidebook-toting tourists; by night it's the domain of foreign students, young Romans and out-of-towners, all out for a good time in its many cafes and bars. The fountain piercing the centre of the square, of Roman

origin, was restored by Carlo Fontana in 1692. The beautiful Romanesque facade of Basilica di Santa Maria in Trastevere, currently under wraps as painstaking restoration takes place, lords over all this.

Basilica di Santa Maria in Trastevere
Basilica

(📞06 581 48 02; Piazza Santa Maria in Trastevere; 🕙7.30am-9pm Sep-Jul, 8am-noon & 4-9pm Aug; 🚊Viale di Trastevere, 🚊Viale di Trastevere) Nestled in a quiet corner of Trastevere's focal square, this is said to be the oldest church dedicated to the Virgin Mary in Rome. In its original form, it dates to the early 3rd century, but a major 12th-century make over saw the addition of a Romanesque bell tower and glittering facade. The portico came later, added by Carlo Fontana in 1702. Inside, the 12th-century mosaics are the headline feature.

Tempietto di Bramante & Chiesa di San Pietro in Montorio
Church

(📞06 581 39 40; www.sanpietroinmontorio.it; Piazza San Pietro in Montorio 2; 🕙chiesa 8.30am-noon & 3-4pm Mon-Fri, tempietto 10am-6pm

Tue-Sun; 🚇Via Garibaldi) Considered the first great building of the High Renaissance, Bramante's sublime Tempietto (Little Temple; 1508) is a perfect surprise, squeezed into the courtyard of the Chiesa di San Pietro in Montorio, on the spot where St Peter is said to have been crucified. It's small, but perfectly formed; its classically inspired design and ideal proportions epitomise the Renaissance zeitgeist.

◉ Vatican City, Borgo & Prati

St Peter's Square   Piazza

(Piazza San Pietro; 🚇Ottaviano-San Pietro) Overlooked by St Peter's Basilica, the Vatican's central square was laid out between 1656 and 1667 to a design by Gian Lorenzo Bernini. Seen from above, it resembles a giant keyhole with two semicircular colonnades, each consisting of four rows of Doric columns, encircling a giant ellipse that straightens out to funnel believers into the basilica. The effect was deliberate – Bernini described the colonnades as representing 'the motherly arms of the church'.

The scale of the piazza is dazzling: at its largest it measures 320m by 240m. There are 284 columns and, atop the colonnades, 140 saints. The 25m **obelisk** in the centre was brought to Rome by Caligula from Heliopolis in Egypt and later used by Nero as a turning post for the chariot races in his circus.

Leading off the piazza, the monumental approach road, **Via della Conciliazione**, was commissioned by Mussolini and built between 1936 and 1950.

Castel Sant'Angelo Museum, Castle

(📞06 681 91 11; www.castelsantangelo.benicul turali.it; Lungotevere Castello 50; adult/reduced €10/5; 🕘9am-7.30pm, ticket office to 6.30pm; 🚇Piazza Pia) With its chunky round keep, this castle is an instantly recognisable landmark. Built as a mausoleum for the emperor Hadrian, it was converted into a papal fortress in the 6th century and named after an angelic vision that Pope Gregory the Great had in 590. Nowadays, it houses the **Museo Nazionale di Castel Sant'Angelo** and its eclectic collection of paintings, sculpture, military memorabilia and medieval firearms.

St Peter's Basilica (p44), Ponte Sant'Angelo and the Tiber River

Villa Borghese & Northern Rome

Villa Borghese   Park

(www.sovraintendenzaroma.it; entrances at Piazzale San Paolo del Brasile, Piazzale Flaminio, Via Pinciana, Via Raimondo, Largo Pablo Picasso; ☉sunrise-sunset; 🚌Via Pinciana) Locals, lovers, tourists, joggers – no one can resist the lure of Rome's most celebrated park. Originally the 17th-century estate of Cardinal Scipione Borghese, it covers about 80 hectares of wooded glades, gardens and grassy banks. Among its attractions are several excellent museums, the landscaped **Giardino del Lago** (boat hire per 20min €3; ☉7am-9pm summer, to 6pm winter), **Piazza di Siena**, a dusty arena used for Rome's top equestrian event in May, and a panoramic terrace on the **Pincio Hill** (Ⓜ Flaminio).

Museo Nazionale Etrusco di Villa Giulia   Museum

(☎06 322 65 71; www.villagiulia.beniculturali. it; Piazzale di Villa Giulia; adult/reduced €8/4; ☉8.30am-7.30pm Tue-Sun; 🚌Via delle Belle Arti)

Pope Julius III's 16th-century villa provides the charming setting for Italy's finest collection of Etruscan and pre-Roman treasures. Exhibits, many of which came from tombs in the surrounding Lazio region, range from bronze figurines and black *bucchero* tableware to temple decorations, terracotta vases and a dazzling display of sophisticated jewellery.

Must-sees include a polychrome terracotta statue of Apollo from a temple in Veio and the 6th-century-BC *Sarcofago degli Sposi* (Sarcophagus of the Betrothed), found in 1881 in Cerveteri.

🎧 TOURS

A Friend in Rome   Tours

(☎340 501 92 01; www.afriendinrome.it) Silvia Prosperi and her team offer a range of private tours covering the Vatican and main historic centre as well as areas outside the capital. They can also organise kid-friendly tours, food and wine itineraries, vintage car drives and horse rides along Via Appia Antica. Rates start at €165 for a basic three-hour tour for up to eight people; add €55 for every additional hour.

Roman Guy
Tours

(https://theromanguy.com) A professional set-up that organises a wide range of group and private tours. Packages, led by English-speaking experts, include skip-the-line visits to the Vatican Museums (US$89), foodie tours of Trastevere and the Jewish Ghetto (US$84), and an evening bar hop through the historic centre's cocktail bars (US$225).

🅐 SHOPPING

Antica Caciara Trasteverina
Food & Drinks

(☑06 581 28 15; www.anticacaciara.it; Via San Francesco a Ripa 140; ☺7am-2pm & 4-8pm Mon-Sat; 🚊Viale di Trastevere, 🚊Viale di Trastevere) The fresh ricotta is a prized possession at this century-old deli, and it's all usually snapped up by lunchtime. If you're too late, take solace in the to-die-for *ricotta infornata* (oven-baked ricotta), 35kg wheels of famous, black-waxed *pecorino romano* DOP (€16.50 per kilo), and aromatic garlands of *guanciale* (pig's jowl) begging to be chopped up, pan-fried and thrown into the perfect carbonara.

Benheart
Fashion & Accessories

(Map p72; ☑06 5832 0801; www.benheart.it; Via del Moro 47; ☺11am-11pm; 🚊Piazza Trilussa) From the colourful resin floor papered with children's drawings to the vintage typewriter, dial-up telephone and old-fashioned tools decorating the interior, everything about this artisanal leather boutique is achingly cool. Benheart, a young Florentine designer, is one of Italy's savviest talents and his fashionable handmade shoes (from €190) and jackets for men and women are glorious.

Artisanal Cornucopia
Design

(☑342 8714597; www.artisanalcornucopia.com; Via dell'Oca 38a; ☺10am-7pm; Ⓜ Flaminio) One of several stylish independent boutiques on Via dell'Oca, this chic concept store showcases exclusive handmade pieces by Italian designers: think a trunk full of Anthony Peto hats, bold sculpture-like lamps by Roman designer Vincenzo Del Pizzo, and delicate gold necklaces and other jewellery crafted by Giulia Barela. It also sells artisan bags, shoes, candles, homewares and other lovely handmade objects.

Bartolucci
Toys

(Map p72; www.bartolucci.com; Via dei Pastini 98; ☺10am-10.30pm; 🚊Via del Corso) It's difficult to resist going into this magical toyshop where everything is carved out of wood. By the main entrance, a Pinocchio pedals his bike robotically, perhaps dreaming of the full-size motorbike parked nearby, while inside there are all manner of ticking clocks, rocking horses, planes and more Pinocchios than you're likely to see in your whole life.

Il Sellaio
Fashion & Accessories

(☑06 321 17 19; www.serafinipelletteria.it; Via Caio Mario 14; ☺9.30am-7.30pm Mon-Fri, 9.30am-1pm & 3.30-7.30pm Sat; Ⓜ Ottaviano-San Pietro) During the 1960s Ferruccio Serafini was one of Rome's most sought-after artisans, making handmade leather shoes and bags for the likes of John F Kennedy, Liz Taylor and Marlon Brando. Nowadays, his daughter Francesca runs the family shop where you can pick up beautiful hand-stitched bags, belts and accessories. You can also have your own designs made to order.

Confetteria Moriondo & Gariglio
Chocolate

(Map p72; ☑06 699 08 56; Via del Piè di Marmo 21-22; ☺9am-7.30pm Mon-Sat; 🚊Via del Corso) Roman poet Trilussa was so smitten with this historic chocolate shop – established by the Torinese confectioners to the royal house of Savoy – that he was moved to mention it in verse. And we agree, it's a gem. Decorated like an elegant tearoom, with crimson walls, tables and glass cabinets, it specialises in delicious handmade chocolates, many prepared according to original 19th-century recipes.

Ibiz – Artigianato in Cuoio
Fashion & Accessories

(Map p72; ✆06 6830 7297; www.ibizroma.it; Via dei Chiavari 39; ⏰9.30am-7.30pm Mon-Sat; 🚇Corso Vittorio Emanuele II) In her diminutive family workshop, Elisa Nepi and her team craft exquisite, soft-as-butter leather wallets, bags, belts and sandals, in simple but classy designs and myriad colours. You can pick up a belt for about €35, while for a bag you should bank on at least €110.

EATING

Rome teems with trattorias, ristoranti, pizzerias, *enoteche* (wine bars serving food) and gelaterie. Excellent places dot the *centro storico,* Trastevere, Prati, Testaccio and San Lorenzo. Be warned that the area around Termini has quite a few substandard restaurants, as does the Vatican, which is packed with tourist traps.

✖ Ancient Rome

Terre e Domus Lazio Cuisine €€

(Map p68; ✆06 6994 0273; Via Foro Traiano 82-4; meals €30; ⏰9am-midnight Mon & Wed-Sat, 10am-midnight Sun; 🚇Via dei Fori Imperiali) This modern white-and-glass restaurant is the best option in the touristy Forum area. With minimal decor and large windows overlooking the Colonna di Traiano, it's a relaxed spot to sit down to traditional local staples, all made with ingredients sourced from the surrounding Lazio region, and a glass or two of regional wine.

✖ Centro Storico

Forno Roscioli Pizza, Bakery €

(Map p72; ✆06 686 40 45; www.anticoforno roscioli.it; Via dei Chiavari 34; pizza slices from €2, snacks €2; ⏰6am-8pm Mon-Sat, 9am-7pm Sun; 🚇Via Arenula) This is one of Rome's top bakeries, much loved by lunching locals who crowd here for luscious sliced pizza, prize pastries and hunger-sating *supplì* (risotto balls). The *pizza margherita* is superb, if messy to eat, and there's also a counter serving hot pastas and vegetable side dishes.

Forno di Campo de' Fiori
Pizza, Bakery €

(Map p72; www.fornocampodefiori.com; Campo de' Fiori 22; pizza slices around €3; ⏰7.30am-2.30pm & 4.45-8pm Mon-Sat, closed Sat dinner Jul & Aug; 🚇Corso Vittorio Emanuele II) This buzzing bakery on Campo de' Fiori, divided into two adjacent shops, does a roaring trade in *panini* and delicious fresh-from-the-oven *pizza al taglio* (pizza by the slice). Aficionados swear by the *pizza bianca* ('white' pizza with olive oil, rosemary and salt), but the *panini* and *pizza rossa* ('red' pizza, with olive oil, tomato and oregano) taste plenty good too.

Emma Pizzeria
Pizza €€

(Map p72; ✆06 6476 0475; www.emmapizz eria.com; Via Monte della Farina 28-29; pizzas €8-18, mains €35; ⏰12.30-3pm & 7-11.30pm; 🚇Via Arenula) Tucked in behind the Chiesa di San Carlo ai Catinari, this smart, modern pizzeria is a top spot for a cracking pizza and smooth craft beer (or a wine from its pretty extensive list). It's a stylish set-up with outdoor seating and a spacious, art-clad interior, and a menu that lists seasonal, wood-fired pizzas alongside classic Roman pastas and mains.

Armando al Pantheon
Roman €€

(Map p72; ✆06 6880 3034; www.armandoal pantheon.it; Salita dei Crescenzi 31; meals €40; ⏰12.30-3pm Mon-Sat & 7-11pm Mon-Fri; 🚇Largo di Torre Argentina) With its cosy wooden interior and unwavering dedication to old-school Roman cuisine, Armando al Pantheon is a regular go-to for local foodies. It's been on the go for more than 50 years and has served its fair share of celebs, but it hasn't let fame go to its head and it remains as popular as ever. Reservations essential.

Casa Coppelle
Ristorante €€€

(Map p72; ✆06 6889 1707; www.casacoppelle. it; Piazza delle Coppelle 49; meals €65, tasting menu €85; ⏰noon-3.30pm & 6.30-11.30pm; 🚇Corso del Rinascimento) Boasting an enviable setting near the Pantheon and a plush, theatrical look – think velvet drapes, black lacquer tables and bookshelves – Casa

Bartolucci (p81)

Coppelle sets a romantic stage for high-end Roman-French cuisine. Gallic trademarks like snails and onion soup feature alongside updated Roman favourites such as pasta *amatriciana* (with tomato sauce and pancetta) and *cacio e pepe* (*pecorino* and black pepper), here reinvented as a risotto with prawns. Book ahead.

🍽 Tridente, Trevi & the Quirinale

Pastificio   Fast Food €

(Via della Croce 8; pasta, wine & water €4; ⊘1-3pm Mon-Sat; Ⓜ Spagna) A brilliant budget find, this old-fashioned pasta shop (1918), with a kitchen hatch, serves up two choices of pasta at lunchtime. It's fast food, Italian style – freshly cooked (if you time it right) pasta, with wine and water included. Grab a space to stand and eat between shelves packed with packets of dry pasta or take it away.

**Fiaschetteria
Beltramme**   Trattoria €€

(☑ 06 6979 7200; Via della Croce 39; meals €40; ⊘12.15-3pm & 7.30-10.45pm; Ⓜ Spagna)

A super spot for authentic Roman dining near the Spanish Steps, Fiaschetteria (meaning 'wine-sellers') is a hole-in-the-wall, stuck-in-time place with a short menu. Fashionistas with appetites dig into traditional Roman dishes made using recipes unchanged since the 1930s when a waiter at the 19th-century wine bar (from 1886 to be precise) started serving food. Seeking the perfect carbonara? This is the address.

These days more creative dishes run alongside the timeless classics.

Il Margutta   Vegetarian €€

(☑ 06 3265 0577; www.ilmargutta.bio; Via Margutta 118; lunch buffet weekdays/weekends €15/25, meals €15-40; ⊘8.30am-11.30pm; ☑ ; Ⓜ Spagna, Flaminio) This chic art-gallery-bar-restaurant gets packed at lunchtime with Romans feasting on its good-value, eat-as-much-as-you-can buffet deal. Everything is organic, the evening menu tempting with creative dishes such as tofu with marinated ginger and smoked tubers, or grilled chicory with almond cream and candied tangerine. Among the various tasting menus is a vegan option.

Colline Emiliane   Italian €€€

(Map p76; ☏06 481 75 38; www.collineemiliane.
com; Via degli Avignonesi 22; meals €45; ⊙12.45-
2.45pm & 7.30-10.45pm Tue-Sun, closed Sun dinner & Mon; Ⓜ Barberini) Sensational regional
cuisine from Emilia-Romagna aside, what
makes this small white-tablecloth dining
address so outstanding is its family vibe
and overwhelmingly warm service. It's been
a stronghold of the Latini family since the
1930s, and today son Luca runs the show
with his mother Paola (dessert queen),
aunt Anna (watch her making fresh pasta
each morning in the glassed-off lab) and
father Massimo.

Imàgo   Italian €€€

(Map p76; ☏06 6993 4726; www.imagorestau
rant.com; Piazza della Trinità dei Monti 6, Hotel
Hassler; tasting menus €120-150; ⊙7-10.30pm
Feb-Dec; ☍; Ⓜ Spagna) Even in a city of great
views, the panoramas from the Hassler
Hotel's Michelin-starred romantic rooftop
restaurant are special, extending over a
sea of roofs to the great dome of St Peter's
Basilica; request the corner table. Comple-
menting the views are the bold, mod-Italian

creations of culinary whizz, chef Francesco
Apreda.

⊗ Monti, Esquilino & San Lorenzo

Panella   Bakery, Cafe €

(☏06 487 24 35; www.panellaroma.com; Via
Merulana 54; meals €7-15; ⊙8am-11pm Mon-Thu,
to midnight Fri & Sat, 8.30am-4pm Sun; Ⓜ Vittorio
Emanuele) Pure heaven for foodies, this
enticing bakery is littered with well-used
trays of freshly baked pastries loaded with
confectioner's custard, wild-cherry fruit
tartlets, *pizza al taglio, arancini* and focaccia – the smell alone is heavenly. Grab a bar
stool between shelves of gourmet groceries
inside or congratulate yourself on scoring a
table on the flowery, sun-flooded terrace –
one of Rome's loveliest.

Mercato Centrale   Food Hall €

(www.mercatocentrale.it/roma; Via Giolitti 36,
Stazione Termini; snacks/meals from €3/10;
⊙7am-midnight; ☍; Ⓜ Termini) A gourmet
oasis for hungry travellers at Stazione
Termini, this dazzling three-storey food
hall is the latest project of Florence's savvy

Al fresco dining in Tridente

SIMON DACK/ALAMY ©

Umberto Montano. You'll find breads, pastries, cakes, veggie burgers, fresh pasta, truffles, pizza and a whole lot more beneath towering vaulted 1930s ceilings, as well as some of the city's most prized producers, including Gabriele Bonci (breads, focaccia and pizza), Roberto Liberati (salami) and Marcella Bianchi (vegetarian).

Ai Tre Scalini
Wine Bar €€

(Map p68; ☑06 4890 7495; www.aitrescalini. org; Via Panisperna 251; meals €25; ☺12.30pm-1am; ⓂCavour) A firm favourite since 1895, the 'Three Steps' is always packed, with crowds spilling out of the funky violet-painted door and into the street. Tuck into a heart-warming array of cheeses, salami and dishes such as *polpette al sugo* (meatballs with sauce), washed down with superb choices of wine or beer.

Said
Italian €€€

(☑06 446 92 04; www.said.it; Via Tiburtina 135; meals €50; ☺6pm-12.30am Mon, 10am-12.30am Tue-Fri, to 1.30am Sat, to midnight Sun; ☜; ☐Via Tiburtina, ☐Via dei Reti) Housed in an early-1920s chocolate factory, this hybrid cafe-bar, restaurant and boutique is San Lorenzo's coolest hipster haunt. Its Japanese pink-tea pralines, indulged in with a coffee or bought wrapped to take home, are glorious, and dining here is urban chic, with battered sofas, industrial antiques and creative cuisine. Lunch and dinner reservations, served from 12.30pm and 8pm, are recommended.

Antonello Colonna Open
Italian €€€

(Map p76; ☑06 4782 2641; www.antonello colonna.it; Via Milano 9a; lunch/brunch €16/30, meals €16-100; ☺12.30-3.30pm & 8-11pm Tue-Sat, 12.30-3.30pm Sun; ☀; ☐Via Nazionale) Spectacularly set at the back of Palazzo delle Esposizioni, super-chef Antonello Colonna's Michelin-starred restaurant lounges dramatically under a dazzling all-glass roof. Cuisine is new Roman – innovative takes on traditional dishes, cooked with wit and flair – and the all-you-can-eat lunch buffet and weekend brunch are unbeatable value.

⦿ Roman Cuisine

Like most Italian cuisines, the *cucina romana* (Roman cooking) was born of careful use of local ingredients – making use of the cheaper cuts of meat, like *guanciale* (pig's cheek), and greens that could be gathered wild from the fields.

There are a few classic Roman dishes that almost every trattoria and restaurant in Rome serves. These carb-laden comfort foods are seemingly simple, yet notoriously difficult to prepare well. Iconic Roman dishes include carbonara (pasta with pig's cheek, egg and salty *pecorino romano;* sheep's milk cheese), *alla gricia* (with pig's cheek and onions), *amatriciana* (invented when a chef from Amatrice added tomatoes to alla gricia) and *cacio e pepe* (with *pecorino romano* and black pepper). As wonderful and deeply gratifying as these timeless dishes are the centuries-old dining traditions that have been meticulously preserved alongside them: many trattorias in Rome, as tradition demands, only cook up gnocchi (dumplings) on Thursdays, *baccalà con ceci* (salted cod with chickpeas) on Fridays, and tripe on Saturdays.

Carbonara

VVOE/SHUTTERSTOCK ©

On sunny days, dine alfresco on the rooftop terrace.

ⓧ San Giovanni & Testaccio
Romeo e Giulietta
Ristorante, Pizza €€

(☑Giulietta 06 4522 9022, Romeo 06 3211 0120; https://romeo.roma.it; Piazza dell'Emporio 28;

pizzas €6.50-12, meals €40; ⏱Romeo 10am-2am, Giulietta 7pm-midnight daily, noon-3pm Sat-Sun; 🚇Via Marmorata) Occupying a former car showroom, this contemporary multispace food hub is the latest offering from top Roman chef, Cristina Bowerman. The centre of operations is Romeo Chef & Baker, a designer deli, cocktail bar and restaurant offering modern Italian and international fare, but there's also Giulietta Pizzeria (https://giuliettapizzeria.it) dishing up sensational wood-fired pizzas and, a short hop away, Frigo, an artisanal gelateria.

Sbanco   Pizza €€
(📞06 78 93 18; Via Siria 1; pizzas €7.50-12.50; ⏱7.30pm-midnight; 🚇Piazza Zama) With its informal warehouse vibe and buzzing atmosphere, Sbanco is one of the capital's hottest pizzerias. Since opening in 2016, it has quickly made a name for itself with its creative, wood-fired pizzas and sumptuous fried starters – try the carbonara *supplì* (risotto balls). To top things off, it serves some deliciously drinkable craft beer.

🍽 Trastevere & Gianicolo
Da Augusto   Trattoria €
(📞06 580 37 98; Piazza de' Renzi 15; meals €25; ⏱12.30-3pm & 8-11pm; 🚇Viale di Trastevere, 🚇Viale di Trastevere) Bag one of Augusto's rickety tables outside and tuck into some truly fabulous mamma-style cooking on one of Trastevere's prettiest piazza terraces. Hearty portions of all the Roman classics are dished up here as well as lots of rabbit, veal, hare and *pajata* (calf intestines). Winter dining is around vintage formica tables in a bare-bones interior, unchanged for decades. Be prepared to queue. Cash only.

La Prosciutteria   Tuscan €
(📞06 6456 2839; www.laprosciutteria.com/roma-trastevere; Via della Scala 71; taglieri €5 per person; ⏱11am-11.30pm; 🚇Piazza Trilussa) For a gratifying taste of Tuscany in Rome, consider lunch or a decadent *aperitivo* at this Florentine *prosciutteria* (salami shop). Made-to-measure *taglieri* (wooden chopping boards) come loaded with different cold cuts, cheeses, fruit and veg and are best devoured over a glass of Brunello di Montalcino or simple Chianti Classico. Bread comes in peppermint-green tin saucepans and dozens of hams and salami dangle overhead.

Da Enzo   Trattoria €
(📞06 581 22 60; www.daenzoal29.com; Via dei Vascellari 29; meals €30; ⏱12.30-3pm & 7-11pm Mon-Sat; 🚇Viale di Trastevere, 🚇Viale di Trastevere) Vintage buttermilk walls, red-checked tablecloths and a traditional menu featuring all the Roman classics: what makes this staunchly traditional trattoria exceptional is its careful sourcing of local, quality products, many from nearby farms in Lazio. The seasonal, deep-fried Jewish artichokes and the *pasta cacio e pepe* (cheese-and-black-pepper pasta) in particular are among the best in Rome.

Panattoni   Pizza €
(Ai Marmi; 📞06 580 09 19; Viale di Trastevere 53; pizzas €6.50-9; ⏱6.30pm-1am Thu-Tue; 🚇Viale di Trastevere, 🚇Viale di Trastevere) Also called 'ai Marmi' or *l'obitorio* (the morgue) because of its vintage marble-slab tabletops, this is Trastevere's most popular pizzeria. Think super-thin pizzas, a clattering buzz, testy waiters, a street terrace and some fantastic fried starters – the *supplì* (Roman rice ball), *baccalà* (salted cod) and zucchini flowers are all heavenly.

Litro   Italian €€
(📞06 4544 7639; http://vinerialitro.it; Via Fratelli Bonnet 5, Monteverde; meals €25; ⏱12.30pm-3.30am & 5.30pm-midnight Mon-Fri, 12.30pm-12.30am Sat; 📶; 🚇Via Fratelli Bonnet) Crunchy brown bread comes in a paper bag and the 1950s clocks on the wall – all three dozen of them – say a different time at this understated vintage-styled bistro-bar in wonderfully off-the-beaten-tourist-track Monteverde. The creative Roman kitchen is predominantly organic, with ingredients sourced from small local producers, and the choice of natural and biodynamic wines is among the best in Rome.

⊗ Vatican City, Borgo & Prati

Pizzarium   Pizza €
(📞06 3974 5416; Via della Meloria 43; pizza slices €5; ⏰11am-10pm; Ⓜ Cipro-Musei Vaticani) When a pizza joint is packed at lunchtime on a wet winter's day, you know it's something special. Pizzarium, the takeaway of Gabriele Bonci, Rome's acclaimed pizza king, serves Rome's best sliced pizza, bar none. Scissor-cut squares of soft, springy base are topped with original combinations of seasonal ingredients and served on paper trays for immediate consumption. Also worth trying are the freshly fried *supplì* (crunchy rice croquettes).

Fa-Bìo   Sandwiches €
(📞06 6452 5810; www.fa-bio.com; Via Germanico 43; sandwiches €5; ⏰10.30am-5.30pm Mon-Fri, to 4pm Sat; 🚇Piazza del Risorgimento, Ⓜ Ottaviano-San Pietro) ✎ Sandwiches, wraps, salads and fresh juices are all prepared with speed, skill and fresh organic ingredients at this friendly takeaway. Locals, Vatican tour guides and in-the-know visitors come here to grab a quick lunchtime bite and, if you can find room in the tiny interior, you'd do well to follow suit.

Fatamorgana   Gelato €
(www.gelateriafatamorgana.it; Via Leone IV 52; gelato €2.50-5; ⏰noon-11pm summer, to 9pm winter; Ⓜ Ottaviano-San Pietro) The Prati branch of the hit gelateria chain. As well as all the classic flavours there are some wonderfully left-field creations, including a strange but delicious *basilico, miele e noci* (basil, honey and hazelnuts).

Ristorante
L'Arcangelo   Ristorante €€€
(📞06 321 09 92; www.larcangelo.com; Via Giuseppe G Belli 59; meals €50; ⏰1-2.30pm Mon-Fri & 8-11pm Mon-Sat; 🚇Piazza Cavour) Styled as an informal bistro with wood panelling, leather banquettes and casual table settings, L'Arcangelo enjoys a stellar local reputation. Dishes are modern and creative yet still undeniably Roman in their use of traditional ingredients such as sweetbreads and *baccalà* (cod). A further plus is the wine list, which boasts some interesting Italian labels.

Italian cheeses

Local dishes in a Trastevere restaurant

🍴 Southern Rome

Eataly Italian €

(www.eataly.net; Piazzale XII Ottobre 1492; meals €10-50; ⊙shops 9am-midnight, restaurants typically noon-3.30pm & 7-11pm; 🛱; MPiramide) Be prepared for some serious taste bud titillation in this state-of-the-art food emporium of gargantuan proportions. Four shop floors showcase every conceivable Italian food product (dried and fresh), while multiple themed food stalls and restaurants offer plenty of opportunity to taste or feast on Italian cuisine.

Doppiozeroo Italian €

(☑06 5730 1961; www.doppiozeroo.com; Via Ostiense 68; meals €15; ⊙7am-2am; 🖳Via Ostiense, MPiramide) This easygoing bar was once a bakery, hence the name ('double zero' is a type of flour). But today the sleek, modern interior attracts hungry, trendy Romans who pile in here for its cheap, canteen-style lunches, famously lavish *aperitivo* (6pm to 9pm) and abundant weekend brunch (12.30pm to 3.30pm).

🍷 DRINKING & NIGHTLIFE

🍷 Ancient Rome

Cavour 313 Wine Bar

(Map p68; ☑06 678 54 96; www.cavour313.it; Via Cavour 313; ⊙12.30-3.15pm daily & 6-11.30pm Mon-Thu, 6pm-midnight Fri & Sat, 7-11pm Sun, closed Aug; MCavour) Close to the Forum, Cavour 313 is a historic wine bar, a snug, wood-panelled retreat frequented by everyone from tourists to actors and politicians. It serves a selection of salads, cold cuts and cheeses (€9 to €12), but the headline act here is the wine. And with more than 1000 labels to choose from, you're sure to find something to please your palate.

0,75 Bar

(Map p68; ☑06 687 57 06; www.075roma.com; Via dei Cerchi 65; ⊙11am-2am; 🛱; 🖳Via dei Cerchi) This welcoming bar overlooking the Circo Massimo is good for a lingering evening drink, an *aperitivo* or casual meal (mains €6 to €16.50). It's a friendly place with a laidback vibe, an international crowd, attractive wood-beam look and cool tunes.

Terrazza Caffarelli
Cafe

(Caffetteria dei Musei Capitolini; Map p68; ☏06 6919 0564; Piazzale Caffarelli 4; ⏱9.30am-7pm; 🚇Piazza Venezia) The Capitoline Museums' stylish terrace cafe is a memorable place to relax over a drink or light lunch (panini, salads, pastas) and swoon over magical views of the city's domes and rooftops. Although it is part of the museum complex, you don't need a ticket to come here as it has an independent entrance on Piazzale Caffarelli.

🔵 Centro Storico

Barnum Cafe
Cafe

(Map p72; ☏06 6476 0483; www.barnumcafe. com; Via del Pellegrino 87; ⏱9am-10pm Mon, to 2am Tue-Sat; 🛜; 🚇Corso Vittorio Emanuele II) A laid-back *Friends*-style cafe, evergreen Barnum is the sort of place you could quickly get used to. With its shabby-chic vintage furniture and white bare-brick walls, it's a relaxed spot for a breakfast cappuccino, a light lunch or a late afternoon drink. Come evening, a coolly dressed-down crowd sips seriously good cocktails.

Open Baladin
Bar

(Map p72; ☏06 683 89 89; www.openbaladin roma.it; Via degli Specchi 6; ⏱noon-2am; 🛜; 🚇Via Arenula) For some years, this cool, modern pub near Campo de' Fiori has been a leading light in Rome's craft beer scene, and with more than 40 beers on tap and up to 100 bottled brews, many from Italian artisanal microbreweries, it's still a top place for a pint. There's also a decent food menu with *panini,* gourmet burgers and daily specials.

Roscioli Caffè
Cafe

(Map p72; ☏06 8916 5330; www.rosciolicaffe. com; Piazza Benedetto Cairoli 16; ⏱7am-11pm Mon-Sat, 8am-6pm Sun; 🚇Via Arenula) The Roscioli name is a sure bet for good food and drink in this town: the family runs one of Rome's most celebrated **delis** (Map p72; ☏06 687 52 87; www.salumeriaroscioli.com; Via dei Giubbonari 21; meals €55; ⏱12.30-4pm & 7pm-midnight Mon-Sat; 🚇Via Arenula) and a hugely popular bakery (p82), and this

Drinking Coffee in Rome

For an espresso (a shot of strong black coffee), ask for *un caffè;* if you want it with a drop of hot or cold milk, order *un caffè macchiato* ('stained' coffee) *caldo/freddo.* Long black coffee (as in a watered-down version) is known as *caffè lungo* (an espresso with more water) or *caffè all'american* (a filter coffee). If you fancy a coffee but one more shot will catapult you through the ceiling, you can drink *orzo,* made from roasted barley but served like coffee.

Then, of course, there's the cappuccino (coffee with frothy milk, served warm rather than hot). If you want it without froth, ask for a *cappuccino senza schiuma;* if you want it hot, ask for it *ben caldo.* Italians drink cappuccino only during the morning and never after meals.

In summer, *cappuccino freddo* (iced coffee with milk, usually already sugared), *caffè freddo* (iced espresso) and *granita di caffè* (frozen coffee, usually with cream) top the charts.

A *caffè latte* is a milkier version of the cappuccino with less froth; a *latte macchiato* is even milkier (warmed milk 'stained' with a spot of coffee). A *caffè corretto* is an espresso 'corrected' with a dash of grappa or something similar.

There are two ways to drink coffee in a Roman bar-cafe: either standing at the bar, in which case you pay first at the till and then, with your receipt, order at the counter; or you can sit down at a table and enjoy waiter service. In the latter case you'll pay up to double what you'd pay at the bar. In both scenarios, a complimentary glass of tap water is invariably served with your coffee – if it isn't, don't be shy to ask for one.

cafe doesn't disappoint either. The coffee is wonderfully luxurious, and the artfully crafted pastries, petits fours and *panini* taste as good as they look.

Football at the Stadio Olimpico

Football is a Roman passion, with support divided between the two local teams: Roma and Lazio. Both play their home games at the **Stadio Olimpico** (☑06 3685 7563; Viale dei Gladiatori 2, Foro Italico; ☐Lungotevere Maresciallo Cadorna), Rome's impressive Olympic stadium. If you go to a game, make sure you get it right – Roma play in red and yellow and their supporters stand in the Curva Sud (South Stand); Lazio play in sky blue and their fans fill the Curva Nord (North Stand).

Roma fans at Stadio Olimpico
MARCO IACOBUCCI EPP/SHUTTERSTOCK ©

La Casa del Caffè
Tazza d'Oro   Coffee
(Map p72; ☑06 678 97 92; www.tazzadorocoffee shop.com; Via degli Orfani 84-86; ☺7am-8pm Mon-Sat, 10.30am-7.30pm Sun; ☐Via del Corso) A busy, stand-up affair with burnished 1940s fittings, this is one of Rome's best coffeehouses. Its espresso hits the mark nicely and there's a range of delicious coffee concoctions, including a cooling *granita di caffè*, a crushed-ice coffee drink served with whipped cream. There's also a small shop and, outside, a coffee *bancomat* for those out-of-hours caffeine emergencies.

🍴 Tridente, Trevi & the Quirinale
Antico Caffè Greco   Cafe
(Map p76; ☑06 679 17 00; Via dei Condotti 86; ☺9am-9pm; Ⓜ Spagna) Rome's oldest cafe, open since 1760, is still working the look with the utmost elegance: waiters in black tails and bow tie, waitresses in frilly white

pinnies, scarlet flock walls and age-spotted gilt mirrors. Prices reflect this amazing heritage: pay €9 for a cappuccino sitting down or join locals for the same (€2.50) standing at the bar.

Il Palazzetto   Cafe, Cocktail Bar
(Map p76; ☑06 6993 4560; Vicolo del Bottino 8; ☺noon-8.30pm Tue-Sun, closed in rain; Ⓜ Spagna) No terrace proffers such a fine view of the comings and goings on the Spanish Steps over an expertly shaken cocktail (€10 to €13). Ride the lift up from the discreet entrance on narrow Via dei Bottino or look for steps leading to the bar from the top of the steps. Given everything is alfresco, the bar is only open in warm, dry weather.

🍴 Trastevere & Gianicolo
Bar San Calisto   Cafe
(Piazza San Calisto 3-5; ☺6am-2am Mon-Sat; ☐Viale di Trastevere, ☐Viale di Trastevere) Those in the know head to 'Sanca' for its basic, stuck-in-time atmosphere and cheap prices (beer from €1.50). It attracts everyone from intellectuals to keeping-it-real Romans, alcoholics and foreign students. It's famous for its chocolate – come for hot chocolate with cream in winter, and chocolate gelato in summer. Try the *sambuca con la mosca* ('with flies' – raw coffee beans). Expect occasional late-night jam sessions.

Freni e Frizioni   Bar
(Map p72; ☑06 4549 7499; www.freniefrizioni. com; Via del Politeama 4-6; ☺7pm-2am; ☐Piazza Trilussa) This perennially cool Trastevere bar is housed in an old mechanic's workshop – hence its name ('brakes and clutches') and tatty facade. It draws a young *spritz*-loving crowd that swells onto the small piazza outside to sip superbly mixed cocktails (€10) and seasonal punches, and fill up on its lavish early-evening *aperitivo* buffet (7pm to 10pm). Table reservations are essential on Friday and Saturday evenings.

Keyhole   Cocktail Bar
(Via Arco di San Calisto 17; ☺10pm-2am; ☐Viale di Trastevere, ☐Viale di Trastevere) The latest in

VENTDUSUD/SHUTTERSTOCK ©

Spritz

a growing trend of achingly hip, underground speakeasies in Rome, Keyhole ticks all the boxes: no identifiable name or signage outside the bar; a black door smothered in keys; and Prohibition-era decor including leather Chesterfield sofas, dim lighting and an electric craft cocktail menu. Not sure what to order? Ask the talented mixologists to create your own bespoke cocktail (around €10).

No password is required to get into Keyhole (originally known as APS Keyhole), but you need to fill in a form to become a member (€5). No phones.

⊕ ENTERTAINMENT

Watching the world go by in Rome is often entertainment enough, but don't overlook the local arts and sports scenes. As well as gigs and concerts in every genre, there are fantastic arts festival performances (especially in summer) with Roman ruins as a backdrop, and football games that split the city asunder.

Auditorium
Parco della Musica   Concert Venue
(☏06 8024 1281; www.auditorium.com; Viale Pietro de Coubertin; 🚋Viale Tiziano) The hub of Rome's thriving cultural scene, the Auditorium is the capital's premier concert venue. Its three concert halls offer superb acoustics, and together with a 3000-seat open-air arena, stage everything from classical music concerts to jazz gigs, public lectures and film screenings.

The Auditorium is also home to Rome's world-class **Orchestra dell'Accademia Nazionale di Santa Cecilia** (www.santa cecilia.it).

ⓘ INFORMATION

TOURIST INFORMATION

Turismo Roma (www.turismoroma.it/?lang=en; 👥) Rome's official tourist website has comprehensive information about sights, accommodation and city transport, as well as itineraries and up-to-date listings.

There are tourist information points at
Fiumicino (International Arrivals, Terminal 3;
⊙8am-8.45pm) and **Ciampino** (Arrivals Hall;
⊙8.30am-6pm) airports, and locations across
the city:

Castel Sant'Angelo (Piazza Pia; ⊙9.30am-7pm;
☒Piazza Pia)

Piazza delle Cinque Lune (Map p72; ⊙9.30am-
7pm; ☒Corso del Rinascimento) Near Piazza
Navona.

Stazione Termini (☒06 06 08; www.turismo
roma.it; Via Giovanni Giolitti 34; ⊙9am-5pm;
Ⓜ Termini) In the hall adjacent to platform 24.

Via dei Fori Imperiali (Map p68; ⊙9.30am-7pm;
☒Via dei Fori Imperiali)

Via Marco Minghetti (Map p72; ☒06 06 08;
www.turismoroma.it; ⊙9.30am-7pm; ☒Via
del Corso) Between Via del Corso and the Trevi
fountain.

Via Nazionale (Map p76; ☒06 06 08; www.
turismoroma.it; Via Nazionale 184; ⊙9.30am-
7pm; ☒Via Nazionale) In front of the Palazzo
delle Esposizioni.

For information about the Vatican, contact the
Ufficio Pellegrini e Turisti (☒06 6988 1662; St
Peter's Square; ⊙8.30am-6.30pm Mon-Sat; ☒Pi-
azza del Risorgimento, ⓂOttaviano-San Pietro).

GETTING THERE & AWAY

AIR

Rome's main international airport, Leonardo da
Vinci (p341), aka Fiumicino, is 30km west of the
city.

Ciampino (p342), 15km southeast of the city
centre, is used by **Ryanair** (☒895 5895509;
www.ryanair.com) for European and Italian
destinations.

TRAIN

Rome's main station and principal transport hub
is **Stazione Termini** (www.romatermini.com;
Piazza dei Cinquecento; ⓂTermini). It has regular

connections to other European countries, all
major Italian cities and many smaller towns.

ⓘ GETTING AROUND

Public transport includes buses, trams, metro
and a suburban train network. The main hub is
Stazione Termini. Tickets, which come in various
forms, are valid for all forms of transport. Children under 10 years travel free.

Metro The metro is quicker than surface
transport but the network is limited. There are
two main lines, A (orange) and B (blue), which
cross at Stazione Termini. Trains run between
5.30am and 11.30pm (to 1.30am on Fridays and
Saturdays).

Bus Most routes pass through Stazione Termini.
Buses run from approximately 5.30am until midnight, with limited services throughout the night.

Foot Walking is the best way of getting around
the *centro storico* (historic centre).

TICKETS & PASSES

Public transport tickets are valid on all of Rome's
bus, tram and metro lines, except for routes to
Fiumicino airport. They come in various forms:

BIT (*biglietto integrato a tempo,* a single ticket
valid for 100 minutes; in that time it can be used
on all forms of transport but only once on the
metro) €1.50.

Roma 24h (valid for 24 hours) €7.

Roma 48h (valid for 48 hours) €12.50.

Roma 72h (valid for 72 hours) €18.

Children under 10 travel free.

Buy tickets at *tabacchi* (tobacconist's shops),
news-stands and from vending machines at main
bus stops and metro stations. They must be
purchased before you start your journey and validated in the machines on buses, at the entrance
gates to the metro, or at train stations. Ticketless
riders risk a fine of at least €50.

The Roma Pass (two/three days €28/38.50)
comes with a two-/three-day travel pass valid
within the city boundaries.

Where to Stay

Rome doesn't really have a low season as such but most hotels drop prices from November to March (excluding Christmas and New Year) and from mid-July through August. Always try to book ahead.

Neighbourhood	Atmosphere
Ancient Rome	Close to major sights such as the Colosseum, Roman Forum and Capitoline Museums; quiet at night. Few budget options; touristy.
Centro Storico	Atmospheric area with everything on your doorstep: sights, restaurants, bars, shops. Most expensive part of town; can be noisy.
Tridente, Trevi & the Quirinale	Good for designer shopping; excellent midrange to top-end options; good transport links. Not cheap; subdued after dark.
Monti, Esquilino & San Lorenzo	Lots of budget accommodation around Stazione Termini; top eating options and good nightlife. Some dodgy streets in Termini area.
San Giovanni & Testaccio	Authentic atmosphere with good eating and drinking options; Aventino a quiet, romantic area; Testaccio a top food and nightlife district. Few options available; not many big sights.
Trastevere & Gianicolo	Gorgeous, atmospheric area; hundreds of bars, cafes and restaurants; some interesting sights. Very noisy; expensive.
Vatican City, Borgo & Prati	Decent range; some excellent shops and restaurants. Not much nightlife; sells out quickly for religious holidays.
Villa Borghese & Northern Rome	Largely residential area good for the Auditorium and some top museums; quiet after dark. Out of the centre; few budget choices.

FLORENCE

Florence at a Glance...

Cradle of the Renaissance – romantic, enchanting and utterly irresistible – Florence (Firenze) is a place to feast on world-class art and gourmet Tuscan cuisine. Few cities are so compact in size or so packed with extraordinary art and architecture at every turn. The urban fabric of this small city, on the banks of the Arno river in northeastern Tuscany, has hardly changed since the Renaissance, and its narrow cobbled streets are a cinematic feast of elegant 15th- and 16th-century palazzi (mansions), medieval chapels, fresco-decorated churches, marble basilicas and world-class art museums. Unsurprisingly, the entire city centre is a Unesco World Heritage site.

Florence in Two Days

Start with a coffee on the Piazza della Repubblica before hitting the **Uffizi** (p99). After lunch visit the **Duomo** (p102) and the **Grande Museo del Duomo** (p105). Next day visit the **Galleria dell'Accademia** (p107) and **Museo di San Marco** (p115). Later, venture across to the Oltrarno, stopping to admire the view from **Ponte Vecchio** (p115) and **Piazzale Michelangelo** (p115).

Florence in Four Days

On day three, explore **Palazzo Pitti** (p116) and the **Giardino di Boboli** (p116). Alternatively, visit the city's major basilicas: **San Lorenzo** (p114), **Santa Croce** (p115) and **Santa Maria Novella** (p111). For dinner, enjoy good food and entertainment at **Il Teatro del Sale** (p121). On day four, take a guided tour of **Palazzo Vecchio** (p110), then explore the city's artisanal shops.

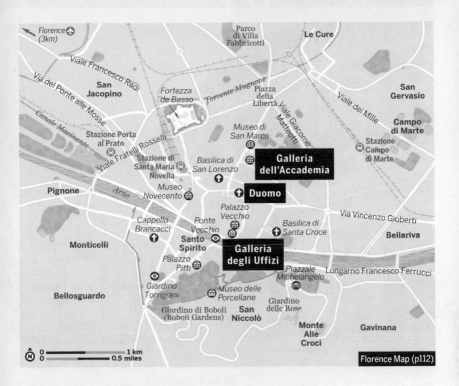

Florence Map (p112)

Arriving in Florence

Florence Airport Shuttle buses to the city centre every 30 minutes between 6am and 8.30pm, then hourly 8.30pm to 11.30pm.

Stazione di Santa Maria Novella Florence's main train station, located in the city centre.

Pisa International Airport Regular trains and buses between 4.30am and 10.25pm to Stazione di Santa Maria Novella (€5 to €10, 1½ hours journey time).

Where to Stay

Advance reservations are essential between Easter and September, while winter ushers in some great deals for visitors – room rates are practically halved. Many top-end boutique options hide in courtyards or behind the inconspicuous door of a *residenza d'epoca* (historical residence) – not listed as hotels or graced with any stars, making such addresses all the more atmospheric and oh-so-Florentine.

For more information about where to stay, see p125.

Galleria degli Uffizi

An art-lover's paradise, the Galleria degli Uffizi houses the world's finest collection of Renaissance paintings, including masterpieces by Giotto, Botticelli, Michelangelo, da Vinci, Raphael, Titian and Caravaggio, in a magnificent 16th-century palazzo.

Great For...

☑ Don't Miss

The reverse side of *The Duke and Duchess of Urbino,* which features the duke and duchess accompanied by the Virtues.

The gallery is undergoing a €65-million refurbishment (the Nuovi Uffizi project) that will eventually see the doubling of exhibition space. Work is pretty much complete on the permanent collection, which has grown over the years from 45 to 101 revamped rooms split across two floors; but there is much to be done still on areas earmarked for temporary exhibitions. Until the project is completed (date unknown), expect some halls to be closed and the contents of others to change.

Tuscan Masters: 13th to 14th Centuries

Starting in the Primo Corridoio (First Corridor) on the 2nd floor, Rooms 2 to 7 are dedicated to pre- and early Renaissance Tuscan art. Among the 13th-century Sienese works displayed in Room 2 are three

❶ Need to Know

Uffizi Gallery; ☎055 29 48 83; www.uffizi.it;
Piazzale degli Uffizi 6; adult/reduced €8/4,
incl temporary exhibition €12.50/6.25;
⊙8.15am-6.50pm Tue-Sun

✕ Take a Break

To clear your head of art overload, stop
by the gallery's rooftop cafe for fresh air
and fabulous views.

★ Top Tip

Save money and visit on the first Sunday of the month – admission is free.

large altarpieces by Duccio di Buoninsegna,
Cimabue and Giotto. These clearly reflect
the transition from the Gothic to the nas-
cent Renaissance style.

The highlight in Room 3 is Simone Martini's shimmering *Annunciazione* (1333),
painted with Lippo Memmi and setting the
Madonna in a sea of gold.

In Room 4 savour the realism of the *Lamentation over the Dead Christ* (1360–65) by
gifted Giotto pupil, Giottino.

Renaissance Pioneers

Florence's victory over the Sienese at the
Battle of San Romano (near Pisa) in 1432
is brought to life with outstanding realism
and increased use of perspective in Paolo
Uccello's magnificent *Battaglia di San
Romano* (1435–40) in Room 8. In the same
room, don't miss the exquisite *Madonna*

con Bambino e due angeli (Madonna and
Child with Two Angels; 1460–65) by Fra'
Filippo Lippi.

In Room 9, Piero della Francesca's
famous profile portraits (1465) of the
crooked-nosed, red-robed duke and
duchess of Urbino are wholly humanist
in spirit: the former painted from the left
side as he'd lost his right eye in a jousting
accident, and the latter painted a deathly
stone-white, reflecting the fact the portrait
was painted posthumously.

In the same room, the seven cardinal and
theological values of 15th-century Florence
by brothers Antonio and Piero del Pollaiolo
– commissioned for the merchants'
tribunal in Piazza della Signoria – radiate
energy. The only canvas in the theological
and cardinal virtues series not to be painted by the Pollaiolos is *Fortitude* (1470), the
first documented work by Botticelli.

Botticelli Room

The spectacular Sala del Botticelli, numbered as Rooms 10 to 14, is one of the Uffizi's hot spots and is always packed. Of the 18

Botticelli works displayed in the Uffizi in all, the iconic *La nascita di Venere* (The Birth of Venus; c 1485), *Primavera* (Spring; c 1482) and *Madonna del Magnificat* (Madonna of the Magnificat; 1483) are the best known by the Renaissance master known for his ethereal figures. Take time to study the lesser-known *Annunciazione* (Annunciation), a 6m-wide fresco painted by Botticelli in 1481 for the San Martino hospital in Florence.

True aficionados rate his twin set of miniatures depicting a sword-bearing Judith returning from the camp of Holofernes and the discovery of the decapitated Holofernes in his tent (1495–1500) as being among his finest works.

La Tribuna

The Medici clan stashed away their most precious masterpieces in this octagonal-shaped treasure trove (Room 18). Perfectly restored to its original exquisite state, a small collection of classical statues and paintings adorn its crimson silk walls and 6000 mother-of-pearl shells painted with crimson varnish encrust the domed ceiling.

Elsewhere in Italy: 15th Century

In Rooms 19 to 23, the ornate vaulted ceilings – frescoed in the 16th and 17th centuries with military objects, allegories, battles and festivals held on piazzas in Florence – are as compelling as the art strung on the walls.

High Renaissance

Passing through the loggia or Secondo Corridoio (Second Corridor), visitors enjoy wonderful views of Florence before entering the Terzo Corridoio (Third Corridor).

Botticelli's *Primavera*

Michelangelo dazzles with the *Doni Tondo,* a depiction of the Holy Family that steals the High Renaissance show in Room 35. The composition is unusual – Joseph holding an exuberant Jesus on his muscled mother's shoulder as she twists round to gaze at him, the colours as vibrant as when they were first applied in 1506–08.

First-Floor Galleries

Head downstairs to the 1st-floor galleries where Rooms 46 to 55 display 16th- to 18th-century works by foreign artists, in-

cluding Rembrandt (Room 49), and Rubens and Van Dyck (who share Room 55). In Room 66, Raphael's *Madonna del cardellino* (Madonna of the Goldfinch; 1505–06) steals the show.

Room 65 is dedicated to Medici portrait artist Agnolo Bronzino (1503–72), who worked at the court of Cosimo I from 1539 until 1555. His 1545 portraits of the Grand Duchess Eleonora of Toleto and her son Giovanni together, and the 18-month-old Giovanni alone holding a goldfinch – symbolising his calling into the Church – are considered masterpieces of 16th-century European portraiture.

As part of the seemingly endless New Uffizi expansion project, four early Florentine works by Leonardo da Vinci are currently displayed in Room 79. His *Annunciazione* (Annunciation; 1472) was deliberately painted to be admired not face on – from where Mary's arm appears too long, her face too light, the angle of buildings not quite right – but rather from the lower right-hand side of the painting.

Room 90, with its canary-yellow walls, features works by Caravaggio, deemed vulgar at the time for his direct interpretation of reality. *The Head of Medusa* (1598–99) is supposedly a self-portrait of the young artist, who died at the age of 39. The biblical drama of an angel steadying the hand of Abraham as he holds a knife to his son Isaac's throat in Caravaggio's *Sacrifice of Isaac* (1601–02) is glorious in its intensity.

★ **Did You Know?**

The Uffizi Gallery presents works in chronological order, giving viewers the opportunity to see the whole panoply of Renaissance art in the manner it developed.

IAN DAGNALL/ALAMY ©

★ **Local Knowledge**

In 1966 flood waters threatened to destroy the Uffizi Gallery. Locals and tourists rushed to the gallery to help rescue the artworks, and these saviours became known as 'mud angels'.

The Duomo's facade

Duomo

Florence's Duomo is the city's most iconic landmark. Capped by Filippo Brunelleschi's red-tiled cupola, it's a staggering construction, and its breathtaking pink, white and green marble facade and graceful campanile (bell tower) dominate the medieval cityscape.

Great For...

Stazione di Santa Maria Novella
Via della Scala
Via de' Panzani
Via Cavour
Via de' Cerretani
Duomo

ℹ Need to Know

Cattedrale di Santa Maria del Fiore; ☏055 230 28 85; www.ilgrandemuseodelduomo. it; Piazza del Duomo; ⊙10am-5pm Mon-Wed & Fri, to 4.30pm Thu, to 4.45pm Sat, 1.30-4.45pm Sun FREE

★ **Top Tip**

Reservations are required to climb the dome. Book online or at the ticket office at Piazza San Giovanni 7, opposite the baptistry's northern entrance.

Sienese architect Arnolfo di Cambio began work on the Duomo in 1296, but construction took almost 150 years and it wasn't consecrated until 1436.

Facade

The neo-Gothic facade was designed in the 19th century by architect Emilio de Fabris to replace the uncompleted original, torn down in the 16th century. The oldest and most clearly Gothic part of the cathedral is its south flank, pierced by the Porta dei Canonici (Canons' Door), a mid-14th-century High Gothic creation (you enter here to climb up inside the dome).

Dome

One of the finest masterpieces of the Renaissance, the **cupola** (Brunelleschi's Dome; adult/reduced incl cupola, baptistry, campanile, crypt & museum €15/3; ⊘8.30am-7pm Mon-Fri, to 5pm Sat, 1-4pm Sun) is a feat of engineering that cannot be fully appreciated without climbing its 463 interior stone steps. It was built between 1420 and 1436 to a design by Filippo Brunelleschi, and is a staggering 91m high and 45.5m wide.

Taking his inspiration from Rome's Pantheon, Brunelleschi arrived at an innovative engineering solution of a distinctive octagonal shape of inner and outer concentric domes resting on the drum of the cathedral rather than the roof itself, allowing artisans to build from the ground up without needing a wooden support frame. Over four million bricks were used in the construction, all of them laid in consecutive rings in horizontal courses using a vertical herringbone pattern.

The climb up the spiral staircase is relatively steep. Make sure to pause when you reach the balustrade at the base of the

Georgio Vasari's and Federico Zuccari's frescoes inside the dome

dome, which gives an aerial view of the octagonal *coro* (choir) in the cathedral below and the seven round stained-glass windows (by Donatello, Andrea del Castagno, Paolo Uccello and Lorenzo Ghiberti) that pierce the octagonal drum.

Interior

After the visual wham-bam of the facade, the sparse decoration of the cathedral's vast interior, 155m long and 90m wide, comes as a surprise – most of its artistic treasures have been removed over the centuries according to the vagaries of ecclesiastical fashion, and many are on show in the **Museo dell'Opera del Duomo** (Cathedral Museum; adult/reduced

> ☑ **Don't Miss**
>
> The flamboyant dome frescoes by Giorgio Vasari and Federico Zuccari.

LUCIANO MORTULA - LGM/SHUTTERSTOCK ©

incl cathedral bell tower, cupola, baptistry & crypt €15/3; ☺9am-7.30pm). The interior is also unexpectedly secular in places (a reflection of the sizeable chunk of the cathedral not paid for by the Church): down the left aisle two immense frescoes of equestrian statues portray two *condottieri* (mercenaries) – on the left Niccolò da Tolentino by Andrea del Castagno (1456), and on the right Sir John Hawkwood (who fought in the service of Florence in the 14th century) by Uccello (1436).

Between the left (north) arm of the transept and the apse is the Sagrestia delle Messe (Mass Sacristy), its panelling a marvel of inlaid wood carved by Benedetto and Giuliano da Maiano. The fine bronze doors were executed by Luca della Robbia – his only known work in the material. Above the doorway is his glazed terracotta *Resurrezione* (Resurrection).

A stairway near the main entrance of the cathedral leads down to the Cripta Santa Reparata (crypt), where excavations between 1965 and 1974 unearthed parts of the 5th-century Chiesa di Santa Reparata that originally stood on the site.

Campanile

The 414-step climb up the cathedral's 85m-tall **campanile** (Bell Tower; adult/ reduced incl campanile, baptistry, cupola, crypt & museum €15/3; ☺8.15am-8pm), begun by Giotto in 1334, rewards with a staggering city panorama. The first tier of bas-reliefs around the base of its elaborate Gothic facade are copies of those carved by Pisano depicting the Creation of Man and the *attività umane* (arts and industries). Those on the second tier depict the planets, the cardinal virtues, the arts and the seven sacraments. The sculpted Prophets and Sibyls in the upper-storey niches are copies of works by Donatello and others.

✖ Take a Break

Take time out over a taste of Tuscan wine at stylish **Coquinarius** (www.coqui narius.com; Via delle Oche 11r; ☺12.30-3pm & 6.30-10.30pm Wed-Mon).

Galleria dell'Accademia

A lengthy queue marks the door to the Galleria dell'Accademia, the late-18th-century gallery that's home to one of the Renaissance's most iconic masterpieces, Michelangelo's David.

Great For...

☑ Don't Miss

David – look for the two pale lines visible on his lower left arm where it was broken in 1527.

David

Fortunately, the world's most famous statue is worth the wait. Standing at over 5m tall and weighing in at 19 tonnes, it's a formidable sight. But it's not just its scale that impresses, it's also the subtle detail – the veins in David's sinewy arms, the muscles in his legs, the change in expression as you move around him. Carved from a single block of marble, Michelangelo's most famous work was also his most challenging – he didn't choose the marble himself; it was veined, and its larger-than-life dimensions were already decided.

When the statue of the boy-warrior, depicted for the first time as a man in the prime of life rather than as a young boy, assumed its pedestal in front of Palazzo Vecchio on Piazza della Signoria in 1504, Florentines immediately adopted it as a powerful emblem of Florentine power, lib-

Michelangelo's *David*

❶ Need to Know

www.firenzemusei.it; Via Ricasoli 60; adult/reduced €8/4, incl temporary exhibition €12.50/6.25; ⏱8.15am-6.50pm Tue-Sun

✕ Take a Break

Grab a pizza slice at the much-loved Pugi (p122), a stone's throw from the Galleria.

★ Top Tip

Cut queuing time by booking tickets in advance at www.firenzemusei.it; the reservation fee is €4.

erty and civic pride. It stayed in the piazza until 1873 when it was moved to its current purpose-built tribune in the Galleria.

Other Works

Michelangelo was also the master behind the unfinished *San Matteo* (St Matthew; 1504–08) and four *Prigioni* ('Prisoners' or 'Slaves'; 1521–30), also displayed in the gallery. The prisoners seem to be writhing and struggling to free themselves from the marble; they were meant for the tomb of Pope Julius II, itself never completed.

Adjacent rooms contain paintings by Andrea Orcagna, Domenico Ghirlandaio, Filippino Lippi and Sandro Botticelli.

What's Nearby?

To the east of the Galleria, Giambologna's equestrian statue of Grand Duke Ferdi-

nando I de' Medici lords it over **Piazza della Santissima Annunziata**, a majestic square dominated by the facades of the **Chiesa della Santissima Annunziata** (⏱7.30am-12.30pm & 4-6.30pm), built in 1250, then rebuilt by Michelozzo et al in the mid-15th century, and the **Ospedale degli Innocenti** (Hospital of the Innocents), Europe's first orphanage, founded in 1421 and now the **Museo degli Innocenti** (☎055 203 73 08; www.museodeglinnocenti.it; Piazza della Santissima Annunziata 13; adult/reduced/family €7/5/10; ⏱10am 7pm). Look up to admire Brunelleschi's classically influenced portico, decorated by Andrea della Robbia (1435–1525) with terracotta medallions of babies in swaddling clothes.

About 200m southeast of the piazza is the **Museo Archeologico** (☎055 23 57, www.archeotoscana.beniculturali.it; Piazza della SS Annunziata 9b; adult/reduced €4/2; ⏱8.30am-7pm Tue-Fri, to 2pm Sat-Mon). Its rich collection of finds, including most of the Medici hoard of antiquities, plunges you deep into the past and offers an alternative to Renaissance splendour.

Heart of the City

Every visitor to Florence spends time navigating the cobbled medieval lanes that run between Via de' Tornabuoni and Via del Proconsolo, but few explore them thoroughly.

Start Piazza della Repubblica
Distance 2km
Duration Two hours

4 Head past the market and along Via Porta Rossa to **Palazzo Davanzati** (p111) with its magnificent studded doors and fascinating museum.

6 Wander down the narrow **Via del Parione** to spy out old mansions and artisans' workshops.

Piazza Santa Trinita

Via Parioncino
Via del Parione
Via de' Tornabuoni
Via Monalda

Lungarno Corsini

5 Hidden behind the unassuming facade of the **Chiesa di Santa Trìnita** are some of the city's finest 15th-century frescoes.

Piazza del Limbo

Classic Photo The River Arno and the Ponte Vecchio.

7 Finish with a sundowner and spectacular Ponte Vecchio views at **La Terrazza Lounge Bar** (p123).

Ⓝ 0 ____ 100 m
0 ____ 0.05 miles

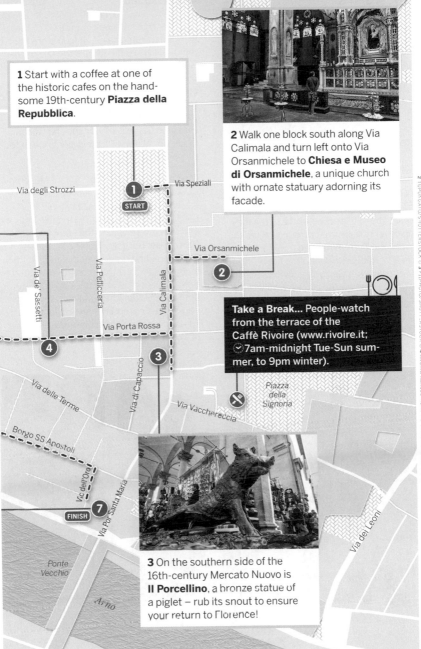

1 Start with a coffee at one of the historic cafes on the handsome 19th-century **Piazza della Repubblica**.

2 Walk one block south along Via Calimala and turn left onto Via Orsanmichele to **Chiesa e Museo di Orsanmichele**, a unique church with ornate statuary adorning its facade.

Via degli Strozzi

Via Speziali

START

Via Orsanmichele

Via de' Sassetti

Via Pellicceria

Via Calimala

Via Porta Rossa

Take a Break... People-watch from the terrace of the Caffè Rivoire (www.rivoire.it; ⊙7am-midnight Tue-Sun summer, to 9pm winter).

Via delle Terme

Via di Capaccio

Via Vaccereccia

Piazza della Signoria

Borgo SS Apostoli

Vic dell'Ora

Via Por Santa Maria

FINISH

Via dei Leoni

Ponte Vecchio

3 On the southern side of the 16th-century Mercato Nuovo is **Il Porcellino**, a bronze statue of a piglet – rub its snout to ensure your return to Florence!

Arno

◉ SIGHTS

◉ Piazza della Signoria & Around

Palazzo Vecchio   Museum

(☏055 276 85 58, 055 27 68 22; www.musefirenze.it; Piazza della Signoria; adult/reduced museum €10/8, tower €10/8, museum & tower €14/12, archaeological tour €4, combination ticket €18/16; ⊘museum 9am-11pm Fri-Wed, to 2pm Thu Apr-Sep, 9am-7pm Fri-Wed, to 2pm Thu Oct-Mar, tower 9am-9pm Fri-Wed, to 2pm Thu Apr-Sep, 10am-5pm Fri-Wed, to 2pm Thu Oct-Mar) This fortress palace, with its crenellations and 94m-high tower, was designed by Arnolfo di Cambio between 1298 and 1314 for the *signoria* (city government). It remains the seat of the city's power, home to the mayor's office and the municipal council. From the top of the **Torre d'Arnolfo** (tower), you can revel in unforgettable rooftop views. Inside, Michelangelo's *Genio della Vittoria* (Genius of Victory) sculpture graces the Salone dei Cinquecento, a magnificent painted hall created for the city's 15th-century ruling Consiglio dei Cinquecento (Council of 500).

Gucci Museo   Museum

(www.gucci.com; Piazza della Signoria 10; adult/reduced €7/5; ⊘10am-8pm, to 11pm Fri) Strut through the chic cafe and icon store to reach this museum. It tells the tale of the Gucci fashion house, from the first luggage pieces in Gucci's signature beige fabric emblazoned with the interlocking 'GG' logo to the 1950s red-and-green stripe and beyond. Don't miss the 1979 Cadillac Seville with gold Gs on the hubcaps and Gucci fabric upholstery. Displays continue to the present day.

Museo del Bargello   Museum

(www.bargellomusei.beniculturali.it; Via del Proconsolo 4; adult/reduced €8/4; ⊘8.15am-1.50pm, closed 2nd & 4th Sun, 1st, 3rd & 5th Mon of month) It was behind the stark walls of Palazzo del Bargello, Florence's earliest public building redecorated in neo-Gothic style in 1845, that the *podestà* (magistrate) meted out justice from the 13th century until 1502. Today the building safeguards Italy's most comprehensive collection of Tuscan Renaissance sculpture with some of Michelangelo's best early works and

Museo del Bargello courtyard

several by Donatello. Michelangelo was just 21 when a cardinal commissioned him to create the drunken grape-adorned *Bacchus* (1496–97). Unfortunately the cardinal didn't like the result and sold it to a banker.

Museo di Palazzo Davanzati   Museum

(☑055 238 86 10; www.polomuseale.firenze. it; Via Porta Rossa 13; adult/reduced €6/3; ⊗8.15am-2pm, closed 1st, 3rd & 5th Mon, 2nd & 4th Sun of month) This is the address to see precisely how Florentine nobles lived in the 16th century. Home to the wealthy Davanzati merchant family from 1578, this 14th-century *palazzo* (mansion) with a wonderful central loggia is a gem. Peep at the carved faces of the original owners on the pillars in the inner courtyard and don't miss the 1st-floor **Sala Madornale** (Reception Room) with its painted wooden ceiling, exotic **Sala dei Pappagalli** (Parrot Room) and **Camera dei Pavoni** (Peacock Bedroom).

Santa Maria Novella

Basilica di Santa Maria Novella   Church

(☑055 21 92 57; www.smn.it; Piazza di Santa Maria Novella 18; adult/reduced €5/3.50; ⊗9am-7pm Mon-Thu, 11am-7pm Fri, 9am-6.30pm Sat, noon-6.30pm Sun summer, shorter hours winter) The striking green-and-white marble facade of 13th- to 15th-century Basilica di Santa Maria Novella fronts an entire monastical complex comprising romantic church cloisters and a frescoed chapel. The basilica itself is a treasure chest of artistic masterpieces, climaxing with frescoes by Domenico Ghirlandaio. The lower section of the basilica's striped marbled facade is transitional from Romanesque to Gothic; the upper section and the main doorway (1456–70) were designed by Leon Battista Alberti. Book tickets in advance online to cut queuing time.

Museo Novecento   Museum

(Museum of the 20th Century; ☑055 28 61 32; www.museonovecento.it; Piazza di Santa Maria Novella 10; adult/reduced €8.50/4; ⊗9am-7pm

Street Levels Gallery

Take a break from Renaissance art with this pioneering urban street-art **gallery** (☑347 3387760, 339 2203607; www.face book.com/pg/StreetLevelsGalleriaFirenze; Via Palazzuolo 74r; ⊗3-7pm). Exhibitions showcase the work of local street artists, including street-sign hacker **Clet** (☑339 2203607, 347 3387760; www.facebook.com/ CLET-108974755823172; Via dell'Olmo 8r; ⊗hours vary), the stencil art of Hogre, and ExitEnter, whose work is easily recognisable by the red balloons holding up the matchstick figures he draws. A highlight is the enigmatic Blub, whose caricatures of historical figures wearing goggles and diving masks adorn many a city wall – his art is known as *L'Arte Sa Nuotare* (Art Knows How to Swim).

Check the gallery's Facebook page for workshops, cultural events, *aperitivi* (pre-dinner drinks) and other uber-cool happenings.

Street art by ExitEnter
ART: MAIL: EXITEXITK@GMAIL.COM; INSTAGRAM: @EXIT.ENTER.K
IMAGE BY MIRIAM DE GIROLAMO/SHUTTERSTOCK ©

Mon-Wed, Sat & Sun, to 2pm Thu, to 11pm Fri summer, 9am-6pm Fri-Wed, to 2pm Thu winter) Don't allow the Renaissance to distract from Florence's fantastic modern-art museum, in a 13th-century *palazzo* previously used as a pilgrim shelter, hospital and school. A well articulated itinerary guides visitors through modern Italian painting and sculpture from the early 20th century to the late 1980s. Installation art makes effective use of the outside space on the 1st-floor loggia. Fashion and theatre get a nod on

Florence

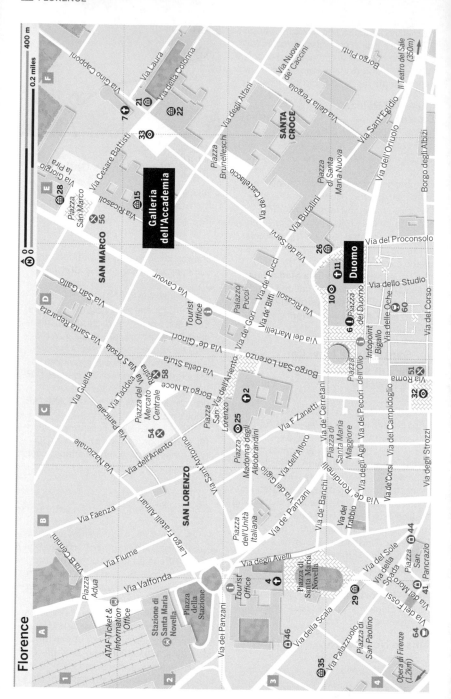

0.2 miles

400 m

SAN MARCO

Galleria dell'Accademia

SANTA CROCE

Duomo

SAN LORENZO

Piazza San Marco

Via Giorgio la Pira

Via Cesare Battisti

Via Gino Capponi

Via Laura

Via della Colonna

Via Nuova de' Caccini

Borgo Pinti

Il Teatro del Sale (350m)

Via degli Alfani

Via della Pergola

Via de' Servi

Via Ricasoli

Via San Gallo

Via Santa Reparata

Via Cavour

Tourist Office

Palazzo Pucci

Via de' Ginori

Via de' Pucci

Via de' Gori

Via de' Biffi

Via dei Martelli

Borgo San Lorenzo

Via del Castellaccio

Piazza Brunelleschi

Via Bufalini

Piazza di Santa Maria Nuova

Via dell'Oriuolo

Via Sant'Egidio

Borgo degli Albizi

Via del Proconsolo

Piazza del Duomo

Via dello Studio

Infopoint Bigallo

Via delle Oche

Via del Corso

Via de' Cerretani

Piazza di Santa Maria Maggiore

Via dei Pecori

Via dell'Olio

Piazza dell'Olio

Via Roma

Via de' Agli

Via del Campidoglio

Via degli Strozzi

Via de' Corsi

Via de' Banchi

Via de' Rondinelli

Via del Trebbio

Via del Sole

Via della Spada

Piazza San Pancrazio

Via del Moro

Via del Fossi

Via F Zanetti

Piazza Madonna degli Aldobrandini

Via dell'Ariento

Via de' Giglio

Via dell'Alloro

Via de' Panzani

Piazza dell'Unità Italiana

Piazza San Lorenzo

Via Santa Antonino

Piazza del Mercato Centrale

Borgo la Noce

Via della Stufa

Via S Orsola

Via Taddea

Piazza del Mercato Centrale

Via Panicale

Via Guelfa

Via Nazionale

Via dell'Ariento

Via Faenza

Largo Fratelli Alinari

Via Fiume

Via B Cennini

Piazza Adua

Stazione di Santa Maria Novella

Piazza della Stazione

Via Valfonda

Via dei Panzani

Tourist Office

Via degli Avelli

Piazza di Santa Maria Novella

Via della Scala

Via del Porcellana

Piazza di San Paolino

Via Palazzuolo

Opera di Firenze (1.2km)

ATAF Ticket & Information Office

7

21

22

33

28

15

56

26

11

10

6

60

51

32

2

25

54

58

44

41

64

4

46

35

29

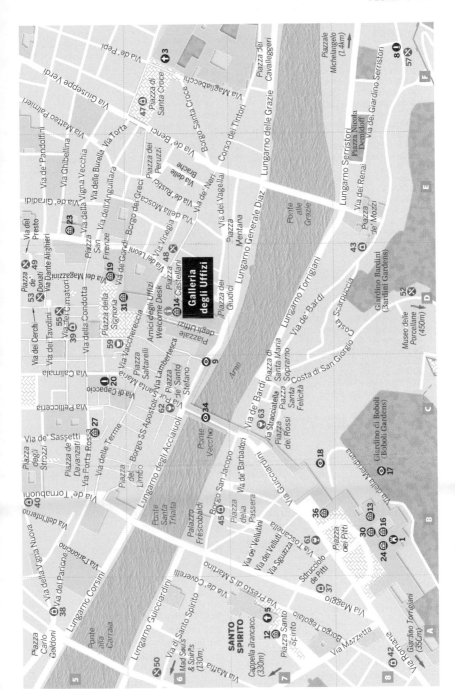

Florence

the 2nd floor, and the itinerary ends with a 20-minute cinematic montage of the best films set in Florence.

⊙ San Lorenzo & San Marco

Museo delle Cappelle Medicee
Mausoleum

(Medici Chapels; www.firenzemusei.it; Piazza Madonna degli Aldobrandini 6; adult/reduced €8/4; ⊗8.15am-1.50pm, closed 1st, 3rd & 5th Mon, 2nd & 4th Sun of month) Nowhere is Medici conceit expressed so explicitly as in the Medici Chapels. Adorned with granite, marble, semi-precious stones and some of Michelangelo's most beautiful sculptures, it is the burial place of 49 dynasty members. Francesco I lies in the dark, imposing

Cappella dei Principi (Princes' Chapel) alongside Ferdinando I and II and Cosimo I, II and III. Lorenzo il Magnifico is buried in the graceful **Sagrestia Nuova** (New Sacristy), which was Michelangelo's first architectural work.

Basilica di San Lorenzo
Basilica

(www.operamedicealaurenziana.org; Piazza San Lorenzo; €6, with Biblioteca Medicea Laurenziana €8.50; ⊗10am-5pm Mon-Sat, plus 1.30-5pm Sun Mar-Oct) Considered one of Florence's most harmonious examples of Renaissance architecture, this unfinished basilica was the Medici parish church and mausoleum. It was designed by Brunelleschi in 1425 for Cosimo the Elder and built over a 4th-century church. In the solemn interior, look for Brunelleschi's austerely beautiful **Sagrestia Vecchia** (Old Sacristy) with its sculptural decoration by Donatello. Michelangelo was commissioned to design the facade in 1518, but his design in white Carrara marble was never executed, hence the building's rough, unfinished appearance.

Museo di San Marco   Museum

(☑055 238 86 08; Piazza San Marco 3; adult/reduced €4/2; ☺8.15am-1.50pm Mon-Fri, 8.15am-4.50pm Sat & Sun, closed 1st, 3rd & 5th Sun, 2nd & 4th Mon of month) At the heart of Florence's university area sits **Chiesa di San Marco** and an adjoining 15th-century Dominican monastery where both gifted painter Fra' Angelico (c 1395–1455) and the sharp-tongued Savonarola piously served God. Today the monastery, aka one of Florence's most spiritually uplifting museums, showcases the work of Fra' Angelico. After centuries of being known as 'Il Beato Angelico' (literally 'The Blessed Angelic One') or simply 'Il Beato' (The Blessed), the Renaissance's most blessed religious painter was made a saint by Pope John Paul II in 1984.

◉ Santa Croce

Basilica di Santa Croce   Church, Museum

(☑055 246 61 05; www.santacroceopera.it; Piazza di Santa Croce; adult/reduced €8/4; ☺9.30am-5.30pm Mon-Sat, 2-5.30pm Sun) The austere interior of this Franciscan basilica is a shock after the magnificent neo-Gothic facade enlivened by varying shades of coloured marble. Most visitors come to see the tombs of Michelangelo, Galileo and Ghiberti inside this church, but frescoes by Giotto in the chapels to the right of the altar are the real highlights. The basilica was designed by Arnolfo di Cambio between 1294 and 1385, and owes its name to a splinter of the Holy Cross donated by King Louis IX of France in 1258.

◉ Oltrarno

Ponte Vecchio   Bridge

Dating from 1345, Ponte Vecchio was the only Florentine bridge to survive destruc-

tion at the hands of retreating German forces in 1944. Above the jewellers' shops on the eastern side, the **Corridoio Vasariano** (Vasari Corridor; ☺by guided tour) is a 16th-century passageway between the Uffizi and Palazzo Pitti (allowing the Medici to wander between their palaces in privacy and comfort) that runs around, rather than through, the medieval **Torre dei Mannelli** at the bridge's southern end. The first documentation of a stone bridge here, at the narrowest crossing point along the entire length of the Arno, dates from 972.

Cappella Brancacci   Chapel

(☑055 238 21 95; http://museicivicifiorentini. comune.fi.it; Piazza del Carmine 14; adult/reduced €6/4.50; ☺10am-5pm Wed-Sat & Mon, 1-5pm Sun) Fire in the 18th century practically destroyed 13th-century **Basilica di Santa Maria del Carmine** (Piazza del Carmine), but it spared the magnificent frescoes in this chapel – a treasure of paintings by Masolino da Panicale, Masaccio and Filippino Lippi commissioned by rich merchant Felice Brancacci upon his return from Egypt in 1423. The chapel entrance is to the right of the main church entrance. Only 30 people can visit at a time, limited to 30 minutes in high season; tickets include admission to the **Fondazione Salvatore Romano** (Cenacolo di Santo Spirito; ☑055 28 70 43; http://museicivicifiorentini.comune.fi.it; Piazza Santo Spirito 29; adult/reduced €7/5; ☺10am-4pm Sat-Mon).

Piazzale Michelangelo   Viewpoint

(🚍13) Turn your back on the bevy of ticky-tacky souvenir stalls flogging David statues and boxer shorts and take in the spectacular city panorama from this vast square, pierced by one of Florence's two David copies. Sunset here is particularly dramatic. It's a 10-minute uphill walk along the serpentine road, paths and steps that scale the hillside from the Arno and Piazza Giuseppe Poggi; from Piazza San Niccolò walk uphill and bear left up the long flight of steps signposted Viale Michelangelo. Or take bus 13 from Stazione di Santa Maria Novella.

From left: Statue of Neptune, Giardino di Boboli; Basilica di San Lorenzo (p114); Artwork inside Palazzo Pitti

Palazzo Pitti   Museum

(www.uffizi.it/palazzo-pitti; Piazza dei Pitti; ⊙8.15am-6.50pm Tue-Sun) Commissioned by banker Luca Pitta and designed by Brunelleschi in 1457, this vast Renaissance palace was later bought by the Medici family. Over the centuries, it served as the residence of the city's rulers until the Savoys donated it to the state in 1919. Nowadays it houses an impressive silver museum, a couple of art museums and a series of rooms recreating life in the palace during House of Savoy times. Stop by at sunset when its entire vast facade is coloured a vibrant pink.

Giardino di Boboli   Gardens

(☎055 29 48 83; www.polomuseale.firenze.it; Palazzo Pitti, Piazza dei Pitti; adult/reduced incl Tesoro dei Granduchi, Museo delle Porcellane & Museo della Moda e del Costume €7/3.50, during temporary exhibition €10/5; ⊙8.15am-7.30pm summer, reduced hours winter, closed 1st & last Mon of month) Behind Palazzo Pitti, the Boboli Gardens were laid out in the mid-16th century to a design by architect Niccolò Pericoli. At the upper, southern limit, beyond the box-hedged rose garden and **Museo delle Porcellane** (Porcelain Museum), beautiful views over the Florentine countryside unfold. Within the lower reaches of the gardens, don't miss the fantastical shell- and gem-encrusted **Grotta del Buontalenti**, a decorative grotto built by Bernardo Buontalenti between 1583 and 1593 for Francesco I de' Medici.

Giardino Torrigiani   Gardens

(☎055 22 45 27; www.giardinotorrigiani.it; Via de' Serragli 144; 1½hr guided tours by donation; ⊙advance reservation via email) Astonishing. Behind the unassuming facades of Via de' Serragli lies a vast, secret garden – Europe's largest privately owned green space within a historic centre, owned by the Torrigiani Malaspina and Torrigiani di Santa Cristina families. Well kept and loved, it's possible to visit this leafy retreat in the engaging company of the charismatic Marquis Vanni Torrigiani Malaspina and his wife, Susanna. Tours (in English or Italian) are intimate and proffer a rare glimpse into a very different and privileged Florentine world.

Basilica di Santo Spirito   Church

(Piazza Santo Spirito; ⏲9.30am-12.30pm
& 4-5.30pm Thu-Tue) The facade of this
Brunelleschi church, smart on Florence's
most shabby chic piazza, makes a striking
backdrop to open-air concerts in summer.
Inside, the basilica's length is lined with 38
semicircular chapels (covered with a plain
wall in the 1960s), and a colonnade of grey
pietra forte Corinthian columns injects
monumental grandeur. Artworks to look
for include Domenico di Zanobi's *Madonna
of the Relief* (1485) in the Cappella Velutti,
in which the Madonna wards off a little red
devil with a club.

TOURS

500 Touring Club   Driving

(📱346 8262324; www.500touringclub.com;
Via Gherardo Silvani 149a) Hook up with
Florence's 500 Touring Club for a guided
tour in a vintage motor – with you behind
the wheel! Every car has a name in this
outfit's fleet of gorgeous vintage Fiat 500s
from the 1960s. Motoring tours are guided
(hop in your car and follow the leader)

and themed – families love the picnic trip,
couples wine tasting.

March to November tours need to be
booked well in advance.

Curious Appetite   Food & Wine

(www.curiousappetitetravel.com) Private and
group food and wine tastings led by Italian-
American Coral Sisk and a small team of
guides. Tastings last 3½ hours (minimum
four people) and are themed: at the market, craft cocktails and *aperitivi*, Italian food
and wine pairings, and artisan gelato.

🔒 SHOPPING

If there is one Italian city that screams
fashion, it's Florence, birthplace of Gucci,
Emilio Pucci, Roberto Cavalli and a bevy of
lesser-known designers. Legendary Via de'
Tornabuoni, a glittering catwalk of designer
boutiques, is the place to start. Nearby, Via
della Vigna Nuova – the street where icon
of Florence fashion Gucci started out as
a tiny saddlery shop in 1921 – is another
fashion hot street. Local designers to look

Bags in the Gucci Museo (p110)

for include Michele Negri, Enrico Coveri, Patrizia Pepe and Ermanno Daelli.

Officina Profumo-Farmaceutica di Santa Maria Novella   Beauty, Gifts

(☑055 21 62 76; www.smnovella.it; Via della Scala 16; ⊙9.30am-8pm) In business since 1612, this exquisite perfumery-pharmacy began life when Santa Maria Novella's Dominican friars began to concoct cures and sweet-smelling unguents using medicinal herbs cultivated in the monastery garden. The shop, with an interior from 1848, sells fragrances, skincare products, ancient herbal remedies and preparations for everything from relief of heavy legs to improving skin elasticity, memory and mental energy.

Benheart   Fashion & Accessories

(☑055 239 94 83; www.benheart.it; Via della Vigna Nuova 97r; ⊙9am-8pm Mon-Sat, 10am-8pm Sun) Evocative of an artisan workshop, this tiny boutique showcases the world-class leather craft of local superstar Benheart. The young Florentine fashion designer went into business with Florentine schoolmate Matteo after undergoing a heart transplant. The pair swore that if Ben survived, they would set up shop on their own. Their handmade shoes (from €250), for men and women, are among the finest in Florence.

Benheart has a second (larger) store on **Via dei Cimatori** (☑055 046 26 38; Via dei Cimatori 25r; ⊙10am-8pm).

Gucci   Fashion & Accessories

(☑055 26 40 11; www.gucci.com; Via de' Tornabuoni 73-81r; ⊙10am-7.30pm) Gucci first made its name with luggage and leather accessories created in a tiny saddlery store around the corner from here, and is now the world's best-known Florentine trademark. Thanks to family feuding there are no Guccis left in the business, but the name still excites aficionados.

La Bottega Della Frutta   Food & Drinks

(☑055 239 85 90; Via dei Federighi 31r; ⊙8.30am-7.30pm Mon-Sat, closed Aug) Follow the trail of knowing Florentines, past the flower-and veg-laden bicycle parked outside, into this enticing food shop bursting with boutique cheeses, organic fruit and veg, biscuits, chocolates, conserved produce, excellent-value wine et al. Mozzarella oozing raw milk arrives fresh from Eboli in Sicily every Tuesday, and if you're looking to buy olive oil, this is the place to taste. Simply ask Elisabeta or husband, Francesco.

Mio Concept   Homewares

(☏055 264 55 43; www.mio-concept.com; Via della Spada 34r; ⏱10am-1.30pm & 2.30-7.30pm Tue-Sat, 3-7pm Mon) A fascinating range of design objects for the home – many upcycled – as well as jewellery, T-shirts and street art cram this stylish boutique created by German-born globetrotter Antje. This is also the only shop in town to sell street-sign artworks by Florence-based street artist Clet (p111); limited edition street signs, of which Clet produces just 13 of each design, start at €2500.

Lorenzo Villoresi   Perfume

(☏055 234 11 87; www.lorenzovilloresi.it; Via de' Bardi 14; ⏱10am-7pm Mon-Sat) Artisan perfumes, bodycare products, scented candles and stones, essential oils and room fragrances crafted by Florentine perfumer Lorenzo Villoresi meld distinctively Tuscan elements such as laurel, olive, cypress and iris with essential oils and essences from around the world. His bespoke fragrances are highly sought after and visiting his elegant boutique, at home in his family's 15th-century *palazzo,* is quite an experience.

Watch this space for a new perfume museum and academy to open in 2018; highlights will include an aromatic courtyard garden scented with plants used in perfumery, and perfume-making workshops and courses.

&Co   Arts & Crafts

(And Company; ☏055 21 99 73; www.andcompanyshop.com; Via Maggio 51r; ⏱10.30am-1pm & 3-7pm Mon-Sat) Souvenir shopping at its best! This Pandora's box of beautiful objects is the love child of Florence-born, British-raised calligrapher and graphic designer

 Tourist Cards

The **Firenze Card** (www.firenzecard.it; €72) is valid for 72 hours and covers admission to some 72 museums, villas and gardens in Florence, as well as unlimited use of public transport and free wi-fi across the city. Its biggest advantage is reducing queuing time in high season – museums have a seperate queue for card-holders. The downside of the Firenze Card is it only allows one admission per museum, plus you need to visit an awful lot of museums to justify the cost. Buy the card online (and collect upon arrival in Florence) or in Florence at tourist offices or ticketing desks of the Uffizi (Gate 2), Palazzo Pitti, Palazzo Vecchio, Museo del Bargello, Cappella Brancacci, Museo di Santa Maria Novella and Giardini Bardini. If you're an EU citizen, your card also covers under 18 year olds travelling with you.

If you prefer to split your Uffizi forays into a couple of visits and/or you're not from the EU and are travelling with kids, the annual Friends of the Uffizi Card (adult/reduced/family of four €60/40/100) is a good deal. Valid for a calendar year (expiring 31 December), it covers admission to 22 Florence museums (including Galleria dell'Accademia, Museo del Bargello and Palazzo Pitti) and allows return visits (have your passport on you as proof of ID to show at each museum with your card). Buy online or from the **Amici degli Uffizi Welcome Desk** (☏055 28 56 10; www.amicidegliuffizi.it; Galleria degli Uffizi, Piazzale degli Uffizi 6; ⏱10am-5pm Tue-Sat) next to Gate 2 at the Uffizi.

Betty Soldi and her vintage-loving husband, Matteo Perduca. Their extraordinary boutique showcases Betty's customised cards, decorative paper products, upcycled homewares and custom fragrances alongside work by other designers (including

¡O¡ Florentine Tripe

When Florentines fancy a fast munch on-the-move, they flit by a *trippaio* – a cart on wheels or mobile stand – for a tripe *panini* (sandwich). Think cow's stomach chopped up, boiled, sliced, seasoned and bunged between bread. Those great bastions of Florentine tradition still going strong include the cart on the southwest corner of Mercato Nuovo, **L'Antico Trippaio** (☑339 7425692; Piazza dei Cimatori; tripe €4.50; ☺9.30am-8pm), and hole in-the-wall **Da Vinattieri** (Via Santa Margherita 4; panini €4.50; ☺10am-7.30pm Mon-Fri, to 8pm Sat & Sun), tucked down an alley next to Dante's Chiesa di Santa Margherita. Pay between €3.50 and €4.50 for a *panini* with tripe doused in *salsa verde* (pea-green sauce of smashed parsley, garlic, capers and anchovies) or garnished with salt, pepper and ground chilli.

DOMENICO TONDINI/ALAMY ©

super-chic leather-printed accessories by Danish design company Edition Poshette).

Obsequium — Wine
(☑055 21 68 49; www.obsequium.it; Borgo San Jacopo 17/39; ☺10am-10pm Mon, to 9pm Tue & Wed, to midnight Thu-Sat, noon-midnight Sun) Tuscan wines, wine accessories and gourmet foods, including truffles, in one of the city's finest wine shops – on the ground floor of one of Florence's best-preserved medieval towers to boot. Not sure which wine to buy? Linger over a glass or indulge in a three-wine tasting with (€20 to €40)

or without (€15 to €30) an accompanying *taglieri* (board) of mixed cheese and salami.

Lorenzo Perrone — Art
(☑340 274402; www.libribianchi.info; Borgo Tegolaio 59r; ☺hours vary) Every book tells a different story in this absolutely fascinating artist's workshop, home to Milan-born Lorenzo Perrone who creates snow-white *Libri Bianchi* (White Books) – aka sublime book sculptures – out of plaster, glue, acrylic and various upcycled objects. His working hours are, somewhat predictably, erratic; call ahead.

EATING
✖ Duomo & Piazza della Signoria
Osteria Il Buongustai — Osteria €
(☑055 29 13 04; Via dei Cerchi 15r; meals €15-20; ☺8am-4pm Mon-Fri, to 11pm Sat) Run with breathtaking speed and grace by Laura and Lucia, this place is unmissable. Lunchtimes heave with locals who work nearby and savvy students who flock here to fill up on tasty Tuscan home cooking at a snip of other restaurant prices. The place is brilliantly no frills – expect to share a table and pay in cash; no credit cards.

Irene — Bistro €€€
(☑055 273 58 91; www.roccofortehotels.com; Piazza della Repubblica 7; meals €60; ☺12.30-10.30pm) Named after the accomplished Italian grandmother of Sir Rocco Forte of the same-name luxury hotel group, Irene (actually part of neighbouring Hotel Savoy) is a dazzling contemporary bistro with a pavement terrace (heated in winter) overlooking iconic Piazza della Repubblica. Interior design is retro-chic 1950s and celebrity chef Fulvio Pierangelini cooks up a playful, utterly fabulous bistro cuisine in his Tuscan kitchen.

✖ Santa Croce
All'Antico Vinaio — Osteria €
(☑055 238 27 23; www.allanticovinaio.com; Via de' Neri 65r; tasting platters €10-30; ☺10am-

4pm & 6-11pm Tue-Sat, noon-3.30pm Sun) The crowd spills out the door of this noisy Florentine thoroughbred. Push your way to the tables at the back to taste cheese and salami in situ (reservations recommended). Or join the queue at the deli counter for a well-stuffed focaccia wrapped in waxed paper to take away – the quality is outstanding. Pour yourself a glass of wine while you wait.

Il Teatro del Sale   Tuscan €€

(☎055 200 14 92; www.teatrodelsale.com; Via dei Macci 111r; lunch/dinner/weekend brunch €15/35/20; ⊗11am-3pm & 7.30-11pm Tue-Sat, 11am-3pm Sun, closed Aug) Florentine chef Fabio Picchi is one of Florence's living treasures who steals the Sant' Ambrogio show with this eccentric, good-value, members-only club (everyone welcome, membership €7) inside an old theatre. He cooks up weekend brunch, lunch and dinner, culminating at 9.30pm in a live performance of drama, music or comedy arranged by his wife, artistic director and comic actress Maria Cassi.

Oltrarno
Essenziale   Tuscan €€

(☎055 247 69 56; http://essenziale.me/; Piazza di Cestello 3r; 3-/5-/7-course tasting menu €35/55/75, brunch €28; ⊗7-10pm Tue-Sat, 11am-4pm Sun; 🛜) There's no finer showcase for modern Tuscan cuisine than this loft-style restaurant in a 19th-century warehouse. Preparing dishes at the kitchen bar, in rolled-up shirt sleeves and navy butcher's apron, is dazzling young chef Simone Cipriani. Order one of his tasting menus to sample the full range of his inventive, thoroughly modern cuisine inspired by classic Tuscan dishes.

Il Santo Bevitore   Tuscan €€

(☎055 21 12 64; www.ilsantobevitore.com; Via di Santo Spirito 64-66r; meals €40; ⊗12.30-2.30pm & 7.30-11.30pm, closed Sun lunch & Aug) Reserve or arrive right on 7.30pm to snag the last table at this ever-popular address, an ode to stylish dining where gastronomes eat by candlelight in a vaulted, white-washed, bottle-lined interior. The menu is a creative reinvention of seasonal classics: risotto with monkfish, red turnip and

Mercato Centrale (p122)

GIANCARLO LIQUORI/SHUTTERSTOCK ©

fennel; *ribollita* (bean, vegetable and bread soup) with kale; or chicken liver terrine with brioche and a Vin Santo reduction.

Burro e Acciughe   Tuscan €€

(Butter & Anchovies; ☑055 045 72 86; www. burroeacciughe.com; Via dell'Orto 35; meals €35; ⊙noon-2pm & 7pm-midnight Fri-Sun, 7pm-midnight Tue-Thu) Carefully sourced, quality ingredients drive this fishy newcomer that woos punters with a short but stylish choice of raw (tartare and carpaccio) and cooked fish dishes. The gnocchi topped with octopus *ragù* (stew) is out of this world, as is the *baccalà* (salted cod) with creamed leeks, turnip and deep-fried polenta wedges. Excellent wine list too.

⊗ San Lorenzo & San Marco

Mercato Centrale   Food Hall €

(☑055 239 97 98; www.mercatocentrale.it; Piazza del Mercato Centrale 4; dishes €7-15; ⊙10am-midnight; 🛜) Wander the maze of stalls crammed with fresh produce at Florence's oldest and largest food market, on the ground floor of a fantastic iron-and-glass structure designed by architect Giuseppe Mengoni in 1874. Head to the 1st floor's buzzing, thoroughly contemporary food hall with dedicated bookshop, cookery school and artisan stalls cooking steaks, burgers, tripe *panini,* vegetarian dishes, pizza, gelato, pastries and pasta.

Load up and find a free table.

Trattoria Mario   Tuscan €

(☑055 21 85 50; www.trattoria-mario.com; Via Rosina 2; meals €25; ⊙noon-3.30pm Mon-Sat, closed 3 weeks Aug; ❋) Arrive by noon to ensure a stool around a shared table at this noisy, busy, brilliant trattoria – a legend that retains its soul (and allure with locals) despite being in every guidebook. Charming Fabio, whose grandfather opened the place in 1953, is front of house while big brother Romeo and nephew Francesco cook with speed in the kitchen. No advance reservations, no credit cards.

Pugi   Bakery €

(☑055 28 09 81; www.focacceria-pugi.it; Piazza San Marco 9b; per kg €15-24; ⊙7.45am-8pm Mon-Sat, closed 2 weeks mid-Aug) The inevitable

Via de Tournabuoni

line outside the door says it all. This bakery is a Florentine favourite for pizza slices and chunks of *schiacciata* (Tuscan flatbread) baked up plain, spiked with salt and rosemary, or topped or stuffed with whatever delicious edible goodies are in season.

🍴 Boboli & San Miniato

San Niccolò 39 Seafood €€

(🕿055 200 13 97; www.sanniccolo39.com; Via di San Niccolò 39; meals €40; ⏰7.30-11pm Mon-Sat; 🛜) With a street terrace at the front and hidden summer garden out the back, this contemporary address in quaint San Niccolò is a gem. Fish – both raw and cooked – is the house speciality, with chef Vanni cooking up a storm with his creative salted-cod burgers, swordfish steak with radicchio, and famous *linguine* (fat spaghetti) with squid ink and Cetara anchovy oil.

The two-course lunch menu for €16, or €20 including a glass of wine and water, is fantastic value.

La Leggenda dei Frati Tuscan €€€

(🕿055 068 05 45; www.laleggendadeifrati.it; Villa Bardini, Costa di San Giorgio 6a; menus €60 & €75, meals €70; ⏰12.30-2pm & 7.30-10pm Tue-Sun; 🛜) Summertime's hottest address. At home in the grounds of historic Villa Bardini, Michelin-starred Legend of Friars enjoys the most romantic terrace with a view in Florence. Veggies are plucked fresh from the vegetable patch, tucked between waterfalls and ornamental beds in Giardino Bardini, and contemporary art jazzes up the classically chic interior. Cuisine is Tuscan, gastronomic and well worth the vital advance reservation.

🍷 DRINKING & NIGHTLIFE

Le Volpi e l'Uva Wine Bar

(🕿055 239 81 32; www.levolpieluva.com; Piazza dei Rossi 1; ⏰11am-9pm Mon-Sat) This unassuming wine bar, hidden away by Chiesa di Santa Felicità, remains as appealing as the day it opened over a decade ago. Its food and wine pairings are first class – taste and buy boutique wines by small producers

from all over Italy, matched perfectly with cheeses, cold meats and the best crostini in town. Wine-tasting classes too.

La Terrazza Lounge Bar Bar

(🕿055 2726 5987; www.lungarnocollection.com; Vicolo dell' Oro 6r; ⏰2.30-11.30pm Apr-Sep) This rooftop bar with wooden-decking terrace accessible from the 5th floor of the 1950s-styled, design Hotel Continentale is as chic as one would expect of a fashion-house hotel. Its *aperitivo* buffet is a modest affair, but who cares with that fabulous, drop-dead-gorgeous panorama of one of Europe's most beautiful cities. Dress the part, or feel out of place. Count on €19 for a cocktail.

Mad Souls & Spirits Cocktail Bar

(🕿055 627 16 21; www.facebook.com/madsoulsandspirits; Borgo San Frediano 38r; ⏰6pm-2am Thu-Sun, to midnight Mon & Wed; 🛜) At this bar of the moment, cult alchemists Neri Fantechi and Julian Biondi woo a discerning fashionable crowd with their expertly crafted cocktails, served in a tiny aqua-green and red-brick space that couldn't be more spartan. A potted cactus decorates each scrubbed wood table and the humorous cocktail menu is the height of irreverence. Check the 'Daily Madness' blackboard for wild 'n' wacky specials.

Santarosa Bistrot Bar

(🕿055 230 90 57; www.facebook.com/santarosa.bistrot; Lungarno di Santarosa; ⏰8am-midnight; 🛜) The living is easy at this hipster garden bistro bar, snug against a chunk of ancient city wall in the flowery Santarosa gardens. Comfy cushioned sofas built from recycled wooden crates sit beneath trees alfresco; food is superb (meals €30); and mixologists behind the bar complement an excellent wine list curated by **Enoteca Pitti Gola e Cantina** (🕿055 21 27 04; www.pittigolaecantina.com; Piazza dei Pitti 16; ⏰1pm-midnight Wed-Mon) with serious craft cocktails.

Todo Modo Cafe

(🕿055 239 91 10; www.todomodo.org; Via dei Fossi 15r; ⏰10am-8pm Tue-Sun) This contemporary bookshop with hip cafe and pocket theatre at the back makes a refreshing change from the usual offerings. A salvaged mix of vintage tables and chairs sits between book- and bottle-lined shelves in the relaxed cafe, actually called 'UqBar' after the fictional place of the same name in a short story by Argentinian writer Jorges Luis Borges.

⊕ ENTERTAINMENT

Opera di Firenze   Opera

(☏055 277 93 09; www.operadifirenze.it; Piazzale Vittorio Gui, Viale Fratelli Rosselli 15; ⊙box office 10am-6pm Tue-Fri, to 1pm Sat) Florence's strikingly modern opera house with glittering contemporary geometric facade sits on the green edge of city park Parco delle Cascine. Its three thoughtfully designed and multifunctional concert halls seat an audience of 5000 and play host to the springtime **Maggio Musicale Fiorentino** (www.operadifirenze.it; ⊙Apr-Jun).

❶ INFORMATION

There are several places in the city to get information, including the following:

Airport Tourist Office (☏055 31 58 74; www.firenzeturismo.it; Florence Airport, Via del Termine 11; ⊙9am-7pm Mon-Sat, to 2pm Sun)

Infopoint Bigallo (☏055 28 84 96; www.firenzeturismo.it; Piazza San Giovanni 1; ⊙9am-7pm Mon-Sat, to 2pm Sun)

Tourist Office (☏055 21 22 45; www.firenzeturismo.it; Piazza della Stazione 4; ⊙9am-6.30pm Mon-Sat, to 1.30pm Sun)

Tourist Office (☏055 29 08 32; www.firenzeturismo.it; Via Cavour 1r; ⊙9am-1pm Mon-Fri)

❶ GETTING THERE & AWAY

AIR

Florence Airport (Aeroporto Amerigo Vespucci; ☏055 3 06 15, 055 306 18 30; www.aeroporto.firenze.it; Via del Termine 11) Also known as Amerigo Vespucci or Peretola airport, 5km northwest of the city centre; domestic and European flights.

Pisa International Airport (Galileo Galilei Airport; ☏050 84 93 00; www.pisa-airport.com) Tuscany's main international airport is a 10-minute drive south of Pisa; it has flights to most major European cities.

TRAIN

Florence's central train station is **Stazione di Santa Maria Novella** (Piazza della Stazione), which is on the main Rome–Milan line. There are at least hourly connections to both cities.

❶ GETTING AROUND

TO/FROM THE AIRPORT

Florence Airport Shuttle buses to the city centre every 30 minutes between 6am and 8.30pm, then hourly 8.30pm to 11.30pm. Taxis are set at €20 to the city centre.

Pisa International Airport Regular trains and buses between 4.30am and 10.25pm to Florence's main train station, Stazione di Santa Maria Novella; count on €5 to €10 and 1½ hours journey time.

PUBLIC TRANSPORT

Buses, electric minibuses and trams run by public transport company ATAF serve the city. Most buses – including bus 13 to Piazzale Michelangelo – start/terminate at the ATAF bus stops opposite the southeastern exit of Stazione di Santa Maria Novella. Tickets are valid for 90 minutes (no return journeys), cost €1.20 (€2 on board – drivers don't give change!) and are sold at kiosks, tobacconists and the **ATAF ticket & information office** (☏800 424500, 199 104245; www.ataf.net; Stazione di Santa Maria Novella, Piazza della Stazione; ⊙6.45am-8pm Mon-Sat) inside the main ticketing hall at Stazione di Santa Maria Novella. A travel pass valid for one/three/seven days is €5/12/18. Upon boarding, time stamp your ticket (punch on board) or risk an on-the-spot €50 fine.

Where to Stay

Florence is unexpectedly small, rendering almost anywhere in the centre convenient.

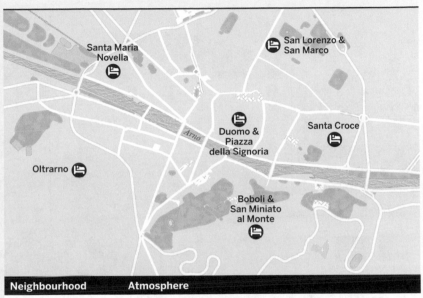

Neighbourhood	Atmosphere
Duomo & Piazza della Signoria	The city's medieval heart, with plenty of accommodation options in all price categories. The tourist crowd is relentless in high season, meaning little peace and quiet.
Santa Maria Novella	Next to Stazione di Santa Maria Novella, with plenty of budget hotels and cheap dining in traditional trattorias. Not the swishest part of town, but hardly rough.
San Lorenzo & San Marco	The market neighbourhood of San Lorenzo has the city's best hostels; San Marco is more upmarket, with elegant *palazzo* hotels, but less eating than elsewhere.
Santa Croce	Few accommodation options in this ancient residential area, refashioned with uber-hip eateries, bars and outstanding nightlife. Some piazzas remain noisy until very late.
Oltrarno	Across the river, with some utterly charming hotels and guesthouses on quiet cobbled lanes. Bohemain wine bars and foodie hot spots on your doorstep. Can feel a step away from the action.
Boboli & San Miniato	The place to stay for a touch of green countryside in the city, with a profusion of parks and panoramic terraces. The city centre and most major sights are a strenuous walk (or bus ride) away.

TUSCANY

Tuscany at a Glance...

With its lyrical landscapes, world-class art and superb cucina contadina (food from the farmer's kitchen), Tuscany offers a splendid array of treats for travellers. No land is more caught up with the fruits of its fertile earth than Tuscany, a gourmet destination where locality, seasonality and sustainability are revered. And oh, the art! During the medieval and Renaissance periods, Tuscany's painters, sculptors and architects created world-class masterpieces. Squirrelled away and safeguarded today in churches, museums and galleries all over the region, Tuscan art is truly unmatched.

Tuscany in Two Days

Start in **Siena** (p136) with its gob-smacking architecture, more than enough for a day or two's exploration on its own. Spend the second day exploring the amazingly well-preserved medieval walled town of **San Gimignano** (p130) with its 14 towers and wonderful setting in the Tuscan landscape.

Tuscany in Four Days

Your third day in Tuscany should be spent on the cobbled streets of **Lucca** (p140) with its cathedral and Renaissance architecture. On day four choose between the hilltop wine town of **Montalcino** (p142), medieval **Montepulciano** (p143) or the churches and museums of **Arezzo** (p146).

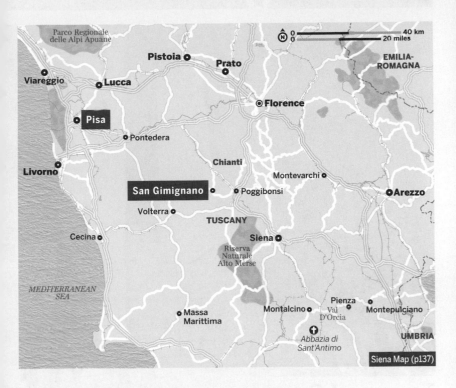

Siena Map (p137)

Arriving in Tuscany

Tuscany's principal international gateway is Pisa International Airport. From there, buses run to Pisa and direct to Florence. Florence also has its own, much smaller, airport serving flights from Italian and European destinations. Regular fast trains run to Florence, which is on the main Rome–Milan rail line. Its main station, Stazione di Santa Maria Novella, is the region's biggest and busiest.

Where to Stay

Tuscany boasts some of Italy's finest accommodation, especially when it comes to *agriturismi* (farm stay accommodation), palace guesthouses and small, characterful B&Bs. However, Tuscany is a very popular destination so be sure to book accommodation in advance, particularly in spring, summer and autumn when the best addresses fill up fast. Check online for cheaper rates.

Towers of San Gimignano

A mecca for day trippers, San Gimignano lies deep in the Tuscan countryside northwest of Siena. Known as the 'medieval Manhattan', it features 15 11th-century towers that soar above its hilltop centro storico (historic centre).

Great For...

☑ Don't Miss

Galleria Continua (📞0577 94 31 34; www.galleriacontinua.com; Via del Castello 11; ⊙10am-1pm & 2-7pm) **FREE**, one of the best contemporary art galleries in Europe.

Originally an Etruscan village, the town was named after the bishop of Modena, San Gimignano, who is said to have saved it from Attila the Hun. It became a *comune* in 1199 and quickly flourished, thanks in no small part to its position on the Via Francigena. Up to 72 towers were built as the town's prosperous burghers sought to outdo their neighbours and flaunt their wealth.

Collegiata

San Gimignano's Romanesque cathedral, the **Collegiata** (Duomo; Basilica di Santa Maria Assunta; 📞0577 94 01 52; www.duomosangimignano.it; Piazza del Duomo; adult/reduced €4/2; ⊙10am-7pm Mon-Sat, 12.30-7pm Sun summer, 10am-4.30pm Mon-Sat, 12.30-4.30pm Sun winter), is named after the college of

priests who originally managed it. Parts of the building were built in the second half of the 11th century, but its remarkably vivid frescoes date from the 14th century.

Entry is via the side stairs and through a loggia that originally functioned as the baptistry. Once in the main space, face the altar and look to your left (north). On the wall are scenes from Genesis and the Old Testament by Bartolo di Fredi, dating from around 1367. On the right (south) wall are scenes from the New Testament by the workshop of Simone Martini, which were completed in 1336. On the inside of the front facade is Taddeo di Bartolo's striking depiction of the *Last Judgment* on the upper-left side is a fresco depicting *Paradiso* (Heaven) and on the upper-right *Inferno* (Hell).

❶ Need to Know

Frequent buses run to/from Florence (€6.80, 1¼ to two hours) and Siena (€6, one to 1½ hours).

✕ Take a Break

Stop by for some earthy local fare at **Locanda Sant'Agostino** (☑0577 94 31 41; Piazza Sant'Agostino 15; meals €35, pizza €8-10; ☻noon-3pm & 7-10pm Thu-Tue).

★ Top Tip

San Gimignano's helpful **tourist office** (☑0577 94 00 08; www.sangimignano.com; Piazza del Duomo 1; ☻10am-1pm & 3-7pm summer, 10am-1pm & 2-6pm winter) **organises a range of English-language tours.**

Palazzo Comunale

The 12th-century **Palazzo Comunale** (☑0577 99 03 12; www.sangimignanomusei.it; Piazza del Duomo 2; combined Civic Museums ticket adult/reduced €9/7; ☻10am-7.30pm summer, 11am-5.30pm winter) has always been the centre of local government – its Sala di Dante is where the great poet addressed the town's council in 1299, urging it to support the Guelph cause. The room (also known as the Sala del Consiglio) is home to Lippo Memmi's early-14th-century *Maestà*, which portrays the enthroned Virgin and Child surrounded by angels, saints and local dignitaries.

Upstairs, the *pinacoteca* (art gallery) has a charming collection of paintings from the Sienese and Florentine schools of the 12th to 15th centuries.

In the Camera del Podestà is a meticulously restored cycle of frescoes by Memmo di Filippuccio, illustrating a moral history – the rewards of marriage are shown in the scenes of a husband and wife naked in a bath and in bed.

After you've enjoyed the art, be sure to climb the 218 steps of the *palazzo's* 54m-tall Torre Grossa for spectacular views of the town and surrounding countryside.

Pisa's Piazza dei Miracoli

Pisans claim that Piazza dei Miracoli is among the world's most beautiful squares. Its walled lawns provide a photogenic setting for the impressive Duomo, but most eyes are drawn to the world-famous Leaning Tower.

Great For...

☑ Don't Miss

Before entering the cathedral, study the three pairs of 16th-century bronze doors at the main entrance.

Leaning Tower

One of Italy's signature sights, the **Torre Pendente** (€18; ⏰8am-8pm Apr-Sep, 9am-7pm Oct, to 6pm Mar, 10am-5pm Nov-Feb) truly lives up to its name, leaning a startling 3.9 degrees off the vertical. The 56m-high tower, officially the Duomo's *campanile* (bell tower), took almost 200 years to build, but was already listing when it was unveiled in 1372. Over time, the tilt, caused by a layer of weak subsoil, steadily worsened until it was finally halted by a major stabilisation project in the 1990s.

Building began in 1173 under the supervision of architect Bonanno Pisano, but his plans came a cropper almost immediately. Only three of the tower's seven tiers had been built when he was forced to abandon construction after it started leaning. Work resumed in 1272, with artisans and masons

The Leaning Tower and the Duomo

ℹ Need to Know

Campo dei Miracoli; ☏050 83 50 11; www.opapisa.it

✕ Take a Break

L'Ostellino (Piazza Cavallotti 1; panini €3.50-7; ⊙noon-4.30pm Mon-Fri, to 6pm Sat & Sun), a short walk from the piazza, is a great place to pick up a tasty sandwich and coffee.

★ Top Tip

Access to the Leaning Tower is limited to groups of 45 and children under eight years are not allowed entrance.

attempting to bolster the foundations, but failing miserably. They kept going, though, compensating for the lean by gradually building straight up from the lower storeys. But once again work had to be suspended – this time due to war – and construction wasn't completed until the second half of the 14th century.

Duomo

Pisa's magnificent Romanesque **cathedral** (Duomo di Santa Maria Assunta; ⊙10am-8pm Apr-Sep, to 7pm Oct, to 6pm Nov-Mar) **FREE** was begun in 1064 and consecrated in 1118. Its striking tiered exterior, with cladding of green-and-cream marble bands, gives on to a vast columned interior capped by a gold wooden ceiling. The elliptical dome, the first of its kind in Europe, was added in 1380.

The cathedral, which served as a blueprint for subsequent Romanesque churches in Tuscany, was paid for with spoils from a 1063 naval battle that the Pisans fought against an Arab fleet off Palermo. To mark the victory, and symbolise Pisa's domination of the Mediterranean, the cathedral was Europe's largest when it was completed.

Battistero

Construction of the cupcake-style **baptistry** (Battistero di San Giovanni; €5, combination ticket with Camposanto or Museo delle Sinopie €7, Camposanto & Museo €8; ⊙8am-8pm Apr-Sep, 9am-7pm Oct, to 6pm Mar, 10am-5pm Nov-Feb) began in 1152, but the building was remodelled and continued by Nicola and Giovanni Pisano more than a century later and finally completed in the 14th century. Don't leave without climbing to the Upper Gallery to listen to the custodian demonstrate the double dome's remarkable acoustics and echo effects.

Driving Tuscany

Taking in Tuscany's two great medieval rivals, Florence and Siena, Chianti's wine-rich hills and the Unesco-listed Val d'Orcia, this drive offers artistic masterpieces, soul-stirring scenery and captivating Renaissance towns.

Start Florence
Distance 185km
Duration Four days

1 Start your journey in the cradle of the Renaissance, **Florence** (p94). Admire Brunelleschi's Duomo dome, wander around the Galleria degli Uffizi, and greet Michelangelo's *David* at the Galleria dell'Accademia.

START **1**

SR222

RA3

Badia a Passignano **2**

Take a Break... Enjoy a meal at **Osteria di Passignano** (www.osteria dipassignano.com; Via di Passignano 33; ⏰12.15-2.15pm & 7.30-10pm Mon-Sat) **in Badia a Passignano, about 20 minutes from Greve.**

3

Riserva Naturale Alto Merse

SR2

SS223

4

3 The medieval cityscape of **Siena** (p136) is one of Italy's most captivating. Be inspired by the Duomo's intricate facade, bustling Piazza del Campo and fine art in the Museo Civico.

4 Take the SR2 (Via Cassia) to **Montalcino** (p142), known to wine buffs around the world for its celebrated local drop, Brunello.

2 Pick up the SR222 (Via Chiantigiana) and head south to Chianti wine country. Stop off in the centuries-old wine centre of **Greve**, then continue south to Siena.

Classic Photo: The idyllic village streets in Pienza.

5 Head east to the Val d'Orcia and pretty **Pienza**. Check out the magnificent Renaissance buildings in and around Piazza Pio II, which went up in just four years in the 15th century and haven't been remodelled since.

6 Steeply stacked **Montepulciano** (p143) harbours a wealth of *palazzi* and fine buildings, plus grandstand views over the Val di Chiana and Val d'Orcia. Round off your trip with a glass or two of the local Vino Nobile.

San Godenzo

Parco Nazionale delle Foreste Casentinesi, Monte Falterona e Campigna

Monte Falterona

40 km

20 miles

FINISH

SR2

Siena

Siena is a city where the architecture soars, as do the souls of many of its visitors. Effectively a giant, open-air museum celebrating the Gothic, Siena has spiritual and secular monuments that have retained both their medieval forms and their extraordinary art collections, providing the visitor with plenty to marvel at.

◎ SIGHTS

Piazza del Campo   Square

Popularly known as 'Il Campo', this sloping piazza has been Siena's civic and social centre since being staked out by the ruling Consiglio dei Nove (Council of Nine) in the mid 12th century. Built on the site of a Roman marketplace, its paving is divided into nine sectors representing the number of members of the *consiglio* and these days acts as a carpet on which young locals meet and relax. The cafes around its perimeter are the most popular coffee and *aperitivi* (pre-dinner drinks) spots in town.

Duomo   Cathedral

(Cattedrale di Santa Maria Assunta; ☑0577 28 63 00; www.operaduomo.siena.it; Piazza Duomo; summer/winter €4/free, when floor displayed €7; ☺10.30am-7pm Mon-Sat, 1.30-6pm Sun summer, to 5.30pm winter) Consecrated on the former site of a Roman temple in 1179 and constructed over the 13th and 14th centuries, Siena's majestic *duomo* (cathedral) showcases the talents of many great medieval and Renaissance architects and artists: Giovanni Pisano designed the intricate white, green and red marble facade; Nicola Pisano carved the elaborate pulpit; Pinturicchio painted the frescoes in the extraordinary **Piccolomini Library** (summer/winter free/€2); and Michelangelo, Donatello and Gian Lorenzo Bernini all produced sculptures.

Pinacoteca Nazionale   Gallery

(☑0577 28 11 61; http://pinacotecanazionale. siena.it; Via San Pietro 29; adult/reduced €4/2; ☺8.15am-7.15pm Tue-Sat, 9am-1pm Sun & Mon) An extraordinary collection of Gothic masterpieces from the Sienese school sits inside the once grand, but now sadly dishevelled, 14th-century **Palazzo Buonsignori**. The highlights are on the 2nd floor, where magnificent works by Guido da Siena, Duccio (di Buoninsegna), Simone Martini, Niccolò di Segna, Lippo Memmi, Ambrogio and Pietro Lorenzetti, Bartolo di Fredi, Taddeo di Bartolo and Sano di Pietro are housed.

Museale Santa
Maria della Scala   Museum

(☑0577 53 45 71, 0577 53 45 11; www.santamaria dellascala.com; Piazza Duomo 1; adult/reduced €9/7; ☺10am-5pm Mon, Wed & Thu, to 8pm Fri, to 7pm Sat & Sun, extended hours in summer) Built as a hospice for pilgrims travelling the Via Francigena, this huge complex opposite the *duomo* dates from the 13th century. Its highlight is the upstairs **Pellegrinaio** (Pilgrims' Hall), featuring vivid 15th-century frescoes by Lorenzo di Pietro (aka Vecchietta), Priamo della Quercia and Domenico di Bartolo. All laud the good works of the hospital and its patrons; the most evocative is di Bartolo's *Il governo degli infermi* (Caring for the Sick; 1440–41), which depicts many activities that occurred here.

Museo Civico   Museum

(Civic Museum; ☑0577 29 22 32; Palazzo Pubblico, Piazza del Campo 1; adult/reduced €9/8; ☺10am-6.15pm summer, to 5.15pm winter) Entered via the Palazzo Pubblico's **Cortile del Podestà** (Courtyard of the Podestà), this wonderful museum showcases rooms richly frescoed by artists of the Sienese school. Commissioned by the city's governing body rather than by the Church, some of the frescoes depict secular subjects – highly unusual at the time. The highlights are two huge frescoes: Ambrogio Lorenzetti's *Allegories of Good and Bad Government* (c 1338–40) and Simone Martini's celebrated *Maestà* (Virgin Mary in Majesty; 1315).

🛍 SHOPPING

Il Magnifico   Food

(☑0577 28 11 06; www.ilmagnifico.siena.it; Via dei Pellegrini 27; ☺7.30am-7.30pm Mon-Sat) Lorenzo Rossi is Siena's best baker, and

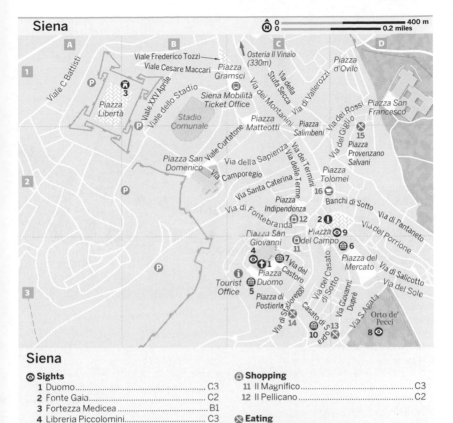

Siena

his *panforte* (spiced fruit and nut cake), *ricciarelli* (sugar-dusted chewy almond biscuits) and *cavallucci* (chewy biscuits flavoured with aniseed and other spices) are a weekly purchase for most local households. Try them at his bakery and shop behind the *duomo,* and you'll understand why.

Il Pellicano Ceramics

(🖉0577 24 79 14; www.siena-ilpellicano.it; Via Diacceto 17a; ⊙10.30am-7pm summer, hours vary in winter) Elisabetta Ricci has been making traditional hand-painted Sienese ceramics for over 30 years. She shapes, fires and paints her creations, often using Renaissance-era styles or typical *contrade* (district) designs. Elisabetta also conducts lessons in traditional ceramic techniques.

⊗ EATING

La Vecchia Latteria Gelato €

(🖉0577 05 76 38; Via San Pietro 10; gelato €2-3.50; ⊙noon-8pm) Sauntering through Siena's historical centre is always more fun

Palazzo Pubblico, home of Museo Civico (p136), in Piazza del Campo (p136)

with a gelato in hand. Just ask one of the many locals who are regular customers at this *gelateria artigianale* (maker of hand-made gelato) near the Pinacoteca Nazionale. Using quality produce, owners Fabio and Francesco concoct and serve fruity fresh or decadently creamy iced treats.

Osteria Il Vinaio Tuscan €

(☑0577 4 96 15; Via Camollia 167; antipasti €6-13, pasta €6-7; ☺10am-10pm Mon-Sat) Wine bars are thin on the ground in Siena, so it's not surprising that Bobbe and Davide's neighbourhood *osteria* (casual tavern serving simple food and drink) is so popular. Join the multigenerational local regulars for a bowl of pasta or your choice from the generous antipasto display, washed down with a glass or two of eminently quaffable house wine.

La Taverna di San Giuseppe Tuscan €€€

(☑0577 4 22 86; www.tavernasangiuseppe.it; Via Dupré 132; meals €45; ☺noon-2.30pm & 7-10pm Mon-Sat) Any restaurant specialising in beef, truffles and porcini mushrooms attracts our immediate attention, but not

all deliver on their promise. Fortunately, this one does. A favoured venue for locals celebrating important occasions, it offers excellent food, an impressive wine list with plenty of local, regional and international choices, a convivial traditional atmosphere and efficient service.

Tre Cristi Seafood €€€

(☑0577 28 06 08; www.trecristi.com; Vicolo di Provenzano 1-7; meals €45, tasting menus €40-65; ☺12.30-2.30pm & 7.30-10pm Mon-Sat) Seafood restaurants are rare in this meat-obsessed region, so the long existence of Tre Cristi (it's been around since 1830) should be heartily celebrated. The menu here is as elegant as the decor, and touches such as a complimentary glass of *prosecco* at the start of the meal add to the experience. Exemplary service.

🍷 DRINKING & NIGHTLIFE

Bar Pasticcheria Nannini Cafe

(☑0577 23 60 09; www.pasticcerienannini.it/en; Via Banchi di Sopra 24; ☺7.30am-9.30pm Mon-Fri, to 11pm Sat, to 10pm Sun) Established

in 1886, Nannini's good coffee and location near the Campo ensure that it remains a local favourite. It's a great place to sample Sienese treats including *cantuccini* (crunchy, almond-studded biscuits), *cavallucci* (chewy biscuits flavoured with aniseed and other spices), *ricciarelli* (chewy, sugar-dusted almond biscuits), *panforte* (dense spiced cake with almonds and candied fruit) and *panpepato* (*panforte* with the addition of pepper and hazelnuts).

Enoteca Italiana — Wine Bar

(②0577 22 88 43; www.enoteca-italiana.it; Fortezza Medicea, Piazza Libertà 1; ⊙noon-7.30pm Mon & Tue, to midnight Wed-Sat) The former munitions cellar and dungeon of this **Medici fortress** (Piazza Caduti delle Forze Armate; ⊙24hr) `FREE` has been artfully transformed into a classy *enoteca* (wine bar) that carries more than 1500 Italian labels. You can take a bottle with you, ship a case home or just enjoy a glass in the attractive courtyard or vaulted interior.

ⓘ INFORMATION

Tourist Office (②0577 28 05 51; www.enjoy siena.it; Piazza Duomo 1, Santa Maria della Scala; ⊙9am-6pm summer, to 5pm winter) Siena's tourist information office is located in the Museale Santa Maria della Scala, and can provide free maps of the city. The entrance is on the right (western) side of the museum building.

ⓘ GETTING THERE & AWAY

Siena isn't on a major train line so buses are generally a better alternative. **Siena Mobilità** (②800 922984; www.sienamobilita.it), part of the Tiemme network, runs services between Siena and other parts of Tuscany. It has a **ticket office** (www.sienamobilita.it; ⊙6.30am-7.30pm Mon-Fri, from 7am Sat) underneath the main bus station in Piazza Gramsci.

ⓘ GETTING AROUND

Within Siena, **Tiemme** (②0577 20 41 11; www. tiemmespa.it) operates *pollicino* (city centre),

 Tuscan Wineries

Stripe upon stripe of vines over undulating, sun-drenched Tuscan hills: try these local wineries to sample some of Italy's finest tipples.

Antinori nel Chianti Classico (②0552 35 97 00; www.antinorichianticlassico.it; Via Cassia per Siena 133, Località Bargino; tour & tasting €25-50, bookings essential; ⊙10am-5pm Mon-Fri, to 5.30pm Sat & Sun winter, to 6.30pm Sat & Sun summer) Visiting this cellar complex is a James Bond–esque experience. Get cleared at the gated, guarded entrance, approach a sculptural main building that's set into the hillside, then explore an exquisitely designed winery full of architectural flourishes and state-of-the-art equipment. Your one-hour guided tour (English and Italian) finishes with a tutored tasting of three Antinori wines beside the family museum.

Badia a Passignano (②0558 07 12 78; www.osteriadipassignano.com; Via di Passignano 33; ⊙10am-7.30pm Mon-Sat) It doesn't get much more atmospheric: an 11th-century abbey, owned by Benedictine monks and set amid vineyards run by the legendary Antinori dynasty. The four-hour 'Antinori at Badia a Passignano' tour (€150, two daily, Monday to Saturday) includes a vineyard and cellar visit and a meal in the estate's restaurant, accompanied by four signature Antinori wines.

Winery in Chianti

 Carnevale in Viareggio

For Tuscany's best winter party head to Viareggio, a popular resort near Lucca. From February to early March, the city stages one of Italy's most flamboyant Carnevale celebrations. Festivities involve fireworks and rampant dusk-to-dawn parties, but the headline attraction is the parade of floats carrying giant satirical effigies of politicians and topical celebrities.

Carnevale parade
ONIGIRI STUDIO/SHUTTERSTOCK ©

urbano (urban) and *suburbano* (suburban) buses (€1.20 per one hour). Buses 3 and 9 run between the train station and Piazza Antonio Gramsci.

Lucca

Lovely Lucca endears itself to everyone who visits. Hidden behind imposing Renaissance walls, its cobbled streets, handsome piazzas and shady promenades make it a perfect destination to explore by foot – as a day trip from Florence or in its own right.

◉ SIGHTS

City Wall   Historic Site

Lucca's monumental *mura* (wall) was built around the old city in the 16th and 17th centuries and remains in almost perfect condition. It superseded two previous walls, the first built from travertine stone blocks as early as the 2nd century BC. Twelve metres high and 4.2km long, today's ramparts are crowned with a tree-lined footpath looking down on the historic centre and –

by the **Baluardo San Regolo** (San Regolo Bastion) – the city's vintage **botanical gardens** (☑0583 44 21 61; Casermetta San Regolo; adult/reduced €4/3; ☺10am-7pm Jul-Sep, to 6pm May & Jun, to 5pm Mar, Apr & Oct) with its magnificent centurion cedar trees.

**Cattedrale di
San Martino**   Cathedral

(☑0583 49 05 30; www.museocattedralelucca. it; Piazza San Martino; adult/reduced €3/2, incl Museo della Cattedrale & Chiesa e Battistero dei SS Giovanni & Reparata €9/5; ☺9.30am-6pm Mon-Fri, to 6.45pm Sat, noon-6pm Sun summer, 9.30am-5pm Mon-Fri, to 6.45pm Sat, noon-6pm Sun winter) Lucca's predominantly Romanesque cathedral dates from the 11th century. Its stunning facade was constructed in the prevailing Lucca-Pisan style and designed to accommodate the pre-existing *campanile* (bell tower). The reliefs over the left doorway of the portico are believed to be by Nicola Pisano, while inside, treasures include the **Volto Santo** (literally, Holy Countenance) crucifix sculpture and a wonderful 15th-century tomb in the **sacristy**.

Torre Guinigi   Tower

(Via Sant'Andrea 45; adult/reduced €4/3; ☺9.30am-7.30pm Jun-Sep, to 6.30pm Apr & May, to 5.30pm Oct & Mar) The bird's-eye view from the top of this medieval, 45m-tall red-brick tower adjoining 14th-century **Palazzo Guinigi** is predictably magnificent. But what impresses even more are the seven oak trees planted in a U-shaped flower bed at the top of the tower. Legend has it that upon the death of powerful Lucchese ruler Paolo Guinigi (1372–1432) all the leaves fell off the trees.

Palazzo Pfanner   Palace

(☑0583 95 21 55; www.palazzopfanner.it; Via degli Asili 33; palace or garden adult/reduced €4.50/4, both €6/5; ☺10am-6pm Apr-Nov) Fire the romantic in you with a stroll around this beautiful 17th-century palace where parts of *Portrait of a Lady* (1996), starring Nicole Kidman and John Malkovich, were shot. Its baroque-styled garden – the only one of substance within the city walls – enchants with ornamental pond, lemon house and

18th-century statues of Greek gods posing between potted lemon trees. Summertime chamber-music concerts hosted here are absolutely wonderful.

Museo della Cattedrale Museum
(Cathedral Museum; ☎0583 49 05 30; www.museocattedralelucca.it; Piazza San Martino; adult/reduced €4/3, with cathedral sacristy & Chiesa e Battistero dei SS Giovanni e Reparata €9/5; ⏱10am-6pm summer, to 5pm Mon-Fri, to 6pm Sat & Sun winter) The cathedral museum safeguards elaborate gold and silver decorations made for the cathedral's Volto Santo, including a 17th-century crown and a 19th-century sceptre.

EATING & DRINKING

Gustevole Gelato €
(☎366 896 03 46; www.facebook.com/gelateriagustevolelucca; Via di Poggio Seconda 26; cones & tubs €2.30-3; ⏱1.30-7pm Tue-Thu, noon-7pm Fri, to 8pm Sat) With enticing flavours like liquorice and mint, ricotta with fig and walnut, or pine kernel made with local Pisan kernels (nuts in sweet, crunchy caramelised clumps), the most recent addition to Lucca's artisan gelato scene is pure gold. Gelato is organic, natural and gluten-free. The key to entering gelato heaven: ask for a dollop of thick whipped cream on top.

Ristorante Giglio Tuscan €€
(☎0583 49 40 58; www.ristorantegiglio.com; Piazza del Giglio 2; meals €40; ⏱noon-2.30pm & 7.30-10pm Thu-Mon, 7.30-10pm Wed) Splendidly at home in the frescoed 18th-century Palazzo Arnolfini, Giglio is stunning. Dine at white-tableclothed tables, sip a complimentary *prosecco,* watch the fire crackle in the marble fireplace and savour traditional Tuscan with a modern twist: think fresh artichoke salad served in an edible parmesan-cheese wafer 'bowl', or risotto simmered in Chianti. End with Lucchese *buccellato* (sweetbread) filled with ice cream and berries.

Bistrot Undici Undici Cafe
(☎0583 189 27 01; www.facebook.com/und1c1und1c1; Piazza Antelminelli 2; ⏱10am-8pm Tue-Thu, to 1am Fri-Sun) With one huge cream-coloured parasol providing shade

Cattedrale di San Martino

HORST LIEBER/SHUTTERSTOCK ©

and a tinkling fountain providing an atmospheric soundtrack, cafe terraces don't get much better than this. And then there is the view at this bucolic cafe (the only cafe) on Piazza San Miniato of the almighty facade of Lucca's lovely cathedral. Live music sets the place rocking after dark.

INFORMATION

Tourist Office (0583 58 31 50; www.turismo.lucca.it; Piazzale Verdi; ☺9am-7pm Apr-Sep, to 5pm Mar-Oct) Free hotel reservations, left-luggage service (two bags €1.50/4.50/7 per hr/half-day/day) and guided city tours in English departing at 2pm daily in summer and on Saturdays and Sundays in winter. The two-hour tour is €10/free per adult/child under 15 years.

ⓘ GETTING THERE & AWAY

BUS

From the bus stops around Piazzale Verdi, **Vaibus Lucca** (www.lucca.cttnord.it) runs services throughout the region, including to the following destinations:

Castelnuovo di Garfagnana (€4.20, 1½ hours, eight daily)

Pisa airport (€3.40, 45 minutes to one hour, 30 daily)

TRAIN

The train station is south of the city walls: take the path across the moat and through the (dank and grungy) tunnel under Baluardo San Colombano. Regional train services:

Florence (€7.50 to €9.60, 1¼ to 1¾ hours, hourly)

Pisa (€3.50, 30 minutes, half-hourly)

Montalcino

This medieval hill town is known throughout the world for its coveted wine, Brunello, and a remarkable number of *enoteche* line its medieval streets.

⊚ SIGHTS

Abbazia di Sant'Antimo   Abbey
(0577 28 63 00; www.antimo.it; Castelnuovo dell'Abate; ☺10am-1pm & 3-7pm summer, till

Montalcino

GABRIELE MALTINTI/SHUTTERSTOCK ©

5pm winter) FREE The serenely beautiful Romanesque Abbazia di Sant'Antimo lies in an isolated valley just below the village of Castelnuovo dell'Abate, 11km from Montalcino. Its Romanesque exterior features stone carvings of various fantastical animals. Inside, there is a particularly intense polychrome 13th-century *Madonna and Child* and a 12th-century Crucifixion above the main altar.

Fortezza   Historic Building

(Piazzale Fortezza; courtyard free, ramparts adult/reduced €4/2; ◷9am-8pm Apr-Oct, 10am-6pm Nov-Mar) This imposing 14th-century structure was expanded under the Medici dukes and now dominates Montalcino's skyline. You can sample and purchase local wines in its **enoteca** (◷0577 84 92 11; www.enotecalafortezza.com; ◷9am-8pm, reduced hours in winter) and also climb up to the fort's ramparts. Buy a ticket for the ramparts at the bar

EATING

Trattoria L'Angolo   Tuscan €

(◷0577 84 80 17; Via Ricasoli 9; meals €20; ◷noon-3pm Wed-Mon Sep-Jun, noon-3pm & 7-11pm Wed-Mon Jul & Aug) We thought about keeping shtum about this place (everyone loves to keep a secret or two), but it seemed selfish not to share our love for its pasta dishes with our loyal readers. Be it vegetarian (ravioli stuffed with ricotta and truffles) or carnivorous (*pappardelle* with wild-boar sauce), the handmade *primi* (first courses) here are uniformly excellent. *Secondi* (main courses) aren't as impressive.

Il Leccio   Tuscan €€

(◷0577 84 41 75; www.illeccio.net; Via Costa Castellare 1/3, Sant'Angelo in Colle; meals €30, 4-course set menu €36; ◷noon-2.30pm & 7-9pm Thu-Tue; ◷) Sometimes simple dishes are the hardest to perfect. And perfection is the only term to use when discussing this trattoria in Brunello heartland. Watching the chef make his way between his stove

and kitchen garden to gather produce for each order puts a whole new spin on the word 'fresh', and both the results and the house Brunello are spectacular.

DRINKING & NIGHTLIFE

Enoteca Osteria Osticcio   Wine Bar

(◷0577 84 82 71; www.osticcio.it; Via Giacomo Matteotti 23; antipasto & cheese plates €7-17, meals €40; ◷noon-4pm & 7-11pm Fri-Wed, plus noon-7pm Thu summer) In a town overflowing with *enoteche,* this is definitely one of the best. Choose a bottle from the huge selection of Brunello and its more modest sibling Rosso di Montalcino to accompany a meal, or opt for a tasting of three Brunelli (€16) or a Brunello and Rosso (€9). The panoramic view, meanwhile, almost upstages it all.

ⓘ INFORMATION

Montalcino's **tourist office** (◷0577 84 93 31; www.prolocomontalcino.com; Costa del Municipio 1; ◷10am-1pm & 2-5.50pm, closed Mon winter) is just off the main square. It can supply free copies of the *Consorzio del Vino Brunello di Montalcino* map of wineries and also books cellar-door visits and winery accommodation.

ⓘ GETTING THERE & AWAY

Tiemme (p139) buses run between Montalcino and Siena (€4.50, 75 minutes, six daily Monday to Saturday). The bus stop is near the **Hotel Vecchia Oliviera**.

Montepulciano

Exploring the medieval town of Montepulciano, perched on a reclaimed narrow ridge of volcanic rock, will push your quadriceps to failure point. When this happens, self-medicate with a generous pour of the highly reputed Vino Nobile while also drinking in the spectacular views over the Val di Chiana and Val d'Orcia.

Assisi

As if cupped in celestial hands, with the plains spreading picturesquely below and Monte Subasio rearing steep and wooded above, the mere sight of Assisi in the rosy glow of dusk is enough to send pilgrims' souls spiralling to heaven. It is at this hour, when the pitter-patter of day-tripper footsteps have faded and the town is shrouded in saintly silence, that the true spirit of St Francis of Assisi, born here in 1181, can be felt most keenly.

Visible for miles around, the **Basilica di San Francesco** (www.sanfrancesco assisi.org; Piazza di San Francesco; ☺upper church 8.30am-6.50pm, lower church & tomb 6am-6.50pm) FREE is the crowning glory of Assisi's Unesco World Heritage ensemble. It's divided into an upper church, the Basilica Superiore, with a celebrated cycle of Giotto frescoes, and beneath, the lower, older Basilica Inferiore, where you'll find frescoes by Cimabue, Pietro Lorenzetti and Simone Martini. Also here, in the Cripta di San Francesco, is St Francis' elaborate and monumental tomb.

The Basilica Superiore, which was built immediately after the lower church between 1230 and 1253, is home to one of Italy's most famous works of art – a series of 28 frescoes depicting the life of St Francis. Vibrant and colourful, they are generally attributed to a young Giotto. From outside the upper church, stairs lead down to the Romanesque Basilica Inferiore, whose half-light and architectural restraint beautifully embody the ascetic, introspective spirit of Franciscan life.

⊙ SIGHTS

Museo Civico & Pinacoteca Crociani
Art Gallery, Museum

(☏0578 71 73 00; www.museocivicomonte pulciano.it; Via Ricci 10; adult/reduced €5/3; ☺10.30am-6.30pm Wed-Mon summer, reduced hours winter) It was a curatorial dream come true: in 2011 a painting in the collection of this modest art gallery was attributed to Caravaggio. The work, *Portrait of a Man,* is thought to portray Cardinal Scipione Borghese, the artist's patron. It's now accompanied by a touch-screen interpretation that allows you to explore details of the painting, its restoration and diagnostic attribution. Other works here include two terracottas by Andrea Della Robbia, and Domenico Beccafumi's painting of the town's patron saint, Agnese.

Palazzo Comunale
Palace

(Piazza Grande; terrace & tower adult/reduced €5/2.50, terrace only €2.50; ☺10am-6pm) Built in the 14th-century in Gothic style and remodelled in the 15th century by Michelozzo, the Palazzo Comunale still functions as Montepulciano's town hall. Head up the 67 narrow stairs to the tower to enjoy extraordinary views – you'll see as far as Pienza, Montalcino and even, on a clear day, Siena.

⊗ EATING & DRINKING

La Dogana
Modern Italian €€

(☏339 5405196; Strada Lauretana Sud 75, Valiano; meals €32, cheese & salumi platter €9; ☺10am-10.30pm Wed-Sun, closed Jan) Chef and cookbook writer Sunshine Manitto presides over the kitchen of this super-chic *enoteca* overlooking the Palazzo Vecchio Winery. Windows frame vistas of vines and cypress trees, but the best seats in the house are on the grassed rear terrace. The menu showcases seasonal produce (much of it grown in the kitchen garden) and offers both snacks and full meals.

La Grotta
Ristorante €€€

(☏0578 75 74 79; www.lagrottamontepulciano. it; Via di San Biagio 15; meals €40; ☺12.30-2pm & 7.30-10pm Thu-Tue, closed mid-Jan–mid-Mar) The dishes here may be traditional, but their flavour and presentation is refined – artfully arranged Parmesan shavings and sprigs of herbs crown delicate towers of pasta, vegetables and meat. The service is exemplary and the courtyard garden divine.

SHCHIPKOVA ELENA /SHUTTERSTOCK ©

Cathedral in Piazza Grande

It's just below town, overlooking the Renaissance splendor of the **Chiesa di San Biago** (0578 75 72 90; www.parrocchiemontepulciano.org; Via di San Biago; incl audio guide €3.50; ⊗ /am-8pm).

Caffè Poliziano   Cafe
(0578 75 86 15; www.caffepoliziano.it; Via di Voltaia 27; ⊗7am-8pm Mon-Fri, to 11pm Sat, to 9pm Sun; ♠) Established as a cafe in 1868, Poliziano was lovingly restored to its original form 20 years ago and is the town's favourite cafe. A sit-down coffee is expensive, but is worth the outlay – especially if you score one of the tiny, precipitous balcony tables.

E Lucevan Le Stelle   Wine Bar
(0578 75 87 25; www.lucevanlestelle.it; Piazza San Francesco 5; ⊗11.30am-11.30pm mid-Mar–Dec; ♠) The decked terrace of this ultra-friendly *osteria* is the top spot in Montepulciano to watch the sun go down. Inside, squishy sofas, modern art and jazz on the sound system give the place a chilled-out vibe. Its food (antipasto plates €4.50 to €8, *piadine* (flat-bread sandwiches) €6, pasta €6.50 to €9) isn't a strength – stick to a glass or two of Nobile (€5 to €7).

ℹ INFORMATION

Strada del Vino Nobile di Montepulciano Information Office (0578 75 78 12; www.stradavinonobile.it; Piazza Grande 7; ⊗9.30am-1.30pm & 2.30-6pm Mon-Fri, 10am-1pm & 2-5pm Sat, 10am-1pm Sun) Books accommodation in Montepulciano and arranges a wide range of courses and tours.

Tourist Office (0578 75 73 41; www.prolocomontepulciano.it; Piazza Don Minzoni 1; ⊗9am-1pm) Reserves last-minute accommodation (in person only), supplies town maps and sells bus tickets.

ℹ GETTING THERE & AWAY

The Montepulciano **bus station** (Piazzo Pietro Nenni) is next to Car Park No 5. Tiemme (p139) runs four buses daily to/from Siena's train station (€6.60, 1½ hours) stopping at Pienza (€2.50, 20 minutes) en route.

Stepped path in Arezzo

Arezzo

Arezzo may not be a Tuscan centrefold, but those parts of its historic centre that survived merciless WWII bombings are as compelling as any destination in the region – the city's central square is as beautiful as it appears in Roberto Benigni's classic film *La vita è bella* (Life is Beautiful).

◉ SIGHTS

Cappella Bacci   Church

(☑0575 35 27 27; www.pierodellafrancesca. it; Piazza San Francesco; adult/reduced €8/5; ⊙9am-6pm Mon-Fri, to 5.30pm Sat, 1-5.30pm Sun) This chapel, in the apse of 14th-century **Basilica di San Francesco**, safeguards one of Italian art's greatest works: Piero della Francesca's fresco cycle of the *Legend of the True Cross*. Painted between 1452 and 1466, it relates the story of the cross on which Christ was crucified. Only 25 people are allowed in every half hour, making advance booking (by telephone or email)

essential in high season. The ticket office is down the stairs by the basilica's entrance.

Museo Archeologico Nazionale 'Gaio Cilnio Mecenate'   Museum

(Gaius Cilnius Maecenas Archaeological Museum; ☑0575 2 08 82; www.facebook.com/archeolog icoarezzo; Via Margaritone 10; adult/reduced €6/3, 1st Sun each month free; ⊙8.30am-7.30pm, to 1.30pm Nov) Overlooking the remains of a Roman amphitheatre that once seated up to 10,000 spectators, this museum – named after Gaius Maecenas (68–8 BC), a patron of the arts and trusted adviser to Roman Emperor Augustus – exhibits Etruscan and Roman artefacts in a 14th-century convent building. The highlight is the *Cratere di Euphronios,* a 6th-century-BC Etruscan vase decorated with vivid scenes showing Hercules in battle.

Chiesa di Santa Maria della Pieve   Church

(Corso Italia 7; ⊙8am-12.30pm & 3-6.30pm) **FREE** This 12th-century church – Arezzo's oldest – has an exotic Romanesque arcaded facade adorned with carved columns, each uniquely decorated. Above the central doorway are 13th-century carved reliefs called *Cyclo dei Mesi* representing each month of the year. The plain interior's highlight – removed for restoration work at the time of writing – is Pietro Lorenzetti's polyptych *Madonna and Saints* (1320–24), beneath the semidome of the apse. Below the altar is a 14th-century silver bust reliquary of the city's patron saint, San Donato.

EATING

Cremì
Gelato €

(☑333 976 63 36; www.facebook.com/gelateria artigianalecremi; Corso Italia 100; cones & tubs €1.80-5; ☺10am-7.30pm Tue-Sun) Follow the locals to this bright, modern *gelateria artigianale* (artisan ice-cream shop) on Arezzo's main *passeggiata* (late afternoon-strolling) strip. Enticing seasonal flavours include pear and vanilla, strawberry cheesecake, peanut, and walnut and fig. Or opt for the luscious and wildly popular house speciality – *mousse di nutella* (a creamy, light-as-air chocolate- and hazelnut-flavoured mousse-cum-ice cream).

Mest Osteria
Tuscan €€

(☑0575 08 08 61; www.osteriamest.it; Via Giorgio Vasari 11; meals €35; ☺7-11.45pm Wed, noon-3pm & 7-11.45pm Thu-Sun) For a thoroughly contemporary Tuscan dining experience, snag a table at this edgy *osteria* with fantastic gnarled old wooden shutters

and dazzling stainless-steel kitchen. The lunch menu features light, smart bites such as 0km club sandwiches, lavishly topped *bruschette,* salmon burgers and creative pasta dishes. Dinner is all about ork with caramelised leeks and mustard-spiced potatoes, and other creative mains.

Le Chiavi d'Oro
Italian €€

(☑0575 40 33 13; www.ristorantelechiavidoro.it; Piazza San Francesco 7; meals €45; ☺12.30-2.30pm & 7.30-10.30pm Tue-Sun) Contemporary Italian cooking is on offer at this game-changing restaurant in central Arezzo. Design lovers are wooed by the minimalist interior with part-resin, part-parquet floor and stylish 1960s Danish chairs, while foodies are quickly won over by the simplistic menu that reads something like a shopping list of ingredients. Bream with artichokes, saffron, breadcrumbs and lime anyone?

ℹ INFORMATION

Tourist Office (☑0575 40 19 45; Piazza della Libertà; ☺2-4pm) You will find another branch of the **tourist office** (☑0575 2 68 50; Piazza della Repubblica 22-23; ☺10.30am-12.30pm) to the right as you exit the train station.

ℹ GETTING THERE & AWAY

Buses operated by **Siena Mobilità** (www.siena mobilita.it) serve Siena (€7, 1½ hours, seven daily). Arezzo is on the Florence–Rome train line, and there are frequent services to both cities.

CINQUE TERRE

Cinque Terre at a Glance...

Set amid some of the most dramatic coastal scenery on the planet, these five ingeniously constructed fishing villages, dating from the early medieval period, can bolster the most jaded of spirits. A Unesco World Heritage site since 1997, Cinque Terre isn't the undiscovered Eden it was 30 years ago, but frankly, who cares? Sinuous paths traverse seemingly impregnable cliffsides, while a 19th-century railway line connects the villages. Thankfully cars were banned over a decade ago.

Cinque Terre in Two Days

Begin your visit to the Cinque Terre by exploring **Monterosso** (p156) before walking the **Sentiero Azzurro** (p155) to **Corniglia** (p157). On day two visit **Riomaggiore** (p158), where you can toast to the sea with a glass of Cinque Terre DOC at **La Conchiglia** (p159), and **Manarola** (p157).

Cinque Terre in Four Days

Spend days three and four hiking the sublimely vertiginous **Sentiero Rosso** (p155) with your head in the clouds.

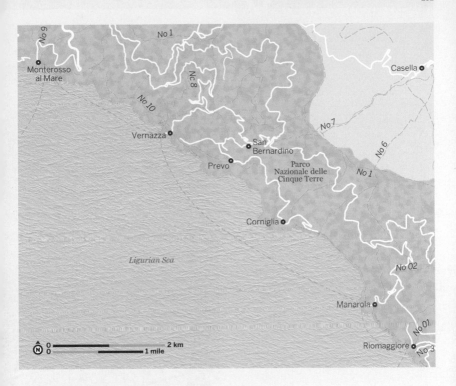

Arriving in Cinque Terre

Between 6.30am and 10pm, one to three trains an hour trundle along the coast between Genoa and La Spezia, stopping at each of the Cinque Terre's villages. Unlimited 2nd-class rail travel between Levanto and La Spezia is covered by the Cinque Terre Train card (one-/two-day €16/29), or you can buy a €4 ticket for travel between any two villages.

Where to Stay

Overnighting here is truly special, but note that hotels can book out for the entire April to October season and are almost all closed outside of that period. They tend to be unremarkable so it's best to book well ahead and be willing to pay if you want something special. Alternatives are apartment rental or making a base in La Spezia.

The Lardarina stairway (p157), Corniglia

Walking in Cinque Terre

With its spectacular scenery, terraced slopes and network of ancient trails, the Cinque Terre offers superlative walking. Routes cater to all levels, ranging from simple 20-minute strolls to daunting hillside hikes.

Great For...

❶ Need to Know

Throughout the day trains ply up and down the coast, linking the Cinque Terre's villages.

★ **Top Tip**

Check www.parconazionale5terre.it for trail details, news and online maps.

Sanctuary Walks

Each of the Cinque Terre's villages is associated with a sanctuary perched high on the cliffsides above the azure Mediterranean. Reaching these religious retreats used to be part of a hefty Catholic penance, but these days the walks through terraced vineyards and across view-splayed cliffs are a heavenly reward in themselves.

Monterosso to Santuario della Madonna di Soviore From Via Roma, follow trail 9 up through forest and past the ruins of an old hexagonal chapel to an ancient paved mule path that leads to Soviore, Liguria's oldest sanctuary, dating from the 11th century. Here you'll find a bar, a restaurant and views as far as Corsica on a clear day.

Vernazza to Santuario della Madonna di Reggio From underneath Vernazza's railway bridge, follow trail 8 up numerous flights of steps and past 14 sculpted Stations of the Cross to this 11th-century chapel with a Romanesque facade.

Corniglia to Santuario della Madonna delle Grazie This sanctuary can be approached from either Corniglia (on trail 7b) or Vernazza (trail 7), though the latter is better. Branch off the Sentiero Azzurro and ascend the spectacular Sella Comeneco to the village of San Bernardino, where you'll find the church with its adored image of Madonna and child above the altar.

Manarola to Santuario della Madonna delle Salute The pick of all the sanctuary walks is this breathtaking traverse (trail 6) through Cinque Terre's finest vineyards to a diminutive Romanesque-meets-Gothic chapel in the tiny village of Volastra.

Vernazza (p157)

Riomaggiore to Santuario della Madonna di Montenero Trail 3 ascends from the top of the village, up steps and past walled gardens to a restored 18th-century chapel with a frescoed ceiling, which sits atop an astounding lookout next to the park's new cycling centre.

Sentiero Azzuro

The **Sentiero Azzurro** (Blue Trail; marked No 2 on maps; admission with Cinque Terre card), a 12km old mule path that once linked all five oceanside villages by foot, is the Cinque Terre's blue-riband hike, narrow and precipitous. The trail dates back to the early

> ☑ **Don't Miss**
>
> The breathtaking views from the Belvedere di Santa Maria (p157) in Corniglia.

ANIBAL TREJO/SHUTTERSTOCK ©

days of the Republic of Genoa in the 12th and 13th centuries and, until the opening of the railway line in 1874, it was the only practical means of getting from village to village.

At the time of writing, the path between Riomagiorre (the famed via dell'Amore) and Manarola and the path between Manarola and Corniglia were closed and will possibly remain so until at least 2019. Only very experienced and well-equipped hikers should attempt the current alternative route from Manarola to Corniglia via Volastra.

Sentiero Rosso

Just a few kilometres shy of a full-blown marathon, the 38km **Sentiero Rosso** (Red trail; marked No 1 on maps) – which runs from Porto Venere to Levanto – dangles a tempting challenge to experienced walkers who aim to complete it in nine to 12 hours.

For every 100 people you see on the Sentiero Azzurro, there are less than a dozen up here plying their way along a route that is mainly flat, tree-covered and punctuated with plenty of shortcuts. An early start is assured by an efficient train and bus connection to Porto Venere (via La Spezia), while refreshments en route are possible in a liberal smattering of welcoming bars and restaurants.

> ✗ **Take a Break**
>
> Sit down to seafood at the Trattoria da Oscar (p156) in Monterosso's old town.

Monterosso

The most accessible village by car and the only Cinque Terre settlement to sport a proper stretch of beach, the westernmost Monterosso is the least quintessential of the quintet. The village, known for its lemon trees and anchovies, is delightful. Split in two, its new and old halves are linked by an underground tunnel burrowed beneath the blustery San Cristoforo promontory.

◉ SIGHTS

Convento dei Cappuccini Church
(Salita San Cristoforo) Monterosso's most interesting church and convent complex is set on the hill that divides the old town from the newer Fegina quarter. Its striped church, the **Chiesa di San Francesco**, dates from 1623 and has a painting attributed to Van Dyck (*Crocifissione*) to the left of the altar. The convent welcomes casual visitors but also has a program of spiritual retreats and workshops.

✖ EATING

Trattoria da Oscar Trattoria €€
(Via Vittorio Emanuele 67; meals €25-30; ⊘noon-2pm & 7-10pm) Behind Piazza Matteoti, in the heart of the old town, this vaulted dining room is run by a young, friendly team and attracts a strong local crowd. The town's famed anchovies dominate the menu; whether you go for the standard fried with lemon, with a white wine sauce or deep-fried, they are all good. There are some lovely laneway tables too. No credit cards.

Miky Seafood €€€
(☏0187 81 76 08; www.ristorantemiky.it; Lungomare Fegina 104; meals €45-65; ⊘noon-2.30pm & 7-10pm Wed-Mon summer) If you're looking for something a little more elegant than a seafront fry-up, Miky does a seasonal fish menu in a moody, modern dining room. Booking ahead is advised. If you miss out on a table, casual beach-side tables are available at its *cantina* (wine bar); ask for directions.

Beach at Monterosso

YRABOTA/SHUTTERSTOCK ©

Vernazza

Vernazza's small harbour – the only secure landing point on the Cinque Terre coast – guards what is perhaps the quaintest, and steepest, of the five villages. Lined with little cafes, a main cobbled street (Via Roma), links seaside Piazza Marconi with the train station. Side streets lead to the village's trademark Genoa-style *caruggi* (narrow lanes), where sea views pop up at every turn.

SIGHTS

Castello Doria Castle

(€1.50; ☉10am-7pm summer, to 6pm winter) This castle, the oldest surviving fortification in the Cinque Terre, commands superb views. Dating to around 1000, it's now largely a ruin except for the circular tower in the centre of the esplanade. To get there, head up the steep, narrow staircase by the harbour.

ACTIVITIES

Vernazza Winexperience Wine

(Deck Giani Franzi; ☏331 3433801; www.vernazza winexperience.com; Via San Giovanni Battista 41; ☉5-9pm Apr-Oct) Sommelier Alessandro Villa's family have lived in Vernazza for over six generations. Let him take you through the rare, small-yield wines that come from the vineyards that tumble down the surrounding hills. While the wine and stupendous sunset view will be pleasure enough, knowing you're also helping keep a unique landscape and culture alive feels good too.

EATING

Gambero Rosso Seafood €€

(☏0187 81 22 65; www.ristorantegamberorosso. net; Piazza Marconi 7; meals €35-45; ☉noon-3pm & 7-10pm Fri-Wed) If you've been subsisting on focaccia, Gambero's house specials – *tegame di Vernazza* (anchovies with baked potatoes and tomatoes), skewered baby octopus or stuffed mussels – will really hit the spot. Bookings recommended.

 Wine on Cinque Terre

Grapes grow abundantly on the Cinque Terre's terraced plots, especially around Manarola. The area's signature wine is Sciacchetrà, a blend of Bosco, Albarola and Vermentino grapes best sampled with cheese or sweet desserts.

Vineyard near Manarola
DPVUESTUDIO/SHUTTERSTOCK ©

Corniglia

Corniglia is the 'quiet' middle village that sits atop a 100m-high rocky promontory surrounded by vineyards. Narrow alleys and colourfully painted four-storey houses characterise the ancient core, a timeless streetscape that was namechecked in Boccaccio's *Decameron*. By virtue of its elevation and central position, it is the only place you can see all five settlements in the same panorama. The dazzling 180-degree sea view is best enjoyed from the **Belvedere di Santa Maria**. To find it, follow Via Fieschi through the village until you eventually reach the clifftop balcony.

It is the only Cinque Terre settlement with no direct sea access, although steep steps lead down to a rocky cove. To reach the village proper from the railway station you must first tackle the **Lardarina**, a 377-step brick stairway, or jump on a shuttle bus (one-way €2.50, free with the Cinque Terre card).

Manarola

Bequeathed with more grapevines than any other Cinque Terre village, Manarola is famous for its sweet Sciacchetrà wine. It's also awash with priceless medieval relics, supporting claims that it is the oldest of the five villages. The spirited locals here speak an esoteric local dialect known as Man-arolese. Due to its proximity to Riomaggiore (852m away), the village is heavily traf-ficked, especially by Italian school parties along with the regular tourists.

◎ SIGHTS

Punta Bonfiglio Viewpoint
Manarola's prized viewpoint is on a rocky promontory on the path out of town towards Corniglia where walkers stop for classic photos of the village. A rest area, including a kids playground, has been constructed here and there's also a bar just below. Nearby are the ruins of an old chapel once used as a shelter by local farmers.

Piazzale Papa Innocenzo IV Piazza
At the northern end of Via Discovolo, you'll come upon this small piazza dominated by a bell tower that was once used as a defen-sive lookout. Opposite, the **Chiesa di San Lorenzo** dates from 1338 and houses a 15th-century polyptych. If you're geared up for a steep walk, from nearby Via Rollandi you can follow a path that leads through vineyards to the top of the mountain.

⊗ EATING

Il Porticciolo Seafood €€
(✆0187 92 00 83; www.ilporticciolo5terre.it; Via Renato Birolli 92; meals €28-37; ⊙11.30am-11pm)
One of several restaurants lining the main route down to the harbour, this is a popular spot for an alfresco seafood feast. Expect seaside bustle and a fishy menu featuring classic crowd-pleasers such as spaghetti with mussels and crispy fried squid.

Riomaggiore

Cinque Terre's easternmost village, Rio-maggiore is the largest of the five and acts as its unofficial HQ (the main park office is based here). Its peeling pastel build-

ings march down a steep ravine to a tiny harbour – the region's favourite postcard view – and glow romantically at sunset. If you are driving, the hills between here and La Spezia are spectacular to explore.

◎ SIGHTS

Fossola Beach Beach
This small pebbly beach is immediately southeast of Riomaggiore marina. It's rug-ged and delightfully secluded. Swimmers should be wary of currents here.

Torre Guardiola Viewpoint
(€1.50; ⊙9am-1pm & 4-7pm Feb-Jul, Sep & Oct, 9am-1pm Aug) Birdlife and local flora can be seen from this lookout on a promon-tory of land just east of Riomaggiore. The building was a former naval installation in WWII known as La Batteria Racchia, and was most recently a nature reserve centre, although its fate is currently undecided. It's reachable via a trail that starts just west of Fossola Beach.

✪ ACTIVITIES

Cooperative Sub 5 Terre Diving
(✆0187 92 00 11; www.5terrediving.it; Via San Giacomo; ⊙10am-4pm Apr-Oct) To dive or snorkel in the translucent waters of the protected marine park, contact this outfit in the subway at the bottom of Via Colombo. It also rents out canoes and kayaks, but book ahead by phone as the office is not always attended.

⊗ EATING

Colle del Telegrafo Ligurian €€
(✆0187 76 05 61; Località Colle del Telegrafo; meals €35-45; ⊙8am-8.30pm) Perched on a ridge south of Riomaggiore, where the old telegraph line used to be strung, the views from the Colle del Telegrafo are spectacu-lar. But they don't overshadow the carefully prepared dishes of pasta with Cinque Terre cooperative pesto, white bean soup and super-fresh whitebait. During the day, join

Dau Cila

hikers for bolstering rounds of cake and espresso.

Dau Cila
Seafood €€

(☏0187 76 00 32; www.ristorantedaucila.com; Via San Giacomo 65; meals €40-45; ☺12.30-3pm & 7-10.30pm) Perched within pebble-lobbing distance of Riomaggiore's wee harbour, Dau Cila is a smart, kitsch-free zone, and specialises in classic seafood and hyper-local wines. Pair the best Cinque Terre whites with cold plates such as smoked tuna with apples and lemon, or lemon-marinated anchovies.

🍷 DRINKING & NIGHTLIFE

La Conchiglia
Bar

(☏0187 92 09 47; Via San Giacomo 149; ☺8am-midnight) A fantastic find: down-to-earth, friendly and unflustered staff; a fantastic well-priced local wine list; absolute waterfront positions; and a menu of big, healthy salads, *panini* and burgers if you've missed lunch or dinner service elsewhere. The shaded waterfront terrace upstairs is a delight.

ⓘ GETTING THERE & AROUND

BOAT

In summer the **Golfo Paradiso SNC** (☏0185 77 20 91; www.golfoparadiso.it) runs boats to the Cinque Terre from Genoa (one-way/return €21/36). Seasonal boat services to/from Santa Margherita (€22.50/34) are handled by the Servizio Marittimo del Tigullio (www.traghetti portofino.it).

CAR & MOTORCYCLE

Private vehicles are not allowed beyond village entrances and during high-volume days roads between villages can be closed. If you're arriving by car or motorcycle, you'll need to pay to park in designated car parks (€12 to €25 per day), though these are often full. In some villages, minibus shuttles depart from the car parks (one-way/return €1.50/2.50) – park offices have seasonal schedules.

TRAIN

Trains link the villages with Genoa and La Spezia.

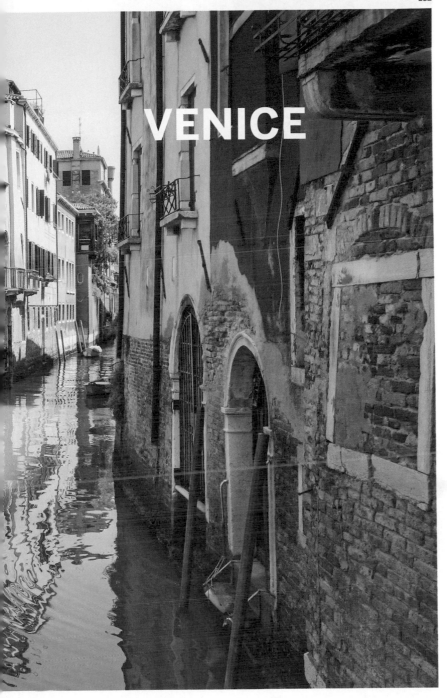

VENICE

Venice at a Glance...

Imagine the audacity of deciding to build a city of marble palaces on a lagoon. Instead of surrendering to acque alte (high tides) like reasonable folk might do, Venetians flooded the world with vivid painting, baroque music, modern opera, spice-route cuisine, bohemian-chic fashions and a Grand Canal's worth of spritz: the signature prosecco and Aperol cocktail. Today, cutting-edge architects and billionaire benefactors are spicing up the art scene, musicians are rocking out 18th-century instruments and backstreet osterie (taverns) are winning a Slow Food following. Your timing couldn't be better: the people who made walking on water look easy are well into their next act.

Venice in Two Days

Rise early to get to **Basilica di San Marco** (p167) and **Palazzo Ducale** (p169). Then choose between the **Gallerie dell'Accademia** (p171) or the **Peggy Guggenheim Collection** (p174). On day two, visit **Ca' Rezzonico** (p175) and **Scuola Grande di San Rocco** (p175) before crossing the **Ponte di Rialto** (p164) to happy hour at one of the city's many bars.

Venice in Four Days

Begin with the **Museo Ebraico** (p178) synagogue tour, followed by Grand Canal views at **Ca' d'Oro** (p179) and the Tintorettos at the **Chiesa della Madonna dell'Orto** (p179). After lunch, cross canals to Castello's many-splendoured **Zanipolo** (p179) and the **Giardini Pubblici** (p179). On the fourth day island-hop to Murano, Burano and Torcello.

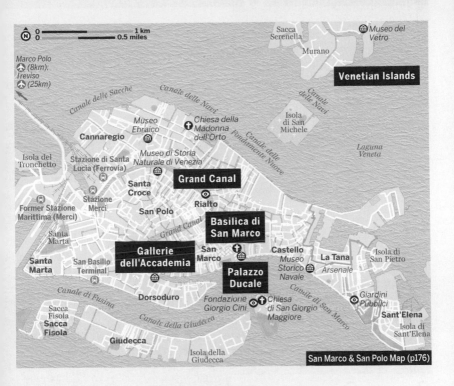

Arriving in Venice

Marco Polo airport Located on the mainland 12km from Venice. Alilaguna operates a ferry service (€15) to Venice from the airport ferry dock. Water taxis cost from €110. Half-hourly buses (€6) connect with Piazzale Roma.

Stazione Santa Lucia Venice's train station. *Vaporetti* (small passenger boats) depart from Ferrovia (Station) docks.

Stazione Venezia Mestre The mainland train station; transfer here to Stazione Santa Lucia.

Where to Stay

Venice offers plenty of luxe hotels along the Grand Canal and Riva degli Schiavoni, and there's also a growing inventory of boutique sleeps. At the same time, the internet has made it much easier for locals to rent out their homes (or extra rooms) and short-term rentals are increasingly popular.

For budget travellers, Venice offers a range of hostels (called *foresterie*). Some bunks even have canal or garden views. During summer, university housing also opens to tourists.

For more information on where to stay see p191.

Grand Canal

Never was a thoroughfare so aptly named as the Grand Canal. Snaking through the heart of the city, Venice's signature waterway is flanked by a magnificent array of Gothic, Moorish, Renaissance and rococo palaces.

For most people, a trip down the Grand Canal starts near the train station, near the Ponte di Calatrava. Officially known as the Ponte della Costituzione (Constitution Bridge), this contemporary bridge, designed by avant-garde Spanish architect Santiago Calatrava in 2008, is one of the few modern structures you'll see in central Venice.

To the Rialto

Leaving the bridge in your wake, one of the first landmarks you'll pass, on your left, is the arcaded Gothic facade of the Ca' d'Oro (p179), a 15th-century *palazzo* (mansion) that now houses an art museum.

Ponte di Rialto & Around

A short way on, the **Ponte di Rialto** (Rialto-Mercato) is the oldest of the four bridges that cross the canal. Nearby, local

---

Great For...

☑ Don't Miss

The Ponte di Rialto, Palazzo Grassi and iconic Basilica di Santa Maria della Salute.

ℹ Need to Know

Take *vaporetti* 1 or 2 from the Ferrovia; it takes 35 to 40 minutes to Piazza San Marco.

✗ Take a Break

Jump off at Rialto and search out **Cantina Do Spade** (☑041 521 05 83; www.cantinadospade.com; Calle delle Do Spade 860, San Polo; ⊙10am-3pm & 6-10pm; 🛜; 🚢Rialto-Mercato) for a cosy drink.

★ Top Tip

Avoid the crowds and tour the canal in the early evening or at night.

shoppers crowd to the **Rialto Market** (☑041 296 06 58; San Polo; ⊙7am-2pm; 🚢Rialto-Mercato) and **Pescaria fish market** (San Polo; ⊙7am-2pm Tue-Sun; 🚢Rialto-Mercato).

Palazzo Grassi

The clean, geometric form of **Palazzo Grassi** (☑041 200 10 57; www.palazzograssi.it; Campo San Samuele 3231; adult/reduced incl Punta della Dogana €18/15; ⊙10am-7pm Wed-Mon mid-Apr–Nov; 🚢San Samuele) comes into view on the first bend after the Rialto. A noble 18th-century palace, it now provides the neoclassical setting for show-stopping contemporary art.

Ponte dell'Accademia & Around

A couple of ferry stops further down and you arrive at the wooden Ponte dell'Accademia, a bridge whose simple design

seems strangely out of place amid Venice's fairy-tale architecture. For an art gallery interlude head to nearby Galleric dell'Accademia (p171) or the Peggy Guggenheim (p174).

Basilica di Santa Maria della Salute

The imperious dome of the Basilica di Santa Maria della Salute (p175) has been overlooking the canal's entrance since the 17th century. Beyond the basilica, the **Punta della Dogana** (☑041 271 90 39; www.palazzograssi.it; Fondamente della Dogana alla Salute 2, Dorsoduro; adult/reduced €15/10, incl Palazzo Grassi €18/15; ⊙10am-7pm Wed-Mon Apr-Nov; 🚢Salute) is a former customs warehouse that now stages contemporary art exhibitions.

St Mark's & Palazzo Ducale

You're now at the mouth of the canal, where you can disembark for Piazza San Marco. Dominating the waterside here is Palazzo Ducale (p169), the historic residence of the Venetian Doges.

Basilica di San Marco

With its profusion of spires and domes, lavish marble-work and 8500 sq metres of luminous mosaics, the Basilica di San Marco, Venice's signature basilica, is an unforgettable sight.

The basilica was founded in the 9th century to house the corpse of St Mark after wily Venetian merchants smuggled it out of Egypt in a barrel of pork fat. When the original burnt down in 932 Venice rebuilt the basilica in its own cosmopolitan image, with Byzantine domes, a Greek cross layout and walls clad in marbles from Syria, Egypt and Palestine.

Exterior & Portals

The front of St Mark's ripples and crests like a wave, its five niched portals capped with shimmering mosaics and frothy stone-work arches. The oldest mosaic on the facade (1270) is in the lunette above the far-left portal, depicting St Mark's stolen body arriving at the basilica. The theme is echoed in three of the other lunettes, including one showing turbaned officials recoiling from the hamper of pork fat containing the sainted corpse.

Great For...

☑ Don't Miss

Loggia dei Cavalli, where reproductions of the four bronze horses gallop off the balcony over Piazza San Marco.

KAMIRA/SHUTTERSTOCK ©

❶ Need to Know

St Mark's Basilica; ☎041 270 83 11; www.
basilicasanmarco.it; Piazza San Marco;
⊙9.45am-5pm Mon-Sat, 2-5pm Sun summer,
to 4pm Sun winter; 🚢San Marco FREE

✕ Take a Break

Treat yourself to a bellini (cocktail of
prosecco and peach purée) at world-
famous **Harry's Bar** (☎041 528 57 77;
www.harrysbarvenezia.com; Calle Vallaresso
1323; ⊙10.30am-11pm; 🚢San Marco).

★ Top Tip

There's no charge to enter the church
and wander around the roped-off
central circuit, although you'll need
to dress modestly, with knees and
shoulders covered, and leave large
bags around the corner at the Ateneo
San Basso Left Luggage Office.

Mosaics

Blinking is natural upon your first glimpse
of the basilica's glittering ceiling mosaics,
many made with 24-carat gold leaf. Just
inside the vestibule are the basilica's oldest
mosaics: Apostles with the Madonna,
standing sentry by the main door for more
than 950 years. Inside the church proper,
three golden domes vie for your attention.
The Pentecost Cupola shows the Holy Spirit, represented by a dove, shooting tongues
of flame onto the heads of the surrounding
saints. In the central 13th-century Ascen-
sion Cupola, angels swirl around the central
figure of Christ hovering among the stars.

Pala d'Oro

Tucked behind the main altar (€2), this
stupendous golden screen is studded with
2000 emeralds, amethysts, sapphires,
rubies, pearls and other gemstones. But
the most priceless treasures here are
biblical figures in vibrant cloisonné, begun
in Constantinople in AD 976 and elaborated
by Venetian goldsmiths in 1209.

Tesoro & Museum

Holy bones and booty from the Crusades
fill the **Tesoro** (Treasury; €3); while ducal
treasures on show in the **museum** (adult/
reduced €5/2.50; ⊙9.45am-4.45pm) would
put a king's ransom to shame. A highlight is
the Quadriga of St Mark's, a group of four
bronze horses originally plundered from
Constantinople and later carted off to Paris
by Napoleon before being returned to the
basilica and installed in the 1st-floor gallery.

Palazzo Ducale

Gothic Palazzo Ducale was the doge's official residence and the seat of the Venetian Republic's government (and location of its prisons) for over seven centuries.

Although the ducal palace probably moved to this site in the 10th century, the current complex only started to take shape in around 1340. In 1424, the wing facing Piazzetta San Marco was added and the palace assumed its final form, give or take a few major fires and refurbishments.

First Floor

The doge's suite of private 1st-floor rooms is now used to house temporary art exhibitions, which are ticketed separately (around €10 extra). The doge lived like a caged lion in his gilded suite in the palace, which he could not leave without permission. The most intriguing room is the Sala dello Scudo (Shield Room), covered with world maps that reveal the extent of Venetian power (and the limits of its cartographers).

Great For...

☑ **Don't Miss**

The face of a grimacing man with his mouth agape at the top of the Scala d'Oro; this was a post box for secret accusations.

TINA BOUR/SHUTTERSTOCK ©

ℹ Need to Know

Ducal Palace; ☎041 271 59 11; www.palazzo
ducale.visitmuve.it; Piazzetta San Marco 1;
adult/reduced incl Museo Correr €19/12, with
Museum Pass free; ⊙8.30am-7pm Apr-Oct, to
5.30pm Nov-Mar; ⚓San Zaccaria

✕ Take a Break

Continue the rarefied vibe within the
jewellery-box interior of Caffè Florian
(p186).

★ Top Tip

Check www.palazzoducale.visitmuve.
it for details of Secret Itineraries tours
and special openings.

Second Floor

Ascend Sansovino's 24-carat gilt stucco-
work Scala d'Oro (Golden Staircase) and
emerge into 2nd-floor rooms covered with
gorgeous propaganda. In the Palladio-
designed Sala delle Quattro Porte (Hall
of the Four Doors), ambassadors awaited
ducal audiences under a lavish display of
Venice's virtues by Giovanni Cambi, Titian
and Tiepolo.

Few were granted an audience in the
Palladio-designed Collegio (Council Room),
where Veronese's 1575–78 *Virtues of the
Republic* ceiling shows Venice as a bewitch-
ing blonde waving her sceptre like a wand
over Justice and Peace. Father–son team
Jacopo and Domenico Tintoretto attempt
similar flattery, showing Venice keeping
company with Apollo, Mars and Mercury in

their *Triumph of Venice* ceiling for the Sala
del Senato (Senate Hall).

Government cover-ups were never so
appealing as in the Sala Consiglio dei Dieci
(Trial Chambers of the Council of Ten),
where Venice's star chamber plotted under
Veronese's *Juno Bestowing Her Gifts on
Venice*. Arcing over the Sala della Bussola
(Compass Room) is his *St Mark in Glory*
ceiling.

Sala del Maggior Consiglio

The cavernous 1419 Sala del Maggior
Consiglio (Grand Council Hall) provides the
setting for Tintoretto's swirling *Paradise*,
a work that's more politically correct than
pretty: heaven is crammed with 500 promi-
nent Venetians, including several Tintoretto
patrons. Veronese's political posturing is
more elegant in his oval *Apotheosis of Venice* ceiling, where gods marvel at Venice's
coronation by angels, with foreign dignitaries and Venetian blondes rubbernecking on
the balcony below.

Gallerie dell'Accademia

Housed in the former Santa Maria della Carità convent complex, the Gallerie dell'Accademia traces the development of Venetian art from the 14th to 18th centuries, with works by Bellini, Titian, Tintoretto, Veronese and Canaletto.

Great For...

☑ Don't Miss

Bernardo Strozzi's *Feast in the House of Simon*. In it, a rather mischievous cat seems intent on stealing the spotlight from Jesus.

Early Works

The grand gallery you enter upstairs features vivid early works that show Venice's precocious flair for colour and drama. Case in point: Jacobello Alberegno's *Apocalypse* (Room 1) shows the whore of Babylon riding a hydra, babbling rivers of blood from her mouth. At the opposite end of the emotional spectrum is Paolo Veneziano's *Coronation of Mary* (Room 1), where Jesus bestows the crown on his mother with a gentle pat on the head to the tune of an angelic orchestra.

Rooms 2–23

UFO arrivals seem imminent in the eerie, glowing skies of Carpaccio's lively *Crucifixion and Glorification of the Ten Thousand Martyrs of Mount Ararat* (Room 2), which offers an intense contrast to Giovanni

Sala dell'Albergo

MARCO BRIVIO/ALAMY ©

❶ Need to Know

📞041 520 03 45; www.gallerieaccademia.
org; Campo della Carità 1050, Dorsoduro;
adult/reduced €12/6, 1st Sun of month free;
🕐8.15am-2pm Mon, to 7.15pm Tue-Sun;
🚤Accademia

✗ Take a Break

Join the locals for delicious *cicheti*
(Venetian tapas) at Cantinone Già
Schiavi (p187).

★ Top Tip

To skip ahead of the queues in high
season, book tickets online (booking
fee €1.50).

Bellini's quietly elegant *Madonna and Child
between St Catherine and Mary Magdalene*
(Room 4). Further along, Room 10 features
paintings by Tintoretto and Titian, as well as
Paolo Veronese's monumental *Feast in the
House of Levi*, originally called *Last Supper*
until Inquisition leaders condemned him
for showing dogs and drunkards, among
others, cavorting with Apostles.

While Rooms 12 to 19 are occasionally
used for temporary exhibitions, it's in Room
12 that you'll find Giambattista Piazzetta's
saucy socialite in *Fortune Teller*. Yet even
her lure is no match for the glorious works
gracing Room 20. Among them is Gentile
Bellini's *Procession in St Mark's Square,*
which offers an intriguing view of Venice's
iconic piazza before its 16th-century makeover. Room 21 is no less captivating, home
to Vittore Carpaccio's *St Ursula Cycle,* a

series of nine paintings documenting the
saint's ill-fated life.

The original convent chapel (Room 23)
is a serene showstopper fronted by a Bellini
altarpiece. Sharing the space is Giorgione's
highly charged *La Tempesta* (The Storm).

Sala dell'Albergo

The Accademia's grand finale is the
newly restored Sala dell'Albergo, with a
lavishly carved ceiling, Antonio Vivarini's
wrap-around 1441–50 masterpiece of
fluffy-bearded saints, and Titian's touching
1534–39 *Presentation of the Virgin*. Here,
a young, tiny Madonna trudges up an
intimidating staircase while a distinctly
Venetian crowd of onlookers point to her
example – yet few of the velvet- and pearl-
clad merchants offer alms to the destitute
mother, or even feed the begging dog.

Venetian Islands

Where other cities have suburban sprawl, Venice has a teal-blue northern lagoon dotted with small islands: Murano, the historic home of Venetian glass-making; Burano, with its colourful streets; and Torcello, the republic's original island settlement.

Great For...

☑ Don't Miss

Museo del Vetro on Murano.

Murano

Venetians have been working in crystal and glass since the 10th century, but due to the fire hazards of glass-blowing, the industry was moved to the island of Murano in the 13th century. Woe betide the glass-blower with wanderlust: trade secrets were so jealously guarded that any glass worker who left the city was guilty of treason and subject to assassination. Today, glass artisans ply their trade at workshops along the **Fondamenta dei Vetrai** marked by *Fornace* (furnace) signs. Tour a factory for a behind-the-scenes look at production or visit the **Museo del Vetro** (Glass Museum; ☎041 527 47 18; www.museovetro.visitmuve. it; Fondamenta Giustinian 8; adult/reduced €10/7.50, free with Museum Pass; ⊙10am-5pm; 🚤Museo) in Palazzo Giustinian near the Museo *vaporetto* stop.

Murano glass

STANISLAV SAMOYLIK/SHUTTERSTOCK ©

✕ **Take a Break**

Feast on fresh seafood at **Acquastan-
ca** (☑041 319 51 25; www.acquastanca.
it; Fondamenta Manin 48, Murano; meals
€40-44; ☺10am-11pm Mon & Fri, 9am-8pm
Tue-Thu & Sat summer, 10am-10pm Mon & Fri,
10am-4pm Tue-Thu & Sat winter; ⚲Faro) on
Murano.

★ **Top Tip**

Hit the outer islands first, then work
your way back to Murano for the early
evening.

If you fancy a stroll, hop across the 60m
bridge to Burano's even quieter sister
island, Mazzorbo. Little more than a broad
grassy knoll, Mazzorbo is a great place for
a picnic or a long, lazy lunch. Line 12 also
stops at Mazzorbo.

Torcello

On the pastoral island of Torcello, a
three-minute ferry-hop from Burano, sheep
outnumber the 14 or so human residents.
This bucolic backwater was the republic's
original island settlement, growing over
time to become a Byzantine metropolis
of 20,000. Little has survived from this
golden age, and of its original nine churches
and two abbeys only the striking brick
Chiesa di Santa Fosca (Piazza Torcello;
☺10am-4.30pm; ⚲Torcello) and splendid
mosaic-filled **Basilica di Santa Maria
Assunta** (☑041 73 01 19; Piazza Torcello; adult/
reduced €5/4, incl museum €8/6, incl museum,
audio guide & campanile €12/10; ☺10am-5pm;
⚲Torcello) remain.

From Fondamente Nove, Line 12 runs
every 15 minutes until midnight. Line 9
connects Torcello with Burano. Follow the
path along the canal, Fondamenta Borgog-
noni, which leads you from the ferry stop to
Torcello's basilica.

Vaporetto services 4.1 and 4.2 run to the
island every 10 minutes throughout the day.

Burano

Venice's lofty Gothic architecture might
leave you feeling slightly loopy, but Burano
will bring you back to your senses with a
reviving shock of colour. The 50-minute ferry
ride (Line 12) from the Fondamente Nove is
packed with photographers bounding into
Burano's backstreets, snapping away at pea-
green stockings hung to dry between hot-
pink, royal-blue and caution-orange houses.

Burano is famed for its handmade
lace, which once graced the décolletage
and ruffs of European aristocracy. Some
women still maintain the traditions, but few
production houses remain – most of the
lace for sale in local shops is of the imported, machine-made variety.

◉ SIGHTS

◉ Piazza San Marco & Around

Museo Correr   Museum

(☏041 240 52 11; www.correr.visitmuve.it; Piazza San Marco 52; adult/reduced incl Palazzo Ducale €19/12, with Museum Pass free; ⊗10am-7pm Apr-Oct, to 5pm Nov-Mar; ☷San Marco) Napoleon bowled down an ancient church to build his royal digs over Piazza San Marco and then filled them with the riches of the doges while taking some of Venice's finest heirlooms to France as trophies. When Austria set up shop the Empress Sisi remodelled the palace, adding ceiling frescoes, silk cladding and brocade curtains. It's now open to the public and full of many of Venice's reclaimed treasures, including ancient maps, statues, cameos and four centuries of artistic masterpieces.

Torre dell'Orologio   Landmark

(Clock Tower; ☏041 4273 0892; www.museicivici veneziani.it; Piazza San Marco; adult/reduced €12/7; ⊗tours by appointment; ☷San Marco) The two hardest-working men in Venice stand duty on a rooftop around the clock, and wear no pants. No need to file workers' complaints: the 'Do Mori' (Two Moors) exposed to the elements atop the Torre dell'Orologio are made of bronze, and their bell-hammering mechanism runs like, well, clockwork. Below the Moors, Venice's gold-leafed, 15th-century timepiece tracks lunar phases. Visits are by guided tour; bookings essential.

◉ Dorsoduro

Peggy Guggenheim Collection   Museum

(☏041 240 54 11; www.guggenheim-venice. it; Palazzo Venier dei Leoni 704; adult/reduced €15/9; ⊗10am-6pm Wed-Mon; ☷Accademia) After losing her father on the *Titanic*, heiress Peggy Guggenheim became one of the great collectors of the 20th century. Her palatial canalside home, Palazzo Venier dei Leoni, showcases her stockpile of surrealist, futurist and abstract expressionist art with works by up to 200 artists, including

> *Venice's gold-leafed, 15th-century timepiece*

Torre dell'Orologio

INU/SHUTTERSTOCK ©

her ex-husband Max Ernst, Jackson Pollock (among her many rumoured lovers), Pablo Picasso and Salvador Dalí.

Basilica di Santa Maria della Salute
Basilica

(La Salute; www.basilicasalutevenezia.it; Campo della Salute 1b; basilica free, sacristy adult/reduced €4/2; ⊕basilica 9.30am-noon & 3-5.30pm, sacristry 10am-noon & 3-5pm Mon-Sat, 3-5pm Sun; ⊛Salute) Guarding the entrance to the Grand Canal, this 17th-century domed church was commissioned by Venice's plague survivors as thanks for their salvation. Baldassare Longhena's uplifting design is an engineering feat that defies simple logic; in fact, the church is said to have mystical curative properties. Titian eluded the plague until age 94, leaving 12 key paintings in the basilica's art-slung sacristy.

Ca' Rezzonico
Museum

(Museum of the 18th Century; ☑041 241 01 00; www.visitmuve.it; Fondamenta Rezzonico 3136; adult/reduced €10/7.50; ⊕10am-6pm Wed-Mon summer, to 5pm winter; ⊛Ca' Rezzonico) Baroque dreams come true at Baldassare Longhena's Grand Canal palace, where a marble staircase leads to gilded ballrooms, frescoed salons and sumptuous boudoirs. Giambattista Tiepolo's **Throne Room ceiling** is a masterpiece of elegant social climbing, showing gorgeous Merit ascending to the Temple of Glory clutching the Golden Book of Venetian nobles' names – including Tiepolo's patrons, the Rezzonico family.

San Polo & Santa Croce

Scuola Grande di San Rocco
Museum

(☑041 523 48 64; www.scuolagrandesanrocco.it; Campo San Rocco 3052; adult/reduced €10/8; ⊕9.30am-5.30pm; ⊛San Tomà) Everyone wanted the commission to paint this building dedicated to the patron saint of the plague-stricken, so Tintoretto cheated: instead of producing sketches like rival Veronese, he gifted a splendid ceiling panel of patron St Roch, knowing it couldn't be refused, or matched by other artists. The

Venice for Kids

Adults think Venice is for them; kids know better. This is where fairy tales come to life, prisoners escape through the roof of a palace, Murano glassblowers breathe life into pocket-sized sea dragons, and spellbound Pescaria fish balance on their tails.

Make an early-morning run down the Grand Canal for cheeky hot chocolates at Caffè Florian (p186); the cafe's fairytale interiors are plucked straight out of a giant storybook. Slip into **Palazzo Mocenigo** (☑041 72 17 98, tour reservations 041 270 03 70; www.visitmuve.it; Salizada di San Stae 1992, Santa Croce; adult/reduced €8/5.50; ⊕10am-5pm Tue-Sun Apr-Oct, to 4pm Nov-Mar; ⊛San Stae) to explore the Cinderella fashions of the past, then roam the secret attic-prisons of the Palazzo Ducale (p168). Check out giant samurai swords at the Museo d'Arte Orientale in Ca' Pesaro (p178), or the massive sea monsters and dinosaurs at the **Museo di Storia Naturale** (Fondaco dei Turchi, Museum of Natural History; ☑041 275 02 06; www.visitmuve.it; Salizada del Fontego dei Turchi 1730, Santa Croce; adult/reduced €8/5.50; ⊕10am-6pm Tue-Sun Jun-Oct, 9am-5pm Tue-Fri, 10am-6pm Sat & Sun Nov-May; ⊛San Stae). Grab your sailor hat and shout out 'Ship Ahoy!' at the **Museo Storico Navale** (Naval History Museum; www.visitmuve.it; Riva San Biagio 2148; ⊛Arsenale), jam-packed with golden princely barges, model warships and enough cannons to make any pirate nervous.

Caffè Florian (p186)
4KCLIPS/SHUTTERSTOCK ©

San Marco & San Polo

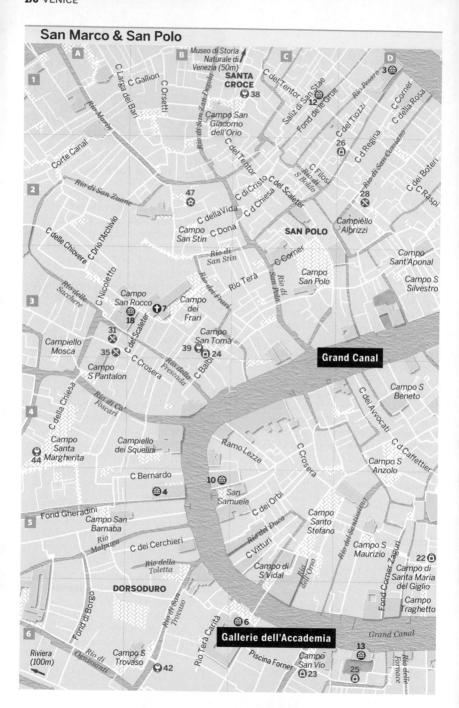

A
B
C
D

1

Museo di Storia
Naturale di
Venezia (50m)

SANTA
CROCE
38

C Larga dei Bari
C Gallion
C Orsetti

C del Tentor
S Stae
12

Rio di San Zuan Degola

Saliz di San Stae
Fond de le Croe

Rio Pesaro
3

C Corner
C della Rosa

C del Tiozzi

Campo San
Giacomo
dell'Orio

C del Tentor

C d Regina

26

Rio Marin

Corte Canal

2

Rio di San Zuane

C delle Chiovere
C Drio l'Archivio
C Nicoletto

47

C della Vida
C di Cristo C del Scaleter
C d Chiesa

C Filosi
Rio di
S Boldo

Rio di San Cassian
C dei Boteri
C C Raspi

28

Campo
San Stin

C Dona
C della Vida

Campiello
Albrizzi

SAN POLO

Campo
Sant'Aponal

Rio di
San Stin

C Corner

Rio Terà

Campo
San Polo

Rio di
San Polo

Campo S
Silvestro

3

Rio delle
Sacchere

C Nicoletto

Campo
San Rocco
18   7

C del Scaleter

Campo
dei Frari

Rio dei Frari

31
35

Campiello
Mosca

Campo
S Pantalon

C Crosera

Campo
San Tomà
39   24

C Balbi

Rio della
Prescada

Grand Canal

4

C della Chiesa

Rio di Cà
Foscari

Campo
Santa
Margherita
44

Campiello
dei Squelini

C Bernardo
4

Ramo Lezze

C Crosera

Campo S
Beneto

C dei Avocati

C d Caffettier

Campo S
Anzolo

5

Fond Gheradini

Campo San
Barnaba

Rio
Malpaga

C dei Cerchieri

Rio della
Toletta

DORSODURO

10

San
Samuele

C dei Orbi

Rio del Duca

C Vitturi

Campo di
S Vidal

Rio
dell'Orso

Campo
Santo
Stefano

Rio del Santissimo

Campo S
Maurizio

Fond Corner Zaguri

22

Campo di
Santa Maria
del Giglio

Campo
Traghetto

6

Riviera
(100m)

Fond di Borgo

Rio di
Ognissanti

Campo S
Trovaso

42

Rio di San
Trovaso

Rio Terà Carità

6

Gallerie dell'Accademia

Piscina Forner

Campo
San Vio
23

13

25

Grand Canal

Rio delle
Fornace

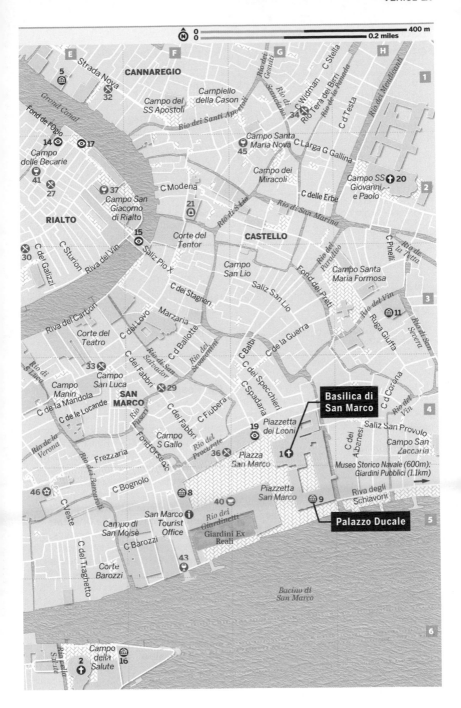

400 m
0.2 miles

CANNAREGIO

5

Strada Nova

32

Campiello della Cason

Campo dei SS Apostoli

Rio dei Gesuiti

C Widman

C Stella

C d Testa

Rio dei Birri

Rio de la Panada

Rio dei Santi Apostoli

34

Grand Canal

Fond de l'Ogio

14

17

Campo delle Becarie

41

27

37

Campo San Giacomo di Rialto

15

RIALTO

C del Galizzi

C Sturion

Riva del Vin

30

Campo Santa Maria Nova

45

C Larga G Gallina

Campo dei Miracoli

C delle Erbe

Rio di San Marina

Campo SS Giovanni e Paolo

20

C Modena

21

Rio di S. Lio

CASTELLO

Corte del Tentor

Saliz Pio X

Campo San Lio

Saliz San Lio

Rio del Paradiso

Fond dei Preti

Campo Santa Maria Formosa

C Pinelli

Rio de la Tetta

C dei Stagneri

C del Lovo

Marzaria

Corte del Teatro

Riva del Carbon

Riva del Vin

11

Ruga Giuffa

Rio di S Luca

Campo Manin

33

Campo San Luca

SAN MARCO

C de la Mandola

C de le Locande

C d Ballotte

Rio di San Salvador

C dei Fabbri

Rio dei Ferali

C dei Fabbri

29

C Fiubera

C dei Specchieri

C Spadaria

C de la Guerra

C Balbi

C Corona

Rio del Vin

19

Piazzetta dei Leoni

Basilica di San Marco

Saliz San Provolo

C dei Albanesi

Campo San Zaccaria

Rio de lo Verona

Frezzaria

Fond Orseolo

Campo S Gallo

Rio del Procurate

36

Piazza San Marco

1

Museo Storico Navale (600m); Giardini Pubblici (1.1km)

46

C Veste

C Bognolo

8

40

Piazzetta San Marco

9

Riva degli Schiavoni

Palazzo Ducale

Campo di San Moisè

San Marco Tourist Office

Rio dei Giardinetti

Giardini Ex Reali

C Barozzi

43

Corte Barozzi

C del Traghetto

Bacino di San Marco

Campo della Salute

16

2

Rio della Salute

San Marco & San Polo

artist documents Mary's life story in the assembly hall, and both Old and New Testament scenes in the Sala Grande Superiore upstairs.

I Frari
Church

(Basilica di Santa Maria Gloriosa dei Frari; ☑041 272 86 18; www.basilicadeifrari.it; Campo dei Frari 3072, San Polo; adult/reduced €3/1.50; ☺9am-6pm Mon-Sat, 1-6pm Sun; ☱San Tomà) A soaring Gothic church, I Frari's assets include marquetry choir stalls, Canova's pyramid mausoleum, Bellini's achingly sweet *Madonna with Child* triptych in the sacristy, and Longhena's creepy Doge Pesaro funereal monument. Upstaging them all, however, is the small altarpiece. This is Titian's 1518 *Assunta* (Assumption), in which a radiant red-cloaked Madonna reaches heavenward, steps onto a cloud and escapes this mortal coil. Titian himself – lost to the plague in 1576 at the age 94 – is buried near his celebrated masterpiece.

Ca' Pesaro
Museum

(Galleria Internazionale d'Arte Moderna e Museo d'Arte Orientale; ☑041 72 11 27; www.visitmuve. it; Fondamenta di Ca' Pesaro 2070, Santa Croce; adult/reduced €14/11.50; ☺10am-6pm Tue-Sun summer, to 5pm winter; ☱San Stae) Like a Carnevale costume built for two, the stately exterior of this Baldassare Longhena–designed 1710 *palazzo* hides two intriguing museums: **Galleria Internazionale d'Arte Moderna** and **Museo d'Arte Orientale**. While the former includes art showcased at La Biennale di Venezia, the latter holds treasures from Prince Enrico di Borbone's epic 1887–89 souvenir-shopping spree across Asia. Competing with the artworks are Ca' Pesaro's fabulous painted ceilings, which hint at the power and prestige of the Pesaro clan.

◎ Cannaregio

Museo Ebraico
Museum

(Jewish Museum; ☑041 71 53 59; www.museo ebraico.it; Campo del Ghetto Nuovo 2902b; adult/

reduced €8/6, incl tour €12/10; ⊘10am-7pm Sun-Fri Jun-Sep, to 5.30pm Sun-Fri Oct-May; 🚇Guglie) This museum explores the history of Venice's Jewish community and showcases its pivotal contributions to Venetian, Italian and world history. Opened in 1955, it has a small collection of finely worked silverware and other objects used in private prayer and to decorate synagogues, as well as early books published in the Ghetto during the Renaissance.

Chiesa della Madonna dell'Orto
Church

(Campo de la Madonna dell'Orto 3520; adult/reduced €3/2; ⊘10am-5pm Mon-Sat; 🚇Orto) This elegantly spare 1365 brick Gothic church remains one of Venice's best-kept secrets. It was the parish church of Venetian Renaissance painter Tintoretto (1518–94), who filled the church with his paintings and is buried in the chapel to the right of the altar.

Galleria Giorgio Franchetti alla Ca' d'Oro
Museum

(☎041 520 03 45; www.cadoro.org; Calle di Ca' d'Oro 3932; adult/reduced €8.50/4.25; ⊘8.15am-2pm Mon, to 7.15pm Tue-Sun; 🚇Ca' d'Oro) One of the most beautiful buildings on the Grand Canal, 15th-century Ca' d'Oro's lacy arcaded Gothic facade is resplendent even without the original gold-leaf details that gave the palace its name (Golden House). Baron Franchetti (1865–1922) bequeathed this treasure-box palace to Venice, packed with his collection of masterpieces, many of which were originally plundered from Veneto churches during Napoleon's conquest of Italy. The baron's ashes are interred beneath an ancient purple porphyry column in the magnificent open-sided, mosaic-floored court downstairs.

◎ Castello

Zanipolo
Basilica

(Basilica di San Giovanni e Paolo; ☎041 523 59 13; www.basilicasantigiovanniepaolo.it; Campo Zanipolo; adult/reduced €2.50/1.25; ⊘9am-6pm Mon-Sat, noon-6pm Sun; 🚇Ospedale) Commenced in 1333 but not finished until the 1430s, this vast church is similar in style and scope to the Franciscan Frari in San Polo, which was being raised at the same time. Both oversized structures feature redbrick facades with high-contrast detailing in white stone. After its completion, Zanipolo quickly became the go-to church for ducal funerals and burials.

Giardini Pubblici
Gardens

(🚇Giardini) Begun under Napoleon as the city's first public green space, these leafy gardens are now the main home of the Biennale. Only around half of the gardens is open to the public all year round as the rest is given over to the permanent **Biennale pavilions**, each representing a different country. Many of them are attractions in their own right, from Carlo Scarpa's daring 1954 raw-concrete-and-glass Venezuelan Pavilion to Denton Corker Marshall's 2015 Australian Pavilion in black granite.

◎ Isola di San Giorgio Maggiore

Chiesa di San Giorgio Maggiore
Church

(☎041 522 78 27; www.abbaziasangiorgio.it; Isola di San Giorgio Maggiore; bell tower adult/reduced €6/4, ⊘8.30am-6pm; 🚇San Giorgio Maggiore) **FREE** Solar eclipses are only marginally more dazzling than Palladio's white Istrian stone facade at this abbey church. Begun in 1565 and completed in 1610, it owes more to ancient Roman temples than the bombastic baroque of Palladio's day. Inside, ceilings billow over a generous nave, with high windows distributing filtered sunshine. Two of Tintoretto's masterworks flank the altar, and a lift whisks visitors up the 60m-high bell tower for stirring panoramas – a great alternative to queuing at San Marco's *campanile*.

Fondazione Giorgio Cini
Cultural Centre

(☎347 3386426; www.cini.it; Isola di San Giorgio Maggiore; adult/reduced €10/8; ⊘tours 10am-5pm Sat & Sun; 🚇San Giorgio Maggiore) In 1951, industrialist and art patron Vittorio Cini – a survivor of the Dachau concentration camp – acquired the monastery of San Giorgio and restored it in memory of his son, Giorgio Cini. The rehabilitated complex is an architectural treasure incorporating designs by Palladio and Baldassare Longhena. Weekend tours allow you to stroll through a garden labyrinth and contemplate the tranquil Cypress Cloister, the oldest extant part of the complex (1526). Check the website for exhibitions, events and performances in the open-air **Teatro Verde**.

◉ The Lido

Only 15 minutes by *vaporetti* 1, 5.1, 5.2, 6, 10 (summer only) and N from San Marco, the Lido has been the beach and bastion of Venice for centuries. In the 19th century, it found a new lease of life as a glamorous bathing resort, attracting monied Europeans to its grand Liberty-style hotels. Thomas Mann's novel *Death in Venice* was set here, and you'll spot plenty of ornate villas that date from those decadent days. Walking itineraries around the most extravagant areas are available to download at www2.comune.venezia.it/lidoliberty.

Lido beaches, such as the Blue Moon complex, line the southern, seaward side of the island and are easily accessed from the *vaporetto* down the Gran Viale. To head further afield, hire a bike from **Lido on Bike** (🖉041 526 80 19; www.lidoonbike.it; Gran Viale Santa Maria Elisabetta 21b, Lido; bicycle rental per 90min/day €5/9; ⊗9am-7pm summer; 🚢Lido SME) and cycle south across the Ponte di Borgo to tiny Malamocco, a miniature version of Venice right down to the lions of St Mark on medieval facades.

⊖ TOURS

Venice Urban Adventures   Food & Drink

(🖉348 980 85 66; www.veniceurbanadventures. com; tours €36-180; ⊗tours 11.30am & 5.30pm Mon-Sat) Knowledgable, enthusiastic, local foodies lead bakery- and *cicheti* (bar snacks)–hopping tours, some of which involve a short stint on a *traghetto* (gondola ferry) or *aperitivo* (pre-dinner drink) on a water taxi. Also offers day trips to wineries around Treviso.

Palazzo Ducale (p168) and views of Chiesa di San Giorgio Maggiore (p179)

Row Venice — Boating

(📞347 7250637; www.rowvenice.org; Fondamenta Gasparo Contarini; 90min lessons 1-2 people €85, 3/4 people €120/140; 🚤Orto) The next best thing to walking on water: rowing a traditional *batellina coda di gambero* (shrimp-tailed boat) standing up like gondoliers do. Tours must be pre-booked, and they commence at the wooden gate of the Sacca Misericordia boat marina.

Context Travel — Cultural

(📞800 691 60 36; www.contexttravel.com; group tours €315-409) Context offers scholarly tours for the curious minded. Groups are small and subjects range from politics to art, history and ecology. Families should try the Art Tour, Lion Hunt, Daily Life in Venice and, for older kids, the Science and Secrets of the Lagoon – led by a marine biologist.

See Venice — Cultural

(📞349 084 8303; www.seevenice.it; tours per hr €75) Intimate and insightful cultural tours are offered by Venetian native Luisella Romeo, whose love and enthusiasm for the city is infectious. She covers all the grand-slam sights, as well as offering off-the-beaten path itineraries, guided tours of contemporary art museums, and visits to artisan studios, design shops and musical venues, which expand visitors' experiences of the city.

Eolo Cruises — Boating

(📞349 7431551; www.cruisingvenice.com; per person €350-450 for 4-6 people) Eolo Cruises covers the lagoon on a double-masted 1946 fishing *bragozzo* (flat-bottomed fishing boat) for one- to eight-day trips (for six to 10 people), including on-board cooking tours. Guests sleep in select villas and *palazzi* (mansions), spend the day sailing and eat seafood lunches on board.

🔒 SHOPPING

Ca' Macana Atelier — Arts & Crafts

(📞041 718 655; www.camacanaatelier.blogspot.it; Rio Terà San Leonardo 1374; ⊙9am-8pm; 🚤San Marcuola) Resist buying inferior

 Gondola Rides

A gondola trip (www.gondolavenezia.it) is anything but pedestrian, with glimpses into *palazzi* courtyards and hidden canals otherwise invisible on foot. Official daytime rates are €80 for 40 minutes (six passengers maximum), and it's €100 between 7pm and 8am, not including songs (negotiated separately) or tips. Additional time is charged in 20-minute increments (day/night €40/50). You may negotiate a price break in low season, overcast weather or around midday, when other travellers get hot and hungry. Agree on a price, time limit and singing in advance to avoid surcharges. Gondolas cluster at *stazi* (stops) along the Grand Canal, at the train station, the Rialto and near major monuments (eg I Frari, Ponte Suspiri and Accademia), but you can also book a pick-up.

SERENAROSSI/SHUTTERSTOCK ©

mass-produced Carnevale masks until you've checked out the traditionally made papier-mâché and leather masks at this long-established shop, with a workshop right at its heart. The steampunk range is exactly as creepy as you'd hope.

Marina e Susanna Sent — Glass

(📞041 520 81 36; www.marinaesusannasent.com; Campo San Vio 669, Dorsoduro; ⊙10am-1pm & 1.30-6.30pm; 🚤Accademia) Wearable waterfalls and soap-bubble necklaces are Venice-style signatures, thanks to the Murano-born Sent sisters. Defying

Shopping in Venice

To find unique pieces, just wander key artisan areas: San Polo around Calle dei Saoneri, Santa Croce around Calle Lunga and Calle del Tentor, San Marco along Frezzeria, Dorsoduro around the Peggy Guggenheim, and Murano.

Glass Venetians have been working in crystal and glass since the 10th century. Murano glass is famous across Italy but items are available around the city and beyond.

Paper Embossing and marbling paper began in the 14th century as part of Venice's burgeoning publishing industry, but these bookbinding techniques and *ebru* (Turkish marbled paper) end papers have taken on lives of their own. You can still watch a Heidelberg press in action at **Veneziastampa** (📋041 71 54 55; www.veneziastampa.com; Campo Santa Maria Mater Domini 2173, Santa Croce; ⊘8.30am-7.30pm Mon-Fri, 9am-12.30pm Sat; 🚤San Stae).

Lace Burano lace was a fashion must for centuries. But the modern master of Venetian textiles is Fortuny, whose showroom, **Fortuny Tessuti Artistici** (📋393 8257651; www.fortuny.com; Fondamenta San Biagio 805, Giudecca; ⊘10am-6pm Mon-Fri; 🚤Palanca) on Giudecca features fabrics created using top-secret techniques.

Marbled paper
TRAMONT_ANA/SHUTTERSTOCK ©

centuries-old beliefs that women can't handle molten glass, their minimalist art-glass statement jewellery is featured in museum

stores worldwide, from Palazzo Grassi to New York's MoMA. See new collections at this store, its flagship Murano studio, or the San Marco branch.

Coin   Department Store
(📋041 520 35 81; www.coinexcelsior.com; Ponte de l'Ogio 5787; ⊘10am-8pm; 🛜; 🚤Rialto) Its glitzy neighbour, Fondaco dei Tedeschi, gets all the attention these days but non-oligarchs will find Coin much more accessible. It's expensive but not stupidly so (especially during the legendary sales), and the range includes streetwear, famous brands and lesser known but top-quality local fashion.

L'Armadio di Coco
Luxury Vintage   Vintage
(📋041 241 32 14; www.larmadiodicoco.it; Campo di Santa Maria del Giglio 2516a; ⊘10.30am-7.30pm; 🚤Giglio) Jam-packed with pre-loved designer treasures from yesteryear, this tiny shop is the place to come for classic Chanel dresses, exquisite cashmere coats and limited-edition Gucci shoulder bags.

ElleElle   Glass
(📋041 527 48 66; www.elleellemurano.com; Fondamenta Manin 52, Murano; ⊘10.30am-1pm & 2-6pm; 🚤Faro) Nason Moretti has been making modernist magic happen in glass since the 1950s, and the third-generation glass designers are in fine form in this showroom. Everything is signed, including an exquisite range of hand-blown drinking glasses, jugs, bowls, vases, tealight holders, decanters and lamps.

Oh My Blue   Jewellery, Handicrafts
(📋041 243 57 41; www.ohmyblue.it; Campo San Tomà 2865, San Polo; ⊘11am-1pm & 2.30-7.30pm; 🚤San Tomà) In her white-on-white gallery, switched-on Elena Rizzi showcases edgy, show-stopping jewellery, accessories and decorative objects from both local and international talent like Elena Camilla Bertellotti, Ana Hagopian and Yoko Takirai. Expect anything from quartz rings and paper necklaces to sculptural bags and ceramics.

Ristorante Quadri

🍴 EATING

🍴 Piazza San Marco & Around

Marchini Time · · · · · · · · · · · Bakery €

(☎041 241 30 87; www.marchinitime.it; Campo San Luca 4589; items €1.20-3.50; ☸7.30am-8.30pm; ⛴Rialto) Elbow your way through the morning crush to bag a warm croissant filled with runny apricot jam or melting Nutella. Everything here is freshly baked, which is why the crowd hangs around as croissants give way to foccacia, *pizette* (mini pizzas) and generously stuffed *panini*.

Bistrot de Venise · · · · · · · Venetian €€€

(☎041 523 66 51; www.bistrotdevenise.com; Calle dei Fabbri 4685; meals €47-78; ☸noon-3pm & 7pm-midnight; 🍴; ⛴Rialto) Indulge in some culinary time travel at this fine-dining bistro where they've revived the recipes of Renaissance chef Bartolomeo Scappi. Dine like a doge in the red-and-gilt dining room on braised duck with wild apple and onion pudding, or enjoy the Jewish recipe of goose, raisin and pine-nut pasta. Even the desserts are beguilingly exotic.

> *Venetian glamour*

Ristorante Quadri · · · · · · Modern Italian €€€

(☎041 522 21 05; www.alajmo.it; Piazza San Marco 121; meals €110-138; ☸12.30-2.30pm & 7.30-10.30pm Tue-Sun; ⛴San Marco) When it comes to Venetian glamour, nothing beats this historic Michelin-starred restaurant overlooking Piazza San Marco. A small swarm of servers greets you as you're shown to your table in a room decked out with silk damask, gilt, painted beams and Murano chandeliers. Dishes are precise and delicious, deftly incorporating Venetian touches into an inventive modern Italian menu.

🍴 Dorsoduro

Pasticceria Tonolo · · · · · · · · · Pastries €

(☎041 532 72 09; Calle dei Preti 3764; pastries €1-4; ☸7.45am-8pm Tue-Sat, 8am-1pm Sun, closed Sun Jul; ⛴Ca' Rezzonico) Long, skinny

Tonolo is the stuff of local legend, a fact confirmed by the never-ending queue of customers. Ditch packaged B&B croissants for flaky *apfelstrudel* (apple pastry), velvety *bignè al zabaione* (marsala cream pastry) and oozing *pain au chocolat* (chocolate croissants). Devour one at the bar with a bracing espresso, then bag another for the road.

Estro   Venetian €€

(☎041 476 49 14; www.estrovenezia.com; Calle dei Preti 3778; meals €35; ☺11am-midnight Wed-Mon; ❄; ⛴San Tomà) Estro is anything you want it to be: wine bar, *aperitivo* pit stop or sit-down degustation restaurant. The 500 wines – all of them naturally processed – are chosen by young-gun owners Alberto and Dario, whose passion for quality extends to the grub, from *cicheti* (Venetian tapas) topped with housemade *porchetta* (roast pork) to roasted guinea fowl and a succulent burger dripping with Asiago cheese.

Riviera   Venetian €€€

(☎041 522 76 21; www.ristoranteriviera.it; Fondamenta Zattere al Ponte Lungo 1473; meals €70-85; ☺12.30-3pm & 7-10.30pm Fri-Tue; ⛴Zattere) Seafood connoisseurs concur that dining at GP Cremonini's restaurant is a Venetian highlight. A former rock musician, GP now focuses his considerable talents on delivering perfectly balanced octopus stew, feather-light gnocchi with lagoon crab, and risotto with langoustine and hop shoots. The setting, overlooking the Giudecca Canal, is similarly spectacular, encompassing views of Venetian domes backed by hot-pink sunsets.

🗶 San Polo & Santa Croce

All'Arco   Venetian €

(☎041 520 56 66; Calle dell'Ochialer 436, San Polo; cicheti from €2; ☺8am-2.30pm Mon, Tue & Sat, to 7pm Wed-Fri summer, 8am-2.30pm Mon-Sat winter; ⛴Rialto-Mercato) Search out this authentic neighbourhood *osteria* (casual tavern) for the best *cicheti* in town. Armed with ingredients from the nearby Rialto Market, father–son team Francesco and Matteo serve miniature masterpieces such as *cannocchia* (mantis shrimp) with pumpkin and roe, and *otrega crudo* (raw

Pastries on display at Pasticceria Tonolo

MATTHIAS SCHOLZ/ALAMY ©

butterfish) with mint-and-olive-oil marinade. Even with copious *prosecco,* hardly any meal here tops €20.

Dai Zemei   Venetian €

(☑041 520 85 96; www.ostariadaizemei.it; Ruga Vecchia San Giovanni 1045, San Polo; cicheti from €1.50; ☉8.30am-8.30pm Mon-Sat, 9am-7pm Sun; ⛴San Silvestro) Running this closet-sized *cicheti* counter are *zemei* (twins) Franco and Giovanni, who serve loyal regulars small meals with plenty of imagination: gorgonzola lavished with *peperoncino* (chilli) marmalade, duck breast drizzled with truffle oil, or chicory paired with leek and marinated anchovies. A gourmet bargain for inspired bites and impeccable wines – try a crisp *nosiola* or invigorating *prosecco* brut.

Antiche Carampane   Venetian €€€

(☑041 524 01 65; www.antichecarampane.com; Rio Terà delle Carampane 1911, San Polo; meals €50; ☉12.45-2.30pm & 7.30-10.30pm Tue-Sat; ⛴San Stae) Hidden in the once shady lanes behind Ponte delle Tette, this culinary indulgence is a trick to find. Once you do, say goodbye to soggy lasagne and hello to a market-driven menu of silky *crudi* (raw fish/seafood), surprisingly light *fritto misto* (fried seafood) and *caramote* prawn salad with seasonal vegetables. Never short of a smart, convivial crowd, it's a good idea to book ahead.

⊗ Cannaregio

Pasticceria Dal Mas   Bakery €

(☑041 71 51 01; www.dalmaspasticceria.it; Rio Terà Lista di Spagna 150; pastries €1.30-6.50; ☉7am-9pm; ⚡; ⛴Ferrovia) Our favourite Venetian bakery-cafe sparkles with mirrors, marble and metal trim, providing a fitting casket for the precious pastries displayed within. Despite the perpetual morning crush, the efficient team dispense top-notch coffee and *cornetti* (croissants) with admirable equanimity. Come mid-morning for mouth-watering, still-warm quiches. The hot chocolate is also exceptional – hardly surprising given its sister chocolate shop next door.

🍽 Cicheti, Bar Snacks Venetian-Style

Even in unpretentious Venetian *osterie* (taverns) and *bacari* (bars)most dishes cost a couple of euros more than they might elsewhere in Italy – not a bad mark-up really, considering all that fresh seafood and produce is brought in by boat. But *cicheti* (Venetian tapas) are some of the best culinary finds in Italy, served at lunch and from around 6pm to 8pm with sensational Veneto wines by the glass. *Cicheti* range from basic bar snacks (spicy meatballs, fresh tomato and basil bruschetta) to highly inventive small plates: think white Bassano asparagus and plump lagoon shrimp wrapped in pancetta or pungent gorgonzola paired with sweet, spicy *peperoncino* (chilli). Prices start at €1 for tasty meatballs and range from €3 to €6 for gourmet fantasias with fancy ingredients, typically devoured standing up or perched atop stools at the bar. Nightly *cicheti* spreads could easily pass as dinner.

PFEIFFER/SHUTTERSTOCK ©

Gelateria Ca' d'Oro   Gelato €

(☑041 522 89 82; Strada Nova 4273b; scoops €1.80; ☉10am-10pm; ⛴Ca' d'Oro) Foot traffic stops here for spectacularly creamy gelato made in-house daily. For a summer pick-me-up, try the *granita di caffe con panna* (coffee shaved ice with whipped cream).

Osteria Boccadoro   Venetian €€€

(☑041 521 10 21; www.boccadorovenezia.it; Campiello Widmann 5405a; meals €40-55; ☉noon-3pm & 7-10pm Tue-Sun; ⛴Fondamente Nove) Birds

From left: Traditional Carnevale masks; Aperol *spritz*; Osteria alla Bifora and neighbouring bars

sweetly singing in this *campo* (square) are probably angling for your leftovers, but they don't stand a chance. Chef-owner Luciano's creative *crudi* (raw seafood) are two-bite delights and cloud-like gnocchi and home-made pasta is gone entirely too soon. Save room for luxuriant desserts.

⊗ Giudecca

Trattoria Altanella   Venetian €€

(🖉041 522 77 80; Calle de le Erbe 268; meals €38-47; ⊙12.30-2.30pm & 7.30-10.30pm Wed-Sun; ❄; 🚤Redentore) Founded by a fisherman and his wife in 1920 and still run by the same family, this cosy restaurant serves fine Venetian fare such as potato gnocchi with cuttlefish and perfectly grilled fish. Inside, the vintage interior is hung with artworks, reflecting the restaurant's popularity with artists, poets and writers, while outside a flower-fringed balcony hangs over the canal.

La Palanca   Venetian €€

(🖉041 528 77 19; Fondamenta Sant'Eufemia 448; meals €25-33; ⊙7am-8pm Mon-Sat; 🚤Palanca)

Locals of all ages pour into this humble bar for *cicheti,* coffee and *spritz*. However, it's at lunchtime that it really comes into its own, serving surprisingly sophisticated fare like swordfish carpaccio with orange zest alongside more rustic dishes, such as a delicious thick seafood soup. In summer, competition for waterside tables is stiff.

🍷 DRINKING & NIGHTLIFE
🍸 Piazza San Marco & Around

Caffè Florian   Cafe

(🖉041 520 56 41; www.caffeflorian.com; Piazza San Marco 57; ⊙9am-11pm; 🚤San Marco) The oldest still-operating cafe in Europe and one of the first to welcome women, Florian maintains rituals (if not prices) established in 1720: besuited waiters serve cappuccino on silver trays, lovers canoodle in plush banquettes and the orchestra strikes up as the sunset illuminates San Marco's mosaics. Piazza seating during concerts costs €6 extra, but dreamy-eyed romantics hardly notice.

🍷 Dorsoduro

Osteria alla Bifora Bar

(📞041 523 61 19; Campo Santa Margherita 2930; ⏱noon-3pm & 5pm-2am Wed-Mon; 🚤Ca' Rezzonico) Other bars around this *campo* cater to *spritz*-pounding students, but this chandelier-lit medieval wine cave sets the scene for gentle flirting over a big-hearted Veneto merlot. Cured-meat platters are carved to order on that Ferrari-red meat slicer behind the bar, but there are placemats to doodle on and new-found friends aplenty at communal tables.

Cantinone Già Schiavi Bar

(📞041 523 95 77; www.cantinaschiavi.com; Fondamenta Nani 992; ⏱8.30am-8.30pm Mon-Sat; 🚤Zattere) Regulars gamely pass along orders to timid newcomers, who might otherwise miss out on smoked swordfish *cicheti* (bar snacks) with top-notch house Soave, or *pallottoline* (mini-bottles of beer) with generous *sopressa* (soft salami) *panini*. Chaos cheerfully prevails at this legendary canalside spot, where Accademia art historians rub shoulders with San

Trovaso gondola builders without spilling a drop.

🍷 San Polo & Santa Croce

Al Mercà Wine Bar

(📞346 8340660; Campo Cesare Battisti 213, San Polo; ⏱10am-2.30pm & 6-8pm Mon-Thu, to 9.30pm Fri & Sat; 🚤Rialto-Mercato) Discerning drinkers throng to this cupboard-sized counter on a Rialto Market square to sip on top-notch *prosecco* and DOC wines by the glass (from €3). Edibles usually include meatballs and mini *panini* (€1.50), proudly made using super-fresh ingredients.

Al Prosecco Wine Bar

(📞041 524 02 22; www.alprosecco.com; Campo San Giacomo dell'Orio 1503, Santa Croce; ⏱10am-8pm Mon-Fri, to 5pm Sat Nov-Mar, to 10.30pm Apr-Oct; 🚤San Stae) 🌿 The urge to toast sunsets in Venice's loveliest *campo* is only natural – and so is the wine at Al Prosecco. This forward-thinking bar specialises in *vini naturi* (natural-process wines) – organic, biodynamic, wild-yeast fermented – from enlightened Italian winemakers like Cinque Campi and Azienda Agricola Barichel. So order a glass of unfiltered 'cloudy' *prosecco* and toast to the good things in life.

Basegò
Bar

(☏041 850 02 99; www.basego.it; Campo San Tomà, San Polo; ⊙9am-11pm; ⛴San Tomà) Focusing on three essential ingredients – good food, good wine and good music – newly opened Basegò has rapidly formed a dedicated group of drinkers. Indulge in a *cicheti* feast of lagoon seafood, Norcia prosciutto, smoked tuna and Lombard cheeses, and on Friday night enjoy live music from the likes of Alessia Obino and Simone Massaron.

Cannaregio

Timon
Wine Bar

(☏041 524 60 66; Fondamenta dei Ormesini 2754; ⊙6pm-1am; ⛴San Marcuola) Find a spot in the wood-lined interior or, in summer, on the boat moored out front along the canal and watch the motley parade of drinkers and dreamers arrive for seafood *crostini* and quality wines by the *ombra* (half-glass) or carafe. Musicians play sets canalside when the weather obliges.

Il Santo Bevitore
Pub

(☏335 8415771; www.ilsantobevitorepub.com; Calle Zancani 2393a; ⊙4pm-2am; ☎; ⛴Ca' d'Oro) San Marco has its glittering cathedral, but beer lovers prefer pilgrimages to this shrine of the 'Holy Drinker' for 20 brews on tap, including Trappist ales and seasonal stouts – alongside a big range of speciality gin, whisky and vodka. The faithful receive canalside seating, footy matches on TV, free wi-fi and the occasional live band.

Un Mondo di Vino
Bar

(☏041 521 10 93; www.unmondodivinovenezia.com; Salizada San Canzian 5984a; ⊙11am-3pm & 5.30-11pm Tue-Sun; ⛴Rialto) Get here early for first crack at marinated artichokes and *sarde in saor* (sardines in tangy onion marinade), and to claim a few square centimetres of ledge for your plate and wineglass.

There are dozens of wines offered by the glass, so take a chance on a freak blend or obscure varietal.

ENTERTAINMENT

To find out what's on the calendar in Venice during your visit, check listings in free mags distributed citywide and online: VeNews (www.venezianews.it), Venezia da Vivere (www.veneziadavivere.com) and 2Venice (www.2venice.it).

La Fenice
Opera

(☏041 78 66 72; www.teatrolafenice.it; Campo San Fantin 1977; restricted view from €30; ⛴Giglio) One of Italy's top opera houses, La Fenice stages a rich roster of opera, ballet and classical music. The cheapest seats are in the boxes at the top, nearest the stage. The view is extremely restricted, but you will get to hear the music, watch the orchestra, soak up the atmosphere and people-watch.

Palazzetto Bru Zane
Classical Music

(Centre du Musique Romantique Française; ☏041 521 10 05; www.bru-zane.com; Palazzetto Bru Zane 2368, San Polo; adult/reduced €15/5; ⊙box office 2.30-5.30pm Mon-Fri, closed late Jul–mid-Aug; ⛴San Tomà) Pleasure palaces don't get more romantic than Palazzetto Bru Zane on concert nights, when exquisite harmonies tickle Sebastiano Ricci angels tumbling across stucco-frosted ceilings. Multi-year restorations returned the 1695–97 Casino Zane's 100-seat music room to its original function, attracting world-class musicians to enjoy its acoustics from late September to mid-May.

ⓘ INFORMATION

Airport Tourist Office (☏041 24 24; www.veneziaunica.it; Arrivals Hall, Marco Polo Airport; ⊙8.30am-7pm)

Piazzale Roma Tourist Office (☏041 24 24, lost & found 041 272 21 79; www.veneziaunica.it; ground fl ASM car park, Piazzale Roma; ⊙7.30am-7.30pm; ⛴Piazzale Roma)

San Marco Tourist Office (041 24 24; www.veneziaunica.it; Piazza San Marco 71f; ⊙9am-7pm; 🚤San Marco)

Stazione Santa Lucia Tourist Office (📞041 24 24; www.veneziaunica.it; ⊙7am-9pm; 🚤Ferrovia)

❶ GETTING THERE & AWAY

AIR

Most flights to Venice fly in to Marco Polo airport (p341), 12km outside Venice, east of Mestre. Ryanair and some other budget airlines also use **Treviso Airport** (📞0422 31 51 11; www.treviso airport.it; Via Noalese 63), about 4km southwest of Treviso and a 26km, one-hour drive from Venice.

TRAIN

Direct intercity services operate out of Venice to most major Italian cities, as well as points in France, Germany, Austria, Switzerland, Slovenia and Croatia.

Local trains linking Venice to the Veneto are frequent, reliable and remarkably inexpensive, including Padua (€4.15, 25 to 50 minutes, three to four per hour) and Verona (€8.85, 1¾ hours, three to four per hour). Expensive, high-speed Le Frecce trains also serve these Veneto destinations, but are a better option for longer journeys to Milan (€60, 2½ hours) and Rome (€86 to €117, 3¾ hours).

❶ GETTING AROUND

TO/FROM THE AIRPORT

BOAT

Alilaguna (📞041 240 17 01; www.alilaguna.it; airport transfer one-way €15) operates four water shuttles that link the airport with various parts of Venice at a cost of €8 to Murano and €15 to all other landing stages. Passengers are permitted one suitcase and one piece of hand luggage. All further bags are charged at €3 per piece. Expect it to take 45 to 90 minutes to reach most destinations; it takes approximately 1¼ hours to reach Piazza San Marco. Lines include the following:

Linea Blu (Blue Line) Stops at the Lido, San Marco, Stazione Marittima and points in between.

 Making the Most of Your Euro

Civic Museum Pass (adult/reduced €24/18) is valid for six months and covers single entry to 11 civic museums, including Palazzo Ducale, Ca' Rezzonico, Ca' Pesaro, Palazzo Mocenigo, Museo Correr and Museo del Vetro (Glass Museum) on Murano.

Chorus Pass (adult/student under 29 years €12/8) allows single entry to 16 historic Venice churches any time within one year (excluding I Frari). Passes are for sale at church ticket booths.

City Pass (adult/junior €39.90/29.90) Valid for seven days, offering entrance to 11 civic museums, 16 Chorus churches and Museo Ebraico.

Rolling Venice Card Visitors aged six to 29 years should pick up this €6 card (from tourist offices and most ACTV public transport ticket points), entitling purchase of a 72-hour public transport pass (€22) and discounts on airport transfers, museums, monuments and cultural events.

Water taxis on the Grand Canal (p164)
VIACHESLAV LOPATIN/SHUTTERSTOCK ©

Linea Rossa (Red Line) Stops at Murano and the Lido.

Linea Arancia (Orange Line) Stops at Stazione Santa Lucia, Rialto and San Marco via the Grand Canal.

Linea Gialla (Yellow Line) Stops at Murano and Fondamente Nove.

BUS

ACTV (Azienda del Consorzio Trasporti Veneziano; 📞041 272 21 11; www.actv.it) Runs bus

5 between Marco Polo Airport and Piazzale Roma (€8, 30 minutes, four per hour) with a limited number of stops en route. Alternatively, a bus+*vaporetto* ticket covering the bus journey and a one-way *vaporetto* trip within a total of 90 minutes costs €14.

ATVO (📞0421 59 46 71; www.atvo.it; Piazzale Roma 497g, Santa Croce; ⊘6.40am-7.45pm) Runs a direct bus service between the airport and Piazzale Roma (€8, 25 minutes, every 30 minutes from 8am to midnight). At Piazzale Roma you can pick up the ACTV *vaporetti* to reach locations around Venice.

WATER TAXI

The dock for water transfers to the historic centre is a 10-minute walk from the arrivals hall via a raised, indoor walkway accessed on the 1st floor of the terminal building. Luggage trolleys (requiring a €1 deposit) can be taken to the dock.

Private water taxis can be booked at the **Consorzio Motoscafi Venezia** (📞041 240 67 12; www.motoscafivenezia.it; ⊘9am-6pm) or **Veneziataxi** (📞information 328 238 96 61; www.veneziataxi.it) desks in the arrivals hall, or directly at the dock. Private taxis cost from €110 for up to four passengers and all their luggage. Extra passengers (up to a limit of 12 or 16) carry a small surcharge.

GETTING AROUND VENICE

VAPORETTO

These small passenger ferries are Venice's main public transport. Single rides cost €7.50; for frequent use, get a timed pass for unlimited travel within a set period (1-/2-/3-/7-day passes cost €20/30/40/60). Tickets and passes are available dockside from ACTV ticket booths and ticket vending machines, or from tobacconists.

GONDOLA

Daytime rates run to €80 for 40 minutes (six passengers maximum) or €100 for 35 minutes from 7pm to 8am, not including songs (negotiated separately) or tips.

TRAGHETTO

Locals use this daytime public gondola service (€2) to cross the Grand Canal between bridges.

WATER TAXI

Sleek teak boats offer taxi services for €15 plus €2 per minute, plus €5 for pre-booked services and extra for night-time, luggage and large groups. Ensure the meter is working when you board.

 Where to Stay

Venice was once known for charmingly decrepit hotels where English poets quietly expired, but new design-literate boutique hotels are spiffing up historic palaces.

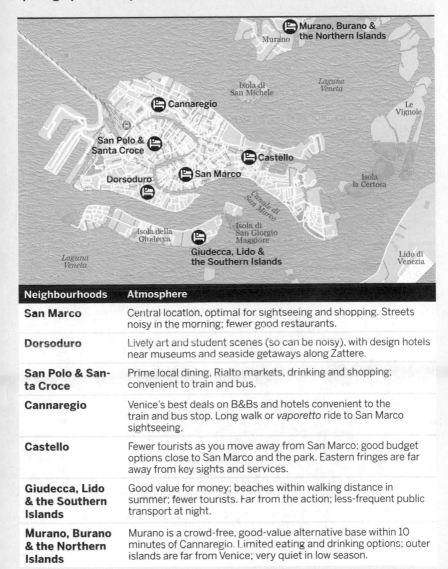

Neighbourhoods	Atmosphere
San Marco	Central location, optimal for sightseeing and shopping. Streets noisy in the morning; fewer good restaurants.
Dorsoduro	Lively art and student scenes (so can be noisy), with design hotels near museums and seaside getaways along Zattere.
San Polo & Santa Croce	Prime local dining, Rialto markets, drinking and shopping; convenient to train and bus.
Cannaregio	Venice's best deals on B&Bs and hotels convenient to the train and bus stop. Long walk or *vaporetto* ride to San Marco sightseeing.
Castello	Fewer tourists as you move away from San Marco; good budget options close to San Marco and the park. Eastern fringes are far away from key sights and services.
Giudecca, Lido & the Southern Islands	Good value for money; beaches within walking distance in summer; fewer tourists. Far from the action; less-frequent public transport at night.
Murano, Burano & the Northern Islands	Murano is a crowd-free, good-value alternative base within 10 minutes of Cannaregio. Limited eating and drinking options; outer islands are far from Venice; very quiet in low season.

MILAN

Milan at a Glance...

Milan is Italy's city of the future, a fast-paced metropolis where creativity is big business, looking good is compulsory and after-work drinks are an art form. Many, however, consider Milan to be vain, distant and dull, and it is true that the city makes little effort to seduce visitors. But this superficial lack of charm disguises a city of ancient roots and many treasures that – unlike in the rest of Italy – you'll often get to experience without the queues. So while the Milanese may not have time to always play nice, jump in and join them in their intoxicating round of pursuits, be that precision shopping, browsing contemporary galleries or loading up a plate with local delicacies.

Milan in Two Days

Start with the blockbuster sights in and around Piazza del Duomo: the **Duomo** (p199), **Galleria Vittorio Emanuele II** (p197) and the **Teatro alla Scala** (p210). Next, immerse yourself in modern art at the **Museo del Novecento** (p203). On day two, stop by Leonardo da Vinci's **The Last Supper** (p201) and the **Pinacoteca di Brera** (p202) before window-shopping in the **Quadrilatero d'Oro** (p196) and an evening canal-side in the Navigli.

Milan in Four Days

Dedicate day three to some lesser-known gems: the **Museo Poldi Pezzoli** (p202) and its cache of Renaissance artworks, the frescoed **Chiesa di San Maurizio** (p203) and the fascinating **Triennale di Milano** (p197). Afterwards, clear your head in **Parco Sempione** (p203) and get in some foodie shopping at legendary deli, **Peck** (p206). On day four, head out of town to the **Certosa di Pavia** (p203), an extraordinary Carthusian monastery.

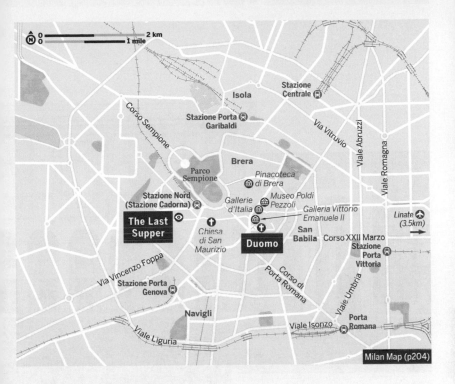

Milan Map (p204)

Arriving in Milan

Malpensa Airport Northern Italy's main international airport, about 50km northwest of Milan. Regular shuttle buses (€10) run to Stazione Centrale. Also, half-hourly express trains (€13) depart Terminal 1 for Stazione Centrale.

Linate Airport Located 7km east of the city, serves domestic and European flights. Half-hourly coaches run to Stazione Centrale.

Stazione Centrale A major national and international rail hub.

Where to Stay

Brera and Parco Sempione have lively art and student scenes and a good selection of historic and design hotels near museums and the park. Duomo and San Babila boast historic and design hotels in a central location, optimal for sightseeing and shopping. Upmarket Corso Magenta and Sant'Ambrogio attract fewer tourists and have some good-value B&Bs and boutique hotels.

Shopping & Design Hot Spots

Milan is a mecca for fashionistas and fans of cutting-edge design. Many of Italy's big-name designers are based here and its streets are lined with flagship stores, showrooms and hip boutiques.

Great For...

☑ **Don't Miss**

Dress up and join the evening *passeggiata* in Galleria Vittorio Emanuele II.

Quadrilatero d'Oro

A stroll around the **Quadrilatero d'Oro** (Golden Quad; Ⓜ Monte Napoleone), the world's most famous shopping district, is a must. This quaintly cobbled quadrangle of streets – bounded by Via Monte Napoleone, Via Sant'Andrea, Via della Spiga and Via Alessandro Manzoni – has always been synonymous with elegance and money (Via Monte Napoleone was where Napoleon's government managed loans). And even if you don't plan on buying anything, the window displays and people-watching are priceless.

Design Heaven

From 19th-century shopping arcades to cutlery and coffee cups, Milanese design marries form, function and style. Judge for yourself at these places:

Triennale di Milano

GIANLUCA DI IOA – COURTESY TRIENNALE DI MILANO ©

iron-and-glass structure known locally
as *il salotto bueno,* the city's fine drawing
room. Shaped like a crucifix, it also marks
the *passeggiata* (evening stroll) route from
Piazza del Duomo to Piazza di Marino and
the doors of Teatro alla Scala (La Scala).
In 2015 a **highline walkway** (☏02 4539
7656; www.highlinegalleria.com; Via Pellico 2;
adult/reduced €12/9; ⊗10am-9pm; ⓂDuomo)
gave access to the Galleria's rooftops for
stunning bird's-eye views of the arcade and
the city.

Studio Museo Achille Castiglioni

Architect, designer and teacher Achille
Castiglioni was one of Italy's most influential 20th-century thinkers. This is the
studio (☏02 805 36 06; http://fondazione
achillecastiglioni.it; Piazza Castello 27; adult/
reduced €10/7; ⊗tours 10am, 11am & noon Tue-
Fri, 6.30pm, 7.30pm & 8.30pm Thu; ⓂCadorna)
where he worked daily until his death in
2002, and the hour-long tours vividly illumi-
nate his intelligent but playful creative process. Details abound and await discovery:
job folders printed with specially produced
numerical stamps; scale models of his Hilly
sofa designed for Cassina; and a host of
inspirational objects from joke glasses to
bicycle seats.

Triennale di Milano

Italy's first Triennale took place in 1923
in Monza. It aimed to promote interest in
Italian design and applied arts, from 'the
spoon to the city', and its success led to
the creation of Giovanni Muzio's **Palazzo
d'Arte** in Milan in 1933. Since then this
exhibition space (☏02 7243 4208; www.
triennaledesignmuseum.it; Viale Emilio Alemanga
6; adult/reduced €10/6.50; ⊗10.30am-8.30pm
Tue-Sun; Ⓟ; ⓂCadorna) has championed design in all its forms, although the triennale
formula has since been replaced by long
annual events, with international exhibits as
part of the program.

Galleria Vittorio Emanuele II

So much more than a shopping arcade, the
neoclassical **Galleria Vittorio Emanuele
II** (Piazza del Duomo; ⓂDuomo) is a soaring

Duomo

Milan's extravagant Gothic Duomo is a soul-stirring sight. Its pearly white facade, adorned with 135 spires and 3400 statues, rises like the filigree of a fairy-tale tiara, wowing the crowds with its extravagant detail.

Commissioned by Giangaleazzo Visconti in 1386 and finished nearly 600 years later, the cathedral boasts a white facade of Candoglia marble and a vast interior punctuated by the largest stained-glass windows in Christendom. Underground, the remains of the saintly Carlo Borromeo are on display in the early Christian baptistry and crypt, while up top the spired roof terraces command stunning views.

Great For...

☑ Don't Miss

The spectacular view through the marble pinnacles on the roof. On a clear day you can see the Alps.

Exterior

During his stint as king of Italy, Napoleon offered to fund the Duomo's completion in 1805, in time for his coronation. The architect piled on the neo-Gothic details and almost all the petrified pinnacles, cusps, buttresses, arches and more than 3000 statues were added in the 19th century.

LEOCHEN66/SHUTTERSTOCK ©

❶ Need to Know

📞02 7202 3375; www.duomomilano.it; Piazza del Duomo; adult/reduced Duomo €2/3, roof terraces via stairs €9/4.50, lift €13/7, archaeological area €7/3; ⏱Duomo 8am-7pm, roof terraces 9am-7pm; Ⓜ Duomo

✕ Take a Break

Head to the sun-trap terrace of **Terrazza Aperol** (📞02 8633 1959; www.terrazzaaperol.it; Piazza del Duomo; cocktails €12 17; ⏱11am-11pm Sun-Fri, to midnight Sat; 📶; Ⓜ Duomo) for a mid-morning *spritz*.

★ Top Tip

It's quicker to walk the stairs to the roof rather than queue for the tiny elevator.

Roof Terraces

Climb to the roof terraces where you'll be within touching distance of the elaborate 135 spires and their forest of flying buttresses. In the centre of the roof rises the 15th-century octagonal lantern and spire, on top of which is the golden *Madonnina* (erected in 1774). For two centuries she was the highest point in the city (108.5m) until the Pirelli skyscraper outdid her in 1958.

Interior

Initially designed to accommodate Milan's then-population of around 40,000, the vast interior is divided into five grandiose naves supported by 52 columns. Looking up you'll see a magnificent set of stained-glass windows, while underfoot the polychrome marble floor sweeps across 12,000 sq metres. Features to look out for include a

1562 figure of St Bartholomew by Marco d'Agrate, a student of Leonardo da Vinci; the *Altar to the Virgin of the Tree*, the most elaborate of the altars in the transept; and the sculpted 17th-century choir.

High up in the apse, a red light marks the location of the cathedral's most precious relic: a nail said to be from Christ's cross.

Crypt

From the ambulatory that encircles the choir, stairs lead down to the crypt, or Winter Choir. This jewel-like circular chapel with its red porphyry pillars, polychrome marble floor and stucco ceiling contains a casket holding the relics of various saints and martyrs.

Through a gap in the crypt's choir stalls, a dark corridor leads to a chapel housing the remains of Carlo Borromeo, cardinal archbishop of Milan (1564–84).

The Last Supper

One of the world's most iconic images, Leonardo da Vinci's **The Last Supper** *depicts Christ and his disciples at the dramatic moment when Christ reveals he's aware of his betrayal.*

Great For...

☑ Don't Miss

Don't miss your allotted visiting time. If you're late you miss out and your ticket will be resold.

The mural, known in Italian as *Il Cenacolo*, is hidden away on a wall of the refectory adjoining the Basilica di Santa Maria delle Grazie. To see it you must book in advance or sign up for a guided city tour.

When Leonardo was at work on the masterpiece, a star-struck monk noted that he would sometimes arrive in the morning, stare at the previous day's efforts, then promptly call it quits for the day. Your visit will be similarly brief (15 minutes to be exact), but the baggage of a thousand dodgy reproductions are quickly shed once standing face to face with the luminous work itself.

Centuries of damage have left the mural in a fragile state despite 22 years of restoration, which was completed in 1999. Da Vinci himself is partly to blame: his experimental mix of oil and tempera was applied between 1495 and 1498, rather than within a week

❶ Need to Know

Il Cenacolo; ☏02 9280 0360; www.cenacolo vinciano.net; Piazza Santa Maria delle Grazie 2; adult/reduced €10/5, plus booking fee €2; ⏲8.15am-6.45pm Tue-Sun; ⓂCadorna

✖ Take a Break

Grab an espresso or beer at **Bar Magenta** (☏02 805 38 08; http://barmagenta. it; Via Giosué Carducci 13; ⏲7.30am-2am; ⓂCadorna).

★ Top Tip

Reservations for *The Last Supper* must be made weeks, if not months, in advance.

as is typical of fresco techniques. The Dominicans didn't help matters when in 1652 they raised the refectory floor, hacking off a lower section of the scene, including Jesus' feet. The most damage was caused by restorers in the 19th century, whose use of alcohol and cotton wool removed an entire layer. But the work's condition does little to lessen its astonishing beauty. Stare at the ethereal, lucent windows beyond the narrative action and you'll wonder if da Vinci's uncharacteristic short-sightedness wasn't divinely inspired.

Basilica di Santa Maria delle Grazie

Any visit to *The Last Supper* should be accompanied by a tour of the **Basilica di Santa Maria delle Grazie** (☏02 467 61 11; www.legraziemilano.it; Piazza Santa Maria delle Grazie; ⏲7am-noon & 3.30-7.30pm Mon-Sat, 7.30am 12.30pm & 4-9pm Sun; ⓂCadorna, ☐16), a Unesco World Heritage site. Designed by Guiniforte Solari, with later additions by Bramante, the basilica encapsulates the magnificence of the Milanese court of Ludovico 'il Moro' Sforza and Beatrice d'Este. Articulated in fine brickwork and terracotta, the building is robust, but fanciful, its apse topped by Bramante's cupola and its interior lined with frescoes.

Codex Atlanticus

The *Codex Atlanticus* is the largest collection of da Vinci's drawings in the world. More than 1700 of them were gathered by sculptor Pompeo Leoni in 12 volumes, so heavy they threatened the preservation of the drawings themselves. The sheets have now been unbound and housed in the **Biblioteca e Pinacoteca Ambrosiana** (☏02 80 69 21; www.ambrosiana.it; Piazza Pio XI 2; adult/reduced €15/10; ⏲10am-6pm Tue-Sun; ⓂDuomo).

◉ SIGHTS

Il Grande Museo del Duomo
Museum

(www.museo.duomomilano.it; Piazza del Duomo 12; adult/reduced €6/4; ⊙10am-6pm Thu-Tue; MDuomo) Stepping through Guido Canali's glowing spaces into the Duomo's museum is like coming upon the sets for an episode of *Game of Thrones*. Gargoyles leer down through the shadows; shafts of light strike the wings of heraldic angels; and a monstrous godhead, once intended for the high altar, glitters awesomely in copper. It's an exciting display, masterfully choreographed through 26 rooms, which tell the 600-year story of the cathedral's construction through priceless sculptures, paintings, stained glass, tapestries and bejewelled treasures.

Museo Poldi Pezzoli
Museum

(☏02 79 48 89; www.museopoldipezzoli.it; Via Alessandro Manzoni 12; adult/reduced €10/7; ⊙10am-6pm Wed-Mon; MMontenapoleone) Inheriting his fortune at the age of 24, Gian Giacomo Poldi Pezzoli also inherited his mother's love of art. During extensive European travels, he was inspired by the 'house museum' that was to become London's V&A and had the idea of transforming his apartments into a series of themed rooms based on the great art periods (the Middle Ages, early Renaissance, baroque etc). Crammed with big-ticket Renaissance artworks, these **Sala d'Artista** are exquisite works of art in their own right.

Pinacoteca di Brera
Gallery

(☏02 72 26 31; www.pinacotecabrera.org; Via Brera 28; adult/reduced €10/7; ⊙8.30am-7.15pm Tue-Wed & Fri-Sun, to 10.15pm Thu; MLanza, Montenapoleone) Located upstairs from the centuries-old Accademia di Belle Arti (still one of Italy's most prestigious art schools), this gallery houses Milan's impressive collection of Old Masters, much of it 'lifted' from Venice by Napoleon. Rubens, Goya and Van Dyck all have a place in the collection, but you're here for the Italians: Titian, Tintoretto, Veronese and the Bellini brothers. Much of the work has tremendous emotional clout, most notably Mantegna's brutal *Lamentation over the Dead Christ*.

Frescoes in Chiesa di San Maurizio

CENZO7/SHUTTERSTOCK ©

Chiesa di San Maurizio   Church

(📞02 8844 5208; Corso Magenta 15; ⏰9.30am-7.30pm Tue-Sun; Ⓜ️Cadorna) This 16th-century royal chapel and one-time Benedictine convent is Milan's hidden crown jewel, every inch of it covered in breathtaking frescoes, most of them executed by Bernardino Luini, who worked with Leonardo da Vinci. Many of the frescoes immortalise Ippolita Sforza, Milanese literary maven, and other members of the powerful Sforza and Bentivoglio clans who paid for the chapel's decoration.

Museo del Novecento   Gallery

(📞02 8844 4061; www.museodelnovecento.org; Via Marconi 1; adult/reduced €10/8; ⏰2.30-7.30pm Mon, 9.30am-7.30pm Tue, Wed, Fri & Sun, to 10.30pm Thu & Sat; Ⓜ️Duomo) Overlooking Piazza del Duomo, with fabulous views of the cathedral, is Mussolini's Arengario, from where he would harangue huge crowds in his heyday. Now it houses Milan's museum of 20th-century art. Built around a futuristic spiral ramp (an ode to the Guggenheim), the lower floors are cramped, but the heady collection, which includes the likes of Umberto Boccioni, Campigli, de Chirico and Marinetti, more than distracts.

Gallerie d'Italia   Museum

(www.gallerieditalia.com; Piazza della Scala 6; adult/reduced €10/8, ⏰9.30am-7.30pm Tue-Wed & Fri-Sun, to 10.30pm Thu; Ⓜ️Duomo) Housed in three fabulously decorated palaces, the enormous art collection of Fondazione Cariplo and Intesa Sanpaolo bank pays homage to 18th- and 19th-century Lombard painting. From a magnificent sequence of bas-reliefs by Antonio Canova to luminous Romantic masterpieces by Francesco Hayez, the works span 23 rooms and document Milan's significant contribution to the rebirth of Italian sculpture, the patriotic romanticism of the Risorgimento (reunification period) and the birth of futurism at the dawn of the 20th century.

Parco Sempione   Park

(⏰6.30am-nightfall; 🚻; Ⓜ️Cadorna, Lanza) Situated behind Castello Sforzesco, Parco Sempione was once the preserve of hunt-

📍 Certosa di Pavia

One of the Italian Renaissance's most notable buildings is the splendid **Certosa di Pavia** (📞0382 92 56 13; www.certosadipavia.com; Viale Monumento; entry by donation; ⏰9-11.30am & 2.30-5.30pm Tue-Sun summer, to 4.30pm winter) **FREE**. Giangaleazzo Visconti of Milan founded the monastery, 10km north of Pavia, in 1396 as a private chapel and mausoleum for the Visconti family. Originally intended as an architectural companion piece to Milan's Duomo, the same architects worked on its design; the final result, however, completed more than a century later, is a unique hybrid between late-Gothic and Renaissance styles.

The church is fronted by a spacious courtyard and flanked by a small cloister, which itself leads onto a much grander, second cloister, under whose arches are 24 cells, each a self-contained living area for one monk. Several cells are open to the public, but you need to join one of the guided tours (Italian only) to access them. In the former sacristy is a giant sculpture, dating from 1409 and made from hippopotamus teeth, including 66 small bas-reliefs and 94 statuettes. In the chapels you'll find frescoes by, among others, Bernardino Luini and the Umbrian master Il Perugino.

Interior of Certosa di Pavia
GIMAS/SHUTTERSTOCK ©

ing Sforza dukes. Then Napoleon came to town and set about landscaping. First the French carved out orchards; next they

Milan

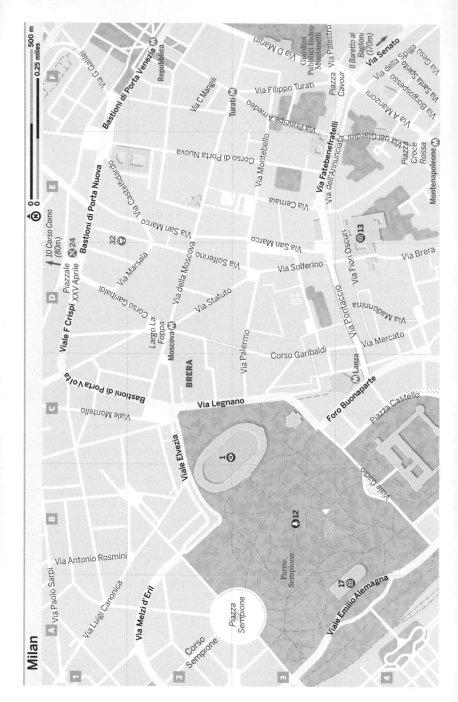

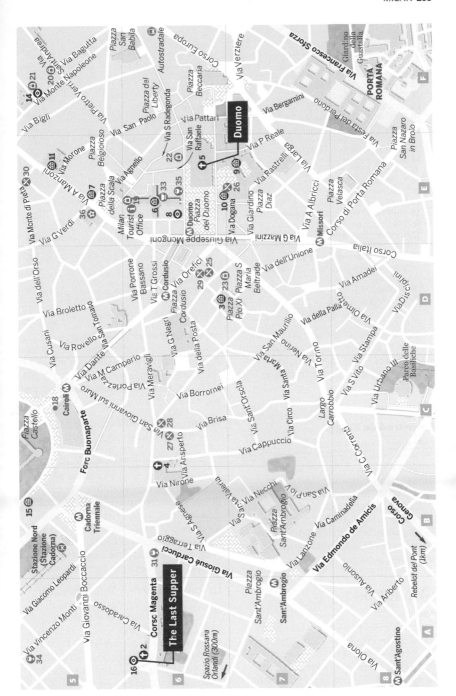

Milan

mooted the idea in 1891 for a vast public park. It was a resounding success and even today Milanese of all ages come to enjoy its winding paths and ornamental ponds.

🎫 TOURS

Autostradale Viaggi　　Tours
(☑02 3008 9900; www.autostradaleviaggi.it; Piazza Castello 1; tours €75; ⊙9am-6pm Mon-Fri, 9am-2pm Sat & Sun; 📠; Ⓜ Cairoli) Autostradale's three-hour city bus tours include admission to *The Last Supper,* Castello Sforzesco and the Teatro alla Scala (La Scala) museum. Tours run Tuesday to Sunday and depart either from the Central Station at 9am or from the taxi rank on the western side of Piazza del Duomo at 9.30am.

🛍 SHOPPING

Peck　　Food & Drinks
(☑02 802 31 61; www.peck.it; Via Spadari 9; ⊙3-8pm Mon, 9am-8pm Tue-Sat, 10am-5pm Sun; 📶; Ⓜ Duomo) Milan's historic deli is a bastion of the city's culinary heritage with three floors below ground dedicated to turning

out the fabulously colourful display of foods that cram every counter. It showcases a mind-boggling selection of cheeses, chocolates, pralines, pastries, freshly made gelato, seafood, meat, caviar, pâté, fruit and vegetables, olive oils and balsamic vinegars.

Brioni　　Fashion & Accessories
(☑02 7639 0086; www.brioni.com; Via Gesù 2-4; ⊙10am-7pm Tue-Sat; Ⓜ Montenapoleone) Founded in Rome in 1945, Brioni has been synonymous with luxury since the get-go. The name was 'borrowed' from the beautiful Brijuni Islands in Croatia, a favoured destination of the European jet set. Nowadays the great and good are catered to in a three-floor flagship store decked out in Eramosa marble, bronze and plate glass, where six experienced tailors offer bespoke services.

La Rinascente　　Department Store
(☑02 8 85 21; www.rinascente.it; Piazza del Duomo; ⊙9.30am-9pm Mon-Thu & Sun, to 10pm Sat; Ⓜ Duomo) Italy's most prestigious department store doesn't let the fashion capital down – come for Italian diffusion lines, French lovelies and LA upstarts. The basement also hides a 'Made in Italy'

design supermarket and chic hairdresser Aldo Coppola is on the top floor. Take away edible souvenirs from the 7th-floor food market.

Borsalino   Fashion & Accessories

(☑02 8901 5436; www.borsalino.com; Galleria Vittorio Emanuele II 92; ⊗3-7pm Mon, 10am-7pm Tue-Sat; ⓂDuomo) Iconic Alessandrian milliner Borsalino has worked with design greats such as Achille Castiglioni, who once designed a pudding-bowl bowler hat. This outlet in the Galleria Vittoria Emanuele II shopping arcade stocks seasonal favourites. The main showroom is at **Via Sant'Andrea 5** (☑02 7601 7072; ⊗10am-7pm Mon-Sat; ⓂMontenapoleone).

**Spazio Rossana
Orlandi**   Homewares

(☑02 467 44 71; www.rossanaorlandi.com; Via Matteo Bandello 14; ⊗10am-7pm Mon-Sat; ⓂSant'Ambrogio) Installed in a former tie factory in the Magenta district, this iconic interior design studio is a challenge to find. Once inside, though, it's hard to leave the dream-like treasure trove stacked with vintage and contemporary limited-edition pieces from young and upcoming artists.

**10 Corso
Como**   Fashion & Accessories

(☑02 2900 2674; www.10corsocomo.com; Corso Como 10; ⊗10.30am-7.30pm Fri-Tue, to 9pm Wed & Thu; ⓂGaribaldi) This might be the world's most hyped 'concept shop', but Carla Sozzani's selection of desirable things (Lanvin ballet flats, Alexander Girard wooden dolls, a demicouture frock by a designer you've not read about *yet*) makes 10 Corso Como a fun window-shopping experience. There's a bookshop upstairs with art and design titles, and a hyper-stylish bar and restaurant in the main atrium and picture-perfect courtyard.

⊗ EATING

Pasticceria Marchesi   Pastries €

(☑02 86 27 70; www.pasticceriamarchesi.it; Via Santa Maria alla Porta 11/a; ⊗7.30am-8pm Mon-

Sat, 8.30am-1pm Sun; ⓂCairoli, Cordusio) This wood-panelled *pasticceria* (pastry shop) has been baking since 1824 and turns out 10 different types of brioche alongside bignes, millefeuilles, croissants, pralines and more. The window displays have the wonky logic of a Hitchcock dream sequence, but with perfect-every-shot coffee, there's no shock ending.

Berberè   Pizza €

(☑02 3670 7820; www.berberepizza.it; Via Sebenico 21; pizza €6.50-14; ⊗7-11.30pm Mon-Fri, 12.30-2.30pm & 7-11.30pm Sat & Sun; 🖈; Ⓜ Isola) Craft pizzas and craft beers is what Bolognese brothers Matteo and Salvatore promise you at this fantastically good pizzeria housed in an atmospheric 1950s cooperative. Everything from the Black Elk flour (they use variations of spelt, enkir and kamut, which give a lighter finish than wheat) to the Ponteré mozzarella, the Torre Guaceto tomatoes and Puglian *fiordilatte* (a semi-soft cheese) is sourced obsessively for the optimum flavour punch. Book ahead.

**Il Luogo di
Aimo e Nadia**   Modern Italian €€€

(☑02 41 68 86; www.aimoenadia.com; Via Montecuccoli 6; meals €95-145; ⊗12.30-2pm & 7.30-10.30pm Mon-Fri, 7.30-10.30pm Sat; ⓂPrimaticcio) For the Milanese, food should be like clothing: excellent, imaginative, seasonal and suitable for all occasions. Not surprisingly, all adore this two-Michelin-starred restaurant, which offers seasonal dishes such as *tagliolini* (a ribbon pasta) with truffles and turnips in winter, and prawns in pistachio crust with artichokes in spring.

Seta   Gastronomy €€€

(Mandarin Oriental; ☑02 8731 8897; www.mandarinoriental.com; Via Andegari 9; meals €120; ⊗12.30-2.30pm & 7.30-10.30pm Mon-Fri, 7.30-10.30pm Sat; 🅿🕸🛜; ⓂMontenapoleone) Smooth as the silk after which it is named, Seta is Michelin-starred dining at its best: beautiful, inventive and full of flavour surprises. Diners sit on the edge of their

Aperitivo

Happy hour elsewhere in the world might mean downing cut-price pints and stale crisps, but not in oh-so-stylish Milan. Its nightly *aperitivo* is a two- or three-hour ritual, starting around 6pm, where for €8 to €20, a cocktail, glass of wine, or beer comes with an unlimited buffet of bruschetta, foccacia, cured meats, salads, and even seafood and pasta. (Occasionally you'll pay a cover charge up front that includes a drink and buffet fare, which generally works out the same.) Take a plate and help yourself; snacks are also sometimes brought to your table. Most of the city's bars offer *aperitivi*, in some form or other.

teal-coloured velvet chairs in keen anticipation of Antonio Guida's inspired dishes such as plum-coloured roe deer with a dazzling splash of mango salsa. It's both solidly traditional and subtly daring, just like Milan.

Cracco — Modern Italian €€€

(☑02 87 67 74; www.ristorantecracco.it; Via Victor Hugo 4; meals €130-160; ⊙12.30-2pm & 7.30pm-12.30am Tue-Fri, 7.30-11pm Mon & Sat; ⓂDuomo) Two Michelin-star chef Carlo Cracco keeps the Milanese in thrall with his off-the-wall inventiveness. The *risotto al sedano, rapa, tartufo nero e caffè* (risotto with celery, turnip, black truffle and coffee) is unlike any northern Italian rice dish you may have stumbled across elsewhere. Let the waiters do the thinking by ordering one of the tasting menus (€130 and €160).

La Brisa — Modern Italian €€€

(☑02 8645 0521; www.ristorantelabrisa.it; Via Brisa 15; meals €50-70; ⊙12.45-2.30pm & 7.45-10.30pm Mon-Fri, 7.45-10.30pm Sun; ✤; ⓂCairoli, Cordusio) Discreet, elegant and exquisitely romantic. Push open the screened door and the maître d' will guide you to a table beneath centuries-old linden trees in a secluded courtyard, where ivy climbs the walls and pink hydrangeas bob in the breeze. Chef Antonio Facciolo's seasonal menus are similarly elegant; his signature dish is a mouth-watering roast pork in a myrtle-berry drizzle.

Il Baretto al Baglioni — Milanese €€€

(☑02 78 12 55; www.ilbarettoalbaglioni.it; Via Senato 7; meals €60; ⊙12.30-3pm & 7.30-11pm; ✤ ⧉; ⓂSan Babila) Il Baretto's cosy, clubby atmosphere and top-notch, no-nonsense Milanese menu keep its wood-pannelled dining rooms packed with silver-haired foxes and their bejewelled partners. The typical Milanese repertoire here includes not only *cotoletta* and osso bucco but an unforgettable white truffle risotto and *riso salto* (pan-fried risotto cakes).

Alice Ristorante — Modern Italian €€€

(☑02 4949 7340; www.aliceristorante.it; Piazza XXV Aprile, Eataly; meals €40-50; ⊙12.30-2pm & 7.30-10pm Mon-Sat; ✤ ⧉; ⓂMoscova, Garibaldi) The one-Michelin -tarred restaurant of talented chef Viviana Varese and sommelier and fish expert Sandra Ciciriello is the pride of Eataly's foodstore. The artful furnishings and views over Piazza XXV Aprile are a match for the superlative food and the menu is full of humour, with dishes such as Polp Fiction (octopus with zucchini trumpets) and That Ball! (truffle ice cream with chocolate, *zabaglione* and cocoa).

🍷 DRINKING & NIGHTLIFE

Pasticceria Marchesi — Cafe

(☑02 9418 1710; www.pasticceriamarchesi. it; Galleria Vittorio Emanuele II; ⊙7.30am-9pm; ⓂDuomo) With an 80% stake in the historic bakery, Prada has opened a luxurious new cafe on the 1st floor of its menswear store in the Galleria. Overlooking the mosaics down below, the lounge is decked out in green floral jacquard and velvet armchairs. Come for high tea or the excellent *aperitivo*, although expect a wait as service is snooze-inducing.

Dry   Cocktail Bar

(📞02 6379 3414; www.drymilano.it; Via Solferino 33; cocktails €8-13, meals €20-25; ⊙7pm-1.30am; 📶; MMoscova) The brainchild of Michelin-starred chef Andrea Berton, Dry pairs its cocktails with gourmet pizzas. The inventive cocktail list includes the Corpse Reviver (London Dry gin, Cointreau, Cocchi Americano and lemon juice) and the Martinez (Boompjes genever, vermouth, Maraschino liqueur and Boker's bitters), the latter inspired by French gold hunters in Martinez, the birthplace of barman Jerry Thomas.

Rebelot del Pont   Cocktail Bar

(📞02 8419 4720; www.rebelotdelpont.com; Ripa di Porta Ticinese 55; ⊙6pm-2am Mon-Sat, noon-midnight Sun; 🚊2, 9, 14, 19) *Rebelot*

means 'pandemonium' in Milanese dialect and this place certainly pushes out the culinary and cocktail boat. Squired by top World Bartender Oscar Quagliarini, you can expect taste sensations such as the Marrakech Souk (blended whisky and spiced honey) and the Garden Sazerac (Monkey 47 gin, cherry liqueur, absinthe and a homemade 'perfume').

Botanical Club   Bar

(📞02 3652 3846; www.thebotanicalclub.com; Via Pastrengo 11; meals €25-30; ⊙12.30-2.30pm & 6.30-10.30pm Mon-Fri, 6.30-10.30pm Sat; 📶; MIsola) This bar, bistro and gin distillery is Italy's first foray into the micro-distillery trend. Behind a bar festooned in greenery, mixologist Katerina Logvinova has over 150 gins to play with, including the house brand, Spleen & Ideal, which experiments with interesting botanicals such as Serbian juniper and tonka beans. To accompany divine concoctions like Chinese Dusk (London Dry gin, sake, plum bitter and fruit liqueur) are contemporary plates of veal tartare and crab salad with green apple.

Chefs at Alice Ristorante

Teatro alla Scala

Ricerca Vini   Wine Bar

(02 4819 3496; www.ricercavini.it; Via Vicenzo Monti 33; ⊙10am-1pm & 3.30-10pm Tue-Sat, 4-10pm Mon; MCadorna) Sure, it's a wine shop, but it's a bar and a rather good restaurant, too. What better place to sample your options before committing to carry home one of the 2500 wines on offer here. It's one of the largest selections in the city, and the *aperitivo* platters of prosciutto and cheese are excellent.

🟆 ENTERTAINMENT

Teatro alla Scala   Opera

(La Scala; 02 7200 3744; www.teatroalla scala.org; Piazza della Scala; tickets €30-300; MDuomo) On one of the most famous opera stages in the world, La Scala's season runs from early December through July. You can also see theatre, ballet and concerts here year-round (except August). Buy tickets online or by phone up to two months before the performance, or from the central box office. On performance days, tickets for

the gallery are available from the box office at Via Filodrammatici 2 (one ticket per customer). Queue early.

🛈 INFORMATION

Milan Tourist Office (02 8845 5555; www. turismo.milano.it; Galleria Vittorio Emanuele II 11-12; ⊙9am-7pm Mon-Fri, to 6pm Sat, 10am-6pm Sun; MDuomo) Centrally located in the Galleria with helpful English-speaking staff and tonnes of maps and brochures.

🛈 GETTING THERE & AWAY

AIR

Linate Airport (LIN; 02 23 23 23; www.milano-linate-airport.com) Located 7km east of the city centre, handles the majority of domestic and a handful of European flights.

Malpensa (p341) Located 50km northwest of Milan and is northern Italy's main airport.

Orio al Serio Airport (035 32 63 23; www. sacbo.it) Located 45km northeast of Milan, and

4km southeast of Bergamo. It receives flights run by a number of budget European carriers, including Ryanair.

BUS

Buses converge on Milan from most major European cities. Most services depart from and terminate in **Lampugnano Bus Terminal** (Via Giulia Natta; MLampugnano).

Autostradale (☎02 3008 9300; www. autostradale.it) is the main national operator. Tickets can be purchased at its offices or at the tourist office.

TRAIN

Milan is a major European rail hub. High-speed services arrive at **Stazione Centrale** (www.mi lanocentrale.it; Piazza Duca d'Aosta; ☺4am-1am; MCentrale) from across Italy, and from France, Switzerland and Germany. An overnight sleeper train also runs from Barcelona (Spain). For train timetables and fares, check out www.trenitalia. com, www.sbb.ch and www.bahn.de.

 GETTING AROUND

TO/FROM THE AIRPORT

BUS

Malpensa Shuttle (☎02 5858 3185; www. malpensashuttle.it; one-way/return €10/16; MCentrale) This Malpensa airport shuttle runs every 20 minutes between 5am and 10.30pm from Stazione Centrale, and hourly throughout the rest of the night. It stops at both terminals and the journey time is 50 minutes.

Airport Bus Express (☎02 3391 0794; www. airportbusexpress.it; one-way/return €5/9; MCentrale) From Linate coaches run to Stazione Centrale (€5 one-way, 25 minutes) every 30 min-

utes between 5.30am and 10pm; ATM city bus 73 departs to Piazza San Babila (€1.50, 25 minutes) every 10 minutes between 5.35am and 12.35am.

Orio al Serio Bus Express (☎02 3008 9300; www.airportbusexpress.it; one-way/return €5/9; MCentrale) This service runs to Stazione Centrale (adult/child €5/4, one hour) every 30 minutes from 4.25am to 10.20pm; Autostradale also runs a half-hourly service to Stazione Centrale (adult/child €5/3.50) between 7.45am and 12.15am.

TAXI

There is a flat fee of €90 between Malpensa Airport and central Milan. The drive should take 50 minutes outside peak traffic times. For travellers to Terminal 2, this might prove the quickest option. The taxi fare to Linate Airport is between €20 and €30.

TRAIN

Malpensa Express (☎02 7249 4949; www. malpensaexpress.it) trains run to the city centre (€13 one-way, 50 minutes) every 30 minutes from 5.40am to 10.40pm.

PUBLIC TRANSPORT

ATM (Azienda Trasporti Milano; ☎02 4860 7607; www.atm.it) runs the metro, buses and trams. The metro is the most convenient way to get around and consists of four underground lines (red M1, green M2, yellow M3 and lilac M5) and a suburban rail network, the blue Passante Ferroviario. Services run from 6am to 12.30am. A ticket costs €1.50 and is valid for one metro ride or up to 90 minutes' travel on buses and trams. Tickets are sold at metro stations, tobacconists and newspaper stands. Tickets must be validated on trams and buses. Bus and tram route maps are available at ATM Info points, or download the IATM app.

ITALIAN LAKES

Italian Lakes at a Glance...

Formed at the end of the last ice age, and a popular holiday spot since Roman times, the Italian Lakes have an enduring, beguiling beauty. Travellers will be greeted by a Mediterranean burst of colour: gardens filled with rose-red camellias, hot-pink oleanders and luxurious palms surrounding cerulean blue lakes. It's impossible not to be seduced. Fishing boats bob in tiny harbours, palaces float in the Borromean Gulf, rustic churches cling to cliff faces and grand belle-époque spas and hotels line the waterfronts.

Italian Lakes in Two Days

Begin in belle-époque **Stresa** (p221) and ferry-hop to the Borromean palaces on **Isola Bella** (p218) and **Isola Madre** (p219). On your second day launch off on a ferry to Verbania to visit the voluptuous gardens at **Villa Taranto** (p222).

Italian Lakes in Four Days

Spend day three in **Como** (p223), where you can amble the flower-laden promenade to **Villa Olmo** (p224), visit the frescoed **Basilica di San Fedele** (p223) and zip up to Brunate for pretty walks and panoramic views. Press on to **Bellagio** (p216) on the fourth day, which sits in the centre of the lake, allowing you to ferry-hop to **Tremezzo** (p225).

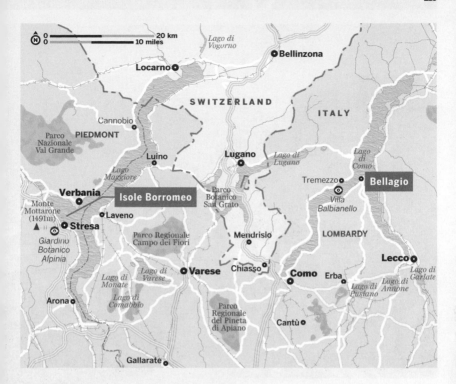

0 / 20 km
0 / 10 miles

Lago di Vogorno

Bellinzona

Locarno

SWITZERLAND

ITALY

Cannobio

Parco Nazionale Val Grande

PIEDMONT

Luino

Lugano

Lago di Lugano

Lago di Como

Tremezzo

Bellagio

Lago Maggiore

Verbania

Isole Borromeo

Parco Botanico San Grato

Villa Balbianello

Monte Mottarone (1491m)

Laveno

Stresa

Parco Regionale Campo dei Fiori

Mendrisio

LOMBARDY

Giardino Botanico Alpinia

Lecco

Lago di Garlate

Lago di Monate

Lago di Varese

Varese

Chiasso

Como

Erba

Lago di Pustano

Lago di Annone

Arona

Lago di Comabbio

Parco Regionale del Pineta di Apiano

Cantù

Gallarate

Arriving in Italian Lakes

For Lago Maggiore, hourly trains leave Milan's Stazione Centrale for Stresa (on the Domodossola line), a convenient base on the lake's western shore. For Lago di Como, hourly services depart Stazione Centrale and Porta Garibaldi to Como San Giovanni. Trains from Milan's Stazione Nord also serve Como's lakeside Stazione FNM (listed on timetables as Como Nord Lago).

Where to Stay

Cannobio on Lake Maggiore, just 5km from the Swiss border, is a dreamy place with some of the best hotels on the lake. Como's pedestrianised core is chock-full of places to sleep, making the town an ideal southern Lago di Como base. Bellagio draws the summer Lake Como crowds – stay overnight for the full magical effect. Seasonal closings are generally from November to February.

Explore Bellagio

It's impossible not to be smitten by Bellagio's waterfront of bobbing boats and its maze of steep stone staircases, red-roofed and green-shuttered buildings, dark cypress groves and rhododendron-filled gardens.

Great For...

☑ Don't Miss

Bellagio's new Lido with sand-scattered decking and diving platforms over the lake.

Bellagio's peerless position on the promontory jutting out into the centre of the inverted Y-shape of **Lago di Como** made it the object of much squabbling between Milan and Como, hence its ruined fortifications and its Romanesque **Basilica di San Giacomo** (Piazza della Chiesa; ⊗9am-5pm), built by Como masters between 1075 and 1125. These days it teems with visitors in summer, but if you turn up out of season, you'll have it almost to yourself.

Villa Serbelloni

Bellagio has been a favoured summer resort since Roman times, when Pliny the Younger holidayed on the promontory where **Villa Serbelloni** (✆031 95 15 55; Piazza della Chiesa 14; adult/child €9/5; ⊗tours 11.30am & 3.30pm Tue-Sun mid-Mar–Oct) now stands. The Romans introduced the olive and laurel trees that dot the villa's 20-hectare gardens, which took on

ORIENTALPRINCESS/SHUTTERSTOCK ©

ℹ️ Need to Know

Useful information is provided by local businesses at **PromoBellagio** (📞031 95 15 55; www.bellagiolakecomo.com; Piazza della Chiesa 14; ⊙9.30am-1pm Mon, 9-11am & 2.30-3.30pm Tue-Sun Apr-Oct).

✕ Take a Break

Dine on the terrace at **Albergo Silvio** (📞031 95 03 22; www.bellagiosilvio.com; Via Carcano 12; meals €28-38; ⊙noon-3pm & 6.30-10pm Mar–mid-Nov & Christmas week).

★ Top Tip

The gardens are at their finest between March and May when the flowers are in bloom.

their Italianate, English and Mediterranean designs at the beginning of the 19th century. The villa, which has hosted Europe's great and good, including Austria's emperor Maximilian I, Ludovico il Moro and Queen Victoria, is now privately owned by the Rockefeller Foundation. The interior is closed to the public, but you can explore the terraced park and gardens by guided tour. Numbers are limited; tickets are sold at the PromoBellagio information office near the church.

Villa Melzi d'Eril

Built in 1808 for Francesco Melzi d'Eril (1753–1816), Napoleon's adviser and vice-president of the First Italian Republic, neoclassical **Villa Melzi d'Eril** (📞339 4573838; www.giardinidivillamelzi.it; Lungo Lario Manzoni; adult/reduced €6.50/4; ⊙9.30am-6.30pm Apr-Oct) is one of the most elegant villas on the lake. The neoclassical temple is where Liszt came over

all romantic and composed his 1837 sonata dedicated to Dante and Beatrice.

The walk to Villa Melzi, south along the lake shore from the Bellagio ferry jetties, reveals views of ranks of gracious residencies stacked up on the waterside hills.

Lake Tours

For a touch of Clooney-esque glamour, consider taking a tour of the lake in one of the slick mahogany cigarette boats operated by **Barindelli's** (📞338 211 03 37; www.barindellitaxiboats.it; Piazza Mazzini; tours per hr €150). Hour-long sunset tours (€140 for up to 12 people) take you around Bellagio's headland, where you can view the splendour of Villa Serbelloni from the water. Alternatively, DIY it on a kayak tour with **Bellagio Water Sports** (📞340 394 93 75; www.bellagiowatersports.com; Pescallo Harbour; rental per 2/4hr €18/30, tours €35; ⊙8.30am-4.30pm Mon-Sat, to 2.30pm Sun), an experienced outfit in Pescallo, on the east side of the Bellagio headland.

Isole Borromeo

The Borromean Gulf forms Lago Maggiore's most beautiful corner, and the Isole Borromeo (Borromean Islands) harbour its most spectacular sights: the privately owned palaces of the Borromeo family.

Great For...

☑ **Don't Miss**

The 3000-year-old fossilised boat displayed in the grotto of Palazzo Borromeo.

Isola Bella

The grandest and busiest of the islands – the crowds can get a little overwhelming on weekends – Isola Bella is the centrepiece of the Borromeo Lake Maggiore empire. The island, the closest to Stresa, took the name of Carlo III's wife, Isabella, in the 17th century, when its centrepiece, **Palazzo Borromeo** (☑0323 3 05 56; www.isoleborromee.it; adult/child €16/8.50, incl Palazzo Madre €21/10; ☻9am-5.30pm mid-Mar–mid-Oct), was built for the Borromeo family.

Presiding over 10 tiers of spectacular terraced gardens, this baroque palace is Lago Maggiore's finest building. Wandering its sumptuous interiors reveals guest rooms, studies and reception halls. Particularly striking are the **Sala di Napoleone**, where the emperor Napoleon stayed with his wife in 1797; the **Sala da Ballo** (Ballroom); the ornate **Sala del Trono** (Throne Room); and

Palazzo Borromeo

ELITRAVO/SHUTTERSTOCK ©

Isola Madre

Baveno

Isola Superiore
(Pescatori) **Isole Borromeo**

Lago Maggiore

Isola Bella

Stresa

❶ Need to Know

A combined ticket covers admission to Palazzo Borromeo and Palazzo Madre.

✕ Take a Break

Stop for lunch on Isola Superiore at **Casabella** (☏0323 3 34 71; www.isola-pescatori.it; Via del Marinaio 1; meals €30-50, five-course tasting menu €55; ⏲noon-2pm & 6-8.30pm Feb-Nov).

★ Top Tip

Give yourself at least half a day to enjoy each palace.

the **Sala delle Regine** (Queen's Room). Paintings from a 130-strong Borromeo collection hang all around.

Isola Madre

The fabulous **Palazzo Madre** *is* the **island of Madre** (☏0323 3 05 56; www.isoleborromee.it; adult/child €13/6.50, incl Palazzo Borromeo €21/10; ⏲9am-5.30pm mid-Mar–mid-Oct). The 16th- to 18th-century *palazzo* is a wonderfully decadent structure crammed full of all manner of antique furnishings and adornments. Highlights include Countess Borromeo's doll collection, a neoclassical puppet theatre designed by a scenographer from Milan's La Scala, and a 'horror' theatre with a cast of devilish marionettes.

Outside, the palace's **gardens** are even more lavish than those of Palazzo Borromeo on Isola Bella, although in June 2006 a freak tornado struck the island, uprooting many of the island's prized plants. Nevertheless, this English-style botanic garden remains full of interest, with azaleas, rhododendrons, camellias, eucalypts, banana trees, hibiscus, fruit orchards, an olive grove and much more. Exotic birdlife, including white peacocks and golden pheasants, roam the grounds.

Isola Superiore (Pescatori)

Tiny 'Fishermen's Island', with a permanent population of around 50, retains much of its original fishing-village atmosphere. Apart from an 11th-century apse and a 16th-century fresco in the charming **Chiesa di San Vittore**, there are no real sights. Many visitors make it their port of call for lunch, but stay overnight and you'll fall in love with the place. Restaurants cluster around the boat landing, all serving grilled fish fresh from the lake (from around €15). On some days in spring and autumn, abundant rainfalls can lift the lake's level a fraction, causing minor flooding on the island. The houses are built with this in mind, with entrance stairs facing internal streets and situated high enough to prevent water entering the houses.

Lago Maggiore

If Lake Maggiore is your first impression of Italy, you're in for a treat. By train or by road, travellers traversing the Alps from Switzerland at the Simplon Pass wind down from the mountains and sidle up to this enormous finger of blue beauty. The star attractions are the Borromean Islands, which, like a fleet of fine vessels, lie at anchor at the Borromean Gulf's (Golfo Borromeo) entrance, an incursion of water between the lake's two main towns, Stresa and Verbania.

More than its siblings to the east, Lake Como and Lake Garda, Lake Maggiore has retained a belle-époque air. All three have mesmerised foreign visitors down the centuries but Lake Maggiore became a popular tourist destination in the late 19th century after the Simplon Pass was opened.

ⓘ GETTING THERE & AROUND

BOAT

Navigazione Lago Maggiore (☑800 551801; www.navigazionelaghi.it) operates passenger ferries and hydrofoils around the lake; its ticket booths are next to embarkation quays. Services include those connecting Stresa with Arona (€6.20, 40 minutes), Angera (€6.20, 35 minutes) and Verbania Pallanza (often just called Pallanza; €5, 35 minutes). Day passes include a ticket linking Stresa with Isola Superiore, Isola Bella and Isola Madre (€16.90). Services are drastically reduced in autumn and winter.

The only car ferry connecting the western and eastern shores sails between Verbania Intra (often just called Intra) and Laveno. Car ferries run every 20 to 30 minutes; one-way transport costs from €8 to €13 for a car and driver; and €5 for a bicycle and cyclist.

BUS

SAF offers a daily Verbania Intra–Milan service that links Stresa with Arona (€2.70, 20 minutes), Verbania Pallanza (€2.70, 20 minutes), Verbania Intra (€2.70, 25 minutes) and Milan (€10.50, 1½ hours).

TRAIN

Stresa is 1¼ hours from Milan (from €8.60, trains every 30 to 90 minutes) on the Domodossola–

Funivia Stresa–Mottarone

Milan train line. Domodossola (€4.15 to €9.90), 30 minutes northwest, is on the Swiss border, from where seven trains daily head to Brig – with four trains continuing on to Geneva.

Stresa

Perhaps more than any other Lake Maggiore town, Stresa, with a ringside view of sunrise over the lake, captures the lake's prevailing air of elegance and bygone decadence. This is most evident in the string of belle-époque confections along the waterfront, a legacy of the town's easy access from Milan, which has made it a favourite for artists and writers since the late 19th century.

People still stream into Stresa to meander along its promenade and explore the little hive of cobbled streets in its old centre (especially pleasant for a coffee break is shady Piazza Cadorna).

⊕ ACTIVITIES

Lago Maggiore Express   Tours
(☑091 756 04 00; www.lagomaggioreexpress.com; adult/child 1-day tour €34/17, 2-day tour €44/22) The Lago Maggiore Express is a picturesque day trip you can do under your own steam. It includes train travel from Arona or Stresa to Domodossola, from where you get the charming Centovalli (Hundred Valleys) train to Locarno in Switzerland, before hopping on a ferry back to Stresa. Tickets are available from the Navigazione Lago Maggiore ticket booths at each port.

The two-day version is better value if you have the time.

⊗ EATING

**Ristorante Il
Vicoletto**   Ristorante €€
(☑0323 93 21 02; www.ristorantevicoletto.com; Vicolo del Pocivo 3; meals €30-45; ⊙noon-2pm & 6.30-10pm Fri-Wed) One of the most popular restaurants in Stresa, Il Vicoletto has a delectable regional menu including lake trout, wild asparagus, and traditional risotto with radicchio and Taleggio (cheese). The dining

 Monte Mottarone

The cable-car trip up **Monte Mottarone** (1492m) from the northwestern end of Stresa offers pretty views over Lake Maggiore, including Isola Bella and Isola Superiore. From the summit on a clear day you can see Lake Orta, several other smaller lakes and Monte Rosa, on the Alpine border with Switzerland.

The 20-minute cable-car journey on the **Funivia Stresa–Mottarone** (☑0323 3 02 95; www.stresa-mottarone.it; Piazzale della Funivia; return adult/reduced €19/12, to Alpino station €13.50/8.50; ⊙9.30am-5.40pm Apr-Oct, 8.10am-5.20pm Nov-Mar) takes you to the Mottarone station at 1385m, from where it's a 15-minute walk or free chairlift (when it's working) up to the summit. At the Alpino midstation (803m) more than a thousand Alpine and sub-Alpine species flourish in the **Giardino Botanico Alpinia** (☑0323 92 71 73; Viale Mottino 26; adult/reduced €4/3.50; ⊙9.30am-6pm mid-Apr–early Oct). On a clear day, the views from here over Maggiore are truly special.

For the more active, there are plenty of good hiking trails on the mountain. Walkers can ask at the cable-car station or the tourist office for a free copy of *Trekking on the Slopes of Mount Mottarone*, which outlines a two-hour walk from Stresa to the Giardino Botanico Alpinia.

Skiing Mottarone's gentle slopes (www.mottaroneski.it) is limited to five green and two blue runs, making it good for beginners. The ski pass includes the cost of the cable car and you can hire gear from the station at the top of Mottarone. The ski pass costs €17 per adult per day (€24 on weekends) and equipment costs extra.

Also possible from the summit is **Alpyland** (☑0323 199 10 07; www.alpyland.com; Mottarone; adult/child €5/4; ⊙10am-5pm Mon-Fri, to 6pm Sat & Sun Apr-Oct, weekends only Dec-Mar, closed Nov; ⊛), a 1200m-long bobsled descent with adjustable speeds that makes it ideal for families.

Verbania's Villa Taranto

The grounds of **Villa Taranto** (☑0323 55 66 67; www.villataranto.it; Via Vittorio Veneto 111, Verbania Pallanza; adult/reduced €10/5.50; ⊘8.30am-6.30pm Apr-Sep, 9am-4pm Oct; ℙ) are one of Lake Maggiore's highlights. A Scottish captain, Neil McEacharn, bought the Normandy-style villa from the Savoy family in 1931 after spotting an ad in the *Times*. He planted some 20,000 plant species over 30 years, and today it's considered one of Europe's finest botanic gardens. Even the main entrance path is a grand affair, bordered by lawns and a cornucopia of colourful flowers. It's a short walk from the Villa Taranto ferry stop.

What you'll see changes with the seasons: the winding dahlia path shows off blooms from more than 300 species from June to October; in April and May, the dogwood and related flowers run riot. In the hothouses you can admire extraordinary equatorial water lilies.

The villa itself is not open to the public as it houses the offices of the local prefecture.

Villa Taranto's botanic gardens
ELESI/SHUTTERSTOCK ©

room is modestly elegant with bottle-lined dressers and linen-covered tables, while the local clientele speaks volumes in this tourist town. Reservations essential.

Piemontese   Piedmontese €€€
(☑0323 3 02 35; www.ristorantepiemontese. com; Via Mazzini 25; meals €40-55; ⊘noon-3pm & 7-11pm Tue-Sun) The name gives a huge

clue as to the focus of this refined dining room. Regional delights include gnocchi with gorgonzola and hazelnuts, and baked perch with black venere rice. The Lake Menu (€39) features carp, trout, perch and pike, while the *menù degustazione* (€55) takes things up a notch with a decadent spread of *lumache* (snails), *capesante* (scallops) and foie gras.

ⓘ INFORMATION

Stresa Tourist Office (☑0323 3 13 08; www. stresaturismo.it; Piazza Marconi 16; ⊘10am-12.30pm & 3-6.30pm summer, closed Sat afternoon & Sun winter) **Has brochures and tips on activities in the area. Located at the ferry dock.**

Lago di Como

Set in the shadow of the snow-covered Rhaetian Alps and hemmed in on both sides by steep wooded hills, Lake Como (aka Lake Lario) is the most spectacular of the region's three major lakes. Shaped like an upside-down Y (or an armless wanderer), its winding shoreline is dotted with ancient villages and exquisite villas.

The lake's main town, Como, sits where the southern and western shores converge.

ⓘ GETTING THERE & AROUND

BOAT

Ferries and hydrofoils operated by Como-based **Navigazione Lago del Como** (☑800 551801; www.navigazionelaghi.it; Lungo Lario Trento) criss-cross the lake, departing year-round from the jetty at the north end of Piazza Cavour. Single fares range from €2.50 (Como–Cernobbio) to €12.60 (Como–Lecco or Como–Gravedona). Return fares are double. Hydrofoil fast services entail a supplement of €1.40 to €4.90, depending on the trip.

Car ferries connect Bellagio with Varenna and Cadenabbia. A whole host of other tickets is available, including those for day cruises with lunch and those that include admission to lakeside villas.

BUS

ASF Autolinee (☑031 24 72 47; www.sptlinea.
it) operates regular buses around Lake Como,
which in Como depart from the bus station on
Piazza Matteotti. Key routes include Como to
Colico (€6.10, two hours, three to five daily), via
all the villages on the western shore, and Como
to Bellagio (€3.40, 70 minutes, hourly).

TRAIN

Como's main train station, **Como San Giovanni**
(Via Corrado e Giulio Venini), is served from
Milan's Stazione Centrale or Porta Garibaldi
(€4.80 to €13.50 depending on type of train,
37 to 90 minutes, at least hourly) that continue
into Switzerland. If travelling between Como and
Lugano or Bellinzona, take the regional trains
(on the Ticino side, look for the S10 train), as the
long-distance trains between Milan and Zürich
cost more.

Trains from Milan's Stazione Nord (€4.80, one
hour, hourly) use Como's lakeside **Como Nord
Lago** (Stazione FNM; Via A Manzoni).

Como

With its charming historic centre, the town
of Como sparkles year-round. Within its
remaining 12th-century city walls, the
beautiful people of this prosperous city
whisk about from shop to cafe, sweeping by
the grandeur of the city's cathedral, villas
and the loveliness of its lake shore with
admirable insouciance. The town is a lovely
spot for an aimless wander, punctuated
with coffee and drink stops, especially in
Piazzas Cavour, Alessandro Volta and San
Fedele.

◎ SIGHTS & ACTIVITIES

Basilica di San Fedele   Basilica
(Piazza San Fedele; ☺8am-noon & 3.30-7pm)
With three naves and three apses, this
evocative basilica is often likened to a clo-
ver leaf. Parts of it date from the 12th century while the facade is the result of a 1914
revamp. The 16th-century rose window and
16th- and 17th-century frescoes enhance
the appeal. The apses are centuries-old and

Duomo (p224) interior

 Villa Balbianello

A 1km walk along the (partially wooded) lake shore from Lenno's main square, **Villa Balbianello** (☎0344 5 61 10; www. fondoambiente.it; Via Comoedia 5, Località Balbianello; villa & gardens adult/reduced €20/10, gardens only adult/reduced €10/5; ◷gardens 10am-6pm Tue & Thu-Sun mid-Mar–mid-Nov) has cinematic pedigree: this was where scenes from *Star Wars: Episode II* and the 2006 James Bond remake of *Casino Royale* were shot. Why? It is one of the most dramatic locations anywhere on Lake Como, providing a genuinely stunning marriage of architecture and lake views.

Though the grounds are lovely, it's well worth joining a guided tour to see the villa's interior. Here you'll see the exquisite collections of the villa's last resident, Guido Monzino, who purchased the estate in 1974. Monzino was an entrepreneur, art collector and explorer, who filled the 18th-century mansion with artwork and mementoes from his adventures in Africa, the Himalayas and the polar regions, among other places.

Built by Cardinal Angelo Durini in 1787, Villa Balbianello was used for a while by Allied commanders at the tail end of WWII. The sculpted gardens, which were restored to Renaissance glory by Monzino, are the perfect place for hopelessly romantic elopers to spend a day. You can access the villa by a 1km path (amid vegetation so florid as to seem Southeast Asian) or take a **taxi boat** (☎333 4103854; www.taxiboatlecco. com; one-way/return €5/7) from Lenno.

MICHAL STIPEK/SHUTTERSTOCK ©

feature some eye-catching sculpture on the right.

Duomo   Cathedral
(Cattedrale di Como; ☎031 331 22 75; Piazza del Duomo; ◷10.30am-5pm Mon-Sat, 1-4.30pm Sun) Although largely Gothic in style, elements of Romanesque, Renaissance and baroque can also be seen in Como's imposing, marble-clad *duomo*. The cathedral was built between the 14th and 18th centuries, and is crowned by a high octagonal dome.

Villa Olmo   Historic Building
(☎031 25 23 52; www.villaolmocomo.it; Via Cantoni 1; gardens free, villa entry varies by exhibition; ◷villa during exhibitions 10am-6pm Tue-Sun, gardens 8am-11pm Apr-Sep, to 7pm Oct-Mar) Set facing the lake, the grand creamy facade of neoclassical Villa Olmo is one of Como's biggest landmarks. The extravagant structure was built in 1728 by the Odescalchi family, related to Pope Innocent XI. If there's an art exhibition showing, you'll get to admire the sumptuous *stile liberty* (Italian art nouveau) interiors. Otherwise, you can enjoy the Italianate and English gardens.

Museo della Seta   Museum
(Silk Museum; ☎031 30 31 80; www.museoseta como.com; Via Castelnuovo 9; adult/reduced €10/7; ◷10am-6pm Tue-Fri, to 1pm Sat) Lake Como's aspiring silk makers still learn their trade in the 1970s-built Istituto Tecnico Industriale di Setificio textile technical school. It's also home to the Museo della Seta, which draws together the threads of the town's silk history. Early dyeing and printing equipment features amid displays that chart the entire fabric production process.

Funicolare Como–Brunate   Cable Car
(☎031 30 36 08; www.funicolarecomo.it; Piazza de Gasperi 4; adult one-way/return €3/5.50, reduced €2/3.20; ◷half-hourly departures 6am-midnight summer, to 10.30pm winter) Prepare for some spectacular views. The Como–Brunate cable car (built in 1894) takes seven minutes to trundle up to the

quiet hilltop village of **Brunate** (720m), revealing a memorable panorama of mountains and lakes. From there, a steep 30-minute walk along a stony mule track leads to **San Maurizio** (907m), where 143 steps climb to the top of a lighthouse.

Lido di Villa Olmo
Swimming

(📞031 338 48 54; www.lidovillaolmo.it; Via Cernobbio 2; adult/reduced €9/5; ⏰9am-7pm mid-May–Sep) What a delight: a compact *lido* (beach) where you can plunge into open-air pools, sunbathe beside the lake, rent boats, sip cocktails at the waterfront bar and soak up mountain views. Bliss.

You'll have to bring a swim cap or purchase one here if you want to use the pool.

⊗ EATING

Natta Café
Cafe €€

(📞031 26 91 23; www.facebook.com/nattacafe como; Via Natta 16; meals €20-35; ⏰12.30-3pm & 7.30-11pm Tue-Sun; 🛜) 🍴 In an atmospheric stone-arched dining room, this *osteria* (tavern) has a proud focus on superb local ingredients and classic wines, while also remaining remarkably warm and inviting. It's a particularly good spot for a light meal, with delectable cheese platters, creative bruschetta and *piadine* (flat-bread sandwiches) and excellent salmon tartare – though pastas and daily specials provide more filling options.

Osteria del Gallo
Italian €€

(📞031 27 25 91; www.osteriadelgallo-como.it; Via Vitani 16; meals €26-32; ⏰12.30-3pm Mon, to 10pm Tue-Sat) An ageless *osteria* that looks exactly the part. In the wood-lined dining room, wine bottles and other goodies fill the shelves, and diners sit at small timber tables to tuck into traditional local food. The menu is chalked up daily and might include a first course of *zuppa di ceci* (chickpea soup), followed by lightly fried lake fish.

❶ INFORMATION

The **Main Tourist Office** (📞031 26 97 12; www. visitcomo.eu; Piazza Cavour 17; ⏰9am-1pm & 2.30-6pm Mon-Sat year-round, 9.30am-1pm Sun Jun-Sep) is on Piazza Cavour. The are also tourist information offices **beside the Duomo** (📞031 26 42 15; www.visitcomo.eu; Via Comacini; ⏰10am-6pm) and inside San Giovanni **train station** (📞342 0076403; www.visitcomo.eu; Como San Giovanni, Piazzale San Gottardo; ⏰9am-5pm summer, 10am-4pm Wed-Mon winter).

Tremezzo

Tremezzo draws a fleet of ferries thanks to its spectacular lake views and 17th-century **Villa Carlotta** (📞034 44 04 05; www.villacarlotta.it; Via Regina 2; adult/reduced €10/8; ⏰9am-7.30pm Apr-Sep, 9.30am-5pm mid-Mar & Oct). The waterfront villa sits high on Como's must-visit list; its botanic gardens are filled with colour from orange trees interlaced with pergolas, while some of Europe's finest rhododendrons, azaleas and camellias bloom. The villa, strung with paintings, sculptures (some by Antonio Canova) and tapestries, takes its name from the Prussian princess who was given the place in 1847 as a wedding present from her mother.

Situated on a steep hillside with panoramic lake views from its terrace, the excellent **Al Veluu** (📞0344 4 05 10; www. alveluu.com; Via Rogaro 11; meals €45-75; ⏰noon-2.30pm & 7-10pm Wed-Mon; 🛋) serves up home-cooked dishes that are prepared with great pride. They also reflect Lago di Como's seasonal produce, so expect butter-soft, milk-fed kid with rosemary at Easter or wild asparagus and polenta in spring. The restaurant terrace is a great place to view the Ferragosto fireworks on 15 August, while in winter the dining room log fire is lit. Upstairs there are two equally comfortable suites (€150 to €250) each sleeping up to four people. Staff even pick you up from the ferry dock.

NAPLES

Naples at a Glance...

Italy's third-largest city is one of its oldest, most artistic and most delicious. Naples' centro storico (historic centre) is a Unesco World Heritage site and its archaeological treasures are among the world's most impressive. Then there's the food. Blessed with rich volcanic soils, a bountiful sea and centuries of culinary know-how, the Naples region is one of Italy's epicurean heavyweights.

Certainly, Naples' urban sprawl can feel anarchic and unloved. But look beyond the grime and graffiti and you'll uncover a city of breathtaking frescoes, sculptures and panoramas, of unexpected elegance, of spontaneous conversations and profound humanity. Welcome to Italy's most unlikely masterpiece.

Naples in Two Days

Start your first day in Naples at the excellent **Museo Archeologico Nazionale** (p230) where you can spend a whole morning. Spend the afternoon checking out the city's historical centre, including the **Cappella Sansevero** (p236) and **Complesso Monumentale di Santa Chiara** (p236). On day two go underground to explore **subterranean Naples** (p234) with its Greek-era grottoes, paleo-Christian burial chambers, catacombs and ancient ruins.

Naples in Four Days

On day three hit **MADRE** (p237) to check out the city's contemporary art collections. The afternoon could be spent at the **Duomo** (p236), followed by a spin round the **Pio Monte della Misericordia** (p237). On day four don't miss the **Palazzo Reale** (p240) or a real Neapolitan pizza, perhaps at **Pizzeria Gino Sorbillo** (p242).

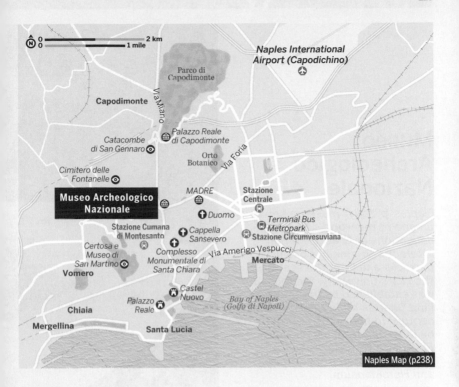

Naples Map (p238)

Arriving in Naples

Naples' **Capodichino airport** (p245) is 7km northeast of the centre. The Alibus shuttle bus connects to Piazza Garibaldi (Stazione Centrale) and Molo Beverello (€3, or €4 on board). Official taxi rates are €23 to a seafront hotel, €19 to Piazza del Municipio or €16 to Stazione Centrale. Naples is southern Italy's main rail hub, with good connections to other Italian cities and towns.

Where to Stay

Where to slumber? The *centro storico* is studded with important churches and sights, artisan studios and student-packed bars. Seafront Santa Lucia delivers grand hotels, while sceney Chiaia is best for fashionable shops and *aperitivo* bars. The lively, laundry-strung Quartieri Spagnoli is within walking distance of all three neighbourhoods.

Farnese Atlante (p233)

Museo Archeologico Nazionale

Naples' premier museum serves up one of the world's finest collections of Graeco-Roman artefacts. Originally a cavalry barracks and later the seat of the city's university, the museum was established by the Bourbon king Charles VII in the late 18th century to house the antiquities he inherited from his mother, Elisabetta Farnese, as well as treasures looted from Pompeii and Herculaneum.

Great For...

❶ Need to Know

📞848 80 02 88, from mobile 06 3996 7050; www.museoarcheologiconapoli.it; Piazza Museo Nazionale 19; adult/reduced €12/6; ⊙9am-7.30pm Wed-Mon; Ⓜ Museo, Piazza Cavour

★ **Top Tip**
You'll need around three hours to cover the museum's greatest hits.

Before tackling the collection, consider investing in the *National Archaeological Museum of Naples* (€12), published by Electa; if you want to concentrate on the highlights, audio guides (€5) are available in English. It's also worth calling ahead to ensure the galleries you want to see are open, as staff shortages often mean that sections of the museum close for part of the day.

Farnese Collection

The basement houses the Borgia collection of Egyptian relics and epigraphs (closed indefinitely on our last visit). The ground-floor Farnese collection of colossal Greek and Roman sculptures features the celebrated *Toro Farnese* (Farnese Bull) and a muscle-bound *Ercole* (Hercules).

Sculpted in the early 3rd century AD and noted in the writings of Pliny, the *Toro Farnese,* probably a Roman copy of a Greek original, depicts the humiliating death of Dirce, Queen of Thebes. According to Greek mythology she was tied to a wild bull by Zeto and Amphion as punishment for her treatment of their mother Antiope, the first wife of King Lykos of Thebes. Carved from a single colossal block of marble, the sculpture was discovered in 1545 near the Baths of Caracalla in Rome and restored by Michelangelo, before eventually being shipped to Naples in 1787.

Ercole was discovered in the same Roman excavations, albeit without his legs. A pair of substitute limbs was made by Guglielmo della Porta, but when the originals turned up at a later dig, the Bourbons had them fitted onto the torso.

La battaglia di Alessandro contro Dario

Mosaics

If you're short on time, take in the *Toro* and *Ercole* before heading straight to the mezzanine floor, home to an exquisite collection of mosaics, mostly from Pompeii. Of the series taken from the Casa del Fauno, it's *La battaglia di Alessandro contro Dario* (The Battle of Alexander against Darius) that really stands out. The best-known depiction of Alexander the Great, the 20-sq-metre mosaic was probably made by Alexandrian craftsmen working in Italy around the end of the 2nd century BC. Other intriguing mosaics include a cat killing a duck and a collection of Nile animals.

☑ Don't Miss

Toro Farnese, La battaglia di Alessandro contro Dario and *Farnese Atlante*.

Gabinetto Segreto

Beyond the mosaics, the Gabinetto Segreto (Secret Chamber) contains a small but much-studied collection of ancient erotica. Pan is caught in the act with a nanny goat in the collection's most famous piece – a small and surprisingly sophisticated statue taken from the Villa dei Papiri in Herculaneum. You'll also find a series of nine paintings depicting erotic positions – a menu for brothel patrons.

Sala Meridiana

Originally the royal library, the enormous Sala Meridiana (Great Hall of the Sundial) on the 1st floor is home to the *Farnese Atlante,* a statue of Atlas carrying a globe on his shoulders, as well as various paintings from the Farnese collection. Look up and you'll find Pietro Bardellino's riotously colourful 1781 fresco depicting the (short-lived) triumph of Ferdinand IV of Bourbon and Marie Caroline of Austria in Rome.

The rest of the 1st floor is largely devoted to fascinating discoveries from Pompeii, Herculaneum, Boscoreale, Stabiae and Cuma. Among them are whimsical wall frescoes from the Villa di Agrippa Postumus and the Casa di Meleagro, extraordinary bronzes from the Villa dei Papiri, as well as ceramics, glassware, engraved coppers and Greek funerary vases.

✕ Take a Break

Head down to boho Piazza Bellini for drinks at **Spazio Nea** (☏081 45 13 58; www.spazionea.it; Via Constantinopoli 53; ☺9am-2am, to 3am Fri & Sat; 🛜; Ⓜ Dante).

Subterranean Naples

Lurking beneath Naples' loud and greasy streets is one of the world's most thrilling urban wonderlands, a silent, mostly undiscovered sprawl of Greek-era grottoes, paleo-Christian burial chambers, catacombs and ancient ruins.

Great For...

☑ **Don't Miss**

The skulls in the Cimitero delle Fontanelle.

Catacombe di San Gennaro

Naples' oldest and most sacred **catacomb** (☏081 744 37 14; www.catacombedinapoli.it; Via Capodimonte 13; adult/reduced €9/5; ⊙1hr tours every hour 10am-5pm Mon-Sat, to 2pm Sun; ☐R4, 178 to Via Capodimonte) became a Christian pilgrimage site when San Gennaro's body was interred here in the 5th century. The carefully restored site allows visitors to experience an evocative otherworld of tombs, corridors and broad vestibules, its treasures including 2nd-century Christian frescoes, 5th-century mosaics and the oldest known portrait of San Gennaro.

Cimitero delle Fontanelle

Holding about eight million human bones, the ghoulish **Fontanelle Cemetery** (☏081 1970 3197; www.cimiterofontanelle.com; Via Fontanelle 80; ⊙10am-5pm; ☐C51 to Via Fontanelle)

Catacombe di San Gennaro

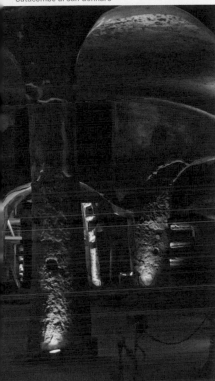

MATYAS REHAK/SHUTTERSTOCK ©

❶ Need to Know

For more on Naples' underground check out www.napoliunplugged.com/locations-category/subterranean-naples.

✕ Take a Break

Test the epic reputation of **Da Ettore** (☏081 764 35 78; Via Gennaro Serra 39; meals €25; ☉12.30-3pm daily, 7.45-10.15pm Tue-Sat; ☐R2 to Via San Carlo), near the Tunnel Borbonico.

★ Top Tip

Tour the Cimitero delle Fontanelle with the **Cooperativa Sociale Onlus 'La Paranza'** (☏081 744 37 14; www.catacombedinapoli.it; Via Capodimonte 13; ☉information point 10am-5pm Mon-Sat, to 2pm Sun; ☐R4, 178 to Via Capodimonte).

16th-century cisterns. An air-raid shelter and military hospital during WWII, this underground labyrinth rekindles the past with evocative wartime artefacts. The standard tour doesn't require pre-booking, though the Adventure Tour (80 minutes, adult/reduced €15/10) and adults-only Speleo Tour (2½ hours, €30) do.

Complesso Monumentale di San Lorenzo Maggiore

Architecture and history buffs shouldn't miss this richly layered religious **complex** (☏081 211 08 60; www.sanlorenzomaggiore napoli.it; Via dei Tribunali 316; church admission free, excavations & museum adult/reduced €9/7; ☉church 8am-7pm, excavations & museum 9.30am-5.30pm; ☐E1, E2 to Via Duomo). Aside from Ferdinando Sanfelice's petite facade, the Cappella al Rosario and the Cappellone di Sant'Antonio, its baroque makeover was stripped away last century to reveal its austere, Gothic elegance. Beneath the basilica, a sprawl of extraordinary **ruins** will transport you back two millennia.

FREE was first used during the 1656 plague, before becoming Naples' main burial site during the 1837 cholera epidemic. At the end of the 19th century it became a hot spot for the anime *pezzentelle* (poor souls) cult, in which locals adopted skulls and prayed for their souls.

Galleria Borbonica

Traverse five centuries along Naples' engrossing **Bourbon Tunnel** (☏366 2484151, 081 764 58 08; www.galleriaborbonica.com; Vico del Grottone 4; 75min standard tour adult/reduced €10/5; ☉standard tour 10am, noon, 3.30pm & 5.30pm Fri-Sun; ☐R2 to Via San Carlo). Conceived by Ferdinand II in 1853 to link the Palazzo Reale to the barracks and the sea, the never-completed escape route is part of the 17th-century Carmignano Aqueduct system, itself incorporating

◉ SIGHTS

◉ Centro Storico

Cappella Sansevero   Chapel

(☑081 551 84 70; www.museosansevero.it; Via Francesco de Sanctis 19; adult/reduced €7/5; ⊙9.30am-6.30pm Wed-Mon; Ⓜ Dante) It's in this Masonic-inspired baroque chapel that you'll find Giuseppe Sanmartino's incredible sculpture, *Cristo velato* (Veiled Christ), its marble veil so realistic that it's tempting to try to lift it and view Christ underneath. It's one of several artistic wonders that include Francesco Queirolo's sculpture *Disinganno* (Disillusion), Antonio Corradini's *Pudicizia* (Modesty) and riotously colourful frescoes by Francesco Maria Russo, the latter untouched since their creation in 1749.

Complesso Monumentale di Santa Chiara   Basilica

(☑081 551 66 73; www.monasterodisantachiara. com; Via Santa Chiara 49c; basilica free, Complesso Monumentale adult/reduced €6/4.50; ⊙basilica 7.30am-1pm & 4.30-8pm, Comp-lesso Monumentale 9.30am-5.30pm Mon-Sat, 10am-2.30pm Sun; Ⓜ Dante) Vast, Gothic and cleverly deceptive, the mighty **Basilica di Santa Chiara** stands at the heart of this tranquil monastery complex. The church was severely damaged in WWII: what you see today is a 20th-century recreation of Gagliardo Primario's 14th-century original. Adjoining it are the basilica's **cloisters**, adorned with brightly coloured 17th-century majolica tiles and frescoes.

Duomo   Cathedral

(☑081 44 90 97; Via Duomo 149; cathedral/baptistry free/€2; ⊙cathedral 8.30am-1.30pm & 2.30-7.30pm Mon-Sat, 8am-1pm & 4.30-7.30pm Sun, baptistry 8.30am-12.30pm & 4-6.30pm Mon-Sat, 8.30am-1pm Sun; ☒E1, E2 to Via Duomo) Whether you go for Giovanni Lanfranco's fresco in the **Cappella di San Gennaro** (Chapel of St Janarius), the 4th-century mosaics in the baptistry, or the thrice-annual miracle of San Gennaro, do not miss Naples' cathedral. Kick-started by Charles I of Anjou in 1272 and consecrated in 1315, it was largely destroyed in a 1456 earthquake,

Tiled cloister in the Complesso Munumentale di Santa Chiara

with copious nips and tucks over the subsequent centuries.

Pio Monte della
Misericordia   Church, Museum
(📞081 44 69 44; www.piomontedellamisericor
dia.it; Via dei Tribunali 253; adult/reduced €7/5;
⊗9am-6pm Mon-Sat, to 2.30pm Sun; 🚌E1, E2
to Via Duomo) The 1st-floor gallery of this
octagonal, 17th-century church delivers
a small, satisfying collection of Renaissance and baroque art, including works by
Francesco de Mura, Giuseppe de Ribera,
Andrea Vaccaro and Paul van Somer. It's
also home to contemporary artworks by
Italian and foreign artists, each inspired by
Caravaggio's masterpiece *Le sette opere
di Misericordia* (The Seven Acts of Mercy).
Considered by many to be the most important painting in Naples, you'll find it above
the main altar in the ground-floor chapel.

MADRE   Gallery
(Museo d'Arte Contemporanea Donnaregina;
📞081 1931 3016; www.madrenapoli.it; Via
Settembrini 79; adult/reduced €7/3.50, Mon
free; ⊗10am-7.30pm Mon & Wed-Sat, to 8pm
Sun; 🚌E1, E2 to Via Duomo, Ⓜ Piazza Cavour)
When *Madonna and Child* overload hits,
reboot at Naples' museum of modern and
contemporary art. Start on level three – the
setting for temporary exhibitions – before
hitting level two's permanent collection of
painting, sculpture, photography and installations from prolific 20th- and 21st-century
artists. Among these are Andy Warhol,
Gilbert & George and Cindy Sherman, as
well as Italian heavyweights Mario Merz
and Michelangelo Pistoletto. Specially
commissioned installations from the likes
of Anish Kapoor and Rebecca Horn round
things off on level one.

◎ Vomero

Certosa e Museo
di San Martino   Monastery, Museum
(📞081 229 45 03; www.polomusealenapoli.beni-
culturali.it; Largo San Martino 5; adult/reduced
€6/3; ⊗8.30am-7.30pm Thu-Tue; Ⓜ Vanvitelli,
🚠 Montesanto to Morghen) The high point
(quite literally) of the Neapolitan baroque,

The Art of the
Neapolitan Presepe

Christmas nativity cribs may not be
exclusive to Naples, but none match the
artistic brilliance of the *presepe napoletano* (Neapolitan nativity crib).

The nobility and bourgeoisie of
18th-century Naples commissioned the
finest sculptors to craft their *presepi*
and used the finest fabrics. Even the
royals got involved: Charles III of Bourbon consulted Dominican monk Padre
Rocco, the esteemed *presepe* expert,
on the creation of his 5000-*pastore*
(crib figure) spectacular, still on show
at the Palazzo Reale (p240). Yet even
this pales in comparison to the upsized
Cuciniello crib on display at the Certosa
e Museo di San Martino, considered the
world's greatest.

Centuries on, the legacy continues.
The craft's epicentre is the *centro
storico* street of Via San Gregorio
Armeno, its clutter of shops and workshops selling everything from doting
donkeys to kitsch celebrity caricatures.

Nativity crib
CENZO7/SHUTTERSTOCK ©

this charterhouse-turned-museum was
founded as a Carthusian monastery in
the 14th century. Centred on one of the
most beautiful cloisters in Italy, it has been
decorated, adorned and altered over the
centuries by some of Italy's finest talent,
most importantly Giovanni Antonio Dosio in
the 16th century and baroque master Cosimo Fanzago a century later. Nowadays, it's
a superb repository of Neapolitan artistry.

Naples

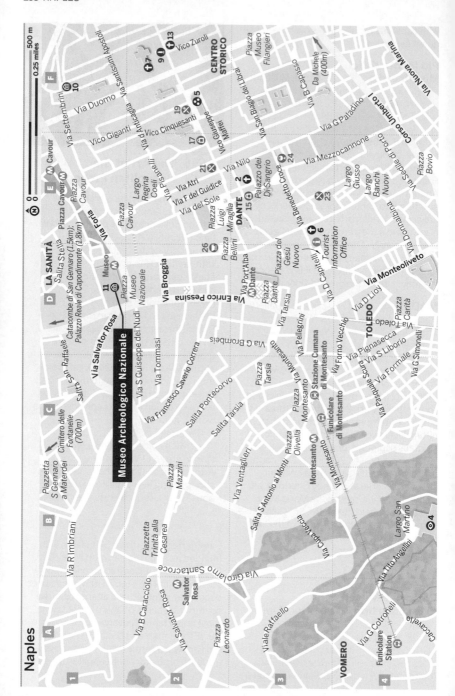

Museo Archeologico Nazionale

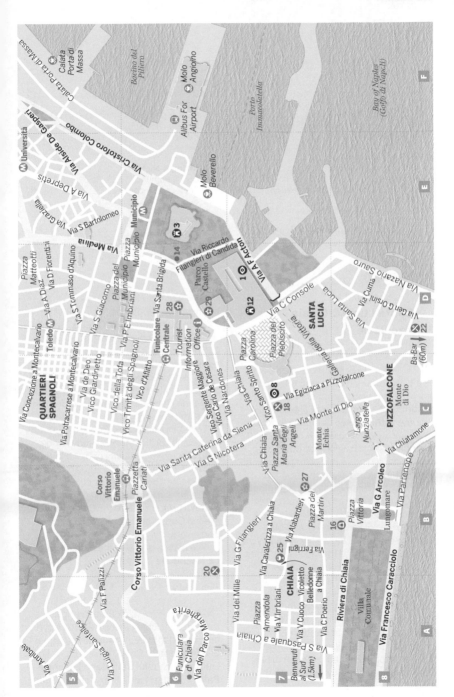

Naples

◎ Santa Lucia & Chiaia

Palazzo Reale   Palace

(Royal Palace; ☑081 40 05 47; Piazza del Plebiscito 1; adult/reduced €4/3; ☺9am-8pm Thu-Tue;
🚃R2 to Via San Carlo, Ⓜ Municipio) Envisaged
as a 16th-century monument to Spanish
glory (Naples was under Spanish rule at
the time), the magnificent Palazzo Reale
is home to the **Museo del Palazzo Reale**,
a rich and eclectic collection of baroque
and neoclassical furnishings, porcelain,
tapestries, sculpture and paintings, spread
across the palace's royal apartments.

Among the many highlights is the Teatrino di Corte, a lavish private theatre created
by Ferdinando Fuga in 1768 to celebrate
the marriage of Ferdinand IV and Marie
Caroline of Austria. Incredibly, Angelo Viva's
statues of Apollo and the Muses set along
the walls are made of papier mâché.

Sala (Room) VIII is home to a pair of
vivid, allegorical 18th-century French
tapestries representing earth and water
respectively. Further along, Sala XII will
leave you sniggering at the 16th-century
canvas Gli esattori delle imposte (The
Tax Collectors). Painted by Dutch artist
Marinus Claesz Van Reymerswaele, it

confirms that attitudes to tax collectors
have changed little in 500 years. Sala XIII
used to be Joachim Murat's study in the
19th century but was used as a snack bar
by Allied troops in WWII. Meanwhile, what
looks like a waterwheel in Sala XXIII is
actually a nifty rotating reading desk made
for Marie Caroline by Giovanni Uldrich in
the 18th century.

The Cappella Reale (Royal Chapel)
houses an 18th-century presepe napoletano (Neapolitan nativity crib). Fastidiously
detailed, its cast of pastori (crib figurines)
were crafted by a series of celebrated
Neapolitan artists, including Giuseppe
Sanmartino, creator of the Cristo velato
(Veiled Christ) sculpture in the Cappella
Sansevero.

The palace is also home to the **Biblioteca Nazionale** (National Library; ☑081 781 91
11; www.bnnonline.it; ☺8.30am-7pm Mon-Fri, to
2pm Sat, papyri exhibition 8.30am-2pm Mon-Fri,
Sezione Lucchesi Palli 8.30am-6.45pm Mon-
Thu, to 3.30pm Fri) 🆓, its own priceless
treasures including at least 2000 papyri
discovered at Herculaneum and fragments
of a 5th-century Coptic Bible. The National
Library's beautiful **Biblioteca Lucchesi
Palli** (Lucchesi Palli Library; closed Satur-

day) – designed by some of Naples' most celebrated 19th-century craftspeople – is home to numerous fascinating artistic artefacts, including letters by composer Giuseppe Verdi. Bring photo ID to enter the Biblioteca Nazionale.

Castel Nuovo   Castle
(☑081 795 77 22; Piazza Municipio; adult/ reduced €6/3, free Sun; ⊙9am-7pm Mon-Sat, to 1.30pm Sun; Ⓜ Municipio) Locals know this 13th-century castle as the Maschio Angioino (Angevin Keep) and its Cappella Palatina is home to fragments of frescoes by Giotto; they're on the splays of the Gothic windows. You'll also find Roman ruins under the glass-floored Sala dell'Armeria (Armoury Hall). The castle's upper floors (closed on Sunday) house a collection of mostly 17th- to early-20th-century Neapolitan paintings. The top floor houses the more interesting works, including landscape paintings by Luigi Crisconio and a watercolour by architect Carlo Vanvitelli.

◎ Capodimonte & La Sanità

Palazzo Reale
di Capodimonte   Museum
(☑081 749 91 11; www.museocapodimonte. beniculturali.it; Via Miano 2; adult/reduced €8/4; ⊙8.30am-7.30pm Thu-Tue; 및R4, 178 to Via Capodimonte, shuttle bus Shuttle Capodimonte) Originally designed as a hunting lodge for Charles VII of Bourbon, this monumental palace was begun in 1738 and took more than a century to complete. It's now home to the **Museo Nazionale di Capodimonte**, southern Italy's largest and richest art gallery. Its vast collection – much of which Charles inherited from his mother, Elisabetta Farnese – was moved here in 1759 and ranges from exquisite 12th-century altarpieces to works by Botticelli, Caravaggio, Titian and Andy Warhol.

⑤ TOURS

Kayak Napoli   Kayaking
(☑331 9874271; www.kayaknapoli.com; tours €20-30; 및140 to Via Posillipo) Popular

kayak tours along the Neapolitan coastline, gliding past often-inaccessible ruins, neoclassical villas and luscious gardens, as well as into secret sea grottoes. Tours cater to rookie and experienced paddlers, with day and night options. The meeting point is at Via Posillipo 68 (Baia delle Rocce Verdi) in the Posillipo neighbourhood. Tours are subject to weather conditions and should be booked ahead.

City Sightseeing Napoli   Bus
(☑081 551 72 79; www.napoli.city-sightseeing.it; adult/reduced €22/11) City Sightseeing Napoli operates a hop-on, hop-off bus service with four routes across the city. All depart from Piazza del Municipio Parco Castello, and tickets are available on board. Tour commentaries are provided in English.

ⓐ SHOPPING

Bottega 21   Fashion & Accessories
(☑081 033 55 42; www.bottegaventuno.it; Vico San Domenico Maggiore 21; ⊙9.30am-8pm Mon-Sat) Top-notch Tuscan leather and traditional, handcrafted methods translate into coveted, contemporary leather goods at Bottega 21. Block colours and clean, simple designs underline the range, which includes stylish totes, handbags, backpacks and duffel bags, as well as wallets and coin purses, unisex belts, notebook covers and tobacco pouches. A solid choice for those who prefer to shop local and independent.

La Scarabattola   Arts & Crafts
(☑081 29 17 35; www.lascarabattola.it; Via dei Tribunali 50; ⊙10.30am-2pm & 3.30-7.30pm Mon-Fri, 10am-6pm Sat; 및E1, E2 to Via Duomo) Not only do La Scarabattola's handmade sculptures of *magi* (wise men), devils and Neapolitan folk figures constitute Jerusalem's official Christmas crèche, the artisan studio's fans include fashion designer Stefano Gabbana and Spanish royalty. Figurines aside, sleek ceramic creations (think Pulcinella-inspired place-card holders) inject Neapolitan folklore with refreshing contemporary style.

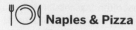

Naples & Pizza

Naples is the spiritual home of pizza and it was already a common street snack when Italian King Umberto I and his wife Queen Margherita visited the city in 1889. Famous *pizzaiola* (pizza maker) Raffaelle Esposito, created a pizza of tomato, mozzarella and basil based on the red, white and green flag of the newly unified Italy. The resulting topping met with the queen's approval and was named in her honour.

Try these legendary pizza hot spots in the *centro storico*:

Pizzeria Gino Sorbillo (☑081 44 66 43; www.sorbillo.it; Via dei Tribunali 32; pizzas from €3; ☺noon-3.30pm & 7-11.30pm Mon-Thu, to midnight Fri & Sat; 🛜; Ⓜ Dante) Day in, day out, this cult-status pizzeria is besieged by hungry hordes. While debate may rage over whether Gino Sorbillo's pizzas are the best in town, there's no doubt that his giant, wood-fired discs – made using organic flour and tomatoes – will have you licking fingertips and whiskers. Head in super early or prepare to wait.

Da Michele (☑081 553 92 04; www.dam-ichele.net; Via Cesare Sersale 1; pizzas from €4; ☺10.30am-midnight Mon-Sat) Veteran pizzeria, Da Michele continues to keep things plain and simple: unadorned marble tabletops, brisk service and two types of pizza – *margherita* or *marinara*. Both are delicious. Just show up, take a ticket and wait (patiently) for your turn.

Di Matteo (☑081 45 52 62; www.pizzeri-adimatteo.com; Via dei Tribunali 94; snacks from €0.50, pizzas from €3; ☺9am-midnight Mon-Sat, to 3.30pm Sun; 🚌C55 to Via Duomo, Ⓜ Duomo) One of Naples' hardcore, low-frills pizzerias, Di Matteo features a popular streetfront stall that sells some of the city's best fried snacks, from *pizza fritta* (Neapolitan fried pizza) to nourishing *arancini* (fried rice balls). Inside, expect trademark sallow lighting, surly waiters and gorgeous pizzas.

E. Marinella Fashion & Accessories
(☑081 764 32 65; www.marinellanapoli.it; Via Riviera di Chiaia 287; ☺7am-8pm Mon-Sat, 9am-1pm Sun; 🚌C25 to Riviera di Chiaia, C24 to Piazza dei Martiri) One-time favourite of Luchino Visconti and Aristotle Onassis, this pocket-sized, vintage boutique is *the* place for prêt-à-porter and made-to-measure silk ties in striking patterns and hues. Match them with an irresistible selection of luxury accessories, including shoes, vintage colognes, and scarves for female style queens.

❎ EATING

Benvenuti al Sud Neapolitan €€
(☑081 1934 9334; Corso Vittorio Emanuele 9; pizzas from €4.50, meals around €25; ☺noon-3.30pm & 6.30pm-midnight Tue-Sat, noon-3.30pm Sun; Ⓜ Mergellina) Its walls splashed with technicolour murals of market produce and Neapolitan vistas, this friendly, upbeat pizzeria-cum-trattoria flips great Neapolitan pie, from simple *marinara* (tomato, oregano, garlic and olive oil) to lesser-known classic *montanara*, which sees the base lightly fried before being topped and baked in the oven for a lovely sheen and crackle. Beyond the pizzas are some fantastic seafood pasta dishes.

Eccellenze Campane Neapolitan €€
(☑081 20 36 57; www.eccellenzecampane.it; Via Benedetto Brin 49; pizza from €6, meals around €30; ☺complex 7am-11pm Sun-Fri, to 12.30am Sat, restaurants 12.30-3.30pm & 7.30-11pm Sun-Fri, to 12.30am Sat; 🛜; 🚌192, 460, 472, 475) This is Naples' answer to Turin-based food emporium Eataly, an impressive, contemporary showcase for top-notch Campanian comestibles. The sprawling space is divided into various dining and shopping sections, offering everything from beautifully charred pizzas and light *fritture* (fried snacks) to finer-dining seafood, lust-inducing pastries, craft beers and no shortage of take-home pantry treats. A must for gastronomes.

L'Ebbrezza di Noè   Neapolitan €€

(📞081 40 01 04; www.lebbrezzadinoe.com; Vico Vetriera 9; meals around €37; ☺6pm-midnight Tue-Thu, to 1am Fri & Sat, noon-3pm Sun; 🛜; Ⓜ Piazza Amedeo) A wine shop by day, 'Noah's Drunkenness' transforms into an intimate culinary hot spot by night. Slip inside for *vino* and conversation at the bar, or settle into one of the bottle-lined dining rooms for seductive, market-driven dishes such as house special *paccheri fritti* (fried pasta stuffed with eggplant and served with fresh basil and a rich tomato sauce).

Topping it off are circa 2800 wines, artfully selected by sommelier owner Luca Di Leva. Book ahead.

Ristorantino dell'Avvocato   Neapolitan €€

(📞081 032 00 47; www.ilristorantinodellavvo cato.it; Via Santa Lucia 115-117; meals €40-45; ☺noon-3pm daily, also 7-11pm Tue-Sat; 🛜; 🚌128 to Via Santa Lucia) This elegant yet welcoming restaurant is a favourite of Neapolitan gastronomes. Apple of their eye is affable lawyer turned head chef Raffaele Cardillo, whose passion for Campania's culinary heritage merges with a knack for subtle, refreshing twists – think coffee *papardelle* (ribbon pasta) served with mullet *ragù* (a rich sauce).

The degustation menus (€45 to €60) are good value, as is the weekday 'three courses on a plate' lunch special. Book ahead Thursday to Saturday.

Salumeria   Bistro €

(📞081 1936 4649; www.salumeriaupnea.it; Via San Giovanni Maggiore Pignatelli 34/35; sandwiches from €4.90, charcuterie platters from €8, meals around €22; ☺noon-5.30pm & 7pm-midnight Mon, Tue & Thu, 7pm-midnight Wed, 7pm-12.30am Fri, 10am-12.30am Sat, 10am-midnight Sun; 🛜; Ⓜ Dante) Small producers, local ingredients and contemporary takes on provincial Campanian recipes drive bistro-inspired Salumeria. Nibble on quality charcuterie and cheeses or fill up on artisanal *panini*, hamburgers and daily specials that might include pasta with a rich *ragù napoletano* sauce slow-cooked over

Marinara pizza

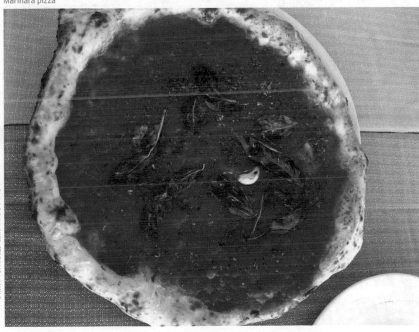

two days. Even the ketchup here is made in-house, using DOP Piennolo tomatoes from Vesuvius.

🍷 DRINKING & NIGHTLIFE

Donna Romita
Bar

(📞081 1851 5074; www.donnaromita.it; Vico Donnaromita 14; ⏰6pm-2am Mon-Sat, from 11am Sun; 🛜) Part of Napoli's new guard of genuinely hip, on-point drinking holes, Donna Romita eschews video screens, unflattering lighting and tacky decor for an architecturally designed combo of minimalist concrete, industrial lighting, sculptural furniture and well-crafted drinks. Not surprisingly, it's a hit with arty, cosmopolitan *centro storico* types.

Ba-Bar
Bar

(📞081 764 35 25; www.ba-bar.it; Via Santa Lucia 169; 🚌128 to Via Santa Lucia) Don't be fooled by the faux British-pub exterior. With its muted colour palette, soft lighting and sub-tle nautical motif, Ba-Bar sets a sophisticated scene for well-crafted cocktails made using fresh ingredients. A short, detail-orientated food menu includes the likes of sesame baguette stuffed with Campanian *provola* cheese, *culatello* (air-cured ham) and hazelnuts, not to mention regional staple *parmigiana di melanzane* (eggplant parmigiana).

Enoteca Belledonne
Bar

(📞081 40 31 62; www.enotecabelledonne.com; Vico Belledonne a Chiaia 18; ⏰10am-2pm & 4.30pm-2am Tue-Sat, 6.30pm-1am Mon & Sun; 🛜; 🚌C24 to Riviera di Chiaia) Exposed-brick walls, ambient lighting and bottle-lined shelves set a cosy scene at Chiaia's best-loved wine bar – just look for the evening crowd spilling out onto the street. Swill, sniff and eavesdrop over a list of well-chosen, mostly Italian wines, including 30 by the glass. The decent grazing menu includes charcuterie and cheese (€16), crostini and *bruschette* (from €6).

Teatro San Carlo

⊛ ENTERTAINMENT

Although Naples is no London, Milan or Melbourne on the entertainment front, it does offer some top after-dark options, from opera and ballet to thought-provoking theatre and cultured classical ensembles. To see what's on, scan daily papers like *Corriere del Mezzogiorno* or *La Repubblica* (Naples edition), click onto www.napoli unplugged.com, or ask at the tourist office. In smaller venues you can usually buy your ticket at the door; for bigger events try the box office inside **Feltrinelli** (☑081 032 23 62; www.azzurroservice.net; Feltrinelli Bookstore, Piazza dei Martiri 23; ⊙11am-2pm & 3-8pm Mon-Sat; 🚇C24 to Piazza dei Martiri), or **Box Office** (☑081 551 91 88; www.boxofficenapoli.it; Galleria Umberto I 17; ⊙9.30am-8pm Mon-Fri, 10am-1.30pm & 4.30-8pm Sat; 🚇R2 to Piazza Trieste e Trento, Ⓜ Municipio).

Teatro San Carlo   Opera, Ballet
(☑081 797 23 31; www.teatrosancarlo.it; Via San Carlo 98; ⊙box office 10am-5.30pm Mon-Sat, to 2pm Sun; 🚇R2 to Via San Carlo, Ⓜ Municipio) San Carlo's opera season usually runs from November or December to June, with occasional summer performances. Reckon on €50 for a place in the sixth tier, €100 for a seat in the stalls or – if you're under 30 (with ID) – €30 for a place in a side box. The ballet season generally runs from late October to April or early May. Ballet tickets range from €35 to €80, with €20 tickets for those under 30.

Be aware that not all shows take place on the main stage, with other venues including the smaller Teatrino di Corte in neighbouring Palazzo Reale.

❶ INFORMATION

Tourist Information Office (☑081 26 87 79; Stazione Centrale; ⊙9am-8pm; Ⓜ Garibaldi) Tourist office inside Stazione Centrale (Central Station).

Tourist Information Office (☑081 551 27 01; www.inaples.it; Piazza del Gesù Nuovo 7; ⊙9am-5pm Mon-Sat, to 1pm Sun; Ⓜ Dante) Tourist office in the *centro storico*.

🗑 Museum Savings

If you're planning to blitz the sights, the **Campania Artecard** (☑800 60 06 01; www.campaniartecard.it) is an excellent investment. A cumulative ticket that covers museum admission and transport, it comes in various forms. The Naples three-day ticket (adult/reduced €21/12) gives free admission to three participating sights, up to 50% off on others and free use of public transport in the city. Other handy options include a seven-day 'Tutta la Regione' ticket (€34), which offers free admission to five sights and discounted admission to others in areas as far afield as Caserta, Ravello (Amalfi Coast) and Paestum. The latter does not cover transport. Cards can be purchased online, at the dedicated artecard booth inside the tourist office at Stazione Central, or at participating sights and museums.

Certosa e Museo di San Martino (p237)

Tourist Information Office (☑081 40 23 94; www.inaples.it; Via San Carlo 9; ⊙9am-5pm Mon-Sat, to 1pm Sun; 🚇R2 to Via San Carlo, Ⓜ Municipio) Tourist office at Galleria Umberto I, directly opposite Teatro San Carlo.

❶ GETTING THERE & AWAY

AIR

Naples International Airport (Capodichino) (☑081 789 62 59; www.aeroportodinapoli.it), 7km northeast of the city centre, is southern Italy's main airport, linking Naples with most

Italian and several other European cities, as well as New York. Budget carrier EasyJet operates several routes to/from Capodichino, including London, Paris, Brussels and Berlin.

BOAT

Fast ferries and hydrofoils for Capri, Ischia, Procida and Sorrento depart from Molo Beverello in front of Castel Nuovo; hydrofoils for Capri, Ischia and Procida also sail from Mergellina.

Ferries for Sicily, the Aeolian Islands and Sardinia sail from Molo Angioino (right beside Molo Beverello) and neighbouring Calata Porta di Massa.

BUS

Most national and international buses leave from **Terminal Bus Metropark** (⏹800 65 00 06; Corso Arnaldo Lucci; ⓂGaribaldi), located on the southern side of Stazione Centrale. The bus station is home to **Biglietteria Vecchione** (⏹331 88969217, 081 563 03 20; www.biglietteria vecchione.it; Corso Arnaldo Lucci, Terminal Bus Metropark; ⊘6.30am-9.30pm Mon-Fri, to 7.30pm Sat & Sun; ⓂGaribaldi), a ticket agency selling national and international bus tickets.

Terminal Bus Metropark serves numerous bus companies offering regional and interregional services, among them **FlixBus** (www.flixbus.com). The bus stop for **SITA Sud** (⏹344 1031070; www.sitasudtrasporti.it) services to the Amalfi Coast is just around the corner on Via Galileo Ferraris (in front of the hulking Istituto Nazionale della Previdenza Sociale office building).

TRAIN

Naples is southern Italy's rail hub and on the main Milan–Palermo line, with good connections to other Italian cities and towns.

National rail company **Trenitalia** (⏹892 021; www.trenitalia.com) runs regular services to Rome (2nd class €12 to €45, 70 minutes to three hours, up to 69 daily). High-speed private rail company **Italo** (⏹892 020; www.italotreno.it) also runs daily services to Rome (2nd class €15 to €39, 70 minutes, up to 17 daily). Most Italo services stop at Roma Termini and Roma Tiburtina stations.

GETTING AROUND

TO/FROM THE AIRPORT

Airport shuttle bus **Alibus** (⏹800 639 525; www.anm.it) connects the airport to Piazza Garibaldi (Stazione Centrale) and Molo Beverello (€3 from selected tobacconists, €4 on board; 45minutes; every 20 minutes). Official taxi fares from the airport are €23 to a seafront hotel or to Mergellina hydrofoil terminal, €19 to Piazza Municipio or Molo Beverello ferry terminal, and €16 to Stazione Centrale.

PUBLIC TRANSPORT

Nonresident vehicles are banned in much of central Naples, though there is no need for a car as a visitor. The city centre is relatively compact and best explored on foot. Furthermore, Naples is generally well served by buses, metro and suburban trains, trams and funiculars.

TIC (Ticket Integrato Campani) tickets – available at kiosks, tobacconists and vending machines – are valid on all city metro, bus, tram and funicular services, including Circumvesuviana and Cumana trains within the Naples city zone. The TIC *biglietto integrato urbano* (€1.60/10 for 90 minutes/3 days) allows for only one trip on each mode of transport (except buses) within 90 minutes of validation. The TIC *biglietto giornaliero integrato urbano* (€4.50, daily), valid until midnight from validation, allows for unlimited travel on all city buses, trams, metro trains and funiculars.

The city's various transport companies offer their own tickets, for use on their services only. For example, ANM – which runs city buses, the four funiculars, and metro lines 1 and 6 – offers a €1.10 single-use ticket. State railway company FS (Ferrovie dello Stato) runs metro line 2, offering a €1.30 single-use ticket for use on that metro line.

BUS

A much cheaper alternative to a taxi, airport shuttle Alibus connects the airport to **Via Novara** (Corso Novara) – in front of the Deutsche Bank branch opposite Stazione Centrale – and the ferry port Molo Angioino (€4, 45 minutes, every 15 to 20 minutes). Buy tickets on board or from selected tobacconists.

ANM (📞800 639525; www.anm.it) buses serve the city and its periphery. Many routes pass through Piazza Garibaldi.

FUNICULAR

Three services connect central Naples to Vomero, while a fourth connects Mergellina to Posillipo.

Funiculare Centrale (www.anm.it; ⏱6.30am-10pm Mon & Tue, to 12.30am Wed-Sun & holidays) Travels from Piazzetta Augusteo to Piazza Fuga. Expected to reopen in early 2018.

Funiculare di Chiaia (www.anm.it; ⏱7am-10pm Wed & Thu, to 12.30am Sun-Tue, to 2am Fri & Sat) Travels from Via del Parco Margherita to Via Domenico Cimarosa.

Funiculare di Montesanto (⏱7am-10pm) Travels from Piazza Montesanto to Via Raffaele Morghen.

Funiculare di Mergellina (⏱7am-10pm) Connects the waterfront at Via Mergellina with Via Manzoni.

METRO

Metro Line 1 (Linea 1; www.anm.it) Runs from Garibaldi (Stazione Centrale) to Vomero and the northern suburbs via the city centre. Useful stops include Duomo and Università (southern edge of the *centro storico*), Municipio (hydrofoil and ferry terminals), Toledo (Via Toledo and Quartieri Spagnoli), Dante (western edge of the *centro storico*) and Museo (Museo Archeologico Nazionale).

Metro Line 2 (Linea 2; www.trenitalia.com) Runs from Gianturco to Garibaldi (Stazione Centrale) and on to Pozzuoli. Useful stops include Piazza Cavour (La Sanità and northern edge of *centro storico*), Piazza Amedeo (Chiaia) and Mergellina (Mergellina ferry terminal). Change between lines 1 and 2 at Garibaldi or Piazza Cavour (known as Museo on Line 1).

Metro Line 6 (Linea 6; www.anm.it) A light-rail service running between Mergellina and Mostra.

TAXI

Official fares from the airport are as follows: €23 to a seafront hotel or to Mergellina hydrofoil terminal; €19 to Piazza del Municipio or Molo Beverello ferry terminal; and €16 to Stazione Centrale and the *centro storico* (historic centre).

Book a taxi by calling any of the following companies:

Consortaxi (📞081 22 22; www.consortaxi.com)

Taxi Napoli (📞081 88 88; www.taxinapoli.it)

Radio Taxi La Partenope (📞081 01 01; www. radiotaxilapartenope.it)

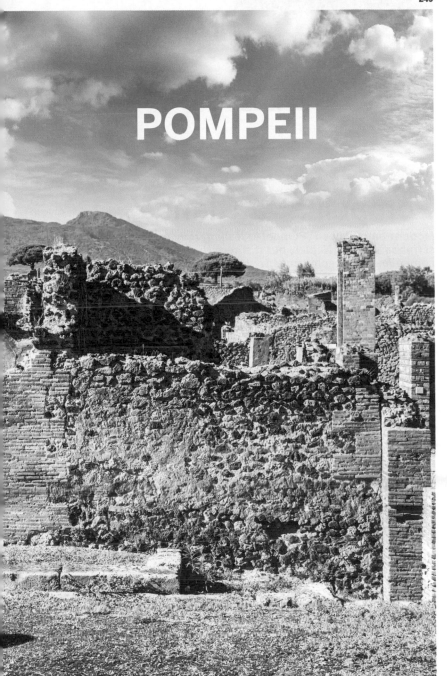

POMPEII

Pompeii at a Glance...

Modern-day Pompeii (Pompei in Italian) may feel like a nondescript satellite of Naples, but it's here that you'll find Europe's most compelling archaeological site: the ruins of ancient Pompeii.

Pompeii's origins are unclear, but it's thought the city was founded in the 7th century BC. Over the next seven centuries it fell to the Greeks and Samnites before becoming a Roman colony in 80 BC. In AD 62, 17 years before Vesuvius erupted, the city was struck by a major earthquake. Damage was widespread and much of the city's 20,000-strong population was evacuated. Fortunately, many had not returned by the time Vesuvius blew, but still 2000 men, women and children perished.

Pompeii in One Day

Dedicate day one to walking the ghostly streets of ancient **Pompeii** (p252) and **Herculaneum** (p258).

Pompeii in Two Days

Spend your final day walking one (or more) of the nature walks around **Mt Vesuvius** (p259).

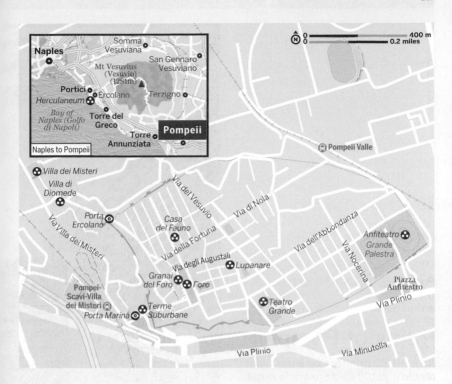

Arriving in Pompeii

To reach the *scavi* (ruins) by Circumvesuviana train (€2.80 from Naples, €2.40 from Sorrento), alight at Pompei-Scavi-Villa dei Misteri station, located beside the main entrance at Porta Marina.

If driving from Naples, head southeast on the A3, using the Pompei exit and following the signs to Pompei Scavi. Car parks (about €5 all day) are clearly marked and vigorously touted.

Where to Stay

There are limited accommodation options around Pompeii itself. The vast majority of visitors come to Pompeii on a day trip from either Naples or Sorrento, both a short train ride away.

Ruins of Pompeii

Around 30 minutes by train from Naples, you'll find Europe's most compelling archaeological site: the ruins of Pompeii. Sprawling and haunting, the site is a remarkably well-preserved slice of ancient life. Here you can walk down Roman streets and snoop around millennia-old houses, temples, shops, cafes, amphitheatres and even a brothel.

Great For...

❶ Need to Know

☎ 081 857 53 47; www.pompeiisites.org; entrances at Porta Marina, Piazza Esedra & Piazza Anfiteatro; adult/reduced €13/7.50, incl Herculaneum €22/12; ⊙9am-7.30pm, last entry 6pm Apr-Oct, to 5pm, last entry 3.30pm Nov-Mar

★ **Top Tip**

The ruins are not well labelled, so pick up a free booklet or an audio guide (€6.50) to enhance your visit.

Visiting the Site

Much of the site's value lies in the fact that the city wasn't blown away by Vesuvius in AD 79, but buried beneath a layer of lapilli (burning fragments of pumice stone). The remains first came to light in 1594, but systematic exploration didn't begin until 1748. Since then 44 of Pompeii's original 66 hectares have been excavated.

Before entering the site through **Porta Marina**, the gate that originally connected the town with the nearby harbour, duck into the **Terme Suburbane**. This 1st-century-BC bathhouse is famous for several erotic frescoes that scandalised the Vatican when they were revealed in 2001. The panels decorate what was once the *apodyterium* (changing room). The room leading to the colourfully frescoed *frigidarium* (cold-water bath) features fragments

of stucco-work, as well as one of the few original roofs to survive at Pompeii.

From the Terme, continue through the city walls to the main part of the site. Highlights to look out for here include:

Foro

A huge grassy rectangle flanked by limestone columns, the foro (forum) was ancient Pompeii's main piazza, as well as the site of gladiatorial battles before the Anfiteatro was constructed. The buildings surrounding the forum are testament to its role as the city's hub of civic, commercial, political and religious activity.

Lupanare

Ancient Pompeii's only dedicated brothel, Lupanare is a tiny two-storey building with five rooms on each floor. Its collection of

Teatro Grande

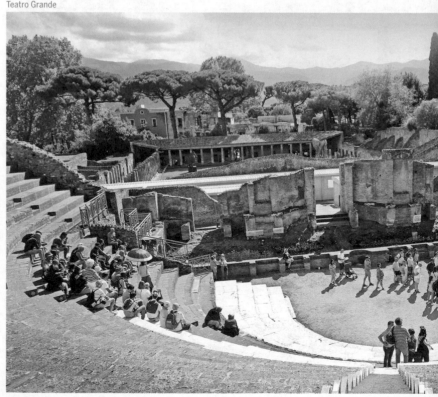

raunchy frescoes was a menu of sorts for clients. The walls in the rooms are carved with graffiti – including declarations of love and hope written by the brothel workers – in various languages.

Teatro Grande

The 2nd-century-BC Teatro Grande was a huge 5000-seat theatre carved into the lava mass on which Pompeii was originally built.

Anfiteatro

Gladiatorial battles thrilled up to 20,000 spectators at the grassy anfiteatro (Am-

phitheatre). Built in 70 BC, it's the oldest known Roman amphitheatre in existence.

Casa del Fauno

Covering an entire *insula* (city block) and boasting two atria at its front end (humbler homes had one), Pompeii's largest private house, Casa del Fauno (House of the Faun), is named after the delicate bronze statue in the *impluvium* (rain tank). It was here that early excavators found Pompeii's greatest mosaics, most of which are now in Naples' Museo Archeologico Nazionale. Valuable on-site survivors include a beautiful, geometrically patterned marble floor.

Body Casts

One of the most haunting sights at Pompeii are the body casts in the Granai del Foro (Forum Granary). These were made in the late 19th century by pouring plaster into the hollows left by disintegrated bodies. Among the casts is a pregnant slave; the belt around her waist would have displayed the name of her owner.

Tours

You'll almost certainly be approached by a guide outside the *scavi* (excavations) ticket office: note that authorised guides wear identification tags. If considering a guided tour of the ruins, reputable tour operators include **Yellow Sudmarine** (☎329 1010328; www.yellowsudmarine.com; 2½hr Pompeii guided tour €135, plus entrance fee) and **Walks of Italy** (www.walksofitaly.com; 3hr Pompeii guided tour per person €59), both of which also offer excursions to other areas of Campania.

> ★ **Top Tip**
> On the first Sunday of the month, all tickets are free.

AVIS DE MIRANDA/SHUTTERSTOCK ©

> ✖ **Take a Break**
> For a memorable bite in Pompeii town, head to Michelin-starred President (p258).

Tragedy in Pompeii

24 AUGUST AD 79

8am Buildings including the **❶ Terme Suburbane** and the **❷ Foro** are still undergoing repair after an earthquake in AD 63 caused significant damage to the city. Despite violent earth tremors overnight, residents have little idea of the catastrophe that lies ahead.

Midday Peckish locals pour into the **❸ Thermopolium di Vetutius Placidus**. The lustful slip into the **❹ Lupanare**, and gladiators practise for the evening's planned games at the **❺ Anfiteatro**. A massive boom heralds the eruption. Shocked onlookers witness a dark cloud of volcanic matter shoot some 14km above the crater.

3pm–5pm Lapilli (burning pumice stone) rains down on Pompeii. Terrified locals begin to flee; others take shelter. Within two hours, the plume is 25km high and the sky has darkened. Roofs collapse under the weight of the debris, burying those inside.

25 AUGUST AD 79

Midnight Mudflows bury the town of Herculaneum. Lapilli and ash continue to rain down on Pompeii, bursting through buildings and suffocating those taking refuge within.

4am–8am Ash and gas avalanches hit Herculaneum. Subsequent surges smother Pompeii, killing all remaining residents, including those in the **❻ Orto dei Fuggiaschi**. The volcanic 'blanket' will safeguard frescoed treasures like the **❼ Casa del Menandro** and **❽ Villa dei Misteri** for almost two millennia.

TOP TIPS

➡ Visit in the afternoon.
➡ Allow three hours.
➡ Wear comfortable shoes and a hat.
➡ Bring drinking water.
➡ Don't use flash photography.

Terme Suburbane
The *laconicum* (sauna), *caldarium* (hot bath) and large, heated swimming pool weren't the only sources of heat here; scan the walls of this suburban bathhouse for some of the city's raunchiest frescoes.

Villa di Diomede

Casa del Poeta Tragico

Porta Ercolano

Casa del Fauno

Basilica

Tempio di Apollo

Porta Marina

Terme del Foro

Macellum

Teatro Grande

Quadriportico dei Teatri

Porta di Stabia

Teatro Piccolo

Foro
An ancient Times Square of sorts, the forum sits at the intersection of Pompeii's main streets and was closed to traffic in the 1st century AD. The plinths on the southern edge featured statues of the imperial family.

Villa dei Misteri

Home to the world-famous *Dionysiac Frieze* fresco. Other highlights at this villa include *trompe l'oeil* wall decorations in the *cubiculum* (bedroom) and Egyptian-themed artwork in the *tablinum* (reception).

Lupanare

The prostitutes at this brothel were often slaves of Greek or Asian origin. Mattresses once covered the stone beds and the names engraved in the walls are possibly those of the workers and their clients.

Thermopolium di Vetutius Placidus

The counter at this ancient snack bar once held urns filled with hot food. The *lararium* (house-hold shrine) on the back wall depicts Dionysus (the god of wine) and Mercury (the god of profit and commerce).

Casa dei Vettii

Porta del Vesuvio

EYEWITNESS ACCOUNT

Pliny the Younger (AD 61–c 112) gives a gripping, first-hand account of the catastrophe (AD 56–117) in his letters to Tacitus.

Porta di Nola

Casa della Venere in Conchiglia

Porta di Sarno

③

⑦

⑥

Grande Palestra

⑤

Tempio di Iside

Orto dei Fuggiaschi

The Garden of the Fugitives showcases the plaster moulds of 13 locals seeking refuge during Vesuvius' eruption – the largest number of victims found in any one area. The huddled bodies make for a moving scene.

Anfiteatro

Magistrates, local senators and the games' sponsors and organisers enjoyed front-row seating at this veteran amphitheatre, home to gladiatorial battles and the odd riot. The parapet circling the stadium featured paintings of com-bat, victory celebrations and hunting scenes.

Casa del Menandro

This dwelling most likely belonged to the family of Poppaea Sabina, Nero's second wife. A room to the left of the atrium features Trojan War paintings and a polychrome mosaic of pygmies rowing down the Nile.

Pompeii

Villa dei Misteri   Archaeological Site
This restored, 90-room villa is one of the most complete structures left standing in Pompeii. The **dionysiac frieze**, the most important fresco still on-site, spans the walls of the large dining room. One of the biggest and most arresting paintings from the ancient world, it depicts the initiation of a bride-to-be into the cult of Dionysus, the Greek god of wine.

A farm for much of its life, the villa's *vino*-making area is still visible at the northern end.

Follow Via Consolare out of the town through **Porta Ercolano**. Continue past **Villa di Diomede**, turn right, and you'll come to Villa dei Misteri.

President   Campanian €€€
(☑081 850 72 45; www.ristorantepresident.
it; Piazza Schettini 12; meals from €40, tasting menus €65-90; ☺noon-3.30pm & 7pm-late Tue-Sun; ☒FS to Pompei, ☒Circumvesuviana to Pompei-Scavi-Villa dei Misteri) At the helm of this Michelin-starred standout is charming owner-chef Paolo Gramaglia, whose passion for local produce, history and culinary creativity translates into bread made to ancient Roman recipes, slow-cooked snapper paired with tomato purée and sweet-onion gelato, and deconstructed *pastiera* (sweet Neapolitan tart).

Around Pompeii

If you're fascinated by Pompeii or the unearthed Roman artefacts at Museo Archeologico Nazionale (p230), check out these nearby ancient sites.

Herculaneum (Ercolano)

Ruins of Herculaneum   Archaeological Site
(☑081 857 53 47; www.pompeiisites.org; Corso Resina 187, Ercolano; adult/reduced €11/5.50, incl Pompeii €22/12; ☺8.30am-7.30pm Apr-Oct, to 5pm Nov-Mar; ☒Circumvesuviana to Ercolano-Scavi) Upstaged by its larger rival, Pompeii, Herculaneum harbours a wealth of archaeological finds, from ancient advertisements and stylish mosaics to carbonised furniture and terror-struck skeletons. Indeed, this superbly conserved Roman fishing town of 4000 inhabitants is easier to navigate than Pompeii, and can be explored with a map and audio guide (€8).

To reach the ruins from Ercolano-Scavi train station, walk downhill to the very end of Via IV Novembre and through the archway across the street. The path leads down to the ticket office, which lies on your left. Ticket purchased, follow the walkway around to the actual entrance to the ruins, where you can also hire audio guides.

Herculaneum's fate runs parallel to that of Pompeii. Destroyed by an earthquake in AD 62, the AD 79 eruption of Mt Vesuvius saw it submerged in a 16m-thick sea of mud that essentially fossilised the city. This meant that even delicate items, such as furniture and clothing, were discovered remarkably well preserved. Tragically, the inhabitants didn't fare so well; thousands of people tried to escape by boat but were suffocated by the volcano's poisonous gases. Indeed, what appears to be a moat around the town is in fact the ancient shoreline. It was here in 1980 that archaeologists discovered some 300 skeletons, the remains of a crowd that had fled to the beach only to be overcome by the terrible heat of clouds surging down from Vesuvius.

The town itself was rediscovered in 1709 and amateur excavations were carried out intermittently until 1874, with many finds carted off to Naples to decorate the houses of the well-to-do or ending up in museums. Serious archaeological work began again in 1927 and continues to this day, although with much of the ancient site buried beneath modern Ercolano it's slow going. Indeed, note that at any given time some houses will invariably be shut for restoration.

MAV   Museum
(Museo Archeologico Virtuale; ☑081 1777 6843; www.museomav.com; Via IV Novembre 44; adult/reduced €7.50/6, with 3D documentary €11.50/10; ☺9am-5.30pm daily Mar-May, 10am-

Frescoes in Villa dei Misteri

6.30pm daily Jun-Sep, 10am-4pm Tue-Sun Oct-Feb; 👶; 🚇Circumvesuviana to Ercolano-Scavi) Using computer-generated recreations, this 'virtual archaeological museum' brings ruins such as Pompeii's forum and Capri's Villa Jovis back to virtual life. Unfortunately, several of the panels are out of order and some of the displays are in Italian only. The short, optional documentary gives an overview of the history of Mt Vesuvius and its infamous eruption in AD 79...in rather lacklustre 3D. The museum is on the main street linking Ercolano-Scavi train station to the ruins of Herculaneum.

Mt Vesuvius

Mt Vesuvius   Volcano
(crater adult/reduced €10/8; ⊘crater 9am-6pm Jul & Aug, to 5pm Apr-Jun & Sep, to 4pm Mar & Oct, to 3pm Nov-Feb, ticket office closes 1hr before crater) Since exploding into history in AD 79, Vesuvius has blown its top more than 30 times. What redeems this slumbering menace is the spectacular panorama from its crater, which takes in

Naples, its world-famous bay, and part of the Apennine mountains. Vesuvius is the focal point of the **Parco Nazionale del Vesuvio** (Vesuvius National Park; www.epnv.it), with nine nature walks around the volcano – download a simple map from the park's website. **Horse Riding Tour Naples** (📞345 8560306; www.horseridingnaples.com; guided tour €60) also runs three daily horse-riding tours (€60).

The mountain is widely believed to have been higher than it currently stands, claiming a single summit rising to about 3000m rather than the 1281m of today. Its violent outburst in AD 79 not only drowned Pompeii in pumice and pushed the coastline back several kilometres but also destroyed much of the mountain top, creating a huge caldera and two new peaks. The most destructive explosion after that of AD 79 was in 1631, while the most recent was in 1944.

Vesuvius is best reached by shuttle bus from either Ercolano or Pompei-Scavi-Villa dei Misteri train stations.

AMALFI COAST

Amalfi Coast at a Glance...

Stretching about 50km along the southern side of the Sorrentine Peninsula, the Amalfi Coast (Costiera Amalfitana) is one of Europe's most breathtaking. Cliffs terraced with scented lemon groves sheer down into sparkling seas, sherbet-hued villas cling precariously to unforgiving slopes, while sea and sky merge in one vast blue horizon.

Yet its stunning topography has not always been a blessing. For centuries after the passing of Amalfi's glory days as a maritime superpower (from the 9th to the 12th centuries), the area was poor and its isolated villages were regular victims of foreign incursions, earthquakes and landslides. But it was this very isolation that first drew visitors in the early 1900s, paving the way for the advent of tourism in the latter half of the century.

Amalfi Coast in Two Days

Wake up in romantic **Ravello** (p272) and greet the day in the gardens of **Villa Rufolo** (p272) and **Villa Cimbrone** (p272). Lunch lazily in town before catching a bus down to **Amalfi** (p270) to explore its extraordinary **cathedral** (p270) and **paper museum** (p270). Dedicate day two to **Positano** (p264) and its chic boutiques, church and beach.

Amalfi Coast in Four Days

Spend the last two days on **Capri** (p266). In **Capri Town** join the local who's-who brigade at the emblematic square **Piazza Umberto I** (p268) before enjoying some of the best views in Capri at **Giardini di Augusto** (p268). Explore **Anacapri** (p269) on the final day. Don't miss **Grotta Azzurra** (p269).

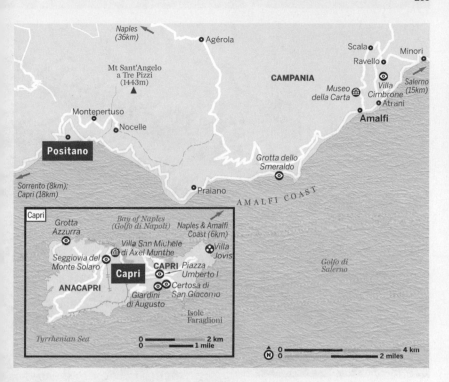

Arriving in the Amalfi Coast

Approaching from Naples there are two main routes to the Amalfi Coast. You can take the Circumvesuviana train to Sorrento and then pick up one of the regular SITA Sud buses to Positano and Amalfi; alternatively, get a train from Naples to Salerno, the Amalfi Coast's main southern gateway, and connect with an onward bus to Amalfi and Positano.

Where to Stay

If you're planning on exploring beyond the coast, Sorrento has the best transport connections, making it a convenient base. Positano, Amalfi and Ravello offer some of the most atmospheric and sophisticated accommodation in Italy, ranging from sumptuous *palazzi* (mansions) to humbler B&Bs with knockout coastal views. Always book ahead in summer and remember that most hotels close over the winter.

A Day in Positano

Positano is the Amalfi Coast's most picturesque town. Its steeply stacked houses are a medley of peach, pink and terracotta, and its near-vertical streets (and steps) are lined with wisteria-draped hotels, smart restaurants and fashionable boutiques.

Great For...

☑ **Don't Miss**

Wandering aimlessly through the narrow streets.

Sights

Positano's most memorable sight is its pyramidal townscape, with its vertiginous pastel-coloured houses tumbling down the slopes to the seafront. Dominating the skyline is the distinct majolica-tiled dome of the **Chiesa di Santa Maria Assunta** (☎089 87 54 80; Piazza Flavio Gioia; ⊘8am-noon & 4-9pm), the town's most famous landmark. Step inside the church to see a delightful classical interior, with pillars topped by gilded Ionic capitals and winged cherubs peeking from above every arch.

Nestled between the colourful boutiques and lemon-themed ceramics shops on Via dei Mulini, **Franco Senesi** (☎089 87 52 57; www.francosenesifineart.com; Via dei Mulini 16; ⊘10am-midnight Apr-Nov) is a light and airy exhibition space showcasing life drawings, colourful surrealistic landscapes and edgy

Spiaggia Grande

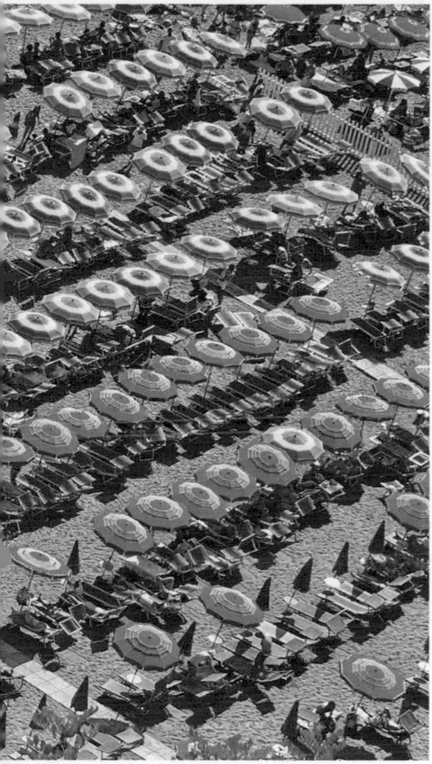

NATALIA BARSUKOVA/SHUTTERSTOCK ©

abstract sculptures by modern Italian artists and sculptors.

Beaches & Boating

Positano's main beach, **Spiaggia Grande**, is nobody's idea of a dream beach, with greyish sand covered by legions of bright umbrellas, but the water is clean and the setting is striking. Hiring a chair and umbrella in the fenced-off areas costs around €20 per person per day, but the crowded public areas are free.

To strike out to sea, **Blue Star** (☎089 81 18 88; www.bluestarpositano.it; Spiaggia Grande; ⊙8.30am-9pm) hires out small motorboats for €60 per hour (€200 for four hours). Consider heading for the archipelago of Li Galli, the four small islands where, according to Homer, the sirens lived. The company also organises popular and fun yacht excursions to Capri and the Grotta dello Smeraldo (€60).

A gentle walk leads from Spiaggia Grande to **Spiaggia di Fornillo**, a more laid-back spot than its swanky *spiaggia* neighbour and home to a handful of summer beach bars, which can get quite spirited after sunset.

Need to Know

Frequent buses connect with Amalfi (€2.50, 40 to 50 minutes) and Sorrento (€2.50, one hour).

Take a Break

Relax on the flower-draped terrace at **La Zagara** (☎089 87 59 64; www.lazagara.com; Via dei Mulini 8; ⊙8am-10pm Apr–mid-Nov).

★ Top Tip

Check www.positano.com for information on local sights, activities, accommodation, transport and more.

Shopping

You can't miss Positano's colourful boutiques – everywhere you look, shop displays scream out at you in a riot of exuberant colour. The humble lemon also enjoys star status; it's not just in *limoncello* (lemon liqueur) and lemon-infused candles but emblazoned on tea towels, aprons and pottery.

La Bottego di Brunella (☎089 87 52 28; www.brunella.it; Viale Pasitea 72; ⊙9am-9pm) is a chic boutique selling locally designed women's fashions in pure linens and silks. To complete the look, head to **La Botteguccia de Giovanni** (☎089 81 18 24; www.labottegucciapositano.it; Via Regina Giovanni 19; ⊙9.30am-9pm May-Oct) for a pair of handmade leather sandals.

Hiking

For more arduous exercise, hikers can tackle the so-called Walk of the Gods. The three-hour, 12km **Sentiero degli Dei** follows a ridge through the hills high above Positano to Praiano. The walk starts at Via Chiesa Nuova in the northern part of town.

Capri

The best known of the islands in the Bay of Naples, Capri is the perfect microcosm of Mediterranean appeal – a smooth cocktail of chichi piazzas and cool cafes, Roman ruins, rugged seascapes and holidaying VIPs. The island has three distinct areas: sophisticated and good-looking Capri Town; more rural, low-key Anacapri; and bustling Marina Grande, the harbour where hydrofoils and ferries dock.

Great For...

ⓘ Need to Know

Ferries and hydrofoils serve Capri from Naples and Sorrento. There are also seasonal connections with Amalfi and Positano.

★ **Top Tip**

To explore the island's azure waters, **Banana Sport** (☏ 348 5949665; Marina Grande; 2hr/day rental €90/220; ☉ May–mid-Oct) **hires out boats in Marina Grande.**

If time is tight, the island's sights may be visited by funicular, bus and/or taxi.

From Marina Grande, the quickest way up to Capri Town is by funicular, but there are also buses and more costly taxis. On foot, it's a tough 2.3km climb along Via Marina Grande. A further bus ride takes you up the hill to Anacapri.

Capri Town & Around

With its whitewashed stone buildings and tiny, car-free streets, Capri Town feels more film set than real life. Taking centre stage is **Piazza Umberto I**, aka la Piazzetta, a showy, open-air salon framed by see-and-be-seen cafes. If that's not your scene, head south along Via Vittorio Emanuele to the 14th-century **Certosa di San Giacomo** (⎇081 837 62 18; Viale Certosa 40; adult/reduced €4/2; ☻10am-7pm Tue-Sun Apr-Aug, to 5pm Sep-Dec, to

2pm Jan-Mar), and, beyond that, the **Giardini di Augusto** (Gardens of Augustus; €1; ☻9am-7.30pm Apr-Oct, 9.30am-5.30pm Nov-Mar). Founded by Emperor Augustus, these colourful gardens rise in a series of flowered terraces to a lookout offering breathtaking views over to the **Isole Faraglioni**, a group of three limestone stacks that rise out of the sea.

A 45-minute walk east of town along Via Tiberio, **Villa Jovis** (Jupiter's Villa; Via A Maiuri; adult/reduced €4/2; ☻10am-6pm Wed-Mon Jun, to 7pm Jul & Aug, reduced hours rest of year, closed Jan–mid-Mar) was the largest and most sumptuous of the island's 12 Roman villas and Tiberius' main Capri residence. A vast pleasure complex, now reduced to ruins, it famously pandered to the emperor's debauched tastes, and included imperial quarters and extensive bathing areas set in dense gardens and woodland.

Rowing boats for Grotta Azzurra tours

Anacapri & Around

Anacapri is smaller and quieter than its traditional rival, though no stranger to tourism. Attention here is largely focused on **Villa San Michele di Axel Munthe** (☎081 837 14 01; www.villasanmichele.eu; Via Axel Munthe 34; €8; ☉9am-6pm May-Sep, reduced hours rest of year), the former home of a Swedish doctor, psychiatrist and animal-rights advocate. Built over the ruins of a Roman villa, the gardens offer stunning views and provide a beautiful setting for a tranquil stroll.

For more sweeping views, jump on the **Seggiovia del Monte Solaro** (☎081 837 14 38; www.capriseggiovia.it; single/return €8/11; ☉9.30am 5pm May-Oct, to 4pm Mar & Apr, to 3.30pm Nov-Feb), a chairlift that whisks you up to Capri's highest peak in a tranquil 12-minute ride. From the top on a clear day you can see the entire Bay of Naples, Amalfi Coast and the islands of Ischia and Procida.

Grotta Azzurra

Capri's single most famous attraction is the **Grotta Azzurra** (Blue Grotto; €14; ☉9am-5pm), a stunning sea cave illuminated by an other-worldly blue light.

Measuring 54m by 30m and rising to a height of 15m, the grotto is said to have sunk by up to 20m in prehistoric times, blocking every opening except the 1.3m-high entrance. And this is the key to the magical blue light. Sunlight enters through a small underwater aperture and is refracted through the water; this, combined with the reflection of the light off the white sandy seafloor, produces the vivid blue effect to which the cave owes its name.

The easiest way to visit is to take a **tour** (☎081 837 56 46; www.motoscafisticapri.com; Private Pier 0, Marina Grande; €15) from Marina Grande; tickets include the return boat trip and a rowing boat into the cave, with the admission fee paid separately.

The grotto is closed if the sea is too choppy and swimming in it is forbidden, although you can swim outside the entrance.

Bay Islands

Capri is one of three islands in the Bay of Naples. The other two, both of which can be reached from Naples, are picturesque Procida, the smallest and quietest of the trio, and Ischia, famous for its thermal waters and spa resorts.

> ☑ **Don't Miss**
>
> The great short walks leading through areas that even in the height of summer are all but deserted. The tourist offices can provide you with maps.

KEVIN BRITLAND/ALAMY ©

> ✕ **Take a Break**
>
> Search out **È Divino** (☎081 837 83 64; www.edivinocapri.com/divino; Vico Sella Orta 10a; meals €30-35; ☉8pm-1am daily Jun-Aug, 12.30-2.30pm & 7.30pm-midnight Tue-Sun rest of the year; ☎) for tasty, market-fresh food in Capri Town.

Amalfi

It is hard to grasp that pretty little Amalfi, with its sun-filled piazzas and small beach, was once a maritime superpower with a population of more than 70,000. For one thing, it's not a big place – you can easily walk from one end to the other in about 20 minutes. For another, there are very few historical buildings of note. The explanation is chilling: most of the old city, and its populace, simply slid into the sea during an earthquake in 1343.

◎ SIGHTS

Cattedrale di Sant'Andrea   Cathedral
(☏089 87 10 59; Piazza del Duomo; ⏱7.30am-7.30pm) A melange of architectural styles, Amalfi's cathedral, one of the few relics of the town's past as an 11th-century maritime superpower, makes a striking impression at the top of its sweeping flight of stairs. Between 10am and 5pm entrance is through the adjacent **Chiostro del Paradiso** (☏089 87 13 24; Piazza del Duomo; adult/

reduced €3/1; ⏱9am-7.45pm Jul-Aug, reduced hours rest of year), a 13th-century cloister.

Museo della Carta   Museum
(☏089 830 45 61; www.museodellacarta.it; Via delle Cartiere 23; €4; ⏱10am-6.30pm daily Mar-Oct, 10am-3.30pm Tue, Wed & Fri-Sun Nov-Feb) Amalfi's paper museum is housed in a rugged, cave-like 13th-century paper mill (the oldest in Europe). It lovingly preserves the original paper presses, which are still in full working order, as you'll see during the 30-minute guided tour (in English), which explains the original cotton-based paper production and the later wood-pulp manufacturing. Afterwards you may well be inspired to pick up some of the stationery sold in the gift shop, alongside calligraphy sets and paper pressed with flowers.

Grotta dello Smeraldo   Cave
(€5; ⏱9am-4pm) Four kilometres west of Amalfi, this grotto is named after the eerie emerald colour that emanates from the water. Stalactites hang down from the 24m-high ceiling, while stalagmites grow up to 10m tall. Buses regularly pass the car

Cattedrale di Sant'Andrea

LEOKS/ALAMY ©

park above the cave entrance (from where you take a lift or stairs down to the rowing boats). Alternatively, **Coop Sant'Andrea** (☎089 87 31 90; www.coopsantandrea.com; Lungomare dei Cavalieri 1) runs boats from Amalfi (€10 return, plus cave admission). Allow 1½ hours for the return trip.

🍴 EATING

Marina Grande   Seafood €€€

(☎089 87 11 29; www.ristorantemarinagrande.com; Viale della Regione 4; tasting menu €70, meals €50; ◷noon-3pm & 6.30-10.30pm Wed-Mon Mar-Oct; 🛜) 🌿 Run by the third generation of the same family, this savvy beachfront favourite serves fish so fresh it's almost flapping. It prides itself on the use of locally sourced organic produce, which, in Amalfi, means superlative seafood. Reservations recommended.

La Pansa   Cafe €

(☎089 87 10 65; www.pasticceriapansa.it; Piazza del Duomo 40; cornetti from €1, pastries from €4.50; ◷7.30am-11pm, closed early Jan-early Feb) A marbled and mirrored 1830 cafe on Piazza del Duomo where black-bow-tied waiters serve a great Italian breakfast: freshly made *cornetti* (croissants), full-bodied espresso and deliciously frothy cappuccino. Standout pastries include the crisp, flaky *coda di aragosta con crema di limone*, a lobster tail–shaped concoction filled with a rich yet light lemon custard cream.

Le Arcate   Italian €€

(☎089 87 13 67; www.learcate.net; Largo Orlando Buonocore, Atrani; pizzas from €6, meals €30; ◷12.30-3.30pm & 7.30-11.30pm Tue-Sun Sep Jun, daily Jul & Aug; 🛜) On a sunny day, it's hard to beat Le Arcate's dreamy location: at the far eastern point of the harbour overlooking the beach, with Atrani's ancient rooftops and majolica-tiled domes before you. Huge parasols shade the sprawl of tables, while the dining room is a stone-walled natural cave. The food is fine, if not exceptional, with decent pizzas and pasta dishes, including gluten-free options.

Paestum

A Unesco World Heritage Site, the temples at **Paestum** (Area Archeologica di Paestum; ☎0828 81 10 23; www.museopaestum.beniculturali.it; adult/reduced incl museum €9/4.50; ◷8.30am-7.30pm, last entry 6.50pm, museum closes 1.40pm 1st & 3rd Mon of month) are among the best-preserved monuments of Magna Graecia, the Greek colony that once covered much of southern Italy. Rediscovered in the late 18th century, the site as a whole wasn't unearthed until the 1950s. Lacking the tourist mobs that can sully better-known archaeological sites, the place has a wonderful serenity. Take sandwiches and prepare to stay at least three hours. In spring the temples are particularly stunning, surrounded by scarlet poppies.

The Tempio di Nettuno, dating from about 450 BC, is the largest and best preserved of the three temples at Paestum; only parts of its inside walls and roof are missing. The two rows of double-storeyed columns originally divided the outer colonnade from the cella, or inner chamber, where a statue of the temple deity would have been displayed.

Almost next door, the so-called basilica (in fact, a temple to the goddess Hera) is Paestum's oldest surviving monument. Dating from the middle of the 6th century BC, it's a magnificent sight, with nine columns across and 18 along the sides.

Save time for the **museum** (☎0828 81 10 23; ◷8.30am-7.30pm, last entry 6.50pm, closes 1.40pm 1st & 3rd Mon of month), which covers two floors and houses a collection of fascinating, if weathered, metopes (bas-relief friezes). This collection includes original metopes from the Tempio di Argiva Hera (Temple of Argive Hera), situated 9km north of Paestum. The most famous of the museum's numerous frescoes is the 5th-century-BC Tomba del Tuffatore (Tomb of the Diver), thought to represent the passage from life to death with its depiction of a diver in mid-air.

Ristorante
La Caravella   Italian €€€

(☑089 87 10 29; www.ristorantelacaravella.it; Via Matteo Camera 12; tasting menus €50-150; ⊘noon-2.30pm & 7-11pm Wed-Mon; ✵) The regional food here recently earned the restaurant a Michelin star, with dishes that offer *nouvelle* zap, like black ravioli with cuttlefish ink, scampi and ricotta, or that are unabashedly simple, like the catch of the day served grilled on lemon leaves. Wine aficionados are likely to find something to try on the seriously impressive *carta dei vini*. Reservations are essential.

Trattoria
Il Mulino   Trattoria, Pizza €€

(☑089 87 22 23; Via delle Cartiere 36; pizzas €6-11, meals €30; ⊘11.30am-4pm & 6.30pm-midnight Tue-Sun) A TV-in-the-corner, kids-running-between-the-tables sort of place, this is about as authentic an eatery as you'll find in Amalfi. There are few surprises on the menu, just hearty, honest pastas, grilled meats and fish. For a taste of local seafood, try the *scialatielli alla pescatore* (ribbon pasta with prawns, mussels, tomato and parsley).

 INFORMATION

Tourist Office (☑089 87 11 07; www.amalfitouristoffice.it; Corso delle Repubbliche Marinare 27; ⊘8.30am-1pm & 2-6pm Mon-Sat Apr-Oct, 8.30am-1pm Mon-Sat Nov-Mar) Just off the main seafront road.

 GETTING THERE & AWAY

BOAT

Between May and October there are daily sailings from Amalfi's ferry terminal east to Salerno and west to Positano, Sorrento and Capri.

BUS

From the **bus station** (Lungomare dei Cavalieri) in Piazza Flavio Gioia, **SITA Sud** (☑344 103 10 70; www.sitasudtrasporti.it; Piazza Flavio Gioia) runs up to 27 buses daily to Ravello (€1.30, 25 minutes).

Eastbound, it runs up to 20 buses daily to Salerno (€2.40, 1¼ hours) via Maiori (20 minutes). Westbound, it runs up to 25 buses daily to Positano (€2, 40 minutes) via Praiano (€1.30, 25 minutes). Many continue to Sorrento (€2.90, 1¾ hours).

You can buy tickets from the *tabacchi* (tobacconist) on the corner of Piazza Flavio Gioia and Via Duca Mansone I (the side street that leads to Piazza del Duomo).

Ravello

Sitting high in the hills above Amalfi, Ravello is a refined, polished town almost entirely dedicated to tourism (and increasingly popular as a wedding venue). Boasting impeccable bohemian credentials – Wagner, DH Lawrence and Virginia Woolf all spent time here – it's today known for its ravishing gardens and stupendous views, the best in the world according to former resident Gore Vidal, and certainly the best on the coast.

◉ SIGHTS

Villa Rufolo   Gardens

(☑089 85 76 21; www.villarufolo.it; Piazza Duomo; adult/reduced €7/5; ⊘9am-9pm May-Sep, reduced hours rest of year, tower museum 11am-4pm) To the south of Ravello's cathedral, a 14th-century tower marks the entrance to this villa, famed for its beautiful cascading gardens. Created by a Scotsman, Francis Neville Reid, in 1853, they are truly magnificent, commanding divine panoramic views packed with exotic colours, artistically crumbling towers and luxurious blooms. Note that the gardens are at their best from May till October; they don't merit the entrance fee outside those times.

Villa Cimbrone   Gardens

(☑089 85 74 59; www.hotelvillacimbrone.com/gardens; Via Santa Chiara 26; adult/reduced €7/4; ⊘9am-sunset) Some 600m south of Piazza Duomo, the Villa Cimbrone is worth a wander, if not for the 11th-century villa itself (now an upmarket hotel), then for the

Flowered terrace in Ravello

shamelessly romantic views from the delightful gardens. They're best admired from the Belvedere of Infinity, an awe-inspiring terrace lined with classical-style statues and busts and overlooking the impossibly blue Tyrrhenian Sea.

Cathedral

Cathedral

(www.chiesaravello.com; Piazza Duomo; museum adult/reduced €3/1.50; ⊗9am-noon & 5.30-7pm) Forming the eastern flank of Piazza Duomo, Ravello's cathedral was built in 1086. Since that time it has undergone various makeovers. The facade is 16th century, but the central bronze door, one of only about two dozen in the country, dates from 1179. The interior is a late-20th-century interpretation of what the original must have once looked like.

INFORMATION

Tourist Office (☑089 85 70 96; www.ravello time.it; Via Roma 18; ⊗10am-8pm) Provides brochures, maps and directions, and can also assist with accommodation.

GETTING THERE & AWAY

From Amalfi's Piazza Flavio Gioia, SITA Sud runs up to 27 buses daily to Ravello (€1.30, 25 minutes).

SICILY

Sicily at a Glance...

Eternal meeting point between East and West, Africa and Europe, Sicily is one of Europe's most alluring destinations. Everything about the Mediterranean's largest island is extreme, from the beauty of its rugged scenery to its hybrid cuisine and flamboyant architecture. After 25 centuries of foreign domination, the island is heir to an impressive cultural legacy, and in a short walk around the regional capital, Palermo, you can see Arab domes, Byzantine mosaics, baroque stucco work and Norman walls. This cultural richness is matched by its startlingly diverse landscape, encompassing everything from bucolic farmlands to smouldering volcanoes, sun-baked hills and island-studded aquamarine seas.

Sicily in Two Days

Spend day one in Catania enjoying the sights such as the Unesco-listed **Piazza del Duomo** (p290), the **Cattedrale di Sant'Agata** (p290) and the city's famous **fish market** (p290). On day two an ascent of **Mt Etna** (p278) is a must, taking either the southern or northern route up.

Sicily in Four Days

On day three make sure you make a beeline for Palermo, Sicily's most vibrant city with its famous **Fontana Pretoria** (p282), glorious churches and wonderful **market** (p282). Spend day four exploring another Unesco site, the **Valley of the Temples** (p280).

Stromboli

Ustica

Panarea

Filicudi

Salina

Alicudi

Lipari

Tyrrhenian Sea

Aeolian Islands

Vulcano

○Mondello

Milazzo ○

◉ Palermo

Messina ○

Trapani
○

Monreale ○

Cefalù
○

Marsala
○

○Castelbuono

Linguaglossa
○

○ Taormina

Parco dell'Etna ▲ **Mt Etna**

Rifugio Sapienza ○

Mazara del Vallo
○

SICILY

Enna
○

Nicolosi

○Catania

Caltanissetta ○

Ionian Coast

Villa Romana del Casale

Ionian Sea

Agrigento ○

Valley of the Temples

Gela ○

Golfo di Gela

○ Syracuse

Mediterranean Sea

Ragusa
○

Vittòria ○

○Noto

Modica

Ⓝ 0 ——————— 100 km
0 ——————— 50 miles

Palermo Map (p284)

Arriving in Sicily

Flights from mainland Italian cities and an increasing number of European destinations serve Sicily's two main airports: Catania's Fontanarossa and Palermo's Falcone-Borsellino. If you're not flying, arriving in Sicily involves a ferry crossing. Regular car/passenger ferries cross the Strait of Messina between Villa San Giovanni and Messina, or Reggio di Calabria and Messina. Ferries also sail to Palermo from Genoa, Civitavecchia and Naples.

Where to Stay

The best place to base yourself in Sicily will depend on your interests and travel style. Cities such as Palermo, Catania, Taormina and Syracuse have the most cosmopolitan mix of higher-end and boutique hotels. If you're happier in a rural setting, the *agriturismi* (farm stay accommodation) of Central Sicily and the Madonie and Nebrodi Mountains are some of the nicest on the island.

Mt Etna

Dominating the landscape of eastern Sicily, Mt Etna is a massive brooding presence. At 3329m it's Italy's highest mountain south of the Alps and the largest active volcano in Europe.

Great For...

☑ Don't Miss

The crater zone: how close you can get will depend on the level of volcanic activity.

Mt Etna is in an almost constant state of activity and locals understandably keep a watchful eye on the smouldering peak. Its most devastating eruptions occurred in 1669 and lasted 122 days. A huge river of lava poured down its southern slope, engulfing a good part of Catania and dramatically altering the landscape. Less destructive eruptions continue to occur frequently, both from its four summit craters and from the fissures and old craters on its flanks.

The volcano is surrounded by the **Parco Naturale dell'Etna**, Sicily's largest remaining unspoilt wilderness, which encompasses a fascinatingly varied natural environment, from the severe, almost surreal summit to the deserts of lava and alpine forests.

The two main approaches to Etna are from the south and north.

Hiking on Mt Etna

ℹ️ Need to Know

The best time for walking is between April and May, and September and October. High summer is very busy and very hot.

✕ Take a Break

There can be few better ways of rounding off a day in the mountains than with a meal at **Antico Orto Dei Limoni** (📞095 91 08 08; www.ortolimoni. it; Via Grotte 4, Nicolosi; pizzas from €5, set menu €27; ⏰1-3pm & 7.30-11pm Wed-Mon), a delightful Nicolosi restaurant.

★ Top Tip

Bring the right kit – it's usually windy up top and temperatures can fall below freezing.

Southern Approach

The southern approach presents the easier ascent to the craters. If travelling by car follow signs for Etna Sud and head up to **Rifugio Sapienza** (1923m), 18km beyond Nicolosi; if reliant on public transport, a daily **AST** (📞095 723 05 11; www.aziendasicilianatrasporti.it) bus runs to Rifugio Sapienza (€6.60 return) from Piazza Giovanni XXIII in Catania.

At the Rifugio, take the **Funivia dell'Etna** (📞095 91 41 41; www.funiviaetna.com; return €30, incl bus & guide €63; ⏰9am-4.15pm Apr-Nov, to 3.45pm Dec-Mar) cable car up to the upper station at 2500m. Fom here it's a 3½- to four-hour return walk up the winding track to the authorised crater zone (2920m). If you plan on doing this, make sure you leave enough time to get up and down before the last cable car leaves. Alternatively, you can pay an extra €30 for a guided 4WD tour to the crater zone.

Northern Approach

The northern route ascends from **Piano Provenzano** (1800m), 16km southwest of Linguaglossa. This area was severely damaged during the 2002 eruptions, as still evidenced by the bleached skeletons of the surrounding pine trees. To reach Piano Provenzano you'll need a car.

Guides

There are many operators offering guided tours up to the craters, and even if your natural inclination is to avoid them, they are well worth considering. Tours typically involve some walking and 4WD transport.

Gruppo Guide Alpine Etna Sud (📞389 3496086, 095 791 47 55; www.etnaguide.eu) is the official guide service on Etna's southern flank, with an office just below Rifugio Sapienza. **Gruppo Guide Alpine Etna** (📞095 777 45 02; www.guidetnanord.com) offers a similar service from Linguaglossa.

Valley of the Temples

The Unesco-listed Valley of the Temples is one of Italy's most mesmerising archaeological sites. Encompassing the ruins of ancient Akragas, it boasts some of the best-preserved Doric temples outside of Greece.

Great For...

☑ Don't Miss

Tempio della Concordia, which was built on a ridge to act as a beacon for home-coming sailors.

Eastern Zone

If you only have time to explore part of the park, make it the eastern zone, where you'll find the park's three best-preserved temples.

Near the eastern ticket office, the 5th-century-BC **Tempio di Hera** (Temple of Hera), also known as the Tempio di Giunone (Temple of Juno), is perched on the ridgetop. Though partly destroyed by an earthquake, the colonnade remains largely intact as does a long sacrificial altar. Traces of red are the result of fire damage, most likely during the Carthaginian invasion of 406 BC.

From here, the path descends past a gnarled 500-year-old olive tree and a series of Byzantine tombs to the **Tempio della Concordia** (Temple of Concord). This remarkable edifice, the model for Unesco's

Tempio di Ercole

ELESI/SHUTTERSTOCK ©

Carthaginian sacking of Akragas. A later earthquake reduced it to the crumbled ruin you see today. Lying amid the rubble is an 8m-tall *telamon* (a sculpted figure of a man with arms raised), originally intended to support the temple's weight. It's actually a copy – the original is in the Museo Archeologico.

A short hop away, you'll find the ruined 5th-century-BC **Tempio dei Dioscuri** (Temple of the Dioscuri, or Temple of Castor and Pollux) and a 6th-century complex of altars and small buildings belonging to the **Santuario delle Divine Chtoniche** (Sanctuary of the Chthonic Deities).

logo, has survived almost entirely intact since its construction in 430 BC, partly due to its conversion into a Christian basilica in the 6th century, and partly thanks to the shock-absorbing, earthquake-dampening qualities of the soft clay underlying its hard rock foundation.

Further downhill, the **Tempio di Ercole** (Temple of Hercules) is Agrigento's oldest, dating from the end of the 6th century BC. Down from the main temples, the miniature **Tomba di Terone** (Tomb of Theron) dates to 75 BC.

Western Zone

The main feature of the western zone is the ruin of the **Tempio di Giove** (Temple of Olympian Zeus). This would have been the world's largest Doric temple had its construction not been interrupted by the

Palermo

For millennia at the crossroads of civilisations, Palermo delivers a heady, heavily spiced mix of Byzantine mosaics, Arabesque domes and frescoed cupolas. This is a city at the edge of Europe and at the centre of the ancient world, a place where souk-like markets rub against baroque churches, where date palms frame Gothic palaces and where the blue-eyed and fair have bronze-skinned cousins.

◉ SIGHTS

◎ Around the Quattro Canti

Fontana Pretoria　　　　Square

(Piazza Pretoria) Fringed by imposing churches and buildings, Piazza Pretoria is dominated by the over-the-top Fontana Pretoria, one of Palermo's major landmarks. The fountain's tiered basins ripple out in concentric circles, crowded with nude nymphs, tritons and leaping river gods. Such flagrant nudity proved a bit much for Sicilian churchgoers, who prudishly dubbed it the Fontana della Vergogna (Fountain of Shame).

La Martorana　　　　Church

(Chiesa di Santa Maria dell'Ammiraglio; Piazza Bellini 3; adult/reduced €2/1; ◷9.30am-1pm & 3.30-5.30pm Mon-Sat, 9-10.30am Sun) On the southern side of Piazza Bellini, this luminously beautiful 12th-century church was endowed by King Roger's Syrian emir, George of Antioch, and was originally planned as a mosque. Delicate Fatimid pillars support a domed cupola depicting Christ enthroned amid his archangels. The interior is best appreciated in the morning, when sunlight illuminates magnificent Byzantine mosaics.

**Chiesa Capitolare
di San Cataldo**　　　　Church

(Piazza Bellini 3; adult/reduced €2.50/1.50; ◷9.30am-12.30pm & 3-6pm) This 12th-century church in Arab-Norman style is one of Palermo's most striking buildings. With its dusky-pink bijou domes, solid square shape, blind arcading and delicate tracery, it illustrates perfectly the synthesis of Arab and Norman architectural styles. The interior, while more austere, is still beautiful, with its inlaid floor and lovely stone-and-brickwork in the arches and domes.

Albergheria

Palazzo dei Normanni　　　Palace

(Palazzo Reale; ☑091 626 28 33; www.federicosecondo.org; Piazza Indipendenza 1; adult/reduced Fri-Mon €12/10, Tue-Thu €10/8; ◷8.15am-5pm Mon-Sat, to 12.15pm Sun) Home to Sicily's regional parliament, this venerable palace dates to the 9th century. However, it owes its current look (and name) to a major Norman makeover, during which spectacular mosaics were added to its royal apartments and magnificent chapel, the **Cappella Palatina** (Palatine Chapel; adult/reduced Fri-Mon €8.50/6.50, Tue-Thu €7/5, plus possible exhibition supplement; ◷8.15am-5.40pm Mon-Sat, 8.15-9.45am & 11.15am-1pm Sun). Visits to the apartments, which are off limits from Tuesday to Thursday, take in the mosaic-lined **Sala dei Venti**, and **Sala di Ruggero II**, King Roger's 12th-century bedroom.

Mercato di Ballarò　　　Market

(◷7.30am-8pm Mon-Sat, to 1pm Sun) Snaking for several city blocks southeast of Palazzo dei Normanni is Palermo's busiest street market, which throbs with activity well into the early evening. It's a fascinating mix of noises, smells and street life, and the cheapest place for everything from Chinese padded bras to fresh produce, fish, meat, olives and cheese – smile nicely for *un assaggio* (a taste).

◎ Capo

Cattedrale di Palermo　　Cathedral

(☑091 33 43 73; www.cattedrale.palermo.it; Corso Vittorio Emanuele; cathedral free, tombs €1.50, treasury & crypt €2, roof €5, all-inclusive ticket adult/reduced €7/5; ◷cathedral 7am-7pm Mon-Sat, 8am-1pm & 4-7pm Sun, royal tombs, treasury & roof 9am-5.30pm Mon-Sat, tombs only 10am-1pm Sun) A feast of geometric patterns, ziggurat crenellations, maioli-ca cupolas and blind arches, Palermo's cathedral has suffered aesthetically from multiple reworkings over the centuries, but remains a prime example of Sicily's unique Arab-Norman architectural style. The interior, while impressive in scale, is essentially a marble shell whose most interesting features are the **royal Norman tombs** (to the left as you enter), the **treasury** (home to Constance of Aragon's gem-encrusted 13th-century crown) and the panoramic views from the **roof**.

◉ Vucciria

Oratorio di Santa Cita   Chapel

(www.ilgeniodipalermo.com; Via Valverde; admission €4, joint ticket incl Oratorio di San Domenico €6; ⊘9am-6pm Mon-Sat) This 17th-century chapel showcases the breathtaking stuccowork of Giacomo Serpotta, who famously introduced rococo to Sicilian churches. Note the elaborate *Battle of Lepanto* on the entrance wall. Depicting the Christian victory over the Turks, it's framed by stucco drapes held by a cast of cheeky cherubs

modelled on Palermo's street urchins. Serpotta's virtuosity also dominates the side walls, where sculpted white stucco figures hold gilded swords, shields and a lute, and a golden snake (Serpotta's symbol) curls around a picture frame.

Museo Archeologico
Regionale   Museum

(⏄091 611 68 07; www.regione.sicilia.it/bbccaa/salinas; Piazza Olivella 24; ⊘9.30am-6.30pm Tue-Sat, to 1.30pm Sun) FREE Situated in a Renaissance monastery, this splendid, wheelchair-accessible museum houses some of Sicily's most valuable Greek and Roman artefacts, including the museum's crown jewel, a series of original decorative friezes from the temples at Selinunte. Undergoing renovations since 2010, the museum has partially reopened, with attractive new exhibition spaces spread around its gracious courtyard.

Oratorio di San Domenico   Chapel

(www.ilgeniodipalermo.com; Via dei Bambini 2; admission €4, joint ticket incl Oratorio di Santa Cita €6; ⊘9am-6pm Mon-Sat) Dominating this

Cappella Palatina's mosaics, Palazzo dei Normanni

ELESI/SHUTTERSTOCK ©

Palermo

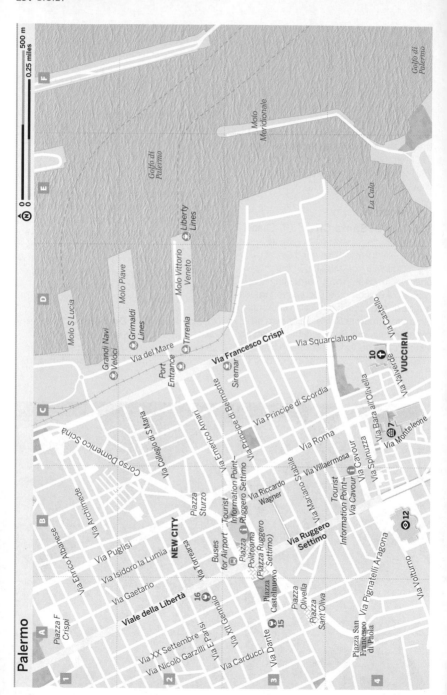

500 m
0.25 miles

Golfo di Palermo

Golfo di Palermo

Molo Meridionale

La Cala

Molo S Lucia

Grandi Navi Veloci

Grimaldi Lines

Molo Piave

Via del Mare

Molo Vittorio Veneto

Liberty Lines

Tirrenia

Port Entrance

Via Francesco Crispi

Via Squarcialupo

Siremar

Corso Domenico Scinà

Via Collegio di S Maria

Via Emerico Amari

Via Principe di Belmonte

Via Principe di Scordia

Via Roma

VUCCIRIA

Via Valverde

Via Castello

10

Via Bara all'Olivella

7

Via Monteleone

Via Archimede

Piazza Sturzo

Tourist Information Point

Via Ruggero Settimo

Via Riccardo Wagner

Via Principe di Belmonte

Via Mariano Stabile

Via Villaermosa

Via Cavour

Via Spinuzza

Tourist Information Point

Via Cavour

Via Enrico Albanese

Via Puglisi

Via Isidoro la Lumia

NEW CITY

Via Torrearsa

Buses for Airport

Piazza Politeama

Piazza (Piazza Ruggero Settimo)

Via Ruggero Settimo

12

Via Pignatelli Aragona

Via Gaetario

Piazza Castelnuovo

Piazza Olivella

Piazza Sant'Oliva

Piazza San Francesco di Paola

Via Volturno

Viale della Libertà

16

15

Piazza Dante

Via XX Settembre

Via Nicolò Garzilli

Via E Parisi

Via XII Gennaio

Via Carducci

Piazza F Crispi

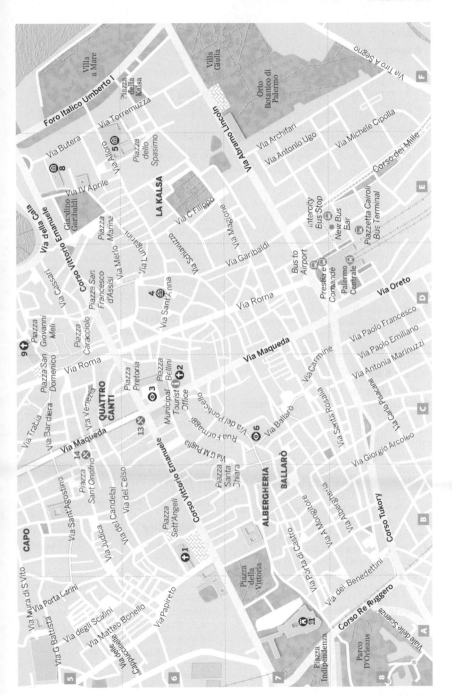

Palermo

small chapel is Anthony Van Dyck's fantastic blue-and-red altarpiece, *The Virgin of the Rosary with St Dominic and the Patronesses of Palermo*. Van Dyck completed the work in Genoa in 1628, after leaving Palermo in fear of the plague. Also gracing the chapel are Giacomo Serpotta's amazingly elaborate stuccoes (1710–17), vivacious and whirling with figures. Serpotta's name meant 'lizard' or 'small snake', and he often included these signature reptiles in his work; see if you can find one!

◎ La Kalsa

Galleria Regionale della Sicilia   Museum
(Palazzo Abatellis; ☏091 623 00 11; Via Alloro 4; adult/reduced €8/4; ⊙9am-6.30pm Tue-Fri, to 1pm Sat & Sun) Housed in the stately 15th-century Palazzo Abatellis, this art museum – widely regarded as Palermo's best – showcases works by Sicilian artists from the Middle Ages to the 18th century. One of its greatest treasures is *Trionfo della Morte* (Triumph of Death), a magnificent fresco (artist unknown) in which Death is represented as a demonic skeleton mounted on a wasted horse, brandishing a wicked-looking scythe while leaping over his hapless victims.

Galleria d'Arte Moderna   Museum
(☏091 843 16 05; www.gampalermo.it; Via Sant'Anna 21; adult/reduced €7/5; ⊙9.30am-6.30pm Tue-Sun) This lovely, wheelchair-accessible museum is housed in a sleekly renovated 15th-century *palazzo,* which

metamorphosed into a convent in the 17th century. Divided over three floors, the wide-ranging collection of 19th- and 20th-century Sicilian art is beautifully displayed. There's a regular program of modern-art exhibitions here, as well as an excellent bookshop and gift shop. English-language audio guides cost €4.

Museo Internazionale delle Marionette   Museum
(☏091 32 80 60; www.museomarionettepalermo.it; Piazzetta Antonio Pasqualino 5; adult/reduced €5/3; ⊙9am-1pm & 2.30-6.30pm Mon-Sat) This whimsical museum houses over 3500 marionettes, puppets, glove puppets and shadow figures from Palermo, Catania and Naples, as well as from further-flung places such as Japan, Southeast Asia, Africa, China and India. Occasional puppet shows (adult/child €10/5) are staged on the museum's top floor in a beautifully decorated traditional theatre complete with a hand-cranked music machine.

◎ New City

Teatro Massimo   Theatre
(☏tour reservations 091 605 32 67; www.teatromassimo.it; Piazza Giuseppe Verdi; guided tours adult/reduced €8/5; ⊙9.30am-6pm) Taking over 20 years to complete, Palermo's neoclassical opera house is the largest in Italy and the second-largest in Europe. The closing scene of *The Godfather: Part III,* with its visually arresting juxtaposition of high culture, crime, drama and death, was filmed here and the building's richly

decorated interiors are nothing short of spectacular. Guided 30-minute tours are offered throughout the day in English, Italian, French, Spanish and German.

Around Palermo

Cattedrale di Monreale   Cathedral

(📞091 640 44 03; Piazza del Duomo; admission to cathedral free, north transept, Roano chapel & terrace €4, cloisters adult/reduced €6/3; ⊙cathedral 8.30am-12.45pm & 2.30-5pm Mon-Sat, 8-10am & 2.30-5pm Sun, cloisters 9am-6.30pm Mon-Sat, to 1pm Sun) Inspired by a vision of the Virgin and determined to outdo his grandfather Roger II, who was responsible for the cathedral in Cefalù and the Cappella Palatina in Palermo, William II set about building the Cattedrale di Monreale, 8km southwest of Palermo. Incorporating Norman, Arab, Byzantine and classical elements, the cathedral is considered the finest example of Norman architecture in Sicily. It's also one of the most impressive architectural legacies of the Italian Middle Ages.

EATING

Trattoria al Vecchio Club Rosanero   Sicilian €

(📞091 251 12 34; Vicolo Caldomai 18; meals €15; ⊙1-3.30pm Mon-Sat & 8-11pm Thu-Sat; 🛜) A veritable shrine to the city's football team (*rosa nero* refers to the team's colours, pink and black), cavernous Vecchio Club scores goals with its bargain-priced, flavour-packed grub. Fish and seafood are the real fortes here; if it's on the menu, order the *caponata e pesce spada* (caponata with swordfish), a sweet-and-sour victory. Head in early to avoid a wait.

Bisso Bistrot   Bistro €

(📞328 1314595, 091 33 49 99; Via Maqueda 172; meals €14-18; ⊙9am-11.30pm Mon-Sat) Frescoed walls, exposed ceiling beams and reasonably priced, lip-smacking appetisers, *primi* (first courses) and *secondi* (main courses) greet diners at this swinging, smart-casual bistro. Located at the northwest corner of the Quattro Canti, its

fabulous edible offerings cover all bases, from morning *cornetti* (croissants) to lunch and dinner meat, fish and pasta dishes (the latter are especially good). Solo diners will appreciate the front bar seating.

DRINKING & NIGHTLIFE

Enoteca Buonivini   Wine Bar

(📞091 784 70 54; Via Dante 8; ⊙9.30am-1.30pm & 4pm-midnight Mon-Thu, to 1am Fri & Sat) Serious oenophiles flock to this bustling, urbane *enoteca* (wine bar), complete with bar seating, courtyard and a generous selection of wines by the glass. There's no shortage of interesting local drops, not to mention artisan cheese and charcuterie boards, beautiful pasta dishes and grilled meats. When you're done, scan the shelves for harder-to-find craft spirits (Australian gin, anyone?) and Sicilian gourmet pantry essentials.

Pizzo & Pizzo   Wine Bar

(📞091 601 45 44; www.pizzoepizzo.com; Via XII Gennaio 1; ⊙12.30-3.30pm & 7.30-11.30pm Mon-Sat) Sure, this sophisticated wine bar is a great place for *aperitivo* (think complimentary morsels like cucumber topped with ricotta mousse, spicy orange marmalade, mustard seed and pistachio), but the buzzing, grown-up atmosphere and the tempting array of cheeses, cured meats and smoked fish might just convince you to stick around for dinner.

INFORMATION

Municipal Tourist Office (📞091 740 80 21; http://turismo.comune.palermo.it; Piazza Bellini; ⊙8.30am-6.30pm Mon-Fri, from 9.30am Sat) The main branch of Palermo's city-run information booths. Other locations include **Piazza Ruggero Settimo** (Teatro Politeama Garibaldi; ⊙8.30am-1.30pm Mon-Fri), **Via Cavour** (⊙8.30am-6.30pm Mon-Fri, 9am-7pm Sun), the Port of Palermo and Mondello, though these are only intermittently staffed, with unpredictable hours.

Tourist Information – Falcone-Borsellino Airport (📞091 59 16 98; www.gesap.it/tourist-information-office; ☺8.30am-7.30pm Mon-Fri, to 6pm Sat) Downstairs in the arrivals hall.

ⓘ GETTING THERE & AWAY

AIR

Falcone-Borsellino Airport (☑800 541880, 091 702 02 73; www.gesap.it) is at Punta Raisi, 35km northwest of Palermo on the A29 motorway. There are regular flights between Palermo and most mainland Italian cities.

BOAT

Numerous ferry companies operate from Palermo's **port** (☑091 604 31 11; cnr Via Francesco Crispi & Via Emerico Amari), just east of the New City.

Grandi Navi Veloci (☑010 209 45 91, 091 6072 6162; www.gnv.it; Calata Marinai d'Italia) runs ferries to Civitavecchia (from €73), Genoa (from €90), Naples (from €44) and Tunis (from €72).

Tirrenia (☑892123; www.tirrenia.it; Calata Marinai d'Italia) sails to Cagliari (from €41, 12 hours, Saturday only) and Naples (from €49, 10 hours, daily). From mid-July to early September, ferries to Cagliari sail on Wednesday and Sunday, not on Saturday.

Grimaldi Lines (☑091 611 36 91, 081 49 64 44; www.grimaldi-lines.com; Via del Mare) runs ferries to Salerno (from €43, 10 to 12 hours) and Tunis (from €35, 11 to 13½ hours) twice weekly, and to Livorno (from €49, 18 hours) thrice weekly.

Società Navigazione Siciliana (☑ferry bookings 090 36 46 01, hydrofoil bookings 0923 87 38 13; www.siremar.it; Via Francesco Crispi 118, Palermo) operates one daily car-ferry service between Ustica and Palermo (€18.35 one-way, three hours), as well as one to three hydrofoil services daily (€25 one-way, 1½ hours).

Liberty Lines (☑0923 87 38 13; www.liberty-lines.it; Molo Vittorio Veneto) runs hydrofoils to Ustica Wednesday to Monday year-round (from €24.45, 1½ hours, one to two daily).

BUS

Offices for all bus companies are located within a block or two of Palermo Centrale train station. The two main departure points are the **Piazzetta Cairoli bus terminal** (Piazzetta Cairoli), just south of the train station's eastern entrance, and

Teatro Massimo (p286)

the **Intercity bus stop** on Via Paolo Balsamo, two blocks due east of the train station. Check locally with your bus company to make sure you're boarding at the appropriate stop.

Salemi, Segesta, SAIS and Interbus tickets are sold at the main bus terminal building at Piazzetta Cairoli. AST and Autoservizi Tarantola tickets can be purchased from the **New Bus Bar** (📞091 617 30 24; Via Paolo Balsamo 32). Cuffaro tickets are purchased from the Cuffaro ticket office at Via Paolo Balsamo 13, opposite New Bus Bar.

Societá Autolinee Licata (SAL; 📞0922 40 13 60; www.autolineesal.it) runs between Palermo's Falcone-Borsellino Airport at Punta Raisi and Agrigento (€12.60, 2¾ hours, three daily Monday to Saturday).

TRAIN

Regular services leave from **Palermo Centrale train station** (Piazza Giulio Cesare; ⏱6am-9pm) to Messina (from €12.80, three to 3¾ hours, eight to 14 daily), Catania (from €13.50, 2¾ to 5½ hours, five to 10 daily) and Agrigento (€9, two hours, six to 10 daily), as well as to nearby towns such as Cefalù (from €5.60, 45 minutes to one hour, nine to 10 daily). There are also Intercity trains to Reggio di Calabria, Naples and Rome.

ⓘ GETTING AROUND

TO/FROM THE AIRPORT

Prestia e Comandè (📞091 58 63 51; www.prestiaecomande.it; one-way/return €6.30/11) runs an efficient half-hourly bus service between 5am and 12.15pm that transfers passengers from the airport to the centre of Palermo, dropping people off outside the **Teatro Politeama Garibaldi** (Via Dante) and Palermo Centrale train station. To find the bus, follow the signs past the downstairs taxi rank and around the corner to the right. Tickets for the journey, which takes anywhere from 35 to 50 minutes depending on traffic, cost €6.30 one-way or €11 return and are purchased on the bus. Return journeys to the airport run between 4am and 10.30pm with the same frequency and pick-up points.

There is a taxi rank outside the arrivals hall and the fare to/from Palermo is between €35

Aeolian Islands

The Aeolian Islands are a little piece of paradise. Stunning cobalt sea, splendid beaches, some of Italy's best hiking, and an awe-inspiring volcanic landscape are just part of the appeal. The islands also have a fascinating human and mythological history that goes back several millennia; the Aeolians figured prominently in Homer's *Odyssey*, and evidence of the distant past can be seen everywhere, most notably in Lipari's excellent archaeological museum.

The seven islands of Lipari, Vulcano, Salina, Panarea, Stromboli, Alicudi and Filicudi are part of a huge 200km volcanic ridge that runs between the smoking stack of Mt Etna and the threatening mass of Vesuvius above Naples. Collectively, the islands exhibit a unique range of volcanic characteristics, which earned them a place on Unesco's World Heritage list in 2000. Highlights include the spectacular volcanic fireworks of Stromboli, the picturesque vineyards and dormant twin cones of Salina and the therapeutic mud baths of Vulcano.

Both Ustica Lines (www.usticalines.it) and Siremar (www.siremar.it) run hydrofoils year-round from Milazzo, the mainland city closest to the islands. Regular hydrofoil and ferry services operate between the islands. Ticket offices with posted timetables can be found close to the docks on all islands.

The pier at Vulcano
MAUDANROS/SHUTTERSTOCK ©

🍴 Sicily's Cuisine

Eating is one of the great joys of a trip to Sicily. In addition to the island's ubiquitous street food, you'll encounter countless specialities.

Pasta alla Norma Named in honour of the opera by Vincenzo Bellini, Catania's signature pasta dish features aubergines, tomatoes, basil and salty ricotta.

Involtini di pesce spada Thinly sliced swordfish rolled up and filled with breadcrumbs, capers, tomatoes and olives.

Couscous di pesce alla trapanese Savour Sicily's North African influences with fish couscous, seasoned with cinnamon, saffron, parsley and garlic.

Bucatini con le sarde A Palermitan staple: tube-shaped pasta with sardines, wild fennel, pine nuts and raisins.

Caponata A kind of Sicilian ratatouille of aubergine, tomatoes, olives and capers.

Arancino (or *arancina* if you're from Palermo) A plump golden rice ball, stuffed with meat or cheese, coated with breadcrumbs and deep-fried.

Crocché Fried potato dumplings flavoured with cheese, parsley and eggs.

Panelle Fried chickpea-flour fritters, often served in sesame rolls.

Pane con la milza A Palermo favourite consisting of a bread roll with boiled calf's spleen and lemon juice.

Cassata siciliana A rich mix of ricotta, sugar, vanilla, candied fruit and diced chocolate, encased by sponge and topped with green icing.

Arancini

and €45, depending on your destination in the city.

Catania

Catania is a true city of the volcano. Much of it is constructed from the lava that engulfed the city during Mt Etna's massive 1669 eruption. The city is lava-black in colour, as if a fine dusting of soot permanently covers its elegant buildings, most of which are the work of baroque master Giovanni Vaccarini.

◎ SIGHTS

Piazza del Duomo   Square

A Unesco World Heritage site, Catania's central piazza is a set piece of contrasting lava and limestone, surrounded by buildings in the unique local baroque style and crowned by the grand Cattedrale di Sant'Agata. At its centre stands Fontana dell'Elefante (1736), a naive, smiling black-lava elephant dating from Roman times and surmounted by an improbable Egyptian obelisk. Another fountain at the piazza's southwest corner, **Fontana dell'Amenano**, marks the entrance to Catania's fish market.

La Pescheria   Market

(Via Pardo; ⊙7am-2pm Mon-Sat) Catania's raucous fish market, which takes over the streets behind Piazza del Duomo every workday morning, is street theatre at its most thrilling. Tables groan under the weight of decapitated swordfish, ruby-pink prawns and trays full of clams, mussels, sea urchins and all manner of mysterious sea life. Fishmongers gut silvery fish and high-heeled housewives step daintily over pools of blood-stained water. It's absolutely riveting. Surrounding the market are a number of good seafood restaurants.

Cattedrale di Sant'Agata   Cathedral

(☎095 32 00 44; Piazza del Duomo; ⊙7am-noon & 4-7pm Mon-Sat, 7.30am-12.30pm & 4.30-7pm Sun) Inside the vaulted interior of this cathedral, beyond its impressive marble facade sporting two orders of columns taken from the Roman amphitheatre, lie the relics of the city's patron saint. Its other famous resident is the world-famous Catanian composer Vincenzo Bellini, his remains transferred here in 1876, 41 years after his death in France. Consider visiting the **Museo Diocesano** (☑095 28 16 35; www. museodiocesanocatania.com; adult/reduced €7/4, incl baths €10/6; ◷9am-2pm Mon, Wed & Fri, 9am-2pm & 3-6pm Tue & Thu, 9am-1pm Sat) next door for access to the Roman baths directly underneath the church.

Fontana dell'Elefante Monument
(Piazza del Duomo) Taking centre stage on Catania's showpiece Piazza del Duomo is the city's most memorable monument, the smiling Fontana dell'Elefante (Fountain of the Elephant; 1736). Made of lava stone and dating from the Roman period, the comical statue is of an adorable elephant, known locally as Liotru and the symbol of the city. The statue is surmounted by an improbable Egyptian obelisk which, according to local folklore, possesses magical powers.

 ENTERTAINMENT

Teatro Massimo Bellini Theatre
(☑095 730 61 35; www.teatromassimobellini. it; Via Perrotta 12; guided tours adult/reduced €6/4; ◷tours 9am-noon Tue-Thu) A few blocks northeast of the *duomo* is Catania's dashing opera theatre. Completed in 1890 and made for homegrown composer Vincenzo Bellini, the building's interiors are suitably lavish, from the stucco-and-marble extravagance of the foyer (known as the *ridotto*) to the glory of the theatre itself, wrapped in four tiers of gilded boxes. The theatre's painted ceiling, by Ernesto Bellandi, depicts scenes from four of Bellini's best-known operas.

 INFORMATION

Airport Tourist Office (☑095 723 96 82; ◷8am-8.15pm Mon-Sat) In the arrivals hall.

Tourist Office (☑095 742 55 73; www.comune. catania.it/la-citta/turismo; Via Vittorio Emanuele 172; ◷8am-7.15pm Mon-Sat, 8.30am-1.30pm Sun) Very helpful city-run tourist office.

Fish at La Pescheria

GETTING THERE & AWAY

AIR

Catania Fontanarossa airport (☑095 723 91 11; www.aeroporto.catania.it) is Sicily's busiest and located 7km southwest of the city centre.

Shuttle-bus service **Alibus** (www.amt.ct.it) runs to the airport from numerous stops in central Catania, including the train station (€4, 30 minutes, every 25 minutes). A **taxi** (☑095 33 09 66; www.radiotaxicatania.org) will cost around €18 to €22.

BOAT

Catania's ferry terminal lies at the southeast edge of the historic centre. From here, **TTT Lines** (☑800 627414, 095 34 85 86; www.tttlines.com) runs a nightly ferry service to Naples.

BUS

All long-distance buses leave from a **terminal** (Via Archimede) 250m north of the train station, with ticket offices across the street on Via D'Amico. As a rule, buses are quicker than trains for most destinations.

Interbus (☑095 53 27 16; www.interbus.it; Via d'Amico 187) runs to Syracuse (€6.20, 1½ hours, 18 daily Monday to Friday, 10 Saturday, seven Sunday) and Taormina (€5.10, 1¼ hours, 11 to 16 daily).

SAIS Autolinee (☑095 53 61 68, 800 211020; www.saisautolinee.it; Via d'Amico 181) serves Palermo (€12.50, 2¾ hours, 12 daily Monday to Saturday, nine Sunday).

SAIS Trasporti (☑090 601 21 36; www. saistrasporti.it; Via d'Amico 181) runs overnight to Rome (€40, one daily, 10½ hours).

TRAIN

Frequent trains depart from Catania Centrale station on Piazza Papa Giovanni XXIII. Destinations include Messina (from €7.60, 1¼ to two hours), Syracuse (from €6.90, 1¼ hours) and Palermo (from €13.50, three hours). Train services are significantly reduced on Sunday.

GETTING AROUND

Several useful **AMT** (☑095 751 91 11, 800 018696; www.amt.ct.it) city buses terminate in front of Catania Centrale train station, including buses 1-4 and 4-7 (both running roughly hourly

from the station to Via Etnea). Also useful is bus D, which runs from Piazza Borsellino (just south of the Cattedrale di Sant'Agata) to the local beaches. Tickets, from *tabacchi* (tobacconists) cost €1 and last 90 minutes. A two-hour combined bus-metro ticket costs €1.20.

Syracuse

More than any other city, Syracuse encapsulates Sicily's timeless beauty. Ancient Greek ruins rise out of lush citrus orchards, cafe tables spill onto dazzling baroque piazzas, and honey-hued medieval lanes lead down to the sparkling blue sea. It's difficult to imagine now but in its heyday this was the largest city in the ancient world, bigger even than Athens and Corinth. Its 'Once upon a Time' begins in 734 BC, when Corinthian colonists landed on the island of Ortygia and founded the settlement, setting up the mainland city four years later. Almost three millennia later, the ruins of that then-new city constitute the Parco Archeologico della Neapolis, one of Sicily's greatest archaeological sites. Across the water from the mainland, Ortygia remains the city's most beautiful corner, a casually chic, eclectic marvel with an ever-growing legion of fans.

SIGHTS

Piazza del Duomo   Piazza

Syracuse's showpiece square is a masterpiece of baroque town planning. A long, rectangular piazza flanked by flamboyant *palazzi*, it sits on what was once Syracuse's ancient acropolis (fortified citadel). Little remains of the original Greek building but if you look along the side of the Duomo, you'll see a number of thick Doric columns incorporated into the cathedral's structure.

Parco Archeologico
della Neapolis   Archaeological Site

(☑0931 6 62 06; Viale Paradiso 14; adult/reduced €10/5, incl Museo Archeologico €13.50/7; ☺9am-1hr before sunset Mon-Sat, 9am-1pm Sun) For the classicist, Syracuse's real attraction is this archaeological park, home to the pearly white, 5th-century-BC **Teatro**

Duomo

Greco. Hewn out of the rocky hillside, this 16,000-capacity amphitheatre staged the last tragedies of Aeschylus (including *The Persians*), first performed here in his presence. In late spring it's brought to life with an annual season of classical theatre.

Duomo   Cathedral

(Piazza del Duomo; adult/reduced €2/1; ⊙9am-6.30pm Mon-Sat Apr-Oct, to 5.30pm Nov-Mar) Built on the skeleton of a 5th-century-BC Greek temple to Athena (note the Doric columns still visible inside and out), Syracuse's cathedral became a church when the island was evangelised by St Paul. Its most striking feature is the columned baroque facade (1728–53) added by Andrea Palma after the 1693 earthquake. A statue of the Virgin Mary crowns the rooftop, in the same spot where a golden statue of Athena once served as a beacon to homecoming Greek sailors.

Museo Archeologico
Paolo Orsi   Museum

(☑0931 48 95 11; www.regione.sicilia.it/benicul-turali/museopaoloorsi; Viale Teocrito 66; adult/ reduced €8/4, incl Parco Archeologico €13.50/7; ⊙9am-6pm Tue-Sat, to 1pm Sun) About 500m east of the archaeological park, this modern museum contains one of Sicily's largest and most interesting archaeological collections. Allow plenty of time to investigate the four sectors charting the area's prehistory, as well as Syracuse's development from foundation to the late Roman period.

Sicily's Baroque Triangle   Area

With a car and a little extra time on your hands, you can explore the so-called 'baroque triangle'. This remote, rocky corner of southeastern Sicily is home to a series of Unesco-listed towns famous for their lavish baroque architecture. Just over 35km south of Syracuse, **Noto** can lay claim to what is arguably Sicily's most beautiful street: Corso Vittorio Emanuele, a pedestrianised boulevard lined with golden baroque *palazzi*. West of Noto, and further inland, **Modica** is a bustling town set in a deep rocky gorge. The headline here is the Chiesa di San Giorgio in Modica Alta, the high part of town. From Modica,

Villa Romana del Casale

Villa Romana del Casale (☎0935 68 00 36; www.villaromanadelcasale.it; adult/reduced €10/5; ☺9am-6pm Apr-Oct, to 4pm Nov-Mar) is sumptuous, even by decadent Roman standards, and is thought to have been the country retreat of Marcus Aurelius Maximianus, Rome's co-emperor during the reign of Diocletian (AD 286–305). Certainly, the size of the complex – four interconnected groups of buildings spread over the hillside – and the 3535 sq metres of astoundingly well-preserved multicoloured floor mosaics suggest a palace of imperial standing.

Following a landslide in the 12th century, the villa lay under 10m of mud for some 700 years, and was thus protected from the damaging effects of air, wind and rain. It was only when serious excavation work began in the 1950s that the mosaics, considered remarkable for their natural, narrative style, the range of their subject matter and the variety of their colour, were brought back to light.

The villa's recent restoration has covered almost the entire complex with a wooden roof (to protect the mosaics from the elements), while an elevated walkway allows visitors to view the tiled floors and the structure itself in its entirety. Architects report a dissatisfaction with the structure for the lack of light, and the shadows that obscure the colours and vivacity of the mosaics, but the condition of the mosaics has been much improved.

Floor mosaic detail
MARCO OSSINO/SHUTTERSTOCK ©

it's a short, twisting, up-and-down drive through rock-littered hills to **Ragusa**, one of Sicily's nine provincial capitals. The town is divided in two, but it's Ragusa Ibla that you want, a claustrophobic warren of grey stone houses and elegant *palazzi* that opens up onto Piazza Duomo, a superb example of 18th-century town planning.

✗ EATING

Caseificio Borderi   Sandwiches €

(www.caseificioborderi.eu; Via Benedictis 6; sandwiches €5; ☺7am-4pm Mon-Sat) No visit to Syracuse's market is complete without a stop at this colourful deli near Ortygia's far northern tip. Veteran sandwich-master Andrea Borderi stands out front with a table full of cheeses, olives, greens, herbs, tomatoes and other fixings, and engages in nonstop banter with customers while creating free-form sandwiches big enough to keep you fed all day.

Sicilia in Tavola   Sicilian €

(☎392 4610889; www.siciliaintavola.eu; Via Cavour 28; meals €20-30; ☺12.30-2.30pm & 7.30-10.30pm Tue-Sun) One of the longest established and most popular eateries on Via Cavour, this snug, simple trattoria has built its reputation on delicious homemade pasta and seafood. To savour both at once, tuck into the *fettuccine allo scoglio* (pasta ribbons with mixed seafood) or the equally fine prawn ravioli, paired with sweet cherry tomatoes and chopped mint. Reservations recommended.

Bistrot Bella Vita   Italian €€

(☎348 1939792; Via Gargallo 60; sweets €1.50, meals €25; ☺cafe 8am-1am summer, to 11pm winter, restaurant noon-3pm & 6.30-11pm, closed Mon) Owned by affable Lombard expat Norma and her Sicilian pastry-chef husband Salvo, this casually elegant cafe-restaurant is one of Ortygia's latest stars. Stop by for good coffee (soy milk available) and made-from-scratch *cornetti, biscotti* and pastries (try the sour orange-and-almond tart). Or book a table in the intimate back dining room, where local, organic produce drives beautifully textured, technically impressive dishes.

Moon
Vegan €€

(☏0931 44 95 16; www.moonortigia.com; Via Roma 112; meals €18-30; ⏰11am-midnight Wed-Mon late Apr–Oct, 6pm-midnight Wed-Mon Nov–mid-Jan & mid-Feb–late Apr; 🛈🅿) If vegan fare usually makes you yawn, subvert your thinking at boho-chic Moon. A cast of mostly organic and biological ingredients beam in decadent, intriguing dishes that might see a tower of thinly sliced pears interlayered with a rich, soy-based cashew cream cheese, or chickpea and tofu conspiring in a smokey *linguine alla carbonara* as wicked as the original.

Don Camillo
Modern Sicilian €€€

(☏0931 6 71 33; www.ristorantedoncamillo.it; Via Maestranza 96; degustation menus €35-70; ⏰12.30-2.30pm & 8-10.30pm Mon-Sat; 🛈🅿) One of Ortygia's most elegant restaurants, Don Camillo specialises in sterling service and innovative Sicilian cuisine. Pique the appetite with mixed shellfish in a thick soup of Noto almonds, swoon over the swordfish with orange-blossom honey and sweet-and-sour vegetables, or (discreetly) lick your whiskers over an outstanding *tagliata di tonno* (tuna steak) with red-pepper 'marmalade'. A must for Slow Food gourmands.

✪ ENTERTAINMENT

Piccolo Teatro dei Pupi
Theatre

(☏0931 46 55 40; www.pupari.com; Via della Giudecca 22; ⏰6 times weekly Apr-Oct, fewer Nov-Mar) Syracuse's beloved puppet theatre hosts regular performances; see its website for a calendar. You can also buy puppets made at the family's workshop across the street.

ⓘ INFORMATION

Tourist Office (☏0931 46 29 46; http://turismo. provsr.it; Via Roma 31; ⏰9am-12.30pm Mon-Fri) City maps and general information.

ⓘ GETTING THERE & AWAY

BUS

Buses are generally faster and more convenient than trains, with long-distance buses arriving and departing from the **bus terminal** (Corso Umberto I), just 180m southeast of the train station.

Interbus (☏0931 6 67 10; www.interbus. it) runs buses to Noto (€3.60, one hour, four daily Monday to Friday, two daily Saturday and Sunday), Catania (€6.20, 1½ hours, 18 daily Monday to Friday, nine Saturday, seven Sunday) and its airport, and Palermo (€13.50, 3¼ to 3½ hours, two to three daily). You can buy tickets at the kiosk by the bus stops.

TRAIN

From Syracuse's **train station** (Via Francesco Crispi) up to 11 trains depart daily for Catania (from €6.90, one to 1½ hours) and Messina (from €10.50, 2½ to 3½ hours). Some go on to mainland Italy.

There are also trains to Noto (€3.80, 30 to 35 minutes, eight daily Monday to Saturday) and Ragusa (€8.30, 2¼ to 2½ hours, three daily Monday to Saturday).

ⓘ GETTING AROUND

Syracuse is home to an innovative system of grey electric minibuses operated by **Sd'A Trasporti** (www.siracusadamare.it; one-way/day pass/week pass €1/3/10). To reach Ortygia from the bus and train stations, catch minibus 1, which loops around the island every half-hour or so, making stops at a number of convenient locations. To reach Parco Archeologico della Neapolis, take minibus 2 from Molo Sant'Antonio (just west of the bridge to Ortygia). Be warned that during the **Ciclo di Rappresentazioni Classiche** (Festival of Greek Theatre; www.indafondazione. org; ⏰mid-May–Jun) festival, minibus 2 can get extremely crowded, with lengthy delays. For route maps see Sd'A Trasporti's website.

SARDINIA

Sardinia at a Glance...

The island of Sardinia captivates with its wild hinterland, out-of-this-world beaches and endearing eccentricities. Here coastal drives thrill, prehistory puzzles and four million sheep rule the roads. Most come here for the amazing beaches with their white sand hemming the bluest of blue seas. But Sardinia is also a place where you can get physical, hiking to ancient ruins in the centre and through boulder-strewn canyons. And if you've spent time in other parts of Italy, Sardinia is, in the words of DH Lawrence, different, with its own takes on wine, cheese, bread and pasta as well as a more laid-back, less gesticulating population.

Sardinia in Two Days

Alghero is Sardinia's most fascinating town – spend day one exploring its **sea walls** (p301), churches and defensive towers. End the day with dinner at **La Botteghina** (p301). On day two head for the **beach** (p301) or take a boat trip to the **Grotta di Nettuno** (p301).

Sardinia in Four Days

From Alghero it's a short drive to the **Valle dei Nuraghi** (p304) where you can spend all day exploring the ruins of these mysterious prehistoric structures. In the evening head south to the capital **Cagliari** (p302). On day four hit the steep streets of the city for its architecture and shopping, ending the day at **Poetto Beach** (p303).

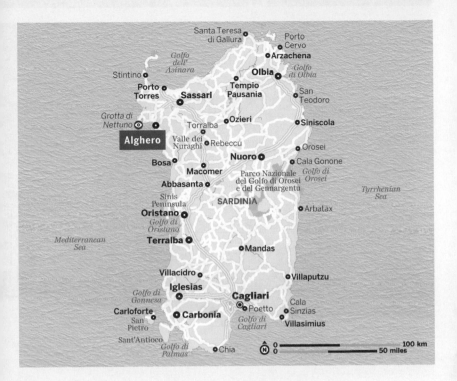

Arriving in Sardinia

Sardinia has three airports – Cagliari Elmas (p304), **Aeroporto di Olbia Costa Smeralda** (☑0789 56 34 44; www. geasar.it) and **Alghero Airport** (☑079 93 50 11; www.aeroportodialghero.it) – all of which are served by budget airlines from across Europe and domestic flights from the mainland. Cagliari Ferry Port handles services operated by Tirrenia ferries to Civitavecchia, Naples and Palermo.

Where to Stay

So what's it to be? A B&B housed in a restored *palazzo* (mansion) in Nuoro, a chic apartment in Cagliari's medieval Il Castello district, or a back-to-nature *agriturismo* (farm stay) snuggled in the depths of Gallura's holm oak forests? With so many atmospheric places to stay, deciding where to base yourself in Sardinia involves so much more than just choosing a bed for the night.

Alghero

One of Sardinia's most beautiful medieval cities, Alghero is the main resort in the northwest. Although largely given over to tourism, the town retains a proud and independent spirit.

Great For...

☑ **Don't Miss**

Alghero's Catalan-style lobster, *aragosta alla catalana*, served with tomato and onion.

Alghero's Past

No one could fail to notice that Alghero (named after the algae that washes up on the coast) has a distinctly Spanish flavour. Ruled by its Genoese founders until the mid-14th century, the Catalan Aragonese took the city in 1353 after a naval battle at Porto Conte. Catalan colonists were encouraged to settle and Alghero became resolutely Catalan Alguer.

The city passed to the Piedmontese House of Savoy in 1720. Poverty meant that by the 1920s the population had fallen to just over 10,000. Heavily bombed in 1943, it remained in poor shape until tourism arrived in the late 1960s.

Old Town

Tourist interest is focused on the old town, the medieval core surrounded by beefy

Medieval tower in Alghero's old town

VALERY ROKHIN/SHUTTERSTOCK ©

Need to Know

English-speaking staff at **InfoAlghero Office** (☎079 97 90 54; www.alghero turismo.eu; Largo Lo Quarter; ⊙9am-1pm & 3.30-6.30pm Mon-Fri, 9am-1pm & 4-7pm Sat year-round, plus 10am-1pm Sun summer only) can provide tourist information on the city and environs.

✕ Take a Break

Gelateria I Bastioni (Bastioni Marco Polo 5; gelato €1.50-4; ⊙2-8pm Apr & Oct, noon-midnight Jun-Sep), the city's best gelateria, is an unmissable part of the Alghero experience. Stop by **La Botteghina** (☎079 973 83 75; www.la botteghina.biz; Via Principe Umberto 63; meals €35; ⊙7-11.30pm Wed-Sun plus noon-3pm Sat & Sun) if you're after Sardinian cuisine.

★ Top Tip

Come in the shoulder seasons (spring and autumn) for a more tranquil experience.

Grotta di Nettuno

An unmissable trip from Alghero takes you to the **Grotta di Nettuno** (☎079 94 65 10; adult/reduced €13/7; ⊙9am-7pm May-Sep, 10am-4pm Apr & Oct, 10am-2pm Jan-Mar, Nov & Dec) across the water on Capo Caccia. Tours of the caves last 45 minutes and take you through narrow walkways flanked by forests of curiously shaped stalactites and stalagmites. The easiest way to get to the caves is to take a ferry from Alghero.

bastions, **sea walls** (Bastioni) and towers. In the centre stands the **Cattedrale di Santa Maria** (☎079 97 92 22; Piazza Duomo 2; ⊙7am-7.30pm, later in summer), its landmark, 16th-century **campanile** (Bell Tower; ☎079 973 30 41; Via Principe Umberto; adult/reduced €2.50/free; ⊙11am-1pm & 7-9pm Mon & Fri Jul & Aug, 11am-1pm Mon, Tue, Thu & Fri & 4-7pm Thu & Fri May, Jun, Sep & Oct, by request Dec & Jan, closed Feb-Apr) rising above the town. Walking the walls and seeking out hidden lunch spots to enjoy the city's signature seafood is how most visitors spend the day, though things really come to life in the evenings when locals hit the streets, chatting, snacking and shopping. The Old Town is also the place to source Alghero's red coral jewellery. On hot days the **Spiaggia di San Giovanni** beach is a short walk to the north.

Cagliari

Sardinia's capital rises in a helter-skelter of golden-hued *palazzi*, domes and facades up to the rocky centrepiece, Il Castello. Although Tunisia is closer than Rome, Cagliari is the most Italian of Sardinia's cities. Vespas buzz down tree-fringed boulevards and locals hang out at busy cafes tucked under arcades in the seafront Marina district.

◉ SIGHTS

Il Castello   Area

This hilltop citadel is c most iconic image, its domes, towers and *palazzi,* once home to the city's aristocracy, rising above the sturdy ramparts built by the Pisans and Aragonese. Inside the battlements, the old medieval city reveals itself like Pandora's box. The university, cathedral, museums and Pisan palaces are wedged into a jigsaw of narrow high-walled alleys. Sleepy though it may seem, the area harbours a number of boutiques, bars and cafes popular with visitors, students and hipsters.

Cattedrale di
Santa Maria   Cathedral

(☏070 864 93 88; www.duomodicagliari.it; Piazza Palazzo 4; ◷8am-noon & 4-8pm Mon-Sat, 8am-1pm & 4.30-8.30pm Sun) Cagliari's graceful 13th-century cathedral stands proudly on Piazza Palazzo. Except for the square-based bell tower, little remains of the original Gothic structure: the clean Pisan-Romanesque facade is a 20th-century imitation, added between 1933 and 1938. Inside, the once-Gothic church has all but disappeared beneath a rich icing of baroque decor, the result of a radical late-17th-century makeover. Bright frescoes adorn the ceilings and the side chapels spill over with exuberant sculptural whirls.

Museo Archeologico
Nazionale   Museum

(☏070 6051 8245; http://museoarcheocagliari. beniculturali.it; Piazza Arsenale; adult/reduced €5/2.50, incl Pinacoteca Nazionale €7/3.50; ◷9am-8pm Tue-Sun) Of the four museums at the **Cittadella dei Musei**, this is the undoubted star. Sardinia's premier archaeological museum showcases

Torre dell'Elefante

CLAUDIO DIVIZIA/SHUTTERSTOCK ©

artefacts spanning thousands of years of history, from the early neolithic, through the Bronze and Iron Ages to the Phoenician and Roman eras. Highlights include a series of colossal figures known as the Giganti di Monte Prama and a superb collection of *bronzetti* (bronze figurines), which, in the absence of any written records, are a vital source of information about Sardinia's mysterious *nuraghic* culture.

Santuario & Basilica di Nostra Signora di Bonaria Church
(☑070 30 17 47; Piazza Bonaria 2; donations welcome; ✆6.30-11.45am & 4.30-8pm summer, 6.30-11.45am & 4-7pm winter) Crowning the Bonaria hill, around 1km southeast of Via Roma, this religious complex is a hugely popular pilgrimage site. Devotees come from all over the world to visit the 14th-century Gothic church (sanctuary) and pray to *Nostra Signora di Bonaria*, a statue of the Virgin Mary and Christ that supposedly saved a ship's crew during a storm. To the right of the sanctuary, the towering basilica still acts as a landmark to returning sailors.

Torre dell'Elefante Tower
(www.beniculturalicagliari.it; Via Santa Croce, cnr Via Università; adult/reduced €3/2; ✆10am-7pm summer, 9am-5pm winter) One of only two Pisan towers still standing, the Torre dell'Elefante was built in 1307 as a defence against the threatening Aragonese. Named after the sculpted elephant by the vicious-looking portcullis, the 42m-high tower became something of a horror show, thanks to the severed heads the city's Spanish rulers used to adorn it with. Climb to the top for far-reaching views over the city's rooftops to the sea.

🛍 SHOPPING
Mercato di San Benedetto Market
(Via San Francesco Cocco Ortu; ✆7am-2pm Mon-Sat) Cagliari's historic morning food market is exactly what a thriving market should be – busy, noisy and packed with fresh, fabulous produce: fish, salami, heavy clusters of

 Poetto Beach

An easy bus ride from the centre, Cagliari's fabulous **Poetto beach** extends for 7km beyond the green Promontorio di Sant'Elia, nicknamed the Sella del Diavola (Devil's Saddle). In summer many of the city's youths decamp here to sunbathe and party in the restaurants and bars that line the sand. Water sports are big and you can hire canoes at the beach clubs. To get to the beach, take bus PF or PQ from Piazza Matteotti.

Promontorio di Sant'Elia
STEFANO GARAU/SHUTTERSTOCK ©

grapes, *pecorino* the size of wagon wheels, steaks, sushi, you name it.

🍴 EATING
La Pola Seafood €€
(☑070 65 06 04; Vico Barcellona 10, meals €30; ✆7-11pm Mon-Sat, plus 1-3pm Sat & Sun) There are many seafood restaurants in the Marina district but few bring in the crowds like this local favourite. To look at, it's nothing out of the ordinary with its murals and orange and yellow walls, but once the food starts arriving you'll appreciate why it's so often packed: multi-dish starters, luxurious lobster mains, beautifully seared tuna.

Luigi Pomata Seafood €€
(☑070 67 20 58; www.luigipomata.com; Viale Regina Margherita 14; meals restaurant €40-50, bistrot €25-30; ✆1-3pm & 8-11pm Mon-Sat) There's always a buzz at chef Luigi Pomata's minimalist seafood restaurant, with

pared-down decor and chefs skilfully preparing super-fresh sushi. For a more casual eating experience, try the Pomata Bistrot, beneath the main restaurant, where you can dine on dishes such as stuffed squid with broccoli cream in a tranquil, relaxed setting.

Dal Corsaro Ristorante €€€
(📞070 66 43 18; www.stefanodeidda.it; Viale Regina Margherita 28; fixed-price menus €70-80; 🕑7.45-11pm Tue-Sun) One of only two Michelin-starred restaurants in Sardinia, Dal Corsaro has long been a bastion of high-end culinary creativity. Calling the shots is chef Stefano Deidda whose artistic brand of cuisine marries technical brilliance with a passion for seasonal Sardinian ingredients. Typical of his style is his *maialino da latte, topinambur e aglio* (roast pork with Jerusalem artichoke and garlic). Bookings required.

🍷 DRINKING & NIGHTLIFE

Caffè Libarium Nostrum Bar
(📞346 5220212; Via Santa Croce 33; 🕑7.30am-2am Tue-Sun) Offering some of the best views in town, this modish Castello bar has panoramic seating on top of the city's medieval ramparts. If the weather's being difficult, make for the brick-lined interior.

Antico Caffè Cafe
(www.anticocaffe1855.it; Piazza Costituzione 10; 🕑7am-2am) DH Lawrence and Grazia Deledda once frequented this grand old cafe, which opened its doors in 1855. Locals come to chat over leisurely coffees, crêpes and salads. There's a pavement terrace, or you can settle inside amid the polished wood, marble and brass.

ℹ INFORMATION

Tourist Office (📞070 677 81 73; www.cagliari turismo.it; Via Roma 145, Palazzo Civico; 🕑9am-8pm summer, 10am-1pm & 2-5pm Mon-Sat winter) Helpful English-speaking staff can provide city information and maps. The office is just inside Palazzo Civico's main entrance, on the right.

ℹ GETTING THERE & AWAY

AIR

Cagliari Elmas Airport (📞070 21 12 11; www. cagliariairport.it) is 9km northwest of the city centre, near Elmas.

Trains run from the airport to Cagliari station approximately every 20 to 30 minutes between 6.37am and 11.07pm. Tickets cost €1.30. A taxi will set you back around €20.

BOAT

Cagliari's ferry port is located just off Via Roma. **Tirrenia** (📞892 123, agency 070 66 95 01; www. tirrenia.it; Via Riva di Ponente 1; 🕑agency 9am-noon Mon-Sat, plus 4-7pm Mon-Wed, 5-8pm Thu, 4.30-7.30pm Fri, 5-7pm Sat) is the main ferry operator serving Cagliari, with year-round services to Civitavecchia (€56 to €66 per person with a *poltrona* seat), Naples (€56 to €98 per person) and Palermo (€58 to €70 per person).

BUS

From the **main bus station** (Piazza Matteotti), **ARST** (Azienda Regionale Sarda Trasporti; 📞800 865042; www.arst.sardegna.it) buses serve destinations across Sardinia.

TRAIN

The main train station is located on Piazza Matteotti. Direct trains serve Sassari (€16.50, 2¾ hours, three daily) where you change for Alghero.

Valle dei Nuraghi

The Valle dei Nuraghi (Valley of the Nuraghi), some 40km south of Sassari, is a verdant area rich in archaeological interest. The hills and fields around the villages of Torralba, Mores, Borutta and Bonarva are littered with the ruins of prehistoric *nuraghi* and *domus de janas,* including one of Sardinia's top archaeological sites, the Nuraghe Santu Antine.

◎ SIGHTS

Nuraghe Santu Antine Archaeological Site
(📞079 84 74 81; www.nuraghesantuantine.it; Torralba; adult/reduced €6/4; 🕑9am-8pm summer, to

5pm winter) One of the largest nuraghic sites in Sardinia, the Nuraghe Santu Antine sits 4km south of Torralba. The complex is focused on a central tower, which now stands 17.5m high but which originally rose to a height of 25m. Around this, walls link three bastions to enclose a triangular compound. The oldest parts of the *nuraghe* date to around 1600 BC, but much of it was built over successive centuries. Visits are by guided tour only.

You enter the compound from the southern side and can walk through the three towers, connected by rough parabolic archways. The entrance to the main tower is separate. Inside, four openings lead into the chamber from an internal hall. Stairs lead up from the hall to the next floor, where a similar but smaller pattern is reproduced. Apart from tiny vents there is no light, and the presence of the dark stone is over-whelming. You ascend another set of steps to reach the floor of what was the final, third chamber, now open to the elements.

On weekdays there are up to eight buses from Sassari to Torralba (€3.10, 45 minutes to 1½ hours), from where it's still a 4km walk to the *nuraghe*.

Necropoli di
Sant'Andrea Priu Archaeological Site
(☑348 5642611; €6; ☺10am-1pm & 3-5pm Mar-May & Oct, 10am-7pm Jun-Sep, by appointment Nov-Feb) About 7km east of Bonorva, the Necropoli di Sant'Andrea Priu is an isolated site, immersed in silence and accessible only by a narrow potholed road. It's made up of around 20 small grottoes carved into trachyte rock, some of which date as far back as 3000 BC.

Dolmen Sa
Coveccada Archaeological Site
`FREE` To the south of Mores, the mighty Dol-men Sa Coveccada is said to be the largest dolmen (a megalithic chambered tomb) in the Mediterranean. Dating to the end of the 3rd millennium BC, the rectangular con-struction consists of three massive stone slabs, roofed by a fourth, weighing around 18 tonnes. As it stands, it reaches a height of 2.7m, is 5m long and 2.5m wide.

  Rebeccu

Between the Necropoli di Sant'Andrea Priu and Bonarva is hilltop Rebeccu, a windswept and largely abandoned medi-eval hamlet carved into calcareous rock. It's worth taking an hour or so to explore the village. According to a local legend, the village was hit by malaria and aban-doned after being cursed by a princess who had been accused of witchcraft and driven out by the villagers.

Museo della
Valle dei Nuraghi Museum
(☑079 84 72 98; Via Carlo Felice 143, Torralba; ☺currently closed) In Torralba, this small museum has a scale model of the Nuraghe Santu Antine and a modest collection of finds lifted from the site. Note that at the time of research the museum was closed for restoration.

EATING

Agriturismo
Sas Abbilas Sardinian €€
(☑347 6758725; www.sasabbilas.it; Località Mariani, Bonorva; fixed-price menus €15 & €30; ☺by reservation) Things don't get much more off the beaten track than this *agriturismo*, ensconced in silent woods 1km or so beyond the Necropoli di Sant'Andrea Priu. Meals are typically abundant affairs featuring cheeses and cured meats, home-grown vegetables, roast meats and classic *seadas* desserts. Just how much you eat depends on whether you opt for the €15 menu or larger €30 option.

GETTING THERE & AWAY

ARST buses serve the main villages (Mores, Tor-ralba, Borutta, Bonorva) from Sassari but that's only half the battle as most of the archaeological sites are some way from the village centres.

To get the best out of the area, you really do need a car.

A trattoria in Trastevere (p86), Rome

In Focus

St Peter's Basilica (p44), Rome

Italy Today

Despite edging closer to the 2020s, Italy's problems have remained unchanged for years. Unemployment and nepotism continue to drive young Italians out of the country, while an ever-increasing number of refugees risk their lives to reach Italian shores. Thankfully, it's not all doom and gloom, with positive developments including urban renewal in Milan and hints of a southern Italian revival.

Regions Rattled

Between August 2016 and January 2017, eight major earthquakes rattled the Appenine areas of central Italy. The deadliest was a 6.2-magnitude quake in August 2016. The earthquake caused close to 300 fatalities. Most of these were in Amatrice, where the collapse of buildings deemed seismically sound exposed a lax approach to building codes. Four strong earthquakes struck Abruzzo in January 2017. Some 29 perished when a post-quake avalanche slammed into a luxury mountain resort.

According to Italy's Civil Protection Agency (Dipartimento Protezione Civile), the bill from the quakes exceeds €23 billion. The tremors have delivered a blow to the regions' tourism and agricultural industries, considered economic backbones. While both the Italian government and the EU have poured millions of euros into recovery efforts, some of Italy's fashion

if Italy were 100 people

92 would be
Italian

4 would be Albanian
& Eastern European

3 would be
Other

1 would be
North African

belief systems
(% of population)

71 — Christian

26 — Other/no religion

3 — Muslim

population per sq km

🚶 ≈ 30 people

Rome — Italy — USA

giants are also pitching in. Among these is luxury footwear company Tod's, whose new factory in Le Marche plans to boost employment there. Meanwhile in Umbria, fashion mogul Brunello Cucinelli announced plans to finance the restoration of the Norcia's Benedictine monastery.

Italexit?

While the UK's Brexit vote has solidified support for the EU across much of the continent, Italy is bucking the trend. Figures released by the Pew Research Centre in 2017 revealed Italy to be the only EU nation where support for the bloc weakened over the previous year. A significant 35% of Italians are now in favour of leaving the EU, compared to 11% in Germany and 22% in France. Italy's figure matches that of Greece, making the two Mediterranean countries the most likely to split with Brussels. Italy's slipping support has been blamed on growing pessimism about the country's economic performance and criticism of the EU's management of economic issues and, of course, the ongoing refugee crisis.

Refugees & Rhetoric

In the first third of 2017, 46,000 asylum seekers reached Italian shores from Africa, an increase of 30% from the previous year. To many Italians, this influx is merely exacerbating the country's already high unemployment and general economic uncertainty. Similar anxieties have been voiced by some of Italy's political figures. In 2017, the District Attorney of Catania, Carmelo Zuccaro, suggested that the very NGOs rescuing refugees at sea could be receiving funding from organised crime syndicates set on flooding Italy with immigrants to destabilise the economy. The accusations have been vehemently refuted by the NGOs, including the Italian branch of Doctors Without Borders.

Cultural Revivals

Despite its challenges, Italy continues to inspire, impress and reinvent. In the north, Milan is back on the global hot list with revamped museums, electric car-sharing schemes and a slew of fresh, contemporary buildings. Parts of southern Italy are also finding their groove. Tourist numbers are soaring in Naples, where improved museums and youth-led cultural initiatives are injecting the city with newfound optimism.

Further south in Basilicata, Matera is drawing greater tourist numbers in the lead-up to its role as Europe's Capital of Culture in 2019. Matera is also one of five Italian cities slated for a 5G mobile network aimed at attracting high-tech research and innovation companies. Across the Tyrrhenian Sea in Sicily, Palermo is slowly but determinedly moving forward from its dark, mafia-riddled past with a string of urban-renewal projects. In 2018, the city is also set to host Manifesta, Europe's top biennial of contemporary art.

Ancient Greek temple in Selinunte, Sicily (p274)

PAOLO TRALLI/SHUTTERSTOCK ©

History

Italy has only been a nation since 1861, prior to which it was last unified as part of the Roman Empire. It has wielded powerful influence as the headquarters of Catholicism, and Italy's dynamic city-states set the modern era in motion with the Renaissance. Italian unity fused north and south in a dysfunctional yet enduring marriage. Even today, Italy still feels like a distinct collection of regions.

c 700,000 BC

Primitive tribes live in caves and hunt elephants, rhinoceroses, hippopotamuses and other hefty wild beasts on the Italian peninsula.

2000 BC

The Bronze Age reaches Italy. Hunter-gatherers have settled as farmers. Copper and bronze are used to fashion tools and arms.

264–241 BC

War rages between Rome and the empire of Carthage. By war's end, Rome is the western Mediterranean's prime naval power.

Roman villa in Herculaneum (p258)

Etruscans, Greeks & Ancient Rome

Long before Renaissance *palazzi* (mansions) and baroque churches, the Italian peninsula was riddled with caves and hill towns built by the Etruscans, who dominated the land by the 7th century BC. Little is known about them, since they spoke a language that today has barely been deciphered. Though impressive as seafarers, warriors and farmers, they lacked cohesion. Greek traders set up a series of independent city-states along the coast and in Sicily in the 8th century BC, collectively known as Magna Graecia. These Greek settlements flourished until the 3rd century BC, and the remains of magnificent Doric temples still stand in Italy's south (at Paestum) and on Sicily (at Agrigento, Selinunte and Segesta). The Etruscans tried and failed to conquer the Greek settlements, but the real threat to both civilisations came from an unexpected source – the grubby but growing Latin town of Rome.

According to legend, Italy's future capital was founded by twins Romulus and Remus on 21 April 753 BC, on the site where they had been suckled by a she-wolf as orphan

AD 79

Mt Vesuvius showers molten rock and ash upon Pompeii and Herculaneum. The towns are only rediscovered in the 18th century.

100–138

The Roman Empire reaches its greatest extent, during the reign of Hadrian.

476

Odovacar proclaims himself king in Rome. The peninsula sinks into chaos and only the eastern half of the empire survives.

infants. Romulus later killed Remus and the settlement was named Rome after him. Over the following centuries, this fearless and often ruthless town become Italy's major power, sweeping aside the Etruscans by the 2nd century AD.

The Roman Republic

Although Roman monuments were emblazoned with the initials SPQR (Senatus Populusque Romanus, or the Senate and People of Rome), the Roman people initially had precious little say in their republic. Known as plebeians (literally 'the many'), the disenfranchised majority slowly wrested concessions from the patrician class by 280 BC, though only a small political class qualified for positions of power in government. Slowly at first, Roman armies conquered the Italian peninsula. Defeated city-states were not taken over directly, but were obliged to become allies, providing troops on demand for the Roman army. Wars with rivals such as Carthage in the east gave Rome control of Sardinia, Sicily, Corsica, mainland Greece, Spain, most of North Africa and part of Asia Minor by 133 BC.

Beware the Ides of March

Born in 100 BC, Gaius Julius Caesar would become one of Rome's most masterful generals, lenient conquerors and capable administrators. After quelling revolts in Spain, Caesar received a Roman mandate in 59 BC to govern Gallia Narbonensis, today's southern France. Caesar raised troops to hold off an invasion of Helvetic tribes from Switzerland, and in 52 to 51 BC stamped out Gaul's last great revolt under the leader Vercingetorix. Diplomatic Caesar was generous to defeated enemies, and the Gauls became his staunchest supporters.

Jealous of the growing power of his one-time protégé, Gnaeus Pompeius Magnus (Pompey) severed his political alliance with Caesar, and convinced the Senate to outlaw Caesar in 49 BC. On 7 January, Caesar crossed the Rubicon River into Italy, sparking civil war. Caesar's three-year campaign ended in decisive victory, and upon his return to Rome in 46 BC, he assumed dictatorial powers.

Caesar launched a series of reforms, overhauled the Senate and embarked on a building program, but by 44 BC, it was clear Caesar had no plans to restore the republic. Dissent grew in the Senate, and on the Ides (15th) of March 44 BC a band of conspirators stabbed Caesar to death in a Senate meeting.

In the years following Caesar's death, his lieutenant, Mark Antony (Marcus Antonius), and nominated heir, great-nephew Octavian, plunged into civil war against Caesar's assassins. Octavian took control of the western half of the empire and Antony headed to the east – but when Antony fell head over heels for Egyptian ruler Cleopatra VII in 31 BC, Octavian and Antony turned on one another. Octavian claimed victory over Antony and Cleopatra in Greece, and when he invaded Egypt, Antony and Cleopatra committed suicide and Egypt became a province of Rome.

902	962	1309
Muslims from North Africa complete the occupation of Sicily, encouraging learning of the Greek classics, mathematics and other sciences.	Otto I is crowned Holy Roman Emperor in Rome. His meddling in Italian affairs leads to clashes between papacy and empire.	Pope Clement V shifts the papacy to Avignon, France, for almost 70 years. Clement had refused to rule in a hostile Rome.

Augustus & the Glories of Empire

By 27 BC Octavian was renamed Augustus (Your Eminence) and conceded virtually unlimited power by the Senate, effectively becoming Rome's emperor. Under Augustus, the arts flourished and buildings were restored and constructed, including the Pantheon.

Over 1.5 million inhabitants thronged the capital's marble temples, public baths, theatres, circuses and libraries. Poverty was rife, and Augustus created Rome's first police force under a city prefect (praefectus urbi) to curb mob violence and quell dissent among the poor, politically underrepresented masses.

Under Hadrian (76–138), the empire reached its greatest extent, including Britain and most of modern-day Middle East, from Turkey to northern Morocco. But by the time Diocletian (245–305) became emperor, the empire was faced with attacks from outside and revolts from within. Diocletian's response to the rise of Christianity was persecution, a policy reversed in 313 under Christian Constantine I (c 272–337).

The empire was later divided in two, with the second capital in Constantinople (modern-day Istanbul) founded by Constantine in 330. The Byzantine eastern empire survived, while Italy and Rome were overrun.

Imperial Insanity

Bribes? Bunga bunga parties? Think they're unsavoury? Spare a thought for the ancient Romans, who suffered their fair share of eccentric leaders. We salute some of the Roman Empire's wackiest, weirdest and downright kinkiest rulers.

Tiberius (14–37) A steady governing hand but prone to depression, Tiberius had a difficult relationship with the Senate and withdrew in his later years to Capri, devoting himself to drinking, orgies and fits of paranoia.

Gaius (Caligula; 37–41) Sex with his sisters and violence were Caligula's idea of entertainment. He emptied the state's coffers and suggested naming a horse consul before being assassinated.

Claudius (41–54) Apparently timid as a child, he was ruthless with enemies and relished watching their executions. According to English historian Edward Gibbon, he was the only one of the first 15 emperors not to take male lovers.

Nero (54–68) Nero had his mum murdered, his first wife's veins slashed, and his second wife kicked to death. The people accused him of fiddling while Rome burned to the ground in 64; Nero blamed the disaster on the Christians. He executed the evangelists Peter and Paul, and had others thrown to wild beasts.

Papal Power & Family Feuds

In a historic twist, the minority religion Emperor Diocletian tried so hard to stamp out preserved Rome's glory. While most of Italy succumbed to invasion from Germanic tribes, Byzantine reconquest and Lombards in the north, the papacy established itself in Rome as a spiritual and secular force.

1321	1714	1805
Dante Alighieri completes his epic poem La divina commedia (The Divine Comedy) and dies the same year.	The end of the War of the Spanish Succession forces the withdrawal of Spanish forces from Lombardy.	Napoleon is proclaimed king of the newly constituted Kingdom of Italy, comprising most of the northern half of the country.

The Last Supper (p200)

★ **Renaissance Wonders**

Duomo (p102), Florence

Galleria degli Uffizi (p99), Florence

Sistine Chapel (p52), Rome

The Last Supper (p201), Milan

Michelangelo's David (p107), Florence

In return for formal recognition of the pope's control of Rome and surrounding Papal States, the Carolingian Franks were granted a powerful position in Italy and their king, Charlemagne, was given the title of Holy Roman Emperor. The bond between the papacy and the Byzantine Empire was broken, and political power shifted north of the Alps, where it remained for more than 1000 years.

Meanwhile, Rome's aristocratic families battled to control the papacy and the right to appoint politically powerful bishops.

The Wonder of the World

Marriage was the ultimate merger between Henry VI, son of Holy Roman Emperor Frederick I (Barbarossa), and Constance de Hauteville, heir to Sicily's Norman throne. The power couple's son, Frederick II (1194–1250), became one of the most colourful figures of medieval Europe. Frederick was a German who grew up in southern Italy and called Sicily home and, as Holy Roman Emperor, allowed freedom of worship to Muslims and Jews. A warrior and scholar, Frederick was nicknamed Stupor Mundi (the Wonder of the World) for his talents as a poet, linguist, mathematician, philosopher and military strategist.

After reluctantly carrying out a (largely diplomatic) Holy Land crusade in 1228–29 under threat of excommunication, Frederick returned to Italy to find papal troops invading Neapolitan territory. Frederick soon had them on the run, and expanded his influence to city-states in central and northern Italy. Battles ensued, which continued after Frederick's death in 1250.

Rise of the City-States

While the south of Italy tended to centralised rule, the north did not. Port cities such as Genoa, Pisa and especially Venice increasingly ignored edicts from Rome, and Florence, Milan, Parma, Bologna, Padua, Verona and Modena resisted Roman meddling in their affairs.

Between the 12th and 14th centuries, these cities developed new forms of government. Venice adopted an oligarchic 'parliamentary' system in a limited democracy. Tuscan and

1814–15

After Napoleon's fall, the Congress of Vienna is held to re-establish the balance of power. The old occupying powers return to Italy.

1848

European revolts spark rebellion in Italy, especially in Austrian-occupied Milan and Venice.

1861

By the end of the Franco-Austrian War (1859–61), Vittorio Emanuele II is proclaimed king of a newly united Italy.

Umbrian city-states created a *comune* (town council), a form of republican government dominated initially by aristocrats, then by wealthy middle classes. Family dynasties shaped their home towns, such as the Medici in Florence. War between the city-states was constant, and Florence, Milan and Venice absorbed their neighbours. Italy's dynamic, independent-minded city-states led a sea change in thinking known as the Renaissance, ushering in the modern era with scientific discoveries, publishing houses and compelling new visions for the world in art.

A Nation Is Born

Centuries of war, plague and occasional religious purges took their toll on Italy's divided city-states, whose role on the world stage was largely reduced by the 18th century to a vacation playground. Napoleon marched into Venice in 1797 without much of a fight, ending 1000 years of Venetian independence and creating the so-called Kingdom of Italy in 1805. But just 10 years later, the reactionary Congress of Vienna restored all the foreign rulers to their places in Italy.

Inspired by the French Revolution and outraged by their subjugation to Napoleon and Austria, Italians began to agitate for an independent, unified nationhood. Count Camillo Benso di Cavour (1810–61) of Turin, prime minister of the Savoy monarchy, became the diplomatic brains behind the Italian unification movement. He won British support for the creation of an independent Italian state and negotiated with the French in 1858 to create a northern Italian kingdom, in exchange for parts of Savoy and Nice.

The bloody 1859–61 Franco-Austrian War ensued, and is now better known as the war for Italian Independence. Pro-Independence forces took over Lombardy and forced the Austrians to relinquish the Veneto. Revolutionary Giuseppe Garibaldi claimed Sicily and southern Italy in the name of Savoy King Vittorio Emanuele II in 1860, and Cavour and the king claimed parts of central Italy (including Umbria and Le Marche). The unified Italian

Florence's Trials by Fire

In 1481 Dominican friar Girolamo Savonarola began prophesying apocalyptic days ahead for Florence unless the city changed its wayward habits. With the horrors of war fresh in their minds and vivid accounts of Florentine plague, Savonarola's blood-curdling predictions struck fear in many Florentine hearts. To appease Savonarola's demands, books, clothes, jewellery, fancy furnishings and art were torched on 'bonfires of the vanities'. Drinking, whoring, partying, gambling, flashy fashion and other sinful behaviours were banned. Florentines soon tired of this fundamentalism. To test Savonarola's commitment to his own methods, the Franciscans invited him to submit to trial by fire. Savonarola sent an emissary instead, but the hapless youth was saved when the trial was cancelled on account of rain. Finally the city government had the fiery friar arrested. He was hanged and burned at the stake as a heretic alongside two supporters on 22 May 1498.

1915	1919	1929
Italy enters WWI on the side of the Allies to win Italian territories still in Austrian hands.	Benito Mussolini forms a right-wing militant group, the Fasci Italiani di Combattimento (Italian Combat Fasces).	Mussolini and Pope Pius XI sign the Lateran Pact, which declares Catholicism Italy's sole religion and the Vatican an independent state.

state was founded in 1861, with Tuscany, the Veneto and Rome incorporated into the fledgling kingdom by 1870 and a parliament established in Rome in 1871.

Mussolini & World Wars

When war broke out in Europe in July 1914, Italy chose to remain neutral, despite being a member of the Triple Alliance with Austria and Germany. Under the terms of the Alliance, Austria was due to hand over northern Italian territory – but Austria refused.

After Austria's deal-breaker, Italy joined the Allies, and plunged into a nightmarish 3½-year war with Austria. When the Austro-Hungarian forces collapsed in November 1918, the Italians marched into Trieste and Trento – but the postwar Treaty of Versailles failed to award Italy the remaining territories it sought.

This humiliation added insult to injury. Italy had lost 600,000 men in the war and, while a few war profiteers had benefited, the majority of the populace was reduced to abject poverty. From this despair rose a demagogue: Benito Mussolini (1883–1945).

A former socialist newspaper editor and one-time draft dodger, Mussolini volunteered for the front and returned wounded in 1917. Frustrated at Italy's treatment in Versailles, Mussolini formed an extremist Italian right-wing militant political group. By 1921 the Fascist Party was feared and admired for its black-shirted street brawlers, Roman salute and self-anointed Duce (Leader), Mussolini. After his march on Rome in 1922 and victory in the 1924 elections, Mussolini took full control of the country by 1926, banning other political parties, independent trade unions and free press.

As the first step to creating a 'new Roman empire', Mussolini invaded Abyssinia (Ethiopia) in 1935–36. Condemned by the League of Nations for his invasion, Mussolini allied with Nazi Germany to back Fascist rebel General Franco in Spain. Yet Italy remained aloof from WWII battles until June 1940, when Germany's blitz of Norway, Denmark and much of France made it look like a winning campaign. Instead, allying with Italy caused Germany setbacks in the Balkans and North Africa.

By the time the Allies landed in Sicily in 1943, the Italians had had enough of Mussolini and his war, and the king had the dictator arrested. Italy surrendered in September – but the Germans rescued Mussolini, occupied the northern two-thirds of the country and reinstalled the dictator. The painfully slow Allied campaign up the peninsula was aided by the Italian Resistance sabotage of German forces, until northern Italy was finally liberated in April 1945. Resistance fighters shot Mussolini and his lover, Clara Petacci, and strung up their corpses in Milan's Piazzale Lotto.

The Grey & Red Years

In the aftermath of war, the left-wing Resistance was disarmed and Italy's political forces scrambled to regroup. The USA, through the economic largesse of the Marshall Plan, wielded considerable political influence and used this to keep the left in check. Immediately after

1940

Italy enters WWII on Nazi Germany's side and invades Greece, which quickly proves to be a mistake.

1944

Mt Vesuvius explodes back into action on 18 March. The eruption is captured on film by USAAF (United States Army Air Forces).

1946

Italians vote in a national referendum to abolish the monarchy and create a republic. King Umberto II refuses to recognise the result.

the war, three coalition governments succeeded one another. The third, which came to power in December 1945, was dominated by the newly formed right-wing Democrazia Cristiana (DC; Christian Democrats), led by Alcide De Gasperi, who remained prime minister until 1953. Italy became a republic in 1946 and De Gasperi's DC won the first elections under the new constitution in 1948.

Until the 1980s, the Partito Comunista Italiano (PCI; Communist Party) played a crucial role in Italy's social and political development, in spite of being systematically kept out of government. The very popularity of the party led to a grey period in the country's history, the *anni di piombo* (years of lead) in the 1970s. Just as the Italian economy was booming, Europe-wide paranoia about the power of the Communists in Italy fuelled a secretive reaction that, it is said, was largely directed by the CIA and NATO.

The 1970s were thus dominated by the spectre of terrorism and considerable social unrest. Neo-Fascist terrorists struck with a bomb blast in Milan in 1969. In 1978 the Brigate Rosse (Red Brigades; a group of young left-wing militants responsible for several bomb blasts and assassinations) claimed their most important victim – former DC prime minister Aldo Moro. His kidnap and murder some 54 days later (the subject of the 2003 film *Buongiorno, notte*) shook the country.

Despite the disquiet, the 1970s also saw positive change. Divorce became legal, legislation allowed women to keep their own names after marriage, and abortion was legalised.

Going the Distance for the Resistance

In 1943 and 1944, the Assisi Underground hid hundreds of Jewish Italians in Umbrian convents and monasteries, while the Tuscan Resistance forged travel documents for them – but the refugees needed those documents fast, before they were deported to concentration camps by Fascist officials. Enter the fastest man in Italy: Gino Bartali, world-famous Tuscan cyclist, Tour de France winner and three-time champion of the Giro d'Italia. After his death in 2003, documents revealed that during his 'training rides' throughout the war years, Bartali had carried Resistance intelligence and falsified documents to transport Jewish refugees to safe locations. Bartali was interrogated at the dreaded Villa Triste in Florence, where suspected anti-Fascists were routinely tortured – but he revealed nothing. Until his death, the long-distance hero downplayed, even to his children, his efforts to rescue Jewish refugees, saying, 'One does these things, and then that's that.'

Clean Hands & Berlusconi

A growth spurt in the aftermath of WWII saw Italy become one of the world's leading economies, but by the 1970s the economy had begun to stagnate, and by the mid-1990s a new and prolonged period of crisis had set in. Economic crisis was coupled with the

1957
Italy signs the Treaty of Rome, which creates the European Economic Community (EEC). The treaty takes effect on 1 January 1958.

1980
A bomb in Bologna kills 85 and injures hundreds more. The Red Brigades and a Fascist cell both claim responsibility.

2001
Silvio Berlusconi's right-wing Casa delle Libertà (Liberties House) coalition wins an absolute majority in national polls.

Tangentopoli (Kickback City) scandal. Led by a pool of Milanese magistrates, investigations known as Mani Pulite (Clean Hands) implicated thousands of public figures in corruption scandals.

The old centre-right political parties collapsed in the wake of these trials, and from the ashes rose what many Italians hoped might be a breath of fresh political air. Media magnate Silvio Berlusconi's Forza Italia (Go Italy) party swept to power in 2001 and again in April 2008. Berlusconi's blend of charisma, confidence, irreverence and promises of tax cuts appealed to many Italian voters. However, Berlusconi's tenure saw the economic situation go from bad to worse, while a series of laws were passed that protected his extensive business interests; for example, granting the prime minister immunity from prosecution while in office.

In 2011 Berlusconi was finally forced to resign due to the deepening debt crisis. A government of technocrats, headed by economist Mario Monti, took over until the inconclusive elections of February 2013. After lengthy postelectoral negotiations, Enrico Letta, a member of the Partito Democratico (PD), was named prime minister, steering a precarious right-left coalition.

Berlusconi's departure ushered in a new era in Italian politics. In 2014, 39-year-old Matteo Renzi, former mayor of Florence, took over as leader of a right-left coalition, making him the third unelected prime minister since Berlusconi's fall (following Monti and Letta). Renzi's cabinet became the youngest in Italian history and the first with an even gender balance.

Renzi resigned in late 2016 after a controversial amendment was turned down by the populace in a referendum. That month Foreign Affairs Minister Paolo Gentiloni became Italy's new prime minister. After resigning as PD leader in February 2017, Renzi won his party's primary election by a landslide on 1 May the same year, returning Renzi as PD leader and reinvigorating the young Tuscan's political ambitions.

2005
Pope John Paul II dies at age 84, prompting a wave of sorrow and chants of *santo subito* (sainthood now).

2011
Berlusconi is forced to step down as the prime minister of Italy. Northern Italian economist Mario Monti is put in charge.

2018
Palermo is crowned Italian Capital of Culture. The Sicilian capital hosts a number of special cultural events.

Botticelli's *Calumny of Apelles* in the Galleria degli Uffizi (p98), Florence

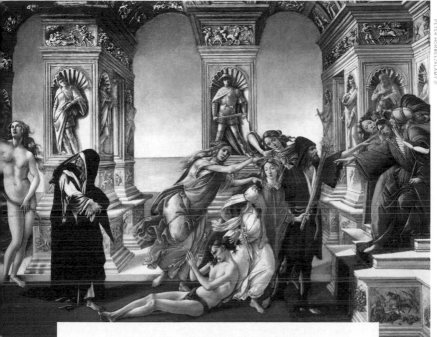

PETER HORREE/ALAMY ©

Art & Architecture

With more Unesco World Heritage sites than any other country, Italy is one place you can hardly throw a stone without hitting a masterpiece. Italian architecture is more than just a wall to hang the art on, with geniuses like Michelangelo creating spaces that alternately give a sense of intimacy and inclusion, steadfastness and momentum.

Classical Era

Only one word describes the buildings of ancient Italy: monumental. The Romans built an empire the size of which had never before been seen and went on to adorn it with buildings cut from the same pattern. From Verona's Roman Arena to Pozzuoli's Anfiteatro Flavio, giant stadiums rose above skylines. Spa centres like Rome's Terme di Caracalla were veritable cities of indulgence, boasting everything from giant marble-clad pools to gymnasiums and libraries. Aqueducts like those below Naples provided fresh water to thousands, while temples such as Pompeii's Tempio di Apollo provided the faithful with awe-inspiring centres of worship.

Antonio Canova's *Venere Vincitrica* (p60), Museo e Galleria Borghese, Rome

LUXERENDERING/SHUTTERSTOCK ©

★ **Italy's Best Museums**

Galleria degli Uffizi (p99), Florence

Vatican Museums (p49), Vatican City

Gallerie dell'Accademia (p171), Venice

Museo del Novecento (p203), Milan

Museo e Galleria Borghese (p60), Rome

Having learned a few valuable lessons from the Greeks, the Romans refined architecture to such a degree that their building techniques, designs and mastery of harmonious proportion underpin much of the world's architecture and urban design to this day.

And though the Greeks invented the architectural orders (Doric, Ionic and Corinthian), it was the Romans who employed them in bravura performances. Consider Rome's Colosseum, with its ground tier of Doric, middle tier of Ionic and penultimate tier of Corinthian columns. The Romans were dab hands at temple architecture too. Just witness Rome's exquisitely proportioned Pantheon, a temple whose huge but seemingly unsupported dome showcases the Roman invention of concrete, an ingredient as essential to the modern construction industry as Ferrari is to the F1 circuit.

Byzantine Glitz

After Constantine became Christianity's star convert, the empire's architects turned their talents to Byzantine churches: domed brick basilicas, plain on the outside, with mosaic-encrusted interiors. One early example is Basilica di Santa Maria Assunta in Torcello. Instead of classical realism, Torcello's *Last Judgment* mosaic conveys a clear message in compelling cartoon shorthand: repent, or snickering devils will drag you off by the hair. Torcello's golden Byzantine mosaics are echoed in Venice's Basilica di San Marco and as far away as Palermo's Cappella Palatina (Palatine Chapel).

Medieval Graces

Italians didn't appreciate over-the-top French Gothic cathedrals; instead, they took Gothic further over the top. A signature Moorish Gothic style graced Venice's *palazzi* (mansions), including the Ca' d'Oro. Milan took Gothic to extremes in its flamboyant Duomo, and the Sienese came up with a novelty for Siena's cathedral: storytelling scenes inlaid in the church floor.

Florentine painter Giotto di Bondone (1266–1337) added another twist. Instead of Byzantine golden cartoon saints, Giotto featured furry donkeys in the life story of St Francis in the Basilica di San Francesco. Pot-bellied pack animals dot Giotto's frescoed Assisi landscape, and when the donkey weeps at the death of the patron saint of animals, it's hard not to well up with him.

Meanwhile, in Siena, Ambrogio Lorenzetti (1290–1348) set a trend for secular painting with his *Allegories of Good and Bad Government* (1337–40), using convincing perspective to make good government seem perfectly achievable, with Peace, Prudence, happy merchants and a wedding party – it's like a medieval Jane Austen novel illustration.

The Renaissance

Plague cut short the talents of many artists and architects in the 14th century, and survivors regrouped. Floating, wide-eyed Byzantine saints seemed far removed from reality, where city-state wars and natural disasters loomed large. Florentine sculptors such as Lorenzo Ghiberti (1378–1455) and Donatello (1386–1466) brought Byzantine ideals down to earth, creating anatomically accurate figures with classical principles of perspective and scale.

Damage to David

Michelangelo's *David* is no stranger to close calls. In 1527, the lower part of his arm was broken off in a riot. In 1843, a hydrochloric 'spruce-up' stripped away some of the original surface, while in 1991 a disturbed, hammer-wielding Italian painter smashed the statue's second left toe.

Architect Filippo Brunelleschi (1377–1446) also looked to the classics as inspiration for Florence's Duomo – specifically Rome's Pantheon – and created a vast dome of mathematically exacting proportions to distribute its massive weight. Critics were sure it would collapse; it still hasn't. But if Brunelleschi studied the classics, neoclassist Palladio pillaged them, borrowing architectural elements of temples, villas and forums for Venice's San Giorgio Maggiore. The idea of creative repurposing wasn't new – the art of reusing old buildings, *spolia,* had been practised in Italy for centuries – but Palladio's conceptual *spolia* was accomplished with easy grace.

Classical laws of harmonious proportions had not been mastered in Roman painting, so Sandro Botticelli (1444–1510) took on the task. Though his early works seem stiff, his *Birth of Venus* (1485) in Florence's Uffizi is a model of poise. Instead of classicism, Leonardo da Vinci (1452–1519) smudged the contours of his lines – a technique called *sfumato,* still visible in his faded *The Last Supper* in Milan. Michelangelo applied the same chiselled perfection to his *David* at Florence's Galleria dell'Accademia and to his image of Adam brought to life by God on the ceiling of the Sistine Chapel.

Mannerism

By 1520, artists such as Michelangelo and Raphael had mastered naturalism, and discovered its expressive limitations – to make a point, the mannerists decided, sometimes you had to exaggerate for effect. One glorious example is *Assunta* (Assumption; 1516–18) by Titian (1490–1576) in Venice's I Frari, where the glowing Madonna rises to heaven in a swirl of red drapery.

Milanese-born Michelangelo Merisi da Caravaggio (1573–1610) had no interest in classical conventions of ideal beauty. Instead he concentrated on revealing and concealing truth through skilful contrasts of light and shadow – or chiaroscuro – evident in his *Conversion of St Paul* and the *Crucifixion of St Peter,* both in Rome's Basilica di Santa Maria del Popolo.

Baroque

The Renaissance's insistence on restraint and pure form led to an exuberant backlash. Baroque religious art served as a kind of spiritual cattle prod, with works by sculptor Gian Lorenzo Bernini (1598–1680), such as his *Ecstasy of St Theresa* in Rome's Chiesa di Santa Maria della Vittoria, simulating religious ecstasy with frantic urgency. While creative boundary pushing was obviously at play, the baroque was also driven by the Counter-Reformation, with much of the work commissioned in an attempt to keep hearts and minds from the clutches of the Protestant church. Baroque artists were early adopters of the sex sells mantra, depicting Catholic spirituality, rather ironically, through worldly

Art Police

Italy's dedicated art police, the Comando Carabinieri Tutela Patrimonio Culturale, tackle the looting of priceless heritage. It's estimated that over 100,000 ancient tombs have been ransacked by *tombaroli* (tomb raiders) alone; contents are sold to private and public collectors around the world.

joy, exuberant decoration and uninhibited sensuality.

With sculptural flourishes, baroque architecture was well suited to the show-place piazzas of Rome and shimmering reflections in Venice's Grand Canal. But in high-density Naples, the only place to go for baroque was indoors – hence the kaleidoscope of coloured, inlaid marbles inside Naples' Certosa di San Martino.

Italian Export Art

By the 18th century, Italy was chafing under foreign domination by Napoleon and Austria. Dependent on foreign admirers, impoverished Italy turned out landscapes for European dandies as 'Grand Tour' souvenirs. The best-known *vedutisti* (landscapists) are Francesco Guardi (1712–93) and Giovanni Antonio Canaletto (1697–1768). Neoclassical sculptor Antonio Canova (1757–1822) took a more daring approach, with a nude sculpture of Napoleon's sister, Paolina Bonaparte Borghese, as a reclining *Venere Vincitrice* (Venus Victrix) in Rome's Museo e Galleria Borghese.

Modern & Contemporary

Stilted by convention and bedraggled by industrialisation, Italy found a creative outlet in European art nouveau, called 'Liberty' in Italian. But some found the style decadent and frivolous. Led by poet Filippo Tommaso Marinetti (1876–1944) and painter Umberto Boccioni (1882–1916), the 1909 *Futurist Manifesto* declared, 'Everything is in movement, everything rushes forward, everything is in constant swift change'. Though the look of futurism was co-opted by Fascism, its impulse could not have been more different: Fascism was an extreme nostalgia for a heroic Italian empire that wasn't exclusively Italian or heroic. Today, futurism is highlighted at Milan's Museo del Novecento. In the 1960s radical Arte Povera (Poor Art) used simple and found materials to trigger associations, and the impact is still palpable at Turin's Galleria Civica d'arte Moderna e Contemporanea (GAM). In architecture, one of the few mid-century high points is the 1956 Pirelli Tower, designed by architect Giò Ponti and engineer Pier Luigi Nervi. Today, Italian architecture is back on the world stage, ranging from Massimiliano Fuksas' whimsical glass sailboat Fiera Milano to Renzo Piano's Turin Fiat factory creatively repurposed into Slow Food showcase, Eataly.

Ribollita (bean, vegetable and bread soup)

The Italian Table

Sit back and enjoy: you're in for a host of treats. Just don't expect the stock-standards that are served at your local Italian back home. In reality, Italian cuisine is a handy umbrella term for the country's diverse regional cuisines. Has anything ever tasted this good? Probably not. Will it ever again? Probably tomorrow. Buon appetito.

Regional Cuisine

Italian city-state rivalries once settled with castle sieges and boiling oil poured on enemies are now settled through considerably friendlier culinary competition – though there may still be some boiling oil involved. In this stiff regional competition for gourmet affections, there is a clear winner: travellers. They get to sample regional variations on Italy's seasonal speciality produce, seafood and meats.

Rome

Italy's capital offers more than just Viagra-strength espresso at La Casa del Caffè Tazza d'Oro (p90) and glorious gelato. Must-try menu items include thin-crust pizza, *saltimbocca* (literally 'leap in the mouth'; veal sautéed with prosciutto and sage) and calorific

Sicilian *cannoli*

pasta classics spaghetti carbonara (with egg, cheese and *guanciale* – pigs' cheeks) and *bucatini all'amatriciana* (pasta with tomato, pancetta and chilli-peppers). Rome is the spiritual home of nose-to-tail noshing, where staples such as *trippa alla romana* (tripe with potatoes, tomato, mint and *pecorino* cheese) and *pajata* (a pasta dish of milk-fed calf's intestines in tomato sauce) beckon brave gourmands.

Liguria & Milan

Milan specialises in *risotto alla milanese con ossobucco* (Milanese-style veal shank and marrow with saffron rice) and *bresaola* (air-dried salted beef), and the latest culinary trend is *latterie* (milk bars), comfort-food restaurants emphasising cheese, vegetables and simple homemade pasta. The Ligurian coast south of Turin is famed for pesto and focaccia, best enjoyed with staggering seaside views in the coves of Cinque Terre.

Bologna to Venice

Culinary culture shock may occur between lunch and dinner in the northeast, where you can lunch on Bologna's namesake *pasta alla bolognese* (a rich beef and pork belly *ragù* usually served with tagliatelle pasta; spaghetti bolognese is a foreign adaptation) and then dine on Venetian polenta with *sarde in saor* (marinated sardines with onions, pine nuts and sultanas).

Venice celebrates its lagoon location and spice-trading past in dishes such as squid-ink risotto and *granseole* (spider crab) graced with star anise. Venetian dandies kicked off the European trend for hot chocolate at cafes ringing Piazza San Marco, and you can still enjoy a decadent, gooey cup in baroque splendour.

Tuscany

The Tuscans have a special way with meat, herbs and olive oil – think whole boar, pheasant, rabbit on a spit, or pampered Maremma beef in *spiedino toscano* (mixed grill). Another must for carnivores is the tender, hulking *bistecca alla fiorentina,* the bone-in steak served in slabs 'three fingers thick' at restaurants such as Florence's Trattoria Mario (p122). Peasant soup (*acquacotta,* literally 'cooked water') becomes a royal feast in the Tuscan town of Lucca, with the addition of farm-fresh eggs, local *pecorino* cheese, toasted bread and Lucca's prized golden olive oil.

Naples, Pompeii & the Amalfi Coast

Sun-soaked Mediterranean flavours sparkle in Naples and its coastal turf, where hot capsicums (peppers), citrus and prized San Marzano tomatoes thrive in the volcanic soils that buried Pompeii. Local buffalo-milk mozzarella with basil and tomato sauce piled on pizza dough makes Naples' most famous export: *pizza margherita*. In Naples' *centro storico* (historic centre) you'll find sublime street food in historic *friggitorie* (fast-food kiosks), from *arancini* (mozzarella-filled rice balls) to tempura-style eggplant. Naples was the playground of French conquerors and Spanish royalty, whose influence is savoured in *sfogliatelle* (pastries filled with cinnamon-laced ricotta) and rum *babà*, French rum cake made Neapolitan with Vesuvius-like eruptions of cream.

South of Naples, you'll know you're approaching the Amalfi Coast when you get a whiff of perfumed Amalfi lemons. The local citrus stars alongside the day's seafood catch and in *limoncello*, Amalfi's sweet lemon digestive.

Sicily & Southern Italy

Ancient Arab influences make Sicily's pasta dishes velvety and complex, and this is one of the best places in Italy to eat dessert. Wild-caught tuna baked in a salt crust, local anchovy-studded *fiori di zucca ripieni* (cheese-stuffed squash blossoms) and *arancini siciliani* (risotto balls) may forever spoil you for lesser versions. Begin southern food adventures at Catania's La Pescheria (p290), the legendary fish market, and look out for Sicilian *dolci* (sweets) that include pistachio gelato and sculpted marzipan.

Menu Decoder

Tutti a tavola! (Everyone to the table!) This is one command every Italian heeds without question. To disobey would be unthinkable – what, you're going to eat your pasta cold? And insult the cook? Even anarchists wouldn't dream of it. You're not obliged to eat three courses – or even two – but here is a rundown of your menu options.

Wine

Which one of Italy's hundreds of speciality wines will best complement the cuisine? When in doubt, keep it local: below are wines to watch for in each region.

Rome & Around Est! Est!! Est!!! (dry herbal/mineral white).

Venice & Verona *Prosecco* (Italy's most popular sparkling white), Amarone (dark, brooding red with velvety tannins), Soave (crisp, minerally white), Tocai (unctuous, fruity/floral white), Valpolicella (versatile, medium-bodied red).

Milan & Lakes Franciacorta (Italy's top-quality sparkling white), Bardolino (light, satiny red).

Piedmont & Around Barolo (Italy's favourite red; elegant and structured), Asti (aka Asti Spumante; sparkling white), Cinque Terre (minerally/grassy white), Gavi (dry, aromatic white), Barbera d'Alba (pleasantly acidic, tomato friendly red), Dolcetto (light-hearted, aromatic red), Sciacchetrá (Cinque Terre's aromatic dessert wine).

Tuscany Chianti Classico (big-hearted red, earthy character), Brunello di Montalcino (Italy's biggest, most complex vintage red), Super Tuscan IGT (bombastic, Sangiovese-based red), Morellino di Scansano (floral, medium-weight red).

Naples & Amalfi Coast Falanghina (dry, minerally white).

Sicily Marsala (sweet fortified wine), Nero d'Avola (volcanic, mineral red).

Antipasti (Appetisers)

Tantalising offerings on the antipasti menu may include the house bruschetta (grilled bread with a variety of toppings, from chopped tomato and garlic to black-truffle spread), seasonal treats such as *prosciutto e melone* (cured ham and cantaloupe) and regional delights including *friarelle con peperoncino* (Neapolitan broccoli with chilli). At this stage, bread (and sometimes *grissini* – Turin-style breadsticks) are deposited on the table as part of your €1 to €4 *pane e coperto* (bread and 'cover', or table service).

Primo (First Course)

Starch is the star in Italian first courses, including pasta and gnocchi (especially in south and central Italy), risotto and polenta (northern Italian specialities). *Primi* menus usually include ostensibly vegetarian or vegan options, such as *pasta con pesto* (the classic north-western pasta with basil, *parmigiano reggiano* (Parmesan) and pine nuts) or *alla Norma* (with eggplant and tomato, Sicilian-style), or the extravagant *risotto al Barolo* (Piedmont risotto cooked in high-end Barolo wine). But even if a dish sounds vegetarian in theory, ask about the stock used in that risotto or polenta, or the ingredients in that suspiciously rich tomato sauce – there may be beef, ham or ground anchovies involved.

Secondo (Second Course)

Light lunchers usually call it a day after the *primo,* or skip the *primo* and just opt for a *secondo*. But if you're up for a long meal, you can follow the *primo* with meat, fish or *contorni* (side dishes) in the second course. Options may range from ambitious meats (especially in Tuscany and Rome) and elegant seafood (notably in Venice and Sicily) to lightly grilled vegetables such as *radicchiodi Treviso* (feathery red rocket). A less inspiring option is *insalata mista* (mixed green salad), typically unadorned greens with vinegar and oil on the side – croutons, cheeses, nuts and other ingredients have no business in classic Italian salads.

Frutti e Dolci

'Siamo arrivati alla frutta' ('We've arrived at the fruit') is an idiom roughly meaning 'we've hit rock bottom' – but hey, not until you've had one last tasty morsel. Your best bets on the fruit menu are local and seasonal. *Formaggi* (cheeses) are an excellent option in Piedmont, but in the south, do the *dolci*. *Biscotti* (twice-baked biscuits) are divine dunked in wine, and consider *zabaglione* (egg and Marsala custard), *tiramisu* (literally 'pick me up', combining eggs, marscapone, coffee and Marsala wine), cream-stuffed profiteroles or Sicily's cream-stuffed shell pastries immortalised in *The Godfather:* 'Leave the gun. Take the cannoli.'

Caffè (Coffee)

Snoozing rather than sightseeing will be most attractive after a proper Italian lunch, so if you want to get things done, it's advisable to administer espresso as a final flourish. Cappuccino (named after the colour of Capuchin monks' habits) is usually only drunk in the morning, before 11am, but later in the day you could indulge in an espresso with a tiny stain of milk as a *caffè macchiato*. On the hottest days of summer, a *granita di caffè* (coffee with shaved ice and whipped cream) is just the ticket.

Caffettiera (coffee maker)

Lifestyle

Imagine you wake up and discover you're Italian.
It's not that obvious at first – your pyjamas just have
a subtly more elegant cut. But when you open your
wardrobe, there's the dead giveaway: the shoes. What
might it be like walking in those butter-soft, richly
coloured shoes for the day, and what could you discover
about Italy?

A Day in the Life of Italy

Sveglia! You're woken not by an alarm but by the burble and clatter of the *caffettiera,* the ubiquitous stovetop espresso maker. If you're between the ages of 18 and 34, there's a 60% chance that's not a room-mate making your morning coffee: it's *mamma* or *papà.* This is not because Italy is a nation of pampered *mammoni* (mama's boys) and spoilt *figlie di papà* (daddy's girls) – at least, not entirely. With youth unemployment high and many university graduates underemployed on short-term contracts, what's the hurry to leave home? Running late, you bolt down your coffee scalding hot (an acquired Italian talent) then get your morning paper from Bucharest-born Nicolae – your favourite news vendor and (as a Romanian) part of Italy's largest migrant community.

On your way to work you scan the headlines: another 24-hour transport strike, more coalition-government infighting and an announcement of new EU regulations on cheese. Outrageous! The cheese regulations, that is; the rest is to be expected. At work, you're buried in paperwork until noon, when it's a relief to join friends for lunch and a glass of wine. Afterwards you toss back another scorching espresso at your favourite bar and find out how your barista's latest audition went – turns out you went to school with the sister of the director of the play, so you promise to put in a good word.

Back at work by 2pm, you multitask Italian-style, chatting with co-workers as you dash off work emails, text your schoolmate about the barista on your *telefonino* (mobile phone) and surreptitiously check *l'Internet* for employment listings – your work contract is due to expire soon. After a busy day like this, *aperitivi* (pre-dinner drinks) are definitely in order, so at 6.30pm you head directly to the latest happy-hour hot spot. Your friends arrive, the decor is *molto* design and the vibe *molto* fashion, until suddenly it's time for your English class – everyone's learning it these days, if only for the slang.

The People

Who are the people you'd encounter every day as an Italian? Just over 19% of your fellow citizens are smokers and around 61% drive (or are driven) to work, compared to only 3.3% who cycle. The average Italian is 44.9 years old, up 0.2 years since 2015. The percentage of Italians aged over 65 is 22.3%, the highest ratio in the EU. This explains the septuagenarians you'll notice on parade with dogs and grandchildren in parks, affably arguing about politics in cafes and ruthlessly dominating bocce tournaments.

You might also notice a striking absence of children. Italy's birth rate is one of the lowest in Europe; an average of 1.43 births per woman compared to 1.89 in the UK, 1.98 in Ireland and 2.07 in France.

From 1876 to 1976, Italy was a country of net emigration. With some 30 million Italian emigrants dispersed throughout Europe, the Americas and Australia, remittances from Italians abroad helped keep Italy's economy afloat during economic crises after independence and WWII.

The tables have since turned. Political and economic upheavals in the 1980s brought new arrivals from Central Europe, Latin America and North Africa, including Italy's former colonies in Tunisia, Somalia and Ethiopia. More recently, waves of Chinese and Filipino immigrants have given Italian streetscapes a East Asian twist. While immigrants account for just over 8% of Italy's population today, the number is growing. In 2001, the country's foreign population (a number that excludes foreign-born people who take Italian citizenship) was 1.3 million. By 2016, that number had almost quadrupled to over five million.

From a purely economic angle, these new arrivals are vital for the country's economic health. While most Italians today choose to live and work within Italy, the country's population is ageing and fewer young Italians are entering blue-collar agricultural and industrial fields. Without immigrant workers to fill the gaps, Italy would be sorely lacking in tomato sauce and shoes. They also keep Italy's tourism economy afloat.

Religion, Loosely Speaking

While almost 80% of Italians identify as Catholics, only around 15% of Italy's population regularly attends Sunday Mass. That said, the Church continues to exert considerable influence on public policy and political parties, especially those of the centre- and far-right.

But in the land of the double park, even God's rules are up for interpretation. Sure, *mamma* still serves fish on Good Friday, but while she might consult *la Madonna* for guidance, chances are she'll get a second opinion from the *maga* (fortune teller) on Channel 32. It's estimated that around 13 million Italians use the services of psychics, astrologers and fortune tellers. While the uncertainties stirred up by Italy's still-stagnant economy help drive these numbers, Italians have long been a highly superstitious bunch. From not toasting with water to not opening umbrellas inside the home, the country offers a long list of tips to keep bad luck at bay.

Superstitious beliefs are especially strong in Italy's south. Here *corni* (horn-shaped charms) adorn everything from necklines to rear-view mirrors to ward off the *malocchio* (evil eye) and devotion to local saints takes on an almost cultish edge. Every year in Naples, thousands cram into the *duomo* to witness the blood of San Gennaro miraculously liquefy in the phial that contains it. When the blood liquefies, the city breathes a sigh of relief – it symbolises another year safe from disaster. When it didn't in 1944, Mt Vesuvius erupted, and when it failed again in 1980, an earthquake struck the city that year. Coincidence? Perhaps. Yet even the most cynical Neapolitans may have wondered what the future holds when the miracle failed once more in December 2016.

Calcio (Football): Italy's Other Religion

Catholicism may be your official faith, but as an Italian your true religion is likely to be *calcio* (football). On any given weekend from September to May, chances are that you and your fellow *tifosi* (football fans) are at the *stadio* (stadium), glued to the TV or checking the score on your mobile phone. Come Monday, you'll be dissecting the match by the office water cooler.

Like politics and fashion, football is in the very DNA of Italian culture. Indeed, they sometimes even converge. Silvio Berlusconi first found fame as the owner of AC Milan and cleverly named his political party after a well-worn football chant. Fashion royalty Dolce & Gabbana declared football players 'the new male icons', using five of Italy's hottest on-field stars to launch its 2010 underwear collection. Decades earlier, 1960s singer Rita Pavone topped the charts with 'La partita di pallone' (The Football Match), in which the frustrated pop princess laments being left alone by her lover, who has gone to watch a football match. It's no coincidence that in Italian *tifoso* means both 'football fan' and 'typhus patient'. When the ball ricochets off the post and slips fatefully through the goalie's hands, when half the stadium is swearing while the other half is euphorically shouting Gooooooooooooooooal!, 'fever pitch' is the term that comes to mind.

Nothing quite stirs Italian blood like a good (or bad) game. Nine months after Italy's 2006 World Cup victory against France, hospitals in northern Italy reported a baby boom. In February the following year, rioting at a Palermo-Catania match in Catania left one policeman dead and around 100 injured. Blamed on the Ultras – a minority group of hardcore football fans – the violence shocked both Italy and the world, leading to a temporary ban of all matches in Italy and increased stadium security. A year earlier, the match-fixing 'Calciopoli' scandals resulted in revoked championship titles and temporary demotion of Serie A (top-tier national) teams, including the mighty Juventus.

Yet, the same game that divides also unites. You might be a Lazio-loathing supporter of AS Roma, but when the national *Azzurri* (The Blues) swag the World Cup, you are nothing but a heart-on-your-sleeve *Italiano* (Italian). In his book *The 100 Things Everyone Needs to Know About Italy,* Australian journalist David Dale writes that Italy's 1982 World Cup win 'finally united twenty regions which, until then, had barely acknowledged that they were part of the one country'.

Versace shirts

Fashion & Design

Better living by design: what could be more Italian? Though the country could get by on its striking good looks, Italy is ever-mindful of design details. They are everywhere you look: the yellow silk lining inside a sober grey suit, the glove compartment of a Fiat 500 car, the toy duck hidden inside your chocolate uova di pasqua (Easter egg).

Italian Fashion

Italians have strong opinions about aesthetics and aren't afraid to share them. A common refrain is *Che brutta!* (How hideous!), which may strike visitors as tactless. But consider it from an Italian point of view – everyone is rooting for you to look good, and who are you to disappoint?

Trendsetters & Fashion Victims

Italians have been style trendsetters since the Middle Ages, when Venetian merchants imported dyes and silks from the East, and Florence's wool guild rose to political prominence and funded a Renaissance. Clothes became markers of social status, and not only nobles set trends: courtesans and trophy wives were so widely imitated that sumptuary laws were passed restricting low necklines and growing train lengths. Italy's local fashions went global through the dissemination of Florentine art and illustrated pamphlets from Venice's publishing houses – predecessors of billboards and Italian *Vogue*. The Venetian innovation of eyeglasses was initially mocked by monocle-sporting English dandies, who eventually saw the light – and their descendants now pay impressive sums for Italian designer sunglasses.

Italy has also had its share of fashion victims over the centuries. After political crusader Savonarola demanded Florentines surrender their extravagant statement jewellery under pain of flagellation, he was burned at the stake. So many Venetian noblewomen were hobbled emulating courtesans in their staggering platform heels that 1430 sumptuary laws set maximum shoe heights of around 60cm (2ft). Siena was more practical, requiring its prostitutes to wear flat shoes. Today, staggering platforms and chic flats still make the rounds of Milan runways.

Italy's Fashion Powerhouses

Cobblers and tailors in Florence who once made only made-to-measure designs began to present seasonal lines in the 1950s to '60s, launching the empires of psychedelic-print maestro Emilio Pucci, logoed leather-goods magnate Guccio Gucci and shoe maven Salvatore Ferragamo. But Milan literally stole the show from Florence in 1958, hosting Italy's first Fashion Week. With its ready factories, cosmopolitan workforce and long-established media, Milan created ready-to-wear fashion for global markets from Armani, Missoni, Versace, Dolce & Gabbana and Prada. Rome remains Italy's political capital and the home of Valentino and his signature red dress, but Milan is Italy's fashion centre, and a key stop on the international design circuit.

Today, Italian fashionistas are combining mass fashion with artisan-made style signatures. This trend is recession friendly: artisan-made items are made to last and singular, hence less trend-sensitive. Fashion-forward artisan hot spots include Florence (cobblers and jewellers), Naples (tailors) and Venice (eyewear, fashion and accessories).

Fashion Family Sagas

Tight as they may be, Italian families are not always examples of heart-warming domesticity. Indeed, some of Italy's most fashionable *famiglie* (families) prove that every clan has its problems, some small, some extra, extra large.

Consider the Versace bunch, fashion's favourite catwalking Calabrians. One of Italy's greatest exports, the familial dynasty was founded by Gianni, inexplicably shot dead outside his Miami mansion by serial killer Andrew Cunanan in 1997. With Gianni gone, creative control was passed to Donatella, Gianni's larger-than-life little sister. The subject of Anna Wintour's most unusual fashion memory – full-body spandex on horseback – the former coke-addled party queen flew herself to rehab on daughter Allegra's 18th birthday.

Then there are the Florentine fashion rivals, the Gucci clan. Established by Guccio Gucci in 1904, the family firm reads like a bad Brazilian soap – power struggles between Rodolfo and Aldo (Guccio's sons) in the 1950s; assault charges by Paolo (Aldo's son) against siblings Roberto and Giorgio, and cousin Maurizio Gucci, in 1982; and a major fallout between Paolo and father Aldo over the offshore siphoning of profits.

The last Gucci to run the company was Maurizio, who sold his share to Bahrain investment bank Investcorp in 1993 for US$170 million. Two years later, Maurizio was dead, gunned down outside his Milan office on the order of ex-wife, Patrizia Reggiani.

Having served only 18 years of her 26-year sentence, Reggiani was released early from custody in late 2016 for good behaviour. Later an appeals court in Milan ruled that despite

★ **Italian Design Icons**

Bialetti caffettiera

Cinzano vermouth

Acqua di Parma cologne

Piaggio Vespa

Olivetti 'Valentine' typewriter

Piaggio Vespa

MASSIMO CAMPANARI/SHUTTERSTOCK ©

her conviction, Gucci's ex-wife remained entitled to an annual allowance of just over €1 million, a deal agreed to by Maurizio in 1993. The court also ruled that Reggiani was owed over €18 million in back payments accrued during her time behind bars.

Modern Italian Design

During centuries of domination by Napoleon and other foreign powers, Italy ceded ground as global taste-maker to French and Austrian art nouveau and English Arts and Crafts – until the industrial era. Italian futurism inspired radical, neoclassical streamlining more suited to Italian manufacturers than French decorators or English craftspeople. The dynamic deco style of futurist paintings was co-opted in Fascist propaganda posters, architecture, furniture and design, like cogs in a political machine.

The rise of Fascism required modern factories for the war industry, and after WWII, repurposed military industrial complexes in Turin and Milan became centrepieces of a new global, consumer-centric economy. Turin's strength was industrial design, from Lavazza espresso machines to the Fiat 500 car; Milan focused on fashion and home decor. As seen in Italian film and pioneering Italian lifestyle magazines such as *Domus,* Italy's mass-produced design objects seemed both aspirational and attainable.

Design Showcases

Though Italian design is distributed globally, seeing it in its home context offers fresh appreciation – and critical perspective. While the Vatican Museums showcase pre-20th-century objects of power, from saints' reliquaries to papal thrones, Milan's Triennale museum focuses on 20th-century secular talismans, including mid-century Vespas to 1980s Memphis Group chairs. Like churches, Italian designer showcases are carefully curated to offer beauty and belonging, from the 1950s Scarpa-designed Olivetti showroom in Venice's Piazza San Marco to Alessi's new flagship store in Milan. Milan's Salone del Mobile is the world's largest design fair, with 2500 companies represented – yet differences in corporate design can seem slight and easily outshone by 700 independent designers in the satellite fair.

BRIAN KINNEY/SHUTTERSTOCK ©

Survival Guide

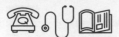

Directory A–Z

Accommodation

Accommodation in Italy is incredibly varied, with everything from family-run *pensioni* and *agriturismi* (farm stays) to idiosyncratic B&Bs, designer hotels, serviced apartments, and even *rifugi* (mountain huts) for weary mountain trekkers.

When considering where to slumber, note the following tips:

○ It pays to book ahead in high season, especially in popular coastal areas in the summer and popular ski resorts in the winter. In the urban centres you can usually find something if you leave it to luck, though reserving a room is essential during key events (such as the furniture and fashion fairs in Milan).

○ Accommodation rates can fluctuate enormously depending on the season, with Easter, summer and the

The Slumber Tax

Visitors may be charged an extra €1 to €7 per night. This is known as a 'tourist tax' or 'room occupancy tax'.

Christmas/New Year period being the typical peak tourist times. Seasonality also varies according to location. Expect to pay top prices in the mountains during the ski season (December to March) or along the coast in summer (July and August). Conversely, summer in the parched cities can equal low season; in August especially, many city hotels charge as little as half price.

○ Price also depends greatly on location. A bottom-end budget choice in Venice or Milan will set you back the price of a decent mid-range option in, say, rural Campania. Where possible, we present the high-season rates for each accommodation option.

○ Most hotels offer breakfast, though this can vary from bountiful buffets to more modest offerings of pastries, packaged yoghurt and fruit. The same is true of B&Bs, where morning food options can sometimes be little more than pre-packaged *cornetti* (Italian croissants), biscuits, jam, coffee and tea.

○ Hotels usually require that reservations be confirmed with a credit-card number. No-shows will be docked a night's accommodation.

B&Bs

B&Bs are a burgeoning sector of the Italian accommodation market and can be found throughout the country in both urban and rural settings. Options

include everything from restored farmhouses, city *palazzi* (mansions) and seaside bungalows to rooms in family houses. In some cases, a B&B can also refer to a self-contained apartment with basic breakfast provisions provided. Tariffs for a double room cover a wide range, from around €60 to €140.

Farmhouse Holidays

Live out your bucolic fantasies at one of Italy's growing number of *agriturismi*. A long-booming industry in Tuscany and Umbria, farm stays are spreading across the country like freshly churned butter. While all *agriturismi* are required to grow at least one of their own products, the farm stays themselves range from rustic country houses with a handful of olive trees to elegant country estates with sparkling pools or fully functioning farms where guests can pitch in.

Hotels & Pensioni

While the difference between an *albergo* (hotel) and a *pensione* is often minimal, a *pensione* will generally be of one- to three-star quality while an *albergo* can be awarded up to five stars. *Locande* (inns) long fell into much the same category as *pensioni,* but the term has become a trendy one in some parts and reveals little about the quality of a place. *Affittacamere* are rooms for rent in private houses. They are generally simple affairs.

Quality can vary enormously and the official star system gives limited clues. One-star hotels/ *pensioni* tend to be basic and usually do not offer private bathrooms. Two-star places are similar, but rooms will generally have a private bathroom. Three-star options usually offer reasonable standards. Four- and five-star hotels offer facilities such as room service, laundry and dry-cleaning.

Prices are highest in major tourist destinations. They also tend to be higher in northern Italy. A *camera* *singola* (single room) costs from around €40, and from around €60 in more expensive cities like Milan. A *camera doppia* (twin beds) or *camera matrimoniale* (double room with a double bed) will cost from around €60 or €70, even more in places like Milan.

Customs Regulations

On leaving the EU, non-EU citizens can reclaim Value Added Tax (VAT) on purchases over €154.94. For more information, visit www.italia.it.

Book Your Stay Online

For more accommodation reviews by Lonely Planet authors, check out http://hotels.lonely planet.com/italy. You'll find independent reviews, as well as recommendations on the best places to stay. Best of all, you can book online.

Discount Cards

Free admission to many galleries and cultural sites is available to those under 18 and over 65 years old, and visitors aged between 18 and 25 often qualify for a discount. In some cases, these discounts only apply to EU citizens.

Some cities or regions offer their own discount passes, such as Roma Pass (three days €38.50), which offers free use of public transport and free or reduced admission to Rome's museums.

In many places around Italy, you can also save money by purchasing a *biglietto cumulativo*, a ticket that allows admission to a number of associated sights for less than the combined cost of separate admission fees.

Climate

Rome

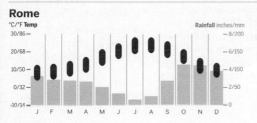

Palermo

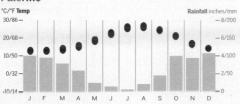

Venice

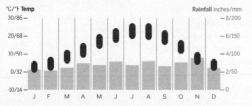

Electricity

Electricity in Italy conforms to the European standard of 220V to 230V, with a frequency of 50Hz. Wall outlets typically accommodate plugs with two or three round pins (the latter grounded, the former not).

230V/50Hz

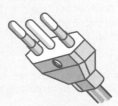

230V/50Hz

Food

The following price ranges refer to a meal of two courses (antipasto/*primo* and *secondo*), a glass of house wine, and *coperto* (cover charge) for one person.

€	under €25
€€	€25-45
€€€	over €45

These figures represent a halfway point between expensive cities such as Milan and Venice and the considerably cheaper towns across the south. Indeed, a restaurant rated as midrange in rural Sicily might be considered dirt cheap in Milan. Note that most eating establishments add *coperto* of around €2 to €3. Some also include a service charge *(servizio)* of 10% to 15%.

Insurance

A travel-insurance policy to cover theft, loss and medical problems is a very good idea. It may also cover you for cancellation or delays to your travel arrangements. Paying for your ticket with a credit card can often provide limited travel accident insurance and you may be able to reclaim the payment if the operator doesn't deliver. Ask your credit-card company what it will cover.

Worldwide travel insurance is available at www.lonelyplanet.com/travel-insurance. You can buy, extend and claim online anytime – even if you're already on the road.

Internet Access

❍ Numerous Italian cities and towns offer public wi-fi hot spots, including Rome and Venice. To use them, you will need to register online using a credit card or an Italian mobile number. An easier option (no need for a local mobile number) is to head to a cafe or bar offering free wi-fi.

❍ Most hotels, B&Bs, hostels and *agriturismi* (farm stays) offer free wi-fi to guests, though signal quality can vary. There will sometimes be a computer for guest use.

Legal Matters

Italy is generally a safe country to travel in. The most likely reason for a brush with the law is to report a theft. If you have something stolen and you want to claim it on insurance, you must make a statement to the police, as insurance companies won't pay up without official proof of a crime.

Police

The Italian police is divided into three main bodies: the *polizia*, who wear navy-blue jackets; the *carabinieri*, in a black uniform with a red stripe; and the grey-clad *guardia di finanza* (fiscal police), responsible for fighting tax evasion and drug smuggling. If you run into trouble, you're most likely to end up dealing with the *polizia* or *carabinieri*.

To contact the police in an emergency, dial 112 or 113.

Drugs & Alcohol

○ If you're caught with what the police deem to be a dealable quantity of hard or soft drugs, you risk prison sentences of between two and 20 years.

○ Possession for personal use is punishable by administrative sanctions, although first-time offenders might get away with a warning.

○ The legal limit for blood-alcohol when driving is 0.05% and random breath tests do occur.

LGBT Travellers

Homosexuality is legal (over the age of 16) and even widely accepted, but Italy is notably conservative in its attitudes, largely keeping in line with those of the Vatican. Overt displays of affection by LGBT couples can attract a negative response, especially in smaller towns.

There are gay venues in Rome and Milan, and a handful in places such as Florence and Naples. Some coastal towns and resorts (such as the Tuscan town of Viareggio or Taormina in Sicily) are popular gay holiday spots in the summer.

Online resources include the following (mostly Italian-language) websites:

Circolo Mario Mieli (www.mariomieli.org) Rome-based cultural centre that organises debates, cultural events and social functions, including Gay Pride.

Coordinamento Lesbiche Italiano (CLR; www.clrbp.it) The national organisation for lesbians, holding regular conferences, literary evenings and other cultural special events.

Gay.it (www.gay.it) Website featuring LGBT news, feature articles and gossip.

Pride (www.prideonline.it) Culture, politics, travel and health with an LGBT focus.

Maps

The city maps provided by Lonely Planet, combined with the good, free local maps available at most Italian tourist offices, will be sufficient for many travellers. For more-specialised maps, browse the good selection at national bookshop chain Feltrinelli (www.lafeltrinelli.it), or consult the websites of the following organisations:

Touring Club Italiano (www.touringclub.com) Italy's largest map publisher offers a comprehensive 1:200,000, 592-page road atlas of Italy (€54.90), as well as 1:400,000 maps of northern, central and southern Italy (€8.50). It also produces 15 regional maps at 1:200,000 (€8.50), as well as a series of walking guides with maps (€14.90).

Tabacco (www.tabaccoeditrice.com) Publishes an excellent 1:25,000 scale series of walking maps (€8.50), covering an area from Livigno in the west to the Slovenia border in the east.

Kompass (www.kompass-italia.it) Publishes 1:25,000 and 1:50,000 scale hiking maps of various parts of Italy, plus a nice series of 1:70,000 cycling maps.

Money

ATMs are widespread in Italy. Major credit cards are widely accepted, but some smaller shops, trattorias and hotels might not take them.

ATMs

○ ATMs (known as 'Bancomat' in Italy) are widely available throughout Italy, and most will accept cards tied into the Visa, MasterCard, Cirrus and Maestro systems.

○ Beware of transaction fees. Every time you withdraw cash, you'll be hit by charges – typically

Practicalities

Smoking Banned in enclosed public spaces, which includes restaurants, bars, shops and public transport.

Newspapers Key national dailies include centre-left *La Repubblica* (www.repubblica.it) and right-wing rival *Corriere della Sera* (www.corriere.it). For the Vatican's take on affairs, *L'Osservatore Romano* (www.osservatore romano.va) is the Holy See's official paper.

Radio As well as the principal Rai channels (Radiouno, Radiodue, Radiotre), there are hundreds of commercial radio stations operating across Italy. Popular Rome-based stations include Radio Capital (www.capital.it) and Radio Città Futura (www.radiocittafutura.it).

TV The main terrestrial channels are RAI 1, 2 and 3 run by Rai (www.rai.it), Italy's state-owned national broad-caster, and Canale 5, Italia 1 and Rete 4 run by Mediaset (www.mediaset.it), the commercial TV company found-ed and still partly owned by Silvio Berlusconi.

Weights & Measures Italy uses the metric system.

your home bank will charge a foreign-exchange fee (usually around 1%) as well as a transaction fee of around 1% to 3%. Fees can sometimes be reduced by withdrawing cash from banks affiliated with your home banking institution; check with your bank.

❂ If an ATM rejects your card, try another one before assuming the problem is with your card.

❂ If your card is lost, stolen or swallowed by an ATM, you can telephone toll-free to have an immediate stop put on its use:

American Express (Amex; ☑06 7290 0347)

Diners Club (☑800 393939)

MasterCard (☑800 870866)

Visa (☑800 819014)

Credit Cards

❂ Major cards such as Visa, MasterCard, Eurocard, Cirrus and Eurocheques are widely accepted. Amex is also recognised, although it's less common than Visa or MasterCard.

❂ Virtually all midrange and top-end hotels accept credit cards, as do most restau-rants and large shops. Some cheaper *pensioni*, trattorias and pizzerias only accept cash.

❂ Do not rely on credit cards at museums or galleries.

❂ Note that using your credit card in ATMs can be costly. On every transaction there's a fee, which can reach US$10 with some credit-card issuers, as well as interest per withdrawal.

Check with your issuer before leaving home.

Currency

Italy's currency is the euro. The seven euro notes come in denominations of €500, €200, €100, €50, €20, €10 and €5. The eight euro coins are in denominations of €2 and €1, then 50, 20, 10, five, and two cents, and finally one cent.

Tipping

Italians are not big tippers. Use the following as a rough guide:

Taxis Optional, but most people round up to the nearest euro.

Hotels Tip porters about €5 at high-end hotels.

Restaurants Service (*servizio*) is generally included in res-taurants – if it's not, a euro or two is fine in pizzerias, 10% in restaurants.

Bars Optional, though many Italians leave small change on the bar when ordering coffee (usually €0.10 per coffee). If drinks are brought to your table, a small tip is generally appreciated.

Opening Hours

Opening hours vary throughout the year. We've provided high-season opening hours; hours will generally decrease in the shoulder and low seasons. 'Summer' times generally refer to the period from April to September or

October, while 'winter' times generally run from October or November to March.

Banks 8.30am–1.30pm and 2.45–4.30pm Monday to Friday

Restaurants noon–3pm & 7.30–11pm or midnight

Cafes 7.30am–8pm, sometimes until 1am or 2am

Bars and clubs 10pm–4am or 5am

Shops 9am–1pm and 4–8pm Monday to Saturday, some also open Sunday

Public Holidays

Most Italians take their annual holiday in August, with the busiest period occurring around 15 August, known locally as Ferragosto. As a result, many businesses and shops close for at least part of that month. Settimana Santa (Easter Holy Week) is another busy holiday period for Italians.

National public holidays include the following:

Capodanno (New Year's Day) 1 January

Epifania (Epiphany) 6 January

Pasquetta (Easter Monday) March/April

Giorno della Liberazione (Liberation Day) 25 April

Festa del Lavoro (Labour Day) 1 May

Festa della Repubblica (Republic Day) 2 June

Ferragosto (Feast of the Assumption) 15 August

Festa di Ognisanti (All Saints' Day) 1 November

Festa dell'Immacolata Concezione (Feast of the Immaculate Conception) 8 December

Natale (Christmas Day) 25 December

Festa di Santo Stefano (Boxing Day) 26 December

Safe Travel

The following government websites offer up-to-date travel advisories.

Australian Department of Foreign Affairs & Trade (www.smartraveller.gov.au)

British Foreign & Commonwealth Office (www.gov.uk/foreign-travel-advice)

Global Affairs Canada (travel.gc.ca/travelling/health-safety)

New Zealand Ministry of Foreign Affairs & Trade (www.safetravel.govt.nz)

US Department of State (travel.state.gov)

Telephone

Directory Enquiries

National and international phone numbers can be requested at 📞1254 (or online at www.1254.it).

Domestic Calls

○ Italian telephone area codes all begin with 0 and consist of up to four digits. The area code is followed by anything from four to eight digits. Area codes are

an integral part of all Italian phone numbers and must be dialled even when calling locally.

○ Mobile-phone numbers begin with a three-digit prefix starting with a 3.

○ Toll-free (free-phone) numbers are known as *numeri verdi* and usually start with 800.

○ Nongeographical numbers start with 840, 841, 848, 892, 899, 163, 166 or 199.

○ Some six-digit national rate numbers are also in use (such as those for Alitalia and Trenitalia).

International Calls

○ To call Italy from abroad, call your international access number, then Italy's country code (📞39) and then the area code of the location you want, including the leading 0.

○ Avoid making international calls from a hotel, as rates are high.

○ The cheapest options are free or low-cost apps such

Important Phone Numbers

Italy country code	📞39
International access code	📞00
Ambulance	📞118
Police	📞112, 113
Fire	📞115

as Skype and Viber, connecting by using the wi-fi at your accommodation or at a cafe or other venue offering free wi-fi.

○ Another cheap option is to use an international calling card. Note, however, that there are very few public payphones left, so consider a pre-paid card that allows you to call from any phone. Cards are available at newsstands and tobacconists.

○ To call abroad from Italy dial 00, then the country and area codes, followed by the telephone number.

○ To make a reverse-charge (collect) international call from a public telephone, dial 170. All phone operators speak English.

Mobile Phones

○ Local SIM cards can be used in European, Australian and some unlocked US phones. Other phones must be set to roaming.

○ Italian mobile phones operate on the GSM 900/1800 network, which is compatible with the rest of Europe and Australia but not always with the North American GSM or CDMA systems – check with your service provider.

○ The cheapest way of using your mobile is to buy a pre-paid *(prepagato)* Italian SIM card. TIM (www.tim.it), Wind (www.wind.it), Vodafone (www.vodafone.it) and Tre (www.tre.it) all offer SIM cards and have retail outlets in most Italian cities

and towns. All SIM cards must be registered in Italy, so make sure you have a passport or ID card with you when you buy one.

○ You can easily top up your Italian SIM with a recharge card *(ricarica),* available from most tobacconists, some bars, supermarkets and banks.

Time

○ All of Italy occupies the Central European Time Zone, which is one hour ahead of GMT. When it is noon in London, it is 1pm in Italy.

○ Daylight-saving time (when clocks move forward one hour) starts on the last Sunday in March and ends on the last Sunday in October.

○ Italy operates on a 24-hour clock, so 3pm is written as 15:00.

Toilets

Beyond museums, galleries, department stores and train stations, there are few public toilets in Italy. If you're caught short, the best thing to do is to nip into a cafe or bar. The polite thing to do is to order something at the bar. You may need to pay to use public toilets at some venues (usually €0.50 to €1.50).

Travellers with Disabilities

Italy is not an easy country for travellers with disabilities, and getting around can be a problem for wheelchair users. Even a short journey in a city or town can become a major expedition if cobblestone streets have to be negotiated. Although many buildings have lifts, they are not always wide enough for wheelchairs. Not a lot has been done to make life easier for the hearing/vision impaired either.

The Italian National Tourist Office in your country may be able to provide advice on Italian associations for travellers with disabilities and information on what help is available.

If travelling by train, ring the national helpline 199 303060 to arrange assistance (6.45am to 9.30pm daily). Airline companies should be able to arrange assistance at airports if you notify them of your needs in advance. Alternatively, contact ADR Assistance (www.adrassistance.it) for help at Fiumicino or Ciampino airports. Some taxis are equipped to carry passengers in wheelchairs; ask for a taxi for a *sedia a rotelle* (wheelchair).

Italy's official tourism website (www.italia.it) offers a number of links for travellers with disabilities.

Accessible Italy (www.accessibleitaly.com) A San Marino–

based company that specialises in holiday services for people with disabilities. This is the best first port of call.

Sage Traveling (www.sage traveling.com) A US-based agency offering advice and tailor-made tours to assist mobility-impaired travellers in Europe.

Visas

○ Italy is a signatory of the Schengen Convention, an agreement whereby participating countries abolished customs checks at common borders. EU citizens do not need a Schengen tourist visa to enter Italy. Nationals of some other countries, including Australia, Canada, Israel, Japan, New Zealand, Switzerland and the USA, do not need a tourist visa for stays of up to 90 days. To check the visa requirements for your country, see www. schengenvisainfo.com/tourist-schengen-visa.

○ All non-EU and non-Schengen nationals entering Italy for more than 90 days or for any reason other than tourism (such as study or work) may need a specific visa. See http://vistoperitalia.esteri.it or contact an Italian consulate for details.

○ Ensure your passport is valid for at least six months beyond your departure date from Italy.

Women Travellers

Italy is not a dangerous country for women to travel in. That said, in some parts of the country, solo women travellers may be subjected to a high level of unwanted attention. Eye-to-eye contact is the norm in Italy's daily flirtatious interplay. Eye contact can become outright staring the further south you travel.

If ignoring unwanted male attention doesn't work, politely tell your interlocutor that you're waiting for your *marito* (husband) or *fidanzato* (boyfriend), and if necessary, walk away.

If you feel yourself being groped on a crowded bus or metro, a loud *'che schifo!'* (how disgusting!) will draw attention to the incident. Otherwise take all the usual precautions you would in any other part of the world.

You can report incidents to the police, who are required to press charges.

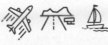

Transport

Getting There & Away

A plethora of airlines link Italy with the rest of the world, and cut-rate carriers have significantly driven down the cost of flights from other European countries. Excellent rail and bus connections, especially with northern Italy, offer efficient overland transport, while car and passenger ferries run to ports throughout the Mediterranean.

Flights, cars and tours can be booked online at lonelyplanet.com/bookings.

Air

Italy's main intercontinental gateway airports are Rome's **Leonardo da Vinci** (Fiumicino; ☑06 6 59 51; www. adr.it/fiumicino) and Milan's **Aeroporto Malpensa** (MXP; ☑02 23 23 23; www. milanomalpensa-airport.com; ☑Malpensa Express). Both are served by nonstop flights from around the world. Venice's **Marco Polo Airport** (☑flight information 041 260 92 60; www.veniceairport.it; Via Galileo Galilei 30/1, Tessera) is also served by a handful of intercontinental flights.

Dozens of international airlines compete with the country's revamped national carrier, Alitalia, rated a three-star airline by UK aviation research company Skytrax. If you're flying from Africa or Oceania, you'll generally need to change planes at least once en route to Italy.

Intra-European flights serve plenty of other Italian cities; the leading mainstream carriers include Alitalia, Air France, British Airways, Lufthansa and KLM.

Climate Change & Travel

Every form of transport that relies on carbon-based fuel generates CO_2, the main cause of human-induced climate change. Modern travel is dependent on aeroplanes, which might use less fuel per kilometre per person than most cars but travel much greater distances. The altitude at which aircraft emit gases (including CO_2) and particles also contributes to their climate change impact. Many websites offer 'carbon calculators' that allow people to estimate the carbon emissions generated by their journey and, for those who wish to do so, to offset the impact of the greenhouse gases emitted with contributions to portfolios of climate-friendly initiatives throughout the world. Lonely Planet offsets the carbon footprint of all staff and author travel.

Cut-rate airlines, led by Ryanair and easyJet, fly from a growing number of European cities to more than two dozen Italian destinations, typically landing in smaller airports such as Rome's **Ciampino** (☑06 6 59 51; www.adr.it/ciampino).

Land

There are plenty of options for entering Italy by train, bus or private vehicle.

Border Crossings

Aside from the coastal roads linking Italy with France and Slovenia, border crossings into Italy mostly involve tunnels through the Alps (open year-round) or mountain passes (seasonally closed or requiring snow chains).

The list below outlines the major points of entry.

Austria From Innsbruck to Bolzano via A22/E45 (Brenner Pass); Villach to Tarvisio via A23/E55.

France From Nice to Ventimiglia via A10/E80; Modane to Turin via A32/E70 (Fréjus Tunnel); Chamonix to Courmayeur via A5/E25 (Mont Blanc Tunnel).

Slovenia From Sežana to Trieste via SR58/E70.

Switzerland From Martigny to Aosta via SS27/E27 (Grand St Bernard Tunnel); Lugano to Como via A9/E35.

Car & Motorcycle

● Every vehicle travelling across an international border should display the nationality plate of its country of registration.

● Always carry proof of vehicle ownership and evidence of third-party insurance. If driving an EU-registered vehicle, your home country insurance is sufficient. Ask your insurer for a European Accident Statement (EAS) form, which can simplify matters in the event of an accident. The form can also be downloaded online at http://cartraveldocs.com/european-accident-statement.

● A European breakdown assistance policy is a good investment and can be obtained through the Automobile Club d'Italia.

● Italy's scenic roads are tailor-made for motorcycle touring, and motorcyclists swarm into the country every summer. With a motorcycle you rarely have to book ahead for ferries and can enter restricted-traffic areas in cities. Crash helmets and a motorcycle licence are compulsory.

Train

Regular trains on two western lines connect Italy with France (one along the coast and the other from Turin into the French Alps). Trains from Milan head north into Switzerland and on towards the Benelux countries. Further east, two main lines head for the main cities in Central and Eastern Europe. Those crossing the Brenner Pass go to Innsbruck, Stuttgart and Munich. Those crossing at Tarvisio proceed to Vienna, Salzburg and Prague. The main international train line to Slovenia crosses near Trieste.

Depending on distances covered, rail can be highly competitive with air travel. Those travelling from neighbouring countries to northern Italy will find it is frequently more comfortable and less expensive, and is only marginally more time-consuming than flying.

Those travelling longer distances (say, from London, Spain, northern Germany or Eastern Europe) will doubtless find flying cheaper and quicker. Bear in mind, however, that the train is a much greener way to go – a trip by rail can contribute up to 10 times fewer carbon dioxide emissions per person than the same trip by air.

The comprehensive European Rail Timetable (UK£16.99, digital version UK£11.99), updated monthly, is available for purchase online at www.europeanrail-timetable.co.uk, as well as at a handful of bookshops in the UK and continental Europe (see the website for details).

Reservations on international trains to/from Italy are always advisable, and sometimes compulsory.

Consider taking long journeys overnight, as the supplemental fare for a sleeper costs substantially less than Italian hotels.

Sea

Multiple ferry companies connect Italy with countries throughout the Mediterranean. Many routes only operate in summer, when ticket prices also rise. Prices for vehicles vary according to their size.

The helpful website www.directferries.co.uk allows you to search routes and compare prices between the numerous international ferry companies servicing Italy. Another useful resource for

ferries from Italy to Greece is www.ferries.gr.

Getting Around

Air

Italy offers an extensive network of internal flights. The privatised national airline, Alitalia, is the main domestic carrier, and numerous low-cost airlines also operate across the country. Useful search engines for comparing multiple carriers' fares (including those of cut-price airlines) are www.skyscanner.com, www.kayak.com and www.azfly.it. Airport taxes are included in the price of your ticket.

Bicycle

Cycling is very popular in Italy. The following tips will help ensure a pedal-happy trip:

o If bringing your own bike, you'll need to disassemble and pack it for the journey, and may need to pay an airline surcharge.

o Make sure to bring tools, spare parts, a helmet, lights and a secure bike lock.

o Bikes can be wheeled onto regional trains displaying the bicycle logo. Simply purchase a separate bicycle ticket *(supplemento bici)*, valid for 24 hours (€3.50). Certain international trains, listed on Trenitalia's 'Travelling with Your Bike' page, also allow transport

of assembled bicycles for €12, paid on board. Bikes dismantled and stored in a bag can be taken for free, even on night trains.

o Most ferries also allow free bicycle passage.

o Bikes are available for hire in most Italian towns. City bikes start at €10/50 per day/week; mountain bikes a bit more. A growing number of Italian hotels offer free bikes for guests.

Boat

Craft *Navi* (large ferries) service Sicily and Sardinia, while *traghetti* (smaller ferries) and *aliscafi* (hydrofoils) service the smaller islands. Most ferries carry vehicles, but hydrofoils do not.

Routes Main embarkation points for Sicily and Sardinia are Genoa, Livorno, Civitavecchia and Naples. Ferries for Sicily also leave from Villa San Giovanni and Reggio Calabria. Main arrival points in Sardinia are Cagliari, Arbatax, Olbia and Porto Torres; in Sicily they're Palermo, Catania, Trapani and Messina.

Timetables and tickets Comprehensive website Direct Ferries (www.directferries.co.uk) allows you to search routes, compare prices and book tickets for ferry routes in Italy.

Overnight ferries Travellers can book a two- to four-person cabin or a *poltrona*, which is an airline-type armchair. Deck class (which allows you to sit/sleep in lounge areas or on deck) is available only on some ferries.

Bus

Routes Everything from meandering local routes to fast, reliable InterCity connections provided by numerous bus companies.

Timetables and tickets Available on bus-company websites and from local tourist offices. Tickets are generally competitively priced with the train and are often the only way to get to smaller towns. In larger cities most of the InterCity bus companies have ticket offices or sell tickets through agencies. In villages and even some good-sized towns, tickets are sold in bars or on the bus.

Advance booking Generally not required, but advisable for overnight or long-haul trips in high season.

Car & Motorcycle

Automobile Associations

The **Automobile Club d'Italia** (ACI; ☏ 803116, from a foreign mobile 800 116800; www.aci.it) is a driver's best resource in Italy. Foreigners do not have to join to get 24-hour roadside emergency service but instead pay a per-incident fee.

Driving Licences

All EU driving licences are recognised in Italy. Travellers from other countries should obtain an International Driving Permit (IDP) through their national automobile association.

Fuel & Spare Parts

Italy's petrol prices vary from one service station (*benzinaio, stazione di servizio*) to another. At the time of writing, lead-free gasoline (*senza piombo; 95 octane*) was averaging €1.44 per litre, with diesel (*gasolio*) costing €1.29 per litre.

Spare parts are available at many garages or via the 24-hour ACI motorist assistance number ☏ 803 116 (or ☏ 800 116800 if calling with a non-Italian mobile-phone account).

Car

o Pre-booking via the internet often costs less than hiring a car once in Italy. Online booking agency Rentalcars.com (www.rentalcars.com) compares the rates of numerous car-rental companies.

o Renters must generally be aged 21 or over, with a credit card and home-country driving licence or IDP.

o Consider hiring a small car, which will reduce your fuel expenses and help you negotiate narrow city lanes and tight parking spaces.

o Check with your credit-card company to see if it offers a Collision Damage Waiver, which covers you for additional damage if you use that card to pay for the car.

Motorcycle

Agencies throughout Italy rent motorbikes, ranging from small Vespas to larger touring bikes. Prices start at around €35/150 per day/week for a 50cc scooter, or upwards of €80/400 per day/week for a 650cc motorcycle.

Road Rules

o Cars drive on the right side of the road and overtake on the left. Unless otherwise indicated, always give way to cars entering an intersection from a road on your right.

o Seatbelt use (front and rear) is required by law; violators are subject to an on-the-spot fine. Helmets are required on all two-wheeled vehicles.

o Day and night, it is compulsory to drive with your headlights on outside built-up areas.

o It's obligatory to carry a warning triangle and fluorescent waistcoat in case of breakdown. Recommended accessories include a first-aid kit, spare-bulb kit and fire extinguisher.

o A licence is required to ride a scooter – a car licence will do for bikes up to 125cc; for anything over 125cc you'll need a motorcycle licence.

o Motorbikes can enter most restricted traffic areas in Italian cities, and traffic police generally turn a blind eye to motorcycles or scooters parked on footpaths.

o The blood alcohol limit is 0.05%; it's zero for drivers under 21 and those who have had their licence for less than three years.

Unless otherwise indicated, speed limits are as follows:

o 130km/h on autostradas

- 110km/h on all main, non-urban roads

- 90km/h on secondary, non-urban roads

- 50km/h in built-up areas

Local Transport
Bus & Metro

- Extensive *metropolitane* (metros) exist in Rome, Milan and Naples.

- Cities and towns of any size have an efficient *urbano* (urban) and *extraurbano* (suburban) bus system. Services are generally limited on Sundays and holidays.

- Purchase bus and metro tickets before boarding and validate them once on board. Passengers with un-validated tickets are subject to a fine (between €50 and €110). Buy tickets from a *tabaccaio* (tobacconist's shop), news-stands, ticket booths or dispensing machines at bus and metro stations. Tickets usually cost around €1 to €2. Many cities offer good-value 24-hour or daily tourist tickets.

Taxi

- You can catch a taxi at the ranks outside most train and bus stations, or simply telephone for a radio taxi.

Radio taxi meters start running from when you've called rather than when you're picked up.

- Charges vary somewhat from one region to another. Most short city journeys cost between €10 and €15. Generally, no more than four people are allowed in one taxi.

Train
Classes & Costs

Prices vary according to the class of service, time of travel and how far in advance you book. Most Italian trains have 1st- and 2nd-class seating; a 1st-class ticket typically costs from a third to half more than 2nd-class.

Travel on Trenitalia's InterCity and Alta Velocità (Frecciarossa, Frecciargento, Frecciabianca) trains means paying a supplement, included in the ticket price, determined by the distance you are travelling. If you have a standard ticket for a slower train and end up hopping on an IC train, you'll have to pay the difference on board. (You can only board an Alta Velocità train if you have a booking, so the problem does not arise in those cases.)

Reservations

- Reservations are obligatory on AV trains.

- Reservations can be made on the Trenitalia and Italo websites, at railway station counters and self-service ticketing machines, or through travel agents.

- Both Trenitalia and Italo offer a variety of advance purchase discounts. Basically, the earlier you book, the greater the saving. Discounted tickets are limited, and refunds and changes are highly restricted. For all ticket options and prices, see the Trenitalia and Italo websites.

Eurail & Interrail Passes

Generally speaking, you'll need to cover a lot of ground to make a rail pass worthwhile. Before buying, consider where you intend to travel and compare the price of a rail pass to the cost of individual tickets on the Trenitalia website (www. trenitalia.com).

InterRail (www.interrail. eu) passes, available online and at most major stations and student-travel outlets, are for people who have been a resident in Europe for more than six months.

Popular High-Velocity Train Routes

From	To	Duration (hr)	Price from (€)
Turin	Naples	5½ 6	50
Milan	Rome	3-3¼	70
Venice	Florence	2	25
Rome	Naples	1¼	17
Florence	Bologna	35min	15

A Global Pass encompassing 30 countries comes in seven versions, ranging from five days' travel within a 15-day period to a full month's unlimited travel. There are four price categories: youth (12 to 27), adult (28 to 59), senior (60+) and family (one adult and up to two children), with different prices for 1st and 2nd class.

The InterRail one-country pass for Italy can be used for three, four, six or eight days in one month. See the website for full price details. Cardholders have access to various discounts and special deals, including on selected accommodation.

Eurail (www.eurail. com) passes, available for non-European residents, are good for travel in 28 European countries (not including the UK). They can be purchased online or from travel agencies outside Europe.

The original Eurail pass, now known as the **Global Pass**, offers a number of options, from five days of travel within a one-month period to three months of unlimited travel.

Youth aged 12 to 27 are eligible for a 2nd-class pass; all others must buy the more expensive 1st-class pass (the family ticket allows up to two children aged 0 to 11 to travel free when accompanied by a paying adult).

Eurail offers several alternatives to the traditional Global Pass:

○ The **Select Pass** allows four to 10 days of travel within a two-month period in two to four bordering countries of your choice.

○ The two-country **Regional Pass** (France/Italy, Switzerland/Italy, Spain/Italy, Greece/Italy, Croatia & Slovenia/Italy) allows four to 10 days of travel within a two-month period.

○ The **One Country Pass** allows three to eight days of travel in Italy within a one-month period.

Language

Italian pronunciation isn't difficult as most sounds are also found in English. The pronunciation of some consonants depends on which vowel follows, but if you read our pronunciation guides below as if they were English, you'll be understood just fine. Just remember to pronounce double consonants as a longer, more forceful sound than single ones. The stressed syllables in words are in italics in our pronunciation guides.

To enhance your trip with a phrasebook, visit **lonelyplanet.com**. Lonely Planet iPhone phrasebooks are available through the Apple App store.

Basics

Hello.
Buongiorno./Ciao. (pol/inf)   bwon·*jor*·no/chow
How are you?
Come sta?   *ko*·me sta
I'm fine, thanks.
Bene, grazie.   be·ne *gra*·tsye
Excuse me.
Mi scusi.   mee *skoo*·zee
Yes./No.
Sì./No.   see/no
Please. (when asking)
Per favore.   per fa·*vo*·re
Thank you.
Grazie.   *gra*·tsye
Goodbye.
Arrivederci./Ciao. (pol/inf)   a·ree·ve·*der*·chee/chow
Do you speak English?
Parla inglese?   *par*·la een·*gle*·ze
I don't understand.
Non capisco.   non ka·*pee*·sko
How much is this?
Quanto costa?   kwan·to *ko*·sta

Accommodation

I'd like to book a room.
Vorrei prenotare   vo·*ray* pre·no·*ta*·re
una camera.   *oo*·na *ka*·me·ra

How much is it per night?
Quanto costa per   kwan·to *kos*·ta per
una notte?   *oo*·na *no*·te

Eating & Drinking

I'd like ..., please.
Vorrei ..., per favore.   vo·*ray* ... per fa·*vo*·re
What would you recommend?
Cosa mi consiglia?   *ko*·za mee kon·*see*·lya
That was delicious!
Era squisito!   e·ra skwee·*zee*·to
Bring the bill/check, please.
Mi porta il conto,   mee *por*·ta eel *kon*·to
per favore.   per fa·*vo*·re
I'm allergic (to peanuts).
Sono allergico/a   so·no a·*ler*·jee·ko/a
(alle arachidi). (m/f)   (a·le a·*ra*·kee·dee)
I don't eat ...
Non mangio ...   non *man*·jo ...
　fish   pesce   *pe*·she
　meat   carne   *kar*·ne
　poultry   pollame   po·*la*·me

Emergencies

I'm ill.
Mi sento male.   mee *sen*·to *ma*·le
Help!
Aiuto!   a·*yoo*·to
Call a doctor!
Chiami un medico!   *kya*·mee oon *me*·dee·ko
Call the police!
Chiami la polizia!   *kya*·mee la po·lee·*tsee*·a

Directions

I'm looking for (a/the) ...
Cerco ...   *cher*·ko ...
　bank
　la banca   la *ban*·ka
　... embassy
　la ambasciata de ...   la am·ba·*sha*·ta de ...
　market
　il mercato   eel mer·*ka*·to
　museum
　il museo   eel moo·*ze*·o
　restaurant
　un ristorante   oon rees·to·*ran*·te
　toilet
　un gabinetto   oon ga·bee·*ne*·to
　tourist office
　l'ufficio del turismo   loo·*fee*·cho del too·*reez*·mo

Behind the Scenes

Writer Thanks

Marc Di Duca

A big *grazie mille* goes to the many tourist offices around the Veneto, especially those in Verona, Vicenza, Padua and Mantua, as well as to Antonio in Belluno. Also huge thanks to Ukrainian grandma and grandpa for looking after my two sons while I was in Italy, and to my wife for suffering my lengthy absences.

Cristian Bonetto

Mille grazie to Raffaele e Silvana, Joe Brizzi, Alfonso Sperandeo, Carmine Romano, Sylvain Bellenger, Federica Rispoli, the team at Cooperativa La Paranza, Vincenzo Mattiucci, Marcantonio Colonna and the many other friends and locals who offered invaluable tips and insight. At Lonely Planet, many thanks to Anna Tyler and my ever-diligent Italy writing team.

Peter Dragicevich

It turns out that it's not hard to find willing volunteers to keep you company on an extended research assignment in Venice, especially when it coincides with Carnevale. Many thanks to my Venice crew of Christine Henderson, Hamish Blennerhassett and Sarah Welch for much masked fun and many good meals. Special thanks to Christine for the unpaid but much appreciated translation services.

Duncan Garwood

A big thank you to Giacomo Bassi for his brilliant tips and suggestions. In Sardinia, *grazie* to everyone who helped and offered advice, in particular Luisa Besalduch, Agostino Rivano, Marianna Mascalchi, Valentina Sanna, Marco Vacca, and the tourist office teams at Alghero, Sassari and Castelsardo. At Lonely Planet, thanks to Anna Tyler

for all her support. And, as always, a big, heartfelt hug to Lidia and the boys, Ben and Nick.

Paula Hardy

Grazie mille to all the fun and fashionable Venetians and Milanese who spilled the beans on their remarkable cities: Paola dalla Valentina, Costanza Cecchini, Sara Porro, Lucia Cattaneo, Monica Cesarato, Francesca Giubilei, Luca Berta, Marco Secchi and Nan McElroy. Thanks, too, to coauthors Regis and Marc for their contributions, and to Anna Tyler for all the support. Finally, much love to Rob for sharing the beauty of the *bel paese*.

Virginia Maxwell

So many locals assisted me in my research for this trip. Many thanks to Tiziana Babbucci, Fernando Bardini, Maricla Bicci, Niccolò Bisconti, Enrico Bracciali, Rita Ceccarelli, Cecilia in Massa Marittima, Stefania Colombini, Ilaria Crescioli, Martina Dei, Paolo Demi, Federica Fantozzi, Irene Gavazzi, Francesco Gentile, Francesca Geppetti, Maria Guarriello, Benedetta Landi, Freya Middleton, Alessandra Molletti, Sonai Pallai, Luigi Pagnotta, Valentina De Pamphilis, Franco Rossi, Fabiana Sciano, Maria Luisa Scorza, Raffaella Senesi, Coral Sisk, Carolina Taddei and Luca Ventresa. Many thanks, too, to my travelling companions: Peter Handsaker, Eveline Zoutendijk, Max Handsaker, Elizabeth Maxwell, Matthew Clarke and Ella Clarke.

Regis St Louis

I'm grateful to the countless tourist office staff, innkeepers, chefs, baristas, market vendors, store clerks, students and many other locals who provided helpful tips and advice along the way. Warm thanks to Cassandra and daughters Magdalena and Genevieve, who make this enterprise all the more worthwhile.

Donna Wheeler

Thanks to Wayne Young, Elena Ciurletti, Gianluca Cannizzo, Emanuela Grandi, Stefano Libardi and the ultra-helpful Duparc Suites team for inspiring local knowledge. To Kathrin Mair, Verena Huf, Caroline Willeit, Antonella Arlotti, Virginia Ciraldo, Elena Boggio, Matteo Paini and Laura Sailis, *grazie* for gracious, warm hospitality. *Soprattutto, molto amore* a Giuseppe Giuseppe Guario.

Nicola Williams

Grazie mille to those who shared their love and insider knowledge with me: in Rome Linda Martinez (The Beehive), Elyssa Bernard, tour guide Fiona Brewer, Sian Lloyd and Lorna Davidson (Roman Guy), Gina Tringali and Eleonora Baldwin at Casa Mia. In Tuscany, Manuele Giovanelli and Zeno Fioravanti, Doreen and Carmello at Florence's Hotel Scoti, Georgette Jupe, Coral Sisk, Nardia Plumridge, Molly McIlwrath, Cailin Swanson and Betti Soldi. Finally, kudos to my expert, trilingual, family-travel research team: Niko, Mischa and Kaya.

Acknowledgements

Climate map data adapted from Peel MC, Finlayson BL & McMahon TA (2007) 'Updated World Map of the Köppen-Geiger Climate Classification', Hydrology and Earth System Sciences, 11, 163344.
Illustrations p58–9, p256–7 by Javier Martinez Zarracina.

This Book

This book was curated by Marc Di Duca and was researched and written by Marc Di Duca, Cristian Bonetto, Peter Dragicevich, Duncan Garwood, Paula Hardy, Virginia Maxwell, Regis St Louis, Donna Wheeler, Nicola Williams. This guidebook was produced by the following:

Destination Editor Anna Tyler
Product Editor Kathryn Rowan
Senior Cartographers Corey Hutchison, Anthony Phelan
Book Designer Clara Monitto
Assisting Editors Anne Mulvaney, Gabbi Stefanos
Assisting Book Designer Nicholas Colicchia
Cover Researcher Naomi Parker
Thanks to Will Allen, Peter Barclay-George, Shona Gray, Anne Mason, Tony Wheeler

Send Us Your Feedback

A – Z
Index

Symbols & Map Key

Look for these symbols to quickly identify listings:

- ◎ Sights
- ✦ Activities
- ◉ Courses
- ◉ Tours
- ✦ Festivals & Events
- ✦ Eating
- ◉ Drinking
- ✦ Entertainment
- ◉ Shopping
- ◉ Information & Transport

These symbols and abbreviations give vital information for each listing:

- ✐ Sustainable or green recommendation
- **FREE** No payment required

- ☏ Telephone number
- ☺ Opening hours
- P Parking
- ☻ Nonsmoking
- ❄ Air-conditioning
- @ Internet access
- ☎ Wi-fi access
- ☒ Swimming pool

- ▢ Bus
- ☗ Ferry
- ▢ Tram
- ▢ Train
- ▢ English-language menu
- ✎ Vegetarian selection
- ❖ Family-friendly

Find your best experiences with these Great For... icons.

 Art & Culture

 Beaches

Budget

 Cafe/Coffee

Cycling

 Detour

 Drinking

 Entertainment

 Events

Family Travel

☩ Food & Drink

 History

Local Life

Nature & Wildlife

◉ Photo Op

Scenery

Shopping

 Short Trip

Sport

Walking

❄ Winter Travel

Sights
- ◉ Beach
- ◉ Bird Sanctuary
- ◉ Buddhist
- ◉ Castle/Palace
- ◉ Christian
- ◉ Confucian
- ◉ Hindu
- ◉ Islamic
- ◉ Jain
- ◉ Jewish
- ◉ Monument
- ◉ Museum/Gallery/ Historic Building
- ◉ Ruin
- ◉ Shinto
- ◉ Sikh
- ◉ Taoist
- ◉ Winery/Vineyard
- ◉ Zoo/Wildlife Sanctuary
- ◉ Other Sight

Points of Interest
- ◉ Bodysurfing
- ◉ Camping
- ◉ Cafe
- ◉ Canoeing/Kayaking
- ● Course/Tour
- ◉ Diving
- ◉ Drinking & Nightlife
- ◉ Eating
- ◉ Entertainment
- ◉ Sento Hot Baths/ Onsen
- ◉ Shopping
- ◉ Skiing
- ◉ Sleeping
- ◉ Snorkelling
- ◉ Surfing
- ◉ Swimming/Pool
- ◉ Walking
- ◉ Windsurfing
- ◉ Other Activity

Information
- ◉ Bank
- ◉ Embassy/Consulate
- ◉ Hospital/Medical
- @ Internet
- ◉ Police
- ◉ Post Office
- ◉ Telephone
- ◉ Toilet
- ◉ Tourist Information
- ● Other Information

Geographic
- ◉ Beach
- ◄ Gate
- ◉ Hut/Shelter
- ◉ Lighthouse
- ◉ Lookout
- ▲ Mountain/Volcano
- ◉ Oasis
- ◉ Park
-)(Pass
- ◉ Picnic Area
- ◉ Waterfall

Transport
- ◉ Airport
- ◉ BART station
- ◉ Border crossing
- ◉ Boston T station
- ◉ Bus
- ◉ Cable car/Funicular
- ◉ Cycling
- ◉ Ferry
- ◉ Metro/MRT station
- ◉ Monorail
- P Parking
- ◉ Petrol station
- ◉ Subway/S-Bahn/ Skytrain station
- ◉ Taxi
- ◉ Train station/Railway
- ◉ Tram
- ◉ Tube Station
- ◉ Underground/ U-Bahn station
- ● Other Transport

Duncan Garwood

From facing fast bowlers in Barbados to sidestepping hungry pigs in Goa, Duncan's travels have thrown up many unique experiences. These days he largely dedicates himself to Spain and Italy, his adopted homeland where he's been living since 1997. He's worked on more than 30 Lonely Planet titles, including guidebooks to Rome, Sardinia, Sicily, Bilbao & San Sebastián, and has contributed to books on food and epic drives. He's also written on Italy for newspapers, websites and magazines.

Paula Hardy

Paula Hardy is an independent travel writer and editorial consultant, whose work for Lonely Planet and other flagship publications has taken her from nomadic camps in the Danakil Depression to Seychellois beach huts and the jewel-like bar at the Gritti Palace on the Grand Canal. Over two decades, she has authored more than 30 Lonely Planet guidebooks and spent five years as commissioning editor of Lonely Planet's bestselling Italian list. These days you'll find her hunting down new hotels, hip bars and up-and-coming artisans primarily in Milan, Venice and Marrakech. Get in touch at www. paulahardy.com.

Virginia Maxwell

Although based in Australia, Virginia spends at least half of her year updating Lonely Planet destination coverage in Europe and the Middle East. Though the Mediterranean is her major area of interest – she has covered Spain, Italy, Turkey, Syria, Lebanon, Israel, Egypt and Morocco for LP guidebooks – Virginia also writes LP guides to Finland, Armenia, Iran and Australia. Follow her @maxwellvirginia on Instagram and Twitter.

Regis St Louis

Regis grew up in a small town in the American Midwest – the kind of place that fuels big dreams of travel – and he developed an early fascination with foreign dialects and world cultures. He spent his formative years learning Russian and a handful of Romance languages, which served him well on journeys across much of the globe. Regis has contributed to more than 50 Lonely Planet titles, covering destinations across six continents. His travels have taken him from the mountains of Kamchatka to remote island villages in Melanesia, and to many grand urban landscapes. When not on the road, he lives in New Orleans.

Donna Wheeler

Donna has written guidebooks for Lonely Planet for over ten years, including the Italy, Norway, Belgium, Africa, Tunisia, Algeria, France, Austria and Australia titles. She is the author of Paris Precincts, a curated photographic guide to the city's best bars, restaurants and shops and is a reporter for Italian contemporary art publisher *My Art Guides*. Donna's work on contemporary art, architecture and design, food, wine, wilderness areas and cultural history also can be found in a variety of other publications. She became a travel writer after various careers as a commissioning editor, creative director, digital producer and content strategist.

Nicola Williams

Border-hopping is a way of life for British writer, runner, foodie, art aficionado and mum-of-three Nicola Williams who has lived in a French village on the southern side of Lake Geneva for more than a decade. Nicola has authored more than 50 guidebooks on Paris, Provence, Rome, Tuscany, France, Italy and Switzerland for Lonely Planet and covers France as a destination expert for the *Telegraph*. She also writes for the *Independent, Guardian*, lonelyplanet.com, Lonely Planet Magazine, French Magazine, *Cool Camping France* and others. Catch her on the road on Twitter and Instagram at @tripalong.

Contributing Writers Kerry Christiani, Gregor Clark, Kevin Raub, Helena Smith

Our Story

A beat-up old car, a few dollars in the pocket and a sense of adventure. In 1972 that's all Tony and Maureen Wheeler needed for the trip of a lifetime – across Europe and Asia overland to Australia. It took several months, and at the end – broke but inspired – they sat at their kitchen table writing and stapling together their first travel guide, *Across Asia on the Cheap*. Within a week they'd sold 1500 copies. Lonely Planet was born.

Today, Lonely Planet has offices in Franklin, London, Melbourne, Oakland, Dublin, Beijing and Delhi, with more than 600 staff and writers. We share Tony's belief that 'a great guidebook should do three things: inform, educate and amuse'.

Our Writers

Marc Di Duca

A travel author for the last decade, Marc has worked for Lonely Planet in Siberia, Slovakia, Bavaria, England, Ukraine, Austria, Poland, Croatia, Portugal, Madeira and on the Trans-Siberian Railway, as well as writing and updating tens of other guides for other publishers. When not on the road, Marc lives between Sandwich, Kent and Mariánské Lázně in the Czech Republic with his wife and two sons.

Cristian Bonetto

Cristian has contributed to over 30 Lonely Planet guides to date, including *New York City, Italy, Venice & the Veneto, Naples & the Amalfi Coast, Denmark, Copenhagen, Sweden* and *Singapore*. Lonely Planet work aside, his musings on travel, food, culture and design appear in numerous publications around the world, including *The Telegraph* (UK) and *Corriere del Mezzogiorno* (Italy). When not on the road, you'll find the reformed playwright and TV scriptwriter slurping espresso in his beloved hometown, Melbourne. Instagram: rexcat75.

Peter Dragicevich

After a successful career in niche newspaper and magazine publishing, both in his native New Zealand and in Australia, Peter finally gave into Kiwi wanderlust, giving up staff jobs to chase his diverse roots around much of Europe. Over the last decade he's written literally dozens of guidebooks for Lonely Planet on an oddly disparate collection of countries, all of which he's come to love. He once again calls Auckland, New Zealand his home – although his current nomadic existence means he's often elsewhere.

◄——— More Writers ———◄

STAY IN TOUCH LONELYPLANET.COM/CONTACT

AUSTRALIA The Malt Store, Level 3, 551 Swanston St, Carlton, Victoria 3053
☏ 03 8379 8000,
fax 03 8379 8111

IRELAND Digital Depot, Roe Lane (off Thomas St), Digital Hub, Dublin 8, D08 TCV4

USA 124 Linden Street, Oakland, CA 94607
☏ 510 250 6400,
toll free 800 275 8555,
fax 510 893 8572

UK 240 Blackfriars Road, London SE1 8NW
☏ 020 3771 5100,
fax 020 3771 5101

 twitter.com/lonelyplanet   facebook.com/lonelyplanet   instagram.com/lonelyplanet   youtube.com/lonelyplanet   lonelyplanet.com/newsletter